BY LANI GUINIER

LIFT EVERY VOICE
   *Turning a Civil Rights Setback
   into a New Vision of Social Justice*

THE TYRANNY OF THE MAJORITY
   Fundamental Fairness in Representative Democracy

With Michelle Fine, Jane Balin
BECOMING GENTLEMEN
   Women, Law School, and Change

Turning a Civil Rights Setback
into a New Vision
of Social Justice

Simon & Schuster

LIFT
EVERY
VOICE

LANI GUINIER

To Dianne
keep the faith

Lani Guinier
Aug 22, 1998

SIMON & SCHUSTER
Rockefeller Center
1230 Avenue of the Americas
New York, NY 10020

Designed by Edith Fowler
Manufactured in the United States of America

10   9   8   7   6   5   4   3   2   1

Library of Congress Cataloging-in-Publication Data

Guinier, Lani.
   Lift every voice : turning a civil rights setback
into a new vision of social justice / Lani Guinier.
      p.   cm.
   Includes bibliographical references and index.
   1. Guinier, Lani.   2. Afro-American women
civil rights workers—Biography.   3. Civil rights
workers—Biography.   4. United States—Politics
and government—1993–   .   5. Clinton, Bill,
1946–   .   6. Civil rights movements—United
States—History—20th century.   I. Title.
E185.97.G94685   1998   98-11876   CIP
323'.092—dc21
[B]
ISBN 0-684-81145-6

Grateful acknowledgment is made for permission
to reprint from the following: "Lift Every Voice and
Sing." Words by James Weldon Johnson; music by
J. Rosamond Johnson. Copyright © 1921 by
Edward B. Marks Music Company. Copyright
renewed. Used by permission of Edward B. Marks
Music Company.

ACKNOWLEDGMENTS

My FRIENDS, family, former clients, and present colleagues helped me retrieve my voice and write this book. Their interventions came in many forms: Dayna Cunningham's energetic red pencil was always poised for combat with my prose. She and her husband, Phil Thompson, brainstormed endlessly about the implications of including criticism of the civil rights leadership in a book that also lovingly recognizes their lasting contributions. Penda Hair wrote me long, single-spaced memorandums and e-mail messages taking issue with much that I say here and pushing me to be more clear about why I am writing this. Gerald Torres generously shared his ideas, his metaphors, and his amazing capacity to take mere prose and make it sing. Il miglior fabbro. Harlon Dalton's editing suggestions were as sharp as his rapier wit, and he never tired of making both insightful and humorous margin comments despite my incorrigible need to solicit his feedback over and over. Susan Sturm, my colleague and collaborator in multiple ways, sat with me for days upon my return to Penn from D.C. in 1993, helping me tape-record my version of events while they were still fresh; put up with my lapses in our joint projects because I was so preoccupied with "the book"; and was always careful to point out in whatever I was doing how I might be heard and ultimately misunderstood, once again. Pamela Karlan brought her many intellectual gifts and litigator's toolbox to fix my manuscript and ended up naming it as well.

Former NAACP LDF lawyers, cooperating attorneys, and clients such as James Ferguson, Albert and Evelyn Turner, Spencer Hogue, J. L. Chestnut, Rose and Hank Sanders, Julius Chambers, G. K. Butterfield, Frank Ballance, Olly Neal, Leslie Winner, and Robert Turner all graciously shared their insights in interviews with me and permitted me to include excerpts from those interviews in this book. Elaine Jones and Donna Gloeckner generously permitted me to review LDF case files and other public documents. Eddie Correia, who dropped everything to help out with the nomination in 1993, Acie Byrd, and Reverend Nelson Johnson, whose vision of "sustainable community" in Greensboro,

North Carolina, has so inspired me, all took time from their busy lives to sit down with me and think about what it all means. Stephanie Camp, an unusually gifted graduate student and budding historian, shared her indomitable appetite for historical context, her instinct for a good story, her passion for getting things right, and her well-honed research skills. Rob Richie proved once again to be a human encyclopedia of information on voting and election systems. Melissa McClenaghan, Christian Grose, and Elizabeth Clement were diligent and resourceful research assistants.

Others who read chapters and offered invaluable advice include dear friends like Roger Wilkins, Marcia Smith, Charles Ogletree, Gwen Parker, and Leroy Clark; committed colleagues such as Bob Shapiro, Bruce Nichols, and Charlotte Sheedy; able students Jean Sbarge, Camille Forbes, Marshella Atkinson, and Elizabeth Valentin; and my mother-in-law, Kathryn Thomas, who encouraged me after she read the first few chapters but then suggested I "watch" my back. Julie Colleluori and the secretarial staff at Penn Law School were just super in providing all manner of support. My mother, Eugenia Guinier, read multiple drafts of the manuscript and despite failing health pushed me always to rethink and rewrite to reach more people. She and my unbelievably nimble, thoughtful, and savvy editor, Michael Korda, patiently reread incarnations of the entire book many times prior to publication. My husband and son, Nolan and Nikolas Bowie, loved me through all of this and gave me the gift of time and space to write and rewrite, to think and rethink, and to heal.

I thank all whom I have mentioned and all who were there in so many other ways, especially those who still come up to me in the street or at the train station to share their observations about politics and to encourage me to keep fighting. You made this book possible.

Writing this book was hard. Initially I told myself it was difficult because I could not use footnotes to explain, clarify, or expand upon my ideas. I had been trained first as a lawyer and then as an academic to be precise and painstakingly exact in telling a story. Some may see the absence of footnotes on these pages, therefore, as a cop-out. Others may see it as liberating. I saw it as an effort to reach a wider audience and to begin a bigger conversation. But as a result of not using traditional academic tools, including notes, there are undoubtedly places where I overstate or overlook.

Moreover, I wrote the first part of this book primarily from memory, assisted by contemporaneous notes, voice mail messages, tape-recorded recollections, and newspaper clippings. Since my memory, like everyone's, is selective, I anticipate that there are others who have different recollections of the same meetings or incidents. I welcome their contribution to what I hope is a continuing conversation about these events and their significance. In the end, I hope at least some who read this book come to understand what I believe is most important: the furor generated when President Clinton nominated me in 1993 to the post of Assistant Attorney General for Civil Rights was not really about me. Nor did I alone pay the price of the abandonment of an ambitious social justice agenda in the aftermath of the president's decision to withdraw the nomination. However, all errors in the recounting or interpreting of these events are mine alone, for which I accept responsibility in advance.

*This book is dedicated to my father, Ewart Guinier,
who taught me to speak in my own voice,
and to my mother, Eugenia Guinier,
who is still teaching me how to lift my voice
in harmony with others*

CONTENTS

Lift Every Voice and Sing

Lift every voice and sing
Till earth and heaven ring
Ring with the harmonies of liberty
Let our rejoicing rise
High as the list'ning skies
Let it resound loud as the rolling sea

Sing a song full of the faith that the dark past has taught us
Sing a song full of the hope that the present has brought us
Facing the rising sun of our new day begun
Let us march on till victory is won

—JAMES WELDON JOHNSON

INTRODUCTION

IT'S TAKEN ME many years, but in my conscious moments I don't regret any of it. Not the decision of the president to nominate me. Not the collapse of the president's support in the face of intense, ideological attack from the right and the center/right. Not the microscopic personal scrutiny I received in the press both before and after. Not the subsequent valedictory treatment I received from people I didn't know, but for whom I clearly came to represent so much. Especially not the belated discovery that this betrayal was not about *me*, but about the collapse of a movement. None of it.

How I came to this point is the story of this book. This book is about the battles fought in the belief that our racial history and our commitment to equality and democracy are essential parts of the same story. It has not always been a pretty story, nor one that follows an inevitable path. This book is not, however, an effort to settle scores. It's the story of the efforts of men and women who believe fundamentally in the promise of the American creed and who act on that belief in their everyday lives. These are people whose lives are without notoriety or fame, but in whose willingness to take risks we see the honor of real heroism.

They are ordinary people in that they do not hold elected office or wield formal power. They do not enjoy great wealth, easy access to the media, lengthy résumés, or "big jobs." Like so many others who have changed the course of our history, they appear ordinary to the unobservant, but on closer scrutiny they are extraordinary in the way we all benefit from the actual work they do.

These are the people, some of whom were once civil rights activists, clients, or sympathizers, who still struggle to connect with others to make a difference, not just for themselves but for their families and their community. These are people who struggle within their own neighborhoods to create the possibility for others to be treated with dignity, to be given an opportunity to speak, and, even more, to be given a meaningful chance to participate in making the decisions that affect all of our lives. These are people with considerable power, but their power depends on commitment and sustained struggle, and not just isolated struggle. These are people whose voices are too often missing from public debate about issues on which they are expert. Their voices are missing not because they don't want to speak but because they don't get a hearing.

When I was trying voting cases as a lawyer for the NAACP Legal Defense Fund during the 1980s, many of these people were my clients. When I say "my clients," I am referring to more than a single person or group of people who retain a lawyer to represent them in a legal case. The term is a metaphor for those whom civil rights lawyers, including myself, undertook to represent when we joined the civil rights movement and fought for civil rights issues. We were lawyers, often playing traditional roles in court or behind the scenes as legislative advocates. But we were also deeply connected to the interests of those whom we sought to represent. Their interests, as we saw them, were not simply an improvement in their individual material conditions or social status. We did not see ourselves as merely litigating on behalf of a set of special or unique interests. We represented *ordinary people*, who fought for the chance to become active citizens in a genuine and inclusive democracy. We believed that if our clients could participate in making decisions that affected their lives, they would change those decisions in ways that enriched all of us.

Participation matters, after all. A seat at the table and a voice at the podium enables each of us to become part of something larger than ourselves.

Self-reliance is an important survival tool. But participation among and with others offers more than simple survival. It nourishes and reinforces both the individual and the community. When individuals participate as citizens, they often realize their fullest potential, supported and affirmed by others. The act of participating in concert reinforces the individual dignity and sense of purpose even of those who fight and fail.

My civil rights clients understood this all too well. They were people who fought back not simply because they were personally aggrieved, but because their injury connected them to a community and a movement that was both as narrow as their local interests and as broad as a nation. My clients were most powerful when they could tell their own stories not having to translate their emotions, their hurts, their hopes, or their fears through the formal categories of a single lawsuit. They understood and believed more deeply than most in the law, but they also knew it is democracy on which the law rests. And democracy demands the ability to participate, the opportunity to act in close association with others, and the right to a hearing. It was only when they could speak plainly through collective actions Americans of any color would understand that their voices were in fact heard.

It was while my nomination to be Assistant Attorney General for Civil Rights was pending in 1993 that I saw, from the inside, the ways in which the commitment to a civil rights vision that is inclusive, democratic, and empowering often means that against you are arrayed the powerful forces of privilege, both public and private. That experience allowed me to understand *why* meaningful participation is so important. It also reminded me, in the most personal way possible, that the civil rights movement, in too many ways, has left that understanding behind.

In seeking the nomination, I wasn't fighting for a specific legal remedy or a specific legal cause, but I experienced the kinds of things my clients did, in a different context. I now knew firsthand what it meant to have no voice. My clients, who fought for the right to vote, were fighting for a voice. By playing according to the rules laid down to me, I surrendered my voice to others. In this book, I describe how I lost and then reclaimed my own voice by interweaving my story with those of others—the men and women who taught me, through their own example, the redemptive value of collective action and the importance of voicing individual grievances within a larger, community-based struggle.

IN RETROSPECT, much has crystalized for me since the nomination. I came to see my "dis-appointment" as an opportunity rather than a defeat. While I was rejected by the political mainstream as a nominee for public office, I was affirmed by others as a "scholar with a heart," what *The New Yorker* called an "Idea Woman." I became myself. I could now speak in my own voice. I could also use this experience to invite others into the conversation.

This, then, is also the story of my own intellectual and political growth and how the nomination debacle moved me to another stage— a broader public platform and a more complex but ultimately satisfying personal and professional identity. In losing a hearing I was pushed back to strength. I discovered the strength that comes from promoting a more inclusive social justice agenda. I found my own voice in listening to others lift theirs.

Trials

CHAPTER ONE

A Low-Tech Lynching

Nearly two years ago, Clarence Thomas sat before the klieg lights and television cameras and declared that he was the victim of a "high-tech lynching." Lani Guinier yearned mightily for that same opportunity, but was denied it by a combination of editorial racism, Senatorial cowardice, and White House incompetence. Lani Guinier was politically lynched, but in a pre-television way. It was a "low-tech lynching."

—*Political Woman*, vol. 1, no. 9
(July 1993)

Ⅰ T WAS JANUARY 23, 1993, the first Saturday night of Bill Clinton's presidency. It was a social gathering, a small dinner party I hosted with two other women. We were law school classmates. Lila, now a psychologist, had wanted to do all the cooking; it would be more "authentic and personal." Nancy, a friend of Hillary's from Wellesley College as well as Yale Law School, thought we should hire a caterer. I compromised—we would cater dinner and serve homemade dessert. Lila got to bake a cake, which, like everything else, was eaten first by the president's official taster, who had arrived early to perform his duties.

The party was held at Lila's family home in northwest Washington, D.C. It was a solid brick house, a corner house, unprepossessing and surprisingly small. In fact, the size of the house had been a useful excuse—we could, in all good faith, limit the guest list. Lila had grown up in this house with her four brothers and one sister. The house was not shabby but it showed signs of age. Little effort had been made to disguise its wear and tear, evidence of a large family with so many boys. That night, however, the house positively glowed. We had even hired an older black man recommended by a friend of Lila's to play the piano.

About thirty minutes after we were all assembled, we got a telephone call from the White House. The president and first lady were on their way. As soon as they arrived, a group of us huddled around Hillary. Confident in our credentials, we nevertheless were giddy with disbelief. Just two days after the official inaugural festivities, the newly minted president of the United States and his wife had left the White House to come to a private home in northwest D.C. Giggling like schoolgirls, we listened eagerly as Hillary described her new digs.

Hillary spoke with the authority of someone in charge. It was important to her, she confided, to maintain an atmosphere of informality in the White House. She wanted to make friends with the staff. By contrast, the Bush family had coped, she sensed, by being detached, maintaining a strict hierarchy, expecting to be served by their "employees."

Hillary and Chelsea had gone exploring the first night. One of their stops was the White House roof, where they noticed the marksmen positioned at the ready. Hillary described the scene with a mixture of awe and shock. She was being protected, for her own safety, for the good of the country. She told the story in a straightforward manner, but I sensed she felt captured, maybe even imprisoned. She had moved into the White House and found herself instead in a fortress.

I began to understand why dinner with "real people," as Hillary had said in accepting our invitation, was important. Casually dressed (except for the designer scarf to complement her headband), eating buffet, here she was "just folks." I began to breathe normally.

Harlon Dalton, a professor at the Yale Law School, adroitly performed the emcee duties. Teaching at Yale Law School was high status in some circles, but little did we know how it had prepared Harlon to reach a much wider audience as a professional comedian. He roasted the president and first lady with gag gifts—a fake hand, big ears, a toy army tank, a black witch's hat. Each present had passed Secret Service scrutiny first, but the sniffing dogs could not detect the contents' significance. Each package was a mere prop, a setup for our master-of-ceremonies' cutting and nimble repartee.

Sitting comfortably, legs outstretched in an armchair in the living room next to the fireplace, the president was a willing audience. His enthusiasm was generous. He laughed and laughed. Big, body laughs. Maybe the president had no choice, since Harlon stood so close he was almost in the president's lap. The first lady, more demure at first, sat upright in a side chair at the president's left. She too quickly responded to Harlon's easy banter. With very little prodding, she and the president cavorted for the amateur photographers among us, modeling the witch's hat and the fake hand. When we joined hands to sing "America the

Beautiful," Hillary grasped my fingers tightly, eager, it appeared, to establish connections.

We considered ourselves—a group of serious, long-standing friends—to be the president and first lady's intellectual if not political peers. Each of us shared the sense of portent, of arrival; we believed in him, in his bigheartedness, in his passion for justice. Congressman Mel Watt, representing the Highway 85 district in North Carolina, was there. Earlier in the evening, he and the president had had a heated conversation in the dining room about voting rights. I remember joining the conversation, challenging the president's interpretation of the motor voter provision, especially, I reminded him, in light of our experience in Arkansas. As a staff lawyer for the NAACP Legal Defense and Education Fund (often referred to simply as LDF or the Legal Defense Fund), I had sued Governor Clinton over Arkansas's deputy voter registration statute. We had settled the case. My co-counsel in that case was Deval L. Patrick. Deval was not there that night, but several other people who would later serve in the Clinton presidential administration were, including the future Solicitor General, the first Solicitor of Labor, counsel to the Army, counsel to the FCC, and the head of an important Justice Department law and order project. Two of us who were there were eventually to be nominated, or at least considered in turn, for the post of Assistant Attorney General for Civil Rights.

This was not a fund-raiser. No one notified the press. It was not a public relations gala. By his own choice, Bill Clinton savored his national debut with people most of whom forty years earlier would not have been able to join him publicly for lunch at the Capitol. In his moment of public triumph, Bill Clinton had simply left his grand House to celebrate in the modest home of an honest-to-goodness black friend.

We were impressed. We knew that Bill Clinton was probably the very first president of the United States to have enough black friends to hold a party, not just convene a photo opportunity.

When we said good-bye at the end of the evening, my husband, Nolan, casually said to Hillary, "Both of us would be happy to serve in this administration," to which she replied, "That is good to know." That was the extent of any direct conversation about a job.

After the party, I received a personal note from the president:

> Dear Lani, Thanks for the party. We loved it. Tell Nolan not to forget about the stuff he promised to send—Hope to see you soon.
>
> Best,
> Bill.

Nolan had talked to "Bill" about his favorite topic—information policy. The "stuff he promised to send" was not a résumé but a position paper.

Then, in early February, Bernard Nussbaum, White House counsel, called and said, "I am not offering you a job but I would like you to cooperate with us in the vetting process. We are thinking about you for a job at Justice. I am going to send you some forms. Please fill them out and return them asap."

Bernie never specified the job, except to say it was a high-ranking senior position at Justice. When I returned the forms, I was interviewed by phone about their contents by Liz Fine, an associate in the White House counsel's office. She advised me that the FBI would begin a background investigation. I did not want that to happen unless I was being offered a position because I had not yet talked to the dean at Penn Law School, where I was a tenured professor. Nevertheless, a week later I got a call from Special Agent Scott Perkins of the FBI, asking to talk to me about the background investigation. I asked him to hold off until I did my own "background investigation" to find out which job I was even being considered for. He gave me his home phone number and his beeper and assured me that he would not proceed. He also made clear that he was under pressure to move forward.

After the call from Special Agent Perkins, I called Bill Kennedy, Liz Fine's boss in the White House counsel's office, to ask what was going on. He was quite put off, suggesting that it was standard procedure to begin a background check at this point. He implied that something was wrong with me for even questioning it. I noted that they might be following standard procedure, but I reminded him that I hadn't been offered a position as yet. Finally, after going back and forth several times, he understood that I needed to be able to tell my dean something before FBI agents began to roam the law school checking up on me. Nussbaum called me back the following Monday. He said, "You are being considered for a senior position; you have not been offered the position but I am confident that you will be given a senior Justice Department position. That is what you should tell your dean."

Bernie Nussbaum called me again at the beginning of March to say he wanted to set up a meeting with Janet Reno, then the nominee for Attorney General. He also advised me to stop by his office to introduce myself to him on my way to see her. At the time, Janet Reno was working out of the Old Executive Office Building. I was unable to arrange both meetings for the same day so I met Bernie first, on a Wednesday at 4:00 P.M.

The television in his office was tuned to the Senate Judiciary Committee vote on Reno. He was staring at the television and occasionally would look up to ask me a question. Except for twenty minutes spent reading and discussing a memo about me that was on his desk, Nussbaum used most of the hour and fifteen minutes that I was in his office

to make small talk or watch television. After the favorable Judiciary
Committee vote sending Reno's nomination to the Senate floor, he
declared he was the second happiest person in America, the first being
the president. I interjected, "Don't you think Janet Reno is also happy?"
"Yes, I guess I am the third happiest person in America," he replied.
Nussbaum then excused himself and raced out to tell the president that
the committee had voted unanimously to confirm Janet Reno as the
first woman Attorney General of the United States. I was left to interview myself in his office.

Bernie wore many different hats. He was my uncle Murray's
friend; he was Hillary's friend. He talked about how he knew Hillary
and how she had been his employee and now she was his client, although some would say she was his boss. He talked about my uncle
Murray, who was a member of the same predominantly Jewish country
club in New York and who, during the transition, had faxed him a
memo saying that Lani Guinier should be considered for the Attorney
General position. I laughed and told Bernie I had not put my uncle up
to it. Bernie said, "In fact your name was on a list to be Attorney
General in December." I laughed again. "Don't worry," he reassured me.
"It was not a short list."

I asked Bernie what the administration's civil rights agenda was. I
wanted to know whether they had a strategy, an affirmative agenda of
areas to emphasize or a negative agenda of issues to minimize. I asked,
"Does the administration have either a positive or a negative agenda on
civil rights?" He answered that it had neither. I asked Bernie about his
personal agenda on civil rights. He said, "To enforce the law." I told him
I certainly had no problem with that.

He asked what I would do if nominated to head the Civil Rights
Division. This was the first time we had even talked about a specific
position. We had been talking around the issue. I was pleased, even
relieved finally to be talking substance. I said it was really important to
revive the morale of the line lawyers, the career civil servants in the
division who had been committed to doing their jobs, and during both
the Bush and Reagan administrations had not been allowed to, or had
been discouraged from doing so in a vigorous and effective way. In some
situations, it would be a challenge to show them how to litigate civil
rights cases again. I had been told that during the last twelve years
some of the Civil Rights Division attorneys spent the day reading the
newspapers.

I also told him that I was interested in talking about different ways
of enforcing some civil rights laws; that some of them possibly had
outlived their usefulness or at least might be more effectively administered in different ways; that an administration interested in embracing
change should be open to change in this arena as well. He said, "I have

no problem with that." He then paused to reread the memorandum on his desk.

He looked away from the television set and directly at me. He said, "I understand that you have done some writing that is controversial. What is that about?" I had written several law review articles as part of the pre-tenure review process of Penn's law school. I received tenure in 1992. Law professors receive tenure based primarily on the theoretical rigor of their academic scholarship. Scholars are also evaluated on whether they make an original contribution to their fields: they must say something new, or something no one else has quite thought of before. Tenure guarantees lifetime employment. It requires a vote of confidence by senior members of the law school faculty, who judge candidates on teaching, institutional citizenship and service, and scholarship. Especially at schools such as Penn, scholarship requires the publication of well-researched, multifootnoted, densely argued analyses.

In my pre-tenure articles, I had written about alternative election systems to remedy violations of the 1965 Voting Rights Act. I told Bernie that the particular system I had described, cumulative voting, was an alternative to single-member districts. Instead of dividing a city with seven elected officials into seven wards or districts, all city voters get seven votes. Voters can use their seven votes in any combination to support candidates of their choice. They could vote all seven for one candidate or divide their votes, putting three on one candidate and four on another. In corporations that use cumulative voting, each shareholder—even so-called minority shareholders—gets the same number of votes as there are directors. If five positions exist for the corporate board of directors, each holder of stock gets five votes per share. In a corporation with one hundred shares of stock, a shareholder with twenty shares can put all her votes on one director-candidate, thus assuring the candidate's election to one of the five seats.

Cumulative voting is race-neutral. It has been used in a variety of ways throughout the United States, including by American corporations to protect minority shareholders from being overwhelmed or ignored by those who own a majority of the stock. It has also been adopted to elect members of local collective decision-making bodies (legislatures, city councils, county school boards) in places like Chilton County, Alabama, in the 1980s; and Illinois throughout most of the middle of this century. Similar election systems are used throughout Europe and most other Western democracies, including Israel, to ensure that minority *viewpoints* are democratically represented. South Africa now uses this kind of a system to assure representation in the national legislature for the white Afrikaners.

The advantage of cumulative voting was that it might encourage the participation of those who felt left out of a system that overrepresented the winners and gave those who lose nothing. It was one of the ideas I drew from the experiences I had gained as a civil rights lawyer in Washington, D.C.; in Selma, Alabama; in Helena, Arkansas; and in Charlotte, North Carolina; as well as from the experiences of my voting rights colleagues in many other places.

But it wasn't just a theoretical notion. Cumulative voting, which was then in place in Chilton County, Alabama, led to the election of the first woman, the first black, and the first Republican in many years. To elect the seven-person school board there, all voters received seven votes. A politically cohesive group of voters could concentrate their seven votes to gain representation. That is exactly what blacks in Chilton County did. Their gains, however, did not come at the expense of other disenfranchised political or religious minorities. Indeed, women also benefited, as did Republicans, then the minority political party in that heavily Democratic county. Cumulative voting also enabled some blacks and whites to form cross-racial coalitions because after voters aggregated some of their votes to express their most intense preferences, they still had other votes left over to support their allies.

Bernie said, "That sounds great. Great. When you talk to Janet Reno, tell her about all those things." That was the end of our conversation.

I returned to D.C. that Friday to meet Janet Reno. She was sworn in that morning. I had a meeting with her in the afternoon. I approached the Justice Department entrance on Tenth Street. The quite ordinary-looking security guard was in a very friendly mood. He greeted me with affection. He didn't know me; he only knew I was here to meet the Attorney General. He told me he knew this was a historic day. His face lit up when he said, with a touch of fatherly pride, "We have a new Attorney General. A woman."

Until that moment, I had been alternately excited and ambivalent about the job. The Assistant Attorney General (AAG) for Civil Rights was a subcabinet post, supervising hundreds of lawyers and other enforcement personnel who brought cases in a range of civil rights areas, including housing discrimination, disability rights, criminal civil rights violations, and voting rights. It was a job I knew well. For four years in the Carter administration I had played right hand to then Assistant Attorney General Drew S. Days III as his lone special assistant. My job under Days came with an impressive title and a spacious office, but I found that the actual chores often allowed limited autonomy. As a public servant, I learned early to swallow my pride when necessary to get the job done. Other people were setting the agenda and they often set it in ways that involved shuffling papers with little results. The AAG for Civil Rights reports directly to the Associate Attorney General, who then reports to the Attorney General. Under no circumstances that I recalled did AAG Drew Days enjoy complete independence. On routine enforcement matters he may have had little oversight from those above him in the chain of command. But in any high-profile case, the back and forth was often mind-boggling. Especially in cases filed in the U.S. Supreme Court, the Solicitor General has final authority and must sign off on the content of all briefs filed by the Civil Rights Division.

The prospect of putting myself in that position again was less than inviting. This was especially true in an administration led by someone who held himself out as a friend but who had not yet made clear the civil rights agenda he intended to follow or his willingness to fight hard for things in which he believed.

My ambivalence returned when I first entered the Justice Department building in March 1993. It was dignified. It was massive. To all comers it announced its importance. But I remembered the frustrations, the endless meetings, the feeling that whatever you filed was written by a committee, often including many people with absolutely no expertise except politics. The brief may have been filed with your name on it, but it was not recognizable as a document you had written. It was not government that was the problem. It was bureaucracy. To some extent, the Justice Department was a euphemism for a bureaucracy filled with lawyers.

I had convinced myself by now, however, that I wanted the job, that I could do the job even if it meant getting up every morning geared for battle. I was confident that if I got the job, the opportunity would present itself for me to fight that battle alongside many of my friends within the administration.

Once I walked into the Attorney General's office on the fifth floor, I got into a celebratory mood right away. "I am just so proud," I gushed when I greeted her. I was really moved to be in the Attorney General's office, now occupied by a woman, for the first time in more than ten years. Reno herself seemed almost dazed. The office was overflowing with flowers and the phone was ringing off the hook. She escorted me through the conference room into her interior chamber. She sat down on the couch opposite an oil painting of Robert Kennedy—the epitome of youth and transcendent mission. It pictured him walking on the windswept beach, hands stuffed in the pocket of his leather jacket, deep in thought about something probably related to his commitment to public service. She announced, "This is the best day of my life and the worst day of my life."

I said, "I can understand why it is the best day. But why is it the worst day?" She paused, then answered. "I am sitting here. I have been in this office two hours. I am sitting across from a portrait of Robert Kennedy, who is one of my heroes, and I just feel overwhelmed." She seemed so genuine, so honest that I immediately liked her. She was treating me as a peer, not a subordinate. I was honored, but I also felt compelled to say: "I heard your testimony about your mom, sitting in the middle of the house that she built with her own hands, sitting in her chair while a hurricane swirled around her, confident that because she had built that house, it was going to stand. I am sure that you are your mother's daughter and that you will be able to stand the hurricane of the next four years." With that, we really hit it off.

She asked me to tell her about myself. I told her I'd always wanted to be a civil rights lawyer. She warmed immediately; it seemed she'd found the person she wanted. We talked about my articles. She said, "Bernie tells me you have written some radical stuff. Is that something that you wrote ten years ago? Is it not important?" And I said, "No, it is something I have written recently and this is what it's about." I repeated what I'd said to Bernie, spending no more than five or ten minutes explaining the premise and the thesis of the articles. She listened politely, but took no notes. When I finished, she said, "Okay. That is fine." And she took some papers from her lap and laid them on the couch as if to say, "Okay. We've moved off that subject. Now we can talk more about you." I then asked her the same questions I had put to Bernie. I asked, "Are there things you definitely want or don't want to do in civil rights?" She said, "No, I just want somebody in here who is going to enforce the law."

Janet Reno, a woman I only just met and about whom I knew very little, became one of the reasons I now desperately wanted the job. Whenever I thought about Janet Reno over the weeks that followed, I softened. Thinking about how overwhelmed she seemed on her first day on the job made me vulnerable, too. I was drawn to her, convinced that her commitment to do what was right came from the heart. She was a steadfast ally. She offered to accompany me on my courtesy calls, should that become necessary. It made me really, really want to work with her, to enforce the law in her shop.

I was worried, however, that no one else in the administration seemed to be taking the nomination process seriously. They treated me as a job applicant, not an administration workhorse. With the exception of Janet Reno herself, the White House and Justice Department staff were almost indifferent to filling in even the broad outlines of an agenda on civil rights.

My concerns were augmented in mid-April when *The Jewish Forward* (edited by Seth Lipsky, who came to the paper from the *Wall Street Journal*) published a critical article about me. I had not spoken

with the reporter, on instructions from the administration, whose cus-
tomary policy was to keep nominees from speaking to the press pending
confirmation hearings. Several of my Jewish friends had taken on the
task of reaching out to the author of the article; they also called some
people they knew within prominent Jewish lobbying organizations.
Their efforts seemed to pay off. There was no further press in the next
few days. But the article reminded me that I could easily become a
lightning rod for controversy.

From the start there was a strong whiff of controversy in the air, as
right-wing ideologues promised revenge after the bruising confirmation
battles over Judge Robert Bork and Justice Clarence Thomas. I was told
that back in December, when my name had surfaced as the leading
candidate for the civil rights position. Early in January 1993, I had
had a conversation with Elaine Jones, Wade Henderson, and Barbara
Arnwine, each of whom had recently assumed leadership positions in a
prominent civil rights organization: the NAACP Legal Defense Fund
(LDF), the Washington office of the NAACP, and the National Lawyers
Committee for Civil Rights Under Law, respectively. They told me I
was their unanimous choice, that they really wanted me to do this job.
They thought I could make a difference; they were pushing for me.
They didn't want to be pushing for me if I was not going to take
the job.

I talked to them about my reservations. I was completely honest. I
told them that the only way I would do the job was if I felt I had a base
of people who would support me in the position. That I couldn't go into
the administration and do this by myself, but that I could work in
conjunction with them. The top priority would be enforcing the civil
rights laws, but I also wanted to initiate the conversation about new
remedies and new ways of thinking about civil rights issues. I shared
with them that I thought we needed fresh approaches that were consistent with where the country was right now, the changing demographics,
and the nature of the problems all Americans were facing. I was awed
by their confidence. It felt as if I was being enlisted to do an important
job by the people I admired the most.

That I did indeed quickly become a lightning rod for controversy
should not have been surprising. After all, I was talking about rebuild-
ing a commitment to civil rights through innovative approaches in a
climate in which much of the constituency for civil rights had been in
hiding, in response to the systemic attacks of the past twelve years. The
civil rights community had experienced the twelve years of Reagan/
Bush Republican administrations as devastating. Under the leadership
of William Bradford Reynolds, the Justice Department Civil Rights
Division had been leading the assault against civil rights as I knew
them. Their agenda, of dismantling the vigorous role that the federal

government had been playing in civil rights enforcement since the mid-1960s, was destroying the federal commitment and eliminating the resources devoted to carrying out that commitment.

The civil rights community had weathered the storm, anonymously infiltrating sympathetic federal agencies, litigating where necessary to hold the line. They were slowly regrouping, but the damage of the Reagan/Bush years would take time to repair. Everyone was eager to move forward quickly, to clean house. But the *Jewish Forward* article tipped me off that the right wing would not sit idly by, and, indeed, would be encouraged by the Justice Department and White House staff's apparent inattention to the substance and process of the civil rights nomination.

I kept pressing for signs of real presidential leadership, or at least a signal from the staff that there was a coherent civil rights vision, even if no one was willing to launch a preemptive strike. No one, however, was listening.

Nor did anyone seem to be in charge. That is, until Ricki Seidman walked into my life. Ricki Seidman is a big woman; she wouldn't get lost easily in a crowd. Her entrance into a room was often a political statement. The day that I was nominated, April 29, 1993, was the day I first saw Ricki in action. A group of us were eating lunch in the Attorney General's dining room. Six among us were about to be introduced in a public ceremony as Justice Department nominees. We had arrived early, assuming we would find an agenda, but none of us had yet seen any evidence of a plan. Webster Hubbell—the president's friend from Little Rock, former justice of the Arkansas Supreme Court, and Hillary's law partner in the Rose Law Firm—sat at the head of the lunch table. He tried hard to make it appear as if someone was in charge. His nomination as Associate Attorney General had already been announced weeks before. The assembled chatted lightly yet nervously. The mindless chatter did nothing to distract me from a feeling that had been growing in the pit of my stomach that at least one of us was a lamb waiting to be taken to slaughter.

As I pondered my fate, the door to the Attorney General's dining room opened wide and Ricki Seidman walked in—marched in was more like it. She arrived alone, but she might have been leading a parade. Her majestic presence was announcement enough: we all stopped in mid-forkful. She bent over to whisper something in Webb Hubbell's ear. He may have been at the head of the table, but now Ricki was in charge. She waved her arms in the air, sweeping away the Justice Department staff minions surrounding the table. By now we were all ears, waiting to be told whatever secrets she had hidden somewhere on her huge frame.

We were not disappointed. With no time to spare, she walked all the nominees through our roles. In a brief fifteen minutes, Ricki restored a sense of order. I saw her then as a true saviour—a get-things-done-now kind of person.

The formal announcement ceremony was scheduled to begin within less than an hour. Ricki Seidman, a staffer in the White House Communications Office, had arrived just in time. Thirty minutes later, I and the other political neophytes were thrust into the public limelight on a platform in the Justice Department courtyard. But while Ricki had prepared us for where to stand and how to walk, neither she nor anyone else had sat down with me to talk about the substance of what to say.

We gathered in the hallway just inside from the courtyard stage and were lined up in the order we would be introduced. We were given our final instructions and then the president arrived. In what we were told was a last-minute decision, President Clinton himself would make the presentations.

The president had a regal bearing. He wore a beautifully tailored blue suit that seemed as much cloak as business uniform of the country's commander in chief. As he strode down the row of nervous nominees, he greeted each of us in his typically physical style: he grasped my hand, congratulated me, and kissed me lightly on the cheek. As he moved on to the others, I remember overhearing one of the nominees pass on a greeting from an old friend from Arkansas. The president stepped back and with a wistful look in his eyes said, "I remember Steve. That was when I had a real life." And I remember the response, "Mr. President, this *is* real life." I pondered the exchange, immediately thinking to myself that it can't get more unreal than this. I realized later I was wrong.

As we were introduced, there were cheers and signs saying: ATTA GIRL, JANET! and the like. I also saw many old friends, including Marie Klimesz and Jerry Hebert, career lawyers in the Civil Rights Division, who were giving the thumbs-up; some were smiling so broadly I thought they would burst. I had not been back in that courtyard in twelve years, yet here I was accepting the nomination to head the Civil Rights Division, determined to enforce the laws as passed by Congress.

As a former staff attorney for the NAACP Legal Defense Fund and now as a law professor reflecting on that experience, I accepted the nomination with a dual sense of mission. I believed it was critical to enforce existing laws. I also wanted to change direction in the fight for civil rights. I was not sanguine about simply recommitting the federal government and its resources to enforcing a 1960s vision of formal equality. I believed that innovative remedies were needed to address a different, more complex set of problems. I wanted to start a genuine dialogue to bridge the different world views on race.

I had hoped to begin that conversation, using this first public announcement to signal a new civil rights commitment and mission. I wanted to use the job to create a space for people to begin to speak for themselves. I wanted to create a space for the constituency of the Civil Rights Division—the disabled, the discriminated against, the marginalized Americans who could enrich our public conversation so that others would learn why they should care that this constituency be represented. I had drafted a written statement to that effect, with the help of my University of Pennsylvania law professor colleagues Susan Sturm and Barbara Woodhouse. No one from the administration had suggested I prepare such a statement, but I had learned from watching Brad Reynolds and other right-wing Republicans that it was a mistake to forgo a public opportunity to define your own agenda.

I also felt it important to establish why exactly I was here *with the president of the United States*. As a staff attorney for the Legal Defense Fund, I had litigated several voting cases against Arkansas Governor Clinton. In introducing me, the president now seemed to take particular pleasure in announcing to the crowd the depth of his commitment to civil rights, symbolized by his nomination of someone who had sued him. Although his remarks were not substantive, his inaugural address had already, in my mind, set the right tone. He recalled Thomas Jefferson's belief that "to preserve the very foundations of our nation we need dramatic change from time to time." "This is our time," the president had said. "Let us embrace it." I believed he would embrace our time in the interests of a genuinely inclusive vision.

I held fast to my hopes on this remarkably sunny April day—even though the president and I had not had a sustained conversation about civil rights policy since our discussion about motor voter laws at the party back in January. I waited patiently as the president and the Attorney General spoke. They were experienced politicians, undaunted by the television cameras or reporters. Both were obviously at ease, despite the many pairs of eyes evaluating their every gesture. Their skilled smoothness contrasted with our visible discomfort. One of the nominees, Walter Dellinger, who had gone to the trouble of memorizing his prepared statement, gripped the written text behind his back, just in case. Another, Sheila Foster, announced that she was "unabashedly ecstatic," but her tight, frozen smile conveyed the opposite.

Several friends who witnessed the ceremony on video, or viewed pictures in news reports, told me I looked radiant and self-possessed, framed by a beaming president in the background. They were kind. I was anxious and used my lawyerly formality to camouflage the butterflies in my stomach. Although I wanted very much to be part of a new, progressive administration and was eager to launch a public education campaign, I was a novice in this new world of "real life."

We each were given first ten, then five, then two and a half minutes to speak. I tried to wedge several themes into my allotted time. I talked about my parents. I spoke first of my black father, who had taught me through the stories of his life how to look injustice in the eye and then to fight back. But I was not just my father's daughter. I told how my mother, who is Jewish, had taught me to see the other person's side, how not to internalize criticism as rejection, and how to try to bridge differences with open, frank dialogue and creative compromise.

Just after announcing my nomination to the world, the president had whispered in my ear, "Thanks for not gloating about the Arkansas registration case. I thought you would boast that you had won." Janet Reno said nothing as she escorted me down the stairs. For her, words were unnecessary. Bill Clinton and Janet Reno were cast from different molds. One had living-room charisma; the other was more self-contained. One talked to the people; the other believed in them.

At the conclusion we were shepherded into a room for our first, and until the Senate confirmation hearings, our only press conference. There I got an inkling of how little I knew about this new, unreal life. I was not skilled at the task of facing down journalists: projecting symbols and reducing complex ideas to sound bites. I was asked about a reference I had made in my acceptance comments on the need to change direction in civil rights enforcement. I chose to respond by explaining in great detail the facts in the case of *Major* v. *Treen*. That was the "Donald Duck" gerrymandering case in Louisiana where a previous Assistant Attorney General for Civil Rights, Brad Reynolds, had declined to enforce the law despite evidence that legislators and interested parties had made explicitly racist comments about how New Orleans didn't need any more "nigger bigshots" and "nigger mayors" to run in voting districts that gave blacks a fair chance to win.

Reynolds's decision had contravened recommendations from his career staff, who were experienced in detecting voting discrimination. I, as attorney for the NAACP Legal Defense Fund, had been forced to go to court. We prevailed in the litigation; yet the weight of my description of how prior administrations had tolerated actual examples of intentional discrimination was more than the reporters wanted to hear that day. Afterwards, my fellow nominees thanked me for what they took as a filibuster. From their perspective, I had successfully distracted the press, whose interest in nonpayment of Social Security taxes could not regain momentum. Momentum is something I would learn much about.

I did not have to wait long. The very next day the *Wall Street Journal* published an opinion piece by Clint Bolick, litigation director of a right-wing organization, the Institute for Justice. Bolick's piece was headlined: BILL CLINTON'S QUOTA QUEENS. The article discussed me and a nominee for a civil rights post in the Department of Education, Norma

Cantu, a former litigator for the Mexican American Legal Defense Fund. Bolick, a protégé of former Assistant Attorney General William Bradford Reynolds and Supreme Court Justice Clarence Thomas, painted both of us with the same broad and hostile brush.

Though "Quota Queens" was coined in the plural the day after the formal nomination, the term was quickly used to target me alone. After all, as a law professor I was the only one with a paper trail. Many of my ideas were complex and thus easily distorted through sound bites. In my law review articles, I expressed reservations about unfettered majority rule—Madison's majority tyranny—and about the need sometimes to disaggregate the majority in order to ensure fair representation for all substantial minorities. Some columnists who attacked me praised remarkably similar ideas, but in a different context. George Will, for example, had opined in a newspaper column: "The Framers also understood that stable, tyrannical majorities can best be prevented by the multiplication of minority interests, so the majority at any moment will be just a transitory coalition of minorities." The difference was that the minority I used to illustrate my academic point about the limitations of winner-take-all majority rule was not, as it was in George Will's example, the minority of well-to-do landlords in New York City. I wrote instead about the political exclusion of the black minority in many local county and municipal governing bodies in the United States.

Fueled by cartoonish caricatures provided by right-wing advocates, the media soon defined me. I kept waiting for the White House to put together a strategy; meanwhile, the right wing had the field to itself. They succeeded in telling their story using my name and most important, my image. I was pigeonholed in a litany of alliteration: "Looney Lani," the "Czarina of Czeparatism," the "Princess of Proportionality," "Real America's Madwoman." The most enduring image—that of Bill Clinton's "Quota Queen"—was a grotesque caricature of a stereotype. Quota Queen conflated three racialized images: welfare, quotas, and unmarried loud, demanding black women. It became part of an organized campaign, that continues still, to convert the 1960s slogan "power to the people" into "quotas" for "unqualified and undeserving *black* people." The right-wing story was that I wanted more for blacks, less for whites—apparently "by any means necessary," including the destruction of democracy. "Quota Queen" made any further communication superfluous; it announced my agenda loud and clear: An imperious black woman who did not know her place, I would do to whites what centuries of whites had done to blacks. "[She's] a black separatist," warned Abigail Thernstrom, a friend of Bolick's and a widely cited neoconservative theorist. I became Reagan's welfare queen tooling around the neighborhood in her Cadillac, mocking the hard work of others and the hard labor undertaken to produce this democratic system.

The image of the undeserving poor was transformed into the image of the undeserving voter who would benefit by me—their champion—manipulating the rules to distort democracy in favor of my chosen few. I was not only asking for what they didn't deserve or hadn't earned. I was willing to corrupt the entire democratic system to get it for them. Who wouldn't be horrified by this racial Rasputin, who would whisper in the president's ear and take the country down the path of division and discord?

Once in play, the term echoed everywhere. During May and June 1993, I was displayed in cartoon and narrative in more than 330 separate articles as a "Quota Queen." *Newsweek* magazine used the term in a headline, CROWNING A QUOTA QUEEN?, to signal a story in which the term "welfare" was also featured prominently. The subtext was that of the welfare mother, with one hand outstretched palm-up, the other resting saucily on her hip as if to say, "I dare you not to give me what is *mine, mine, mine.*" It no longer mattered that I had not even written on welfare. No one cared that, in fact, I did not believe in or advocate quotas. That I was a democratic idealist became irrelevant. No one bothered to try to understand my vision of dispersed and shared power.

Although the term "Quota Queen" was coined the day after the formal nomination by a headline writer for the *Wall Street Journal,* it was used to great effect by the author of the *Journal* op-ed piece, Clint Bolick. Interviewed in *The New York Times,* Bolick said, "Clinton has not had to expend any political capital on the issue of quotas and with her [Guinier] we believe we could inflict a heavy political cost." Clint Bolick had been a political appointee in the Reagan administration; he had helped draft many of the policies I criticized. Bolick was rarely identified as having a personal ax to grind; even Nina Totenberg, in an otherwise evenhanded piece on National Public Radio, quoted Bolick as if he were simply an informed critic, not an ideologue supported primarily by right-wing organizations like the Lynde and Harry Bradley Foundation.

Bolick, leading the attack on me, said I possessed "the most radical notion of government" he had "seen presented in America" in his lifetime. "It amounts to tyranny of the minority." Never mind that many hallowed practices of our existing democracy—including the creation of the Senate with two seats from every state regardless of their population or size—were based on these "radical notions."

Bolick's critique was an instant hit on the nation's opinion pages, where it was echoed in the *Wall Street Journal* itself by its columnist Paul Gigot, by John Leo at *U.S. News & World Report,* and by Stuart Taylor at *Legal Times,* among others. As the distortions were repeated, they gained credence, both on the editorial and news pages. Yet I was still cautioned to remain silent. I cooperated, following administration protocol not to speak to the press pending Senate confirmation hearings.

Lending some credible cover to the right-wing assault was a bizarre series of articles written for *The Jewish Forward* and continuing the trajectory initiated even before the formal nomination announcement. On May 7, David Twersky, writing under the headline AJ CONGRESS READIES FIGHT AGAINST GUINIER, tied my nomination to "a growing series of courtroom confrontations between Jewish and black civil rights groups over redistricting of Congressional and other election jurisdictions." Twersky wrote that "Jewish groups, already preparing to take a fresh look at the Voting Rights Act, are being drawn into the battle over President Clinton's decision to nominate" Lani Guinier. The article noted that I had many supporters, "including Jewish colleagues. But there are others in the community who fear her views, including staffers at the American Jewish Committee."

My nomination, the article concluded, attracted attention in the Jewish community "because groups that monitor voting rights enforcement believe the legal interpretations with which she is associated could, if carried to the extreme, limit the ability of Jews to win elective office." The *Forward* article emphasized the unease of "officials with Jewish groups," who found "disquieting the possibility of giving Ms. Guinier the executive authority to pursue even a watered down version of her published views." I would accelerate the process of balkanization "if confirmed by the Judiciary Committee."

In response to the growing controversy, my supporters sent numerous faxes back and forth between New York and Washington, but they were largely talking to themselves. And even then, the diffidence was evident. For example, on May 11, Legal Defense Fund attorney Dayna Cunningham faxed her Washington colleagues suggesting that "it *may* be time" to mobilize a national press strategy that emphasizes constituency support. "It won't be enough," Dayna concluded, "to debate these people on the merits. They are moving very fast to define the storyline. We've got to snatch it back, don't you think?"

A public relations firm working for the NAACP LDF (where I had been director of the voting rights project during the 1980s) sent a follow-up fax on May 14:

> As mentioned earlier, the press coverage thus far has concentrated on Lani's views and has not provided the momentum we need to serve notice to opponents or to shore up supporters in Congress. Beyond defending Lani's writings, it was critical that we relay the message that she has wide support and that she is not the Bork of the Clinton Administration as she is being portrayed by her right-wing opponents.

Even the stories that have been favorable have not been helpful in galvanizing support, building momentum or effectively responding to the negative attacks that distort her writings.

Those with press credentials urged me in early May to respond to the gathering tidal wave, but I was persuaded by the Justice Department's public information officer, Carl Stern, not to respond to the negative press coverage—it would only draw attention to the controversy, he said. Finally, LDF's consultants, nine days later, had had enough silence. They urged LDF and other civil rights and women's groups to hold a press conference—despite the administration's objections that public statements would merely engage us further in the budding controversy: "The initial hesitation and misgivings about the news conference centered around the potential for escalating attacks in the press. The reality is that the right-wing has already launched an effective attack and it's not likely to subside, but intensify. It is critical that we turn up the volume."

I was catapulted from the solitude of my cramped, paper-strewn law professor's office into the chaos of the public sphere. In a matter of days after I had been tapped for public service, I had in essence been put on trial, charged with writing controversial law review articles. I was accused of being "antidemocratic" for suggesting that simple majority voting rules may not fairly resolve conflict in special circumstances when the majority and minority are permanently divided; and yet, for most of the period while the charges were prosecuted, the administration that masterminded my nomination neither provided defense counsel nor allowed me to speak for myself. They expected the storm to subside on its own. They were wrong.

Dayna Cunningham was astounded, she said, by "the virulence of some of the reporters who had absolutely no interest in the truth." Dayna is a protégée of mine; she left a well-paid position at a highly regarded New York law firm and signed on as assistant counsel at LDF in part because of the work she had done as a law student on a voting fraud case I tried in Selma, Alabama, in the shadow of the infamous Edmund Pettus Bridge. In 1985, the Edmund Pettus Bridge loomed large in our consciousness. Twenty years earlier, a small band of civil rights workers, marching in the long shadow of that bridge from Selma to Montgomery in 1965, were "beaten for democracy." Dayna was only a law student at the time we tried the voting case in Selma, Alabama, in 1985, but she now knew what it felt like to be "part of something," something that "was urgent and truly meaningful," something that "involved people who were passionately committed." Dayna Cunningham wanted to be one of those people. As she later told me, from that day on "the only thing I ever wanted to do—in terms of the law—was to practice voting rights law at the NAACP Legal Defense Fund."

Dayna had read every article I had ever written and the reporters she spoke to couldn't, as she put it, "catch [her] up short taking things out of context." Dayna knew, for example, that other democracies like Germany and the Netherlands frequently employ alternatives to winner-take-all-majority voting in order to form a more inclusive and representative government. Likewise, she knew that the supermajority remedies I had proposed for racially polarized communities in the deep South had been used to great effect in places like Mobile, Alabama, to make sure blacks and whites worked together to run the city. They were also commonplace in the United States Senate itself, where votes to end debate or override a presidential veto required more than a simple majority. Dayna recalls some of her conversations with reporters with great dismay:

> They would ask over the phone: "What do you think about this?" and then I would turn to that page and I would read the whole thing in context and then I would say to them "there is no lack of clarity" and sometimes I would even get them to agree, but none of that would show up in their stories the next day. They were like attack dogs. Even when you say "Stop" they cannot stop; they were on automatic pilot. They had not read the articles; they had been given quotes from some editor to check and that was the extent of their research

To the press, I was news to the extent I was controversial. The more they covered me as news, the more I became controversial. Journalists failed to consult many others with firsthand information, such as black or white political scientists. But, as Dayna's experience suggests, even when "consulted," the fix was in: I was controversial. That was the story. My experience became yet one more example of journalists validating one another's "expert" opinion in an environment in which facts matter less than opinions and opinions matter only to the extent they feed the fight.

WITHIN A WEEK of the first avalanche of negative press coverage, the president began wavering. He talked about me at a press conference on May 7, but now he was fumbling. In response to questions about my nomination, the president said that he was concerned that I didn't believe in one person/one vote, and he alleged there were some other things that I may have written that were problems; but basically he was behind my nomination because it was the first time a full-time civil rights lawyer had been nominated to this position.

I knew I couldn't get to the president directly. Having seen Ricki Seidman in action, I called Ricki, even though she was not then formally assigned to my nomination. I urged her to fix the mess the president seemed to be stepping in. Please, I begged her, inform the president that I do believe in one person/one vote, remind him that Solicitor General–designate Drew S. Days had been a full-time civil rights lawyer when he was nominated as AAG by President Carter, and help the president draft a clearer, affirmative statement explaining why he had nominated me.

Ricki tried. She fought valiantly on my behalf against a small group of men who formed a protective phalanx around the president. The president's men in waiting were all too preoccupied playing tactics, as if Washington were a giant video game that rewarded hand-eye coordination and little else.

I knew that courtesy calls were key. Normally, presidential nominees are encouraged to meet privately with senators prior to confirmation hearings. Early in May, I had met Pennsylvania senator Arlen Specter. In the first two weeks following my nomination announcement, he was the only senator I was allowed to visit. Specter was friendly with Bill Coleman, Jr., secretary of transportation in the Ford administration, chairman of the LDF board, co-author of the brief LDF filed in the seminal *Brown v. Board of Education* school desegregation case, a Republican Party stalwart, and a longtime mentor. Bill Coleman had arranged lunch. Senator Specter, to demonstrate his goodwill, had us meet him in the Senators' Dining Room, so I "could be seen." He framed the discussion with three questions: What would I do, if confirmed? How did I get the nomination? Was what the *Wall Street Journal* saying about me true?

Bill Coleman set the tone with his introduction. He told the senator, "I've known her a long time. She has only one flaw—she didn't marry my son." Following Bill Coleman's lead, Specter's manner was mildly flirtatious, pulling out my chair, carefully watching me sit down, and then asking questions like, "How tall are you?" But he moved on promptly, trying to nail down press reports. "How well do you know the Clintons?" he asked. He really pressed me on the question whether I was nominated as "Hillary's" buddy. "Have you talked to them since the nomination?" "No," I replied. "Did you talk to them before the nomination?" he probed. "About what?" I responded. He followed up quickly, "About the nomination." "No," I stated matter-of-factly.

Ever the former prosecutor, Specter was seeing what kind of witness I'd make. At one point he asked me, "What were Bill Clinton's thoughts about the lawsuits" I'd filed against him as governor of Arkansas. To which I replied, "I don't know what he thought, but I'll tell you what he said." He seemed satisfied with my answers. He was friendly, circumspect, scrutinizing. I was impressed with Specter's style of informal interrogation, and I thought the discussion went well. The Philadelphia papers quoted the senator as saying I was "energetic" and a "very prepossessing woman." He later went further, saying I deserved a hearing. He told reporters that nothing in what he had read of my writing was "alarming." Indeed, Specter argued, "if you turn down Guinier on the state of this record, no potential nominee with any intellect or courage or guts is going to come forward."

But for some weeks after my meeting with Senator Specter I was not allowed any further courtesy calls. In fact, on May 17, I was asked by Justice Department staffers not to proceed with several previously scheduled meetings. I was to cancel all courtesy calls because Webb Hubbell, Philip Heymann, and Drew Days were testifying (as designees respectively for the positions of Associate Attorney General, Deputy Attorney General, and Solicitor General) before the Senate Judiciary Committee that day.

Webb, Phil, and Drew had been nominated first. Their jobs were more important; it made sense that their hearings came first. But, at that point, I alone was being attacked in the press. Yet the Justice Department staffers did not want me to talk informally to senators while other Justice Department officials were testifying publicly. Given their "chronological," who's-on-first strategy, the Justice staffers had also mishandled the "questionnaire." The Senate Judiciary Committee insists on receiving responses to a committee questionnaire before scheduling confirmation hearings. Indeed, the committee waits for at least three weeks to schedule confirmation hearings following receipt of the questionnaire on the Hill. Since six of us were nominated together on April 29, the staff waited until 7:00 P.M. on May 20 to transmit the questionnaires of all the assistant attorneys general en masse. The explanation was that they "didn't want the questionnaires of any assistant attorneys general to go before the committee while Drew, Phil, and Webb were having their hearings." Here too the Justice Department staff was in denial, refusing to respond to the mounting public criticism, instead acting unilaterally to keep me quiet, hidden, out of sight. Eerily, the night that the questionnaires were finally sent up, someone shot a BB gun through my window at the University of Penn Law School.

I knew that Joseph Biden, the Democratic chair of the Senate Judiciary Committee, had problems with the nomination. Senator Biden had presidential aspirations at one time, even though he represented a small state (Delaware), had had major surgery, and was caught plagiarizing speeches during an earlier unsuccessful presidential bid. Senator Biden liked the limelight, as long as he was portrayed in a dignified way. During the hearings on Supreme Court nominations, he liked to ask lengthy and often convoluted questions about arcane legal theories.

He had taken a lot of heat for the Anita Hill/Clarence Thomas hearings and was clearly not looking forward to another messy set of confirmation hearings in which he would have to confront a black woman law professor.

Given Biden's important role, I didn't rely on the Justice Department staff to arrange a personal meeting. I myself tried and tried to get a face-to-face meeting with the senator. I went by his office in person several times to arrange it. Finally, the Thursday before Memorial Day (three weeks from the day I had been nominated), Senator Biden called me about 7:30 or 8:00 P.M. at the Justice Department. I had just left to meet NAACP LDF lawyer Penda Hair, the friend with whom I was staying during this transition period, pending my move to D.C. I met Penda at the LDF office, en route to dinner. We were walking out of her office building when a co-worker came racing out of the stairway. From his pained expression, I thought he'd come to warn us of a terrible automobile accident he'd witnessed from the window above. It turned out the pain was merely shortness of breath; he was trying to catch us before we left the building to tell us that Biden's office was on the phone.

I went back up and was told that the senator would call me from the cloakroom. He was on the floor of the Senate, but his staff would page him immediately. I sat waiting for about fifteen or twenty minutes. When my impatience took over, I called back. The staff patched me through to Senator Biden in the cloakroom.

Biden came on the line without introduction, saying, "Look, I don't have a problem with you. I am not trying to avoid meeting with you. I admire you a lot. You helped me out with Brad Reynolds [referring to testimony I gave when Reynolds was being considered for promotion from AAG for Civil Rights to Associate Attorney General, the number three position in the Reagan Justice Department], but there are other people who have problems. You need to meet with them, not me." He added, "I just want you to know I made a statement today saying you deserve a hearing, an opportunity to defend yourself and put your views in context."

I responded, "I appreciate that. And I do not want to sound impertinent, but I do have a quarrel with the way you are characterizing the issue. Your statement assumes that my views are the views that have been reported in the media and the fact is my views have been caricatured in the media. I would appreciate the opportunity to defend my views. At minimum, it might be helpful to acknowledge that the views the press ascribes to me are not the views I hold."

He said, "I have read your work. I know what you are talking about. I have some problems, or, er, questions."

"It is because you have those questions that I would like to sit down and talk to you," I replied. "Maybe we could ride back to Philadelphia, from Washington to Delaware? I am just one stop further on the Metroliner."

He seemed somewhat charmed by that offer, that I would meet him at his convenience. "But," he replied, "your problem is not with me. I have had thirty senators come to me and say they are opposed to you." When, I asked, did this happen? He didn't answer directly. I continued, "I have just recently started making courtesy calls."

One such call was with Senator Alan Simpson (Republican of Wyoming) in his office. The senator sat behind his desk. I sat on a chair facing him. Completing the semicircle in front of Senator Simpson's desk was a middle-aged male staffer who took notes but was mostly silent, and a youngish woman from the Justice Department. The Justice staffer kept giggling inappropriately, creating strange lulls in the conversation. Nonetheless, after the meeting she asserted that it had gone very well. We had tried to get Vernon Jordan to come. Vernon had told me he could be helpful with Simpson. During a relaxed, one-on-one meeting in his law office on May 5, Vernon had offered to meet or call Simpson on my behalf should that become necessary. When Vernon was subsequently asked to follow up with Simpson, he reportedly said, "I don't do that kind of thing."

My first-year law school legal writing instructor collected fossils with Senator Simpson and had faxed a warm letter of introduction. After a freewheeling, open exchange, Senator Simpson paused, gestured with his right arm, and told me he had a "bombshell question." "I was going to save this question for the hearing and watch your eyes bug out when you tried to answer it," he told me, pausing for emphasis. But, he said, "I will be fair and give you the question in advance." I thanked him, noting it is always better to be prepared.

"What," he asked, "if the white minority in South Africa read your writings?" I smiled. The analogy to South Africa had occurred to me, too. In fact, I had been asked to address it the year before in a talk in Philadelphia. "That would be fine," I said matter-of-factly, "because what I am describing is applicable in South Africa, too. That is, the majority should rule, but it should rule in a way that is respectful and that recognizes the interests of the minority in being part of the governing coalition. The minority has to feel that the government is legitimate in order to go along with its policies."

Senator Simpson greeted my response with visible astonishment. He leaned in toward me as if to make sure those words had issued from my lips. "You really believe that?" he quizzed me in shock. "Of course," I answered. "It's a matter of principle." And I told him that I had given a speech to that effect at the Law and Society meeting a year earlier on a panel moderated by Federal Appeals Court Judge A. Leon Higginbotham, Jr. The senator seemed honestly to be grappling with the dilemma I posed, contrasting the image he expected and the persona he met. This was why courtesy calls were so valuable: if I could get behind the public image, a personal relationship was always possible despite profound disagreements on substance.

The meeting was scheduled for forty-five minutes but it lasted almost an hour and a half. At the end of our very full conversation, Senator Simpson reached across his desk and handed me a ten-page outline someone had prepared of my purported views that the senator had been using as his "script." Simpson then said, "You are going to need this. I don't know yet how I am going to vote. But you are not what I expected. I guess I should say now I am undecided." I heard that Simpson later confided to Senator Paul Simon that he was on the fence.*

I reported these conversations to Senator Biden. Of course, I had no notes of the Simpson conversation to share with Senator Biden because the Justice Department staffer who accompanied me wrote nothing down. Biden's response: "I will bet my life that Simpson votes against you."

"That may be true," I answered, "but I am telling you that the courtesy calls are going very well. I am finally, and for the first time, meeting people face-to-face. In the last three days, how many people have told you they were opposed to me?"

He replied, "Three were in the last few days. And I overheard a female senator tell the Attorney General she would vote no."

I took this to be a reference to Dianne Feinstein. I told Senator Biden that Feinstein's office indicated to me that she did not have a problem with me and that she would be happy to meet with me after the recess.

Biden testily replied, "People are obviously telling you something different than they are telling me. But you should just keep doing what you are doing because you are getting better results than I am."

I knew from Harvard professor of law and constitutional guru Larry Tribe that Biden had asked him to read my writing. About a week earlier, Tribe had been in Washington at the Watergate Hotel awaiting a call from Biden about my writings. Professor Tribe had called me

---

* I subsequently received a telephone call in mid-July 1993 from Senator Paul Simon, in response to an article he had just read in *The Washington Post.* In that article I was portrayed as speaking out, a spokesperson "not just for race but for good causes." Senator Simon used the call to ruminate briefly about what had happened two months earlier. He told me, "When the White House called, my advice was to go ahead. I told them I supported you, that I knew of at least three others on the committee who did; that there was nothing wrong with losing in the interests of a good cause. I told them that Alan Simpson might have been in your corner."

while he was waiting for Biden's call. "I just want you to know I have immersed myself in your work over the past three days and I think it is brilliant. I know that this isn't relevant to what is going on, but I have really learned a lot and I have a lot of respect for you as a scholar." I was very grateful for the comment, even though I knew it would have no effect on the political process.

Larry Tribe's assessment would not save me from the media spectacle I had become. The opinion of a renowned constitutional law scholar would not counteract an imagistic sound bite: a "Quota Queen." Tribe and I discussed the way that the *Wall Street Journal* editors were sharpening the attack and bringing it closer and closer to home. Paul Gigot, in an op-ed piece captioned HILLARY'S CHOICE ON CIVIL RIGHTS, wrote that I proposed "a system of proportional representation to ensure that blacks are elected in direct relation to their share of the population. Presumably this means that many of those white Southern Democrats now in the Senate would have to resign." The only problem with Gigot's analysis is that the words and the sentences that he attributed to me were not direct quotations. Indeed, I had never written the sentences he quoted. As Tribe pointed out, the words "proportional representation" and "ensure" are lifted from a passage in one of my articles, but they do not appear in the order or with anything resembling the meaning of Gigot's usage. On page 1080 of that article in the 1991 *Michigan Law Review*, the particular passage reads: "[E]ven in jurisdictions with *proportionate* black *representation*, black electoral success has neither mobilized the black community nor realized the promised community-based reforms." Almost two paragraphs away, toward the bottom of the same page, the word "ensures" is found: "Thus, although it *ensures* more representatives, district-based black electoral success may not necessarily result in more responsive government."

Larry Tribe and I agreed. Not only were the words Gigot quoted taken totally out of context, but the context makes clear that I was criticizing the very idea that elections should be based solely on the race of the candidate. Indeed, the next sentence in the same article makes it crystal clear I was engaged in a "critique of the black electoral success theory," not an endorsement. I was "put[ting] forth suggestions for a different approach to voting rights reform." I was *not* advocating simple election of more black faces, but an election system that might encourage *all* politicians to be more responsive to their constituents. In such a system, *all* voters are represented in a collective decision-making body by someone they actually voted for. I was arguing that black voters (as well as all other voters) should be represented by the people the voters choose, given a real set of choices. I focused on maximizing the ability of every voter to choose; it was a voter-based, not candidate-centered approach.

Given Biden's refusal to meet with me, I was dubious that anything Professor Tribe said would rescue me from either the "Quota Queen" or "Hillary's choice" departments. It would make no immediate political difference. But Tribe's praise definitely made a psychic mark. His support helped me maintain my dignity and self-esteem.

Tribe's call, in fact, was critical. It affirmed me in a deeply personal way. It renewed my resolve to fight back. I thought of how different the reaction to my articles generally had been in the academy. Much of my writing was an effort at political theory. The format of a law review article was such that you couldn't just criticize, you had to analyze; and you couldn't just analyze, you also had to propose alternative ways to look at a problem. These articles were the beginning of a creative and innovative framework that I was developing, not yet even a theory. I had gotten tenure, but one of the criticisms in the process was that I wasn't theoretical enough. As a scholar I should not feel constrained by politics or pragmatism. There was a real push toward theory in legal academia, and so a good deal of what I was writing was an effort to respond to the demands of the job as a law professor. My law review articles were not a manifesto for America. They were part of a conversation with other legal scholars and judges.

Within the first two weeks after the April 29 announcement, two op-ed pieces in the *Philadelphia Inquirer* (one by a law school colleague and the other by a friend on the editorial board) were the only really favorable things written about me in *the entire time* since I was nominated. Somebody said that the piece in the *L.A. Times* was not bad (I also knew that Michigan law professor Alex Aleinikoff had an op-ed under submission to the *Wall Street Journal*), but considering the onslaught of negative criticism, there was no comparison. My husband, Nolan Bowie, who is a professor of communications and information policy, kept telling me, "What do you expect, given that the media are looking for controversy to sell newspapers? They want to dramatize everything; they don't do the work; they just recycle someone else's work product." But if all that were true, why hadn't they at least made the controversy fair—why hadn't they at least presented my side? I reminded myself these were the questions that only someone like me would ask; someone as politically naive as an obscure law professor whose job before this was to spend hours musing in front of a computer and who was now being called upon to explain myself and my ideas to a national audience. As Nolan had said, when I had my hearings, it would be the biggest class I'd ever taught.

Meanwhile, Republican senators were having a field day, making daily statements that went unchallenged. On May 20, Senator Robert Dole, with whom I had worked on the 1982 amendments to the Voting Rights Act, blasted my nomination on the Senate floor. He charged that my views "redefine the meaning of the term 'out-of-the-mainstream.' " In fact, he concluded, "her views are not only out of the American mainstream, but out of the mainstream of the Democratic party." He embraced the claim that I advocated quotas: "I never thought," Dole said, "I would see the day when a nominee for the top civil rights post at Justice would argue, not that quotas go too far, but rather that they don't go far enough."

Senator Dole claimed that I supported vote-rigging schemes that made "quotas look mild." He asserted that I had been "consistently hostile to the principle of 'one person-one vote.' " In announcing on the floor of the Senate that he was prepared to "keep an open mind," he declared, "I have never met, nor have I ever spoken to, Ms. Guinier. We have never exchanged correspondence."

This was the same senator who had sent me a letter thanking me for my assistance on the 1982 Voting Rights Act amendments. This was the same senator who said, in a speech before the Annual Civil Rights Institute of the NAACP Legal Defense Fund on May 16, 1986: "I see new friends like . . . Lani Guinier—people I got to know during the 1982 effort to extend the landmark Voting Rights Act of 1965 and who I have been pleased to work with since then on other issues of mutual concern. Of all the steps I have taken in my public life. . . . I've never been prouder than in fighting for an extension of this landmark civil rights statute, and never more impressed with my legislative allies."

I had mysteriously changed from "legislative ally" and "new friend" to an unknown and unworthy advocate of "vote rigging." Yet no one within the administration thought to question the transformation.

On May 7, Al Kamen had written in *The Washington Post*, "There are rumblings at the Senate Judiciary Committee that Republicans there may be mounting an effort against University of Pennsylvania law professor Lani Guinier, the administration's pick for assistant attorney general for civil rights. The effort would be to attack some of her writings as too liberal, but it is unclear how serious an effort will be mounted, and the White House does not appear worried." Paul Gigot was busy editorializing in the *Wall Street Journal* that "Republicans have been handed a gift horse" in the form of the nomination of a "young, black, tart-tongued law professor." The White House was busy turning the other cheek.

IT WAS A MONTH of laissez-faire treatment by the White House. Even if they were not worried, I was. I was particularly troubled by their absence of visible support. On the third Friday in May, Ricki Seidman gave me a tour of the West Wing. She thought it might cheer me up to see the Oval Office after a meeting. We were walking down the hallway when Hillary and her deputy chief of staff, Melanne Verveer, passed us.

Hillary said to me, "Hey kiddo!" and just kept walking. About ten steps down the hall she paused. She looked back over her shoulder to where I was still standing. She stopped in mid stride. She was half an hour late for a luncheon, she said breezily. Then she raced off.

I knew even more trouble was brewing. One hot, muggy Philadelphia Sunday, I woke up hoping to be able to read the newspaper once through without seeing more negative press. No such luck. David Boldt, then editor of the editorial page of the *Philadelphia Inquirer,* was railing against me as a "madwoman" with "cockamamie ideas." The day before, another columnist, Roger Hernandez, had repeated the old charges against me and then "dismissed" me. Columnists in my hometown newspaper were recycling the *Wall Street Journal* mantra. I was outside the mainstream, an unfamiliar voice with some unfamiliar-sounding ideas. But unfamiliar meant strange, and strange meant weird, or maybe even worse, a "reverse racist."

All of these things really hurt—not because they were true, or because I even thought that the people writing them believed them, but because they went unanswered. I wanted to respond publicly to what was being said. I wanted to correct the record. But by now what I might say, and whether I could speak at all, was governed by White House policy. I was ordered by both Justice Department and White House staff not to speak to the press in advance of confirmation hearings. This was the one area in which the White House both took charge and remained unambiguous in its directives: as an executive branch nominee, I must remain silent.

Meanwhile, Carl Stern kept trying to calm me down. In response to my panic-stricken calls, Carl simply said, "Oh don't worry. It's still just the *Wall Street Journal* types. Don't worry. If *The New York Times* comes out with an editorial against you, then you have to worry."

The *Times* lead editorial appeared on May 23. It was the final blow. The editors of the *Times* had written: "The core question is whether Ms. Guinier, a veteran litigator, has the philosophy and political sense to be the custodian of [the Voting Rights Act]. These matters are in doubt and must be tested in hearings still weeks away."

On May 24, Attorney General Janet Reno convened a meeting for those of us who had been nominated on April 29. We were told for the first time to hire someone to spearhead our "nomination campaign." The operating assumption was that people at this level would not be targeted. Except that I had been targeted from day one. For most of the other nominees, this was an opportunity to get in gear. Phil and Webb had been voted out by committee by then, and they talked about how helpful it was to be told what to say and what they couldn't say. They described the object of the game. Your goal was not to answer the question but to tell the senator what it was they wanted to know. We were told: the first answer to any question has to be a short, declarative platitude. Phil talked about being coached for his confirmation hearing. During the dry runs, he was asked about the criminal justice reform bill. His first response had been substantive: "That is an area of great interest to me and these are the kinds of things that I would like to do about it." He was told by his handlers that he had given the wrong answer. The right answer is, "Senator, I think crime is a real problem." Don't mention the criminal justice reform bill; give a political speech: "I agree with you, Senator, that we need to build more prisons," or some similarly superficial response. When Phil gave that answer at his actual hearing, whoever asked him the question beamed and moved on because Phil had given the right answer.

Webb talked about being a failure at his initial dry run. At some level it was useful to hear that these other people were being manipulated and handled in a fashion that was inconsistent with their training and their intellectual capacity. But for the most part it struck me that I was in a category all by myself, and yet I was treated as if I were the same as the other nominees, none of whom had encountered much, if any, media notice.

Whether the administration would ever defend me was now in doubt. That had been a secret worry all along. It had been a source of angst in at least two corners of the world beginning the very moment my nomination was announced. My mother worried as any mother would; she became increasingly agitated by the hostile press coverage and the absence of a serious White House response. The other person who was worried was Dayna Cunningham, my protégée at LDF. Dayna was happy for me, but she herself was not happy. She was wise from her own experience litigating cases when Bill Clinton was governor of Arkansas. Even though she worked with Clinton then as the lead defendant, Dayna saw him primarily as a politician and she doubted whether he had an inner core. She had tried to warn me.

Dayna is a rail-thin, light-skinned black woman, a combination of New York sophisticate and zealous civil rights attorney. She is striking, with a wide, open face, high cheekbones, and big, dark eyes that beam at you as she speaks. She talked with her whole body, a compelling study in contrasts—the string of pearls around her neck, the white cashmere sweater, the short, tight black wool skirt, the dark stockings, the slip-on black high heels; that is what you noticed first. But your memory of Dayna was not based on what you saw with your eyes. It was what you heard with your heart. Dayna was a lawyer whose face lit up the room when she talked about her work. She was unswerving in her commitments, her passion about remedying injustice seemingly born full-blown.

Dayna was apprehensive that Bill Clinton would not be an aggressive defender of principle, that he would fight only when his own political neck was on the line. After all, this was the Bill Clinton she had witnessed firsthand in Arkansas: a politician first and foremost, a man who liked to kibbitz, but even more, a man who believed primarily in himself. Dayna was a fine storyteller, unflinching in her recollection of the telling detail, the fidgety hands, the physicality of the touch. In the late 1980s, at a particularly tense meeting in southeastern Arkansas —a section of the Mississippi Delta region where antebellum social relations are still in many respects the order of the day—Dayna and a local LDF cooperating lawyer were one of a handful of black people there to discuss remedies for a highly contentious LDF voting rights suit. The meeting turned sour when one of the local whites demanded to know why, in his view, the whites always were made to pay for others' problems. Other whites in the group began to echo his charge. Dayna felt herself trembling in fear. She huddled closer to Olly Neal, the local black lawyer with whom she was sitting.

Bill Clinton, the lead defendant in the case, took the podium to respond. In a tone of resignation, Clinton said, "We have to pay because we lost."

At the time, Dayna recalled, she wasn't sure if the reference was to the lawsuit or the Civil War.

Later, Governor Clinton came to the rear of the room to talk to Dayna and Olly Neal. Dayna remembers:

He asked me whether I was from LDF. I said I was. "You must know Lani Guinier," he continued. I said, "I do." Grabbing the flesh of my upper arm and squeezing as he talked, he looked at me, nonchalant in his assumed intimacy. Still holding my arm, he declared, "I am in love with Lani Guinier."

Dayna was outraged as she continued:

Only moments before, Bill Clinton had so irresponsibly pandered to the backwards feeling of the white constituency. Then, as if nothing had happened, he became all sweetness, seductively ambiguous in his charm. He turned to me, touched me to make certain I heard, and said, "I love the Legal Defense Fund. I love Lani Guinier."

I thought, "Where is your core? What do you stand for?"

Dayna never trusted Bill Clinton after that.

I knew that President Clinton was averse to conflict, that his default position would always be to fashion a compromise in which everyone split the difference. But I was not prepared to be "the difference." Fore-warned by Dayna's cautionary stories from eastern Arkansas, I still was not prepared to question Bill Clinton's fundamental commitment to do the right thing. I assumed he ultimately wanted to be judged by history rather than public opinion polls. I knew he was nervous as a result of his administration's weak start, but I believed him nevertheless to be fundamentally centered, even anchored in his understanding that greatness required courage, vision, and faith.

We had known each other a long time, after all. When we were in law school, Bill Clinton and Hillary Rodham were directors of the Yale Barristers' Union. They came to my rescue after another student supervisor neglected to recommend me for inclusion in the Prize Trial Competition. My buddies, some of whom saw the slight in racial terms, had appealed to Bill and Hillary, whose intervention assured me an honest chance to compete, which I did successfully. They were admired. We looked up to them, respected them because they were known to be fair. They were among the half dozen or so friends from law school who had attended my wedding.

I had run into them in the 1980s at a Renaissance Weekend in South Carolina. Hillary and I were on a panel entitled "Whatever Happened to the Sixties?" By then I was a lawyer with the NAACP Legal Defense Fund. I spoke about a voting rights case I had just won in Perry County, Alabama, defending black civil rights workers, including Albert Turner, who had led the mule train at Dr. Martin Luther King, Jr.'s, funeral. We had charged selective prosecution by the Reagan Justice Department, and a jury of five blacks and seven whites acquitted our clients. My point was that the sixties were not over; they were being fast-forwarded and replayed in the eighties. Bill Clinton, governor of Arkansas, was in the audience at the panel. He had been jogging and was casually dressed. He listened and glowed.

Later, at the same retreat, Governor Clinton gave an extraordinary talk about his own coming of age, when politics and family collided in the drug investigation of his younger brother. After the talk, everyone in the audience buzzed about how effective he was, how charismatic, how real. Hillary leaned over the table, where we were sitting together in the audience, and whispered her own surprise. She had never seen him, in all his years as governor of Arkansas, speak so honestly in public about this particular episode. She saw it as both a tribute to the trust he felt in this retreat atmosphere and his own coming to terms with the public/private tensions of political life. David Gergen was also at the retreat, as I remember, but he and I had merely exchanged pleasantries.

The president and I were social friends, but what connected us was more than mere association over time. We had close friends in common. We also had a professional relationship. I had sued him; I had negotiated the settlement of a major voter registration lawsuit in Arkansas. At one point in the case, a state clerk who was defending the Arkansas system of selectively deputizing registrars gave my co-counsel, Deval L. Patrick, one of their buttons, which Deval wore proudly. That button, given to him by one of the defendants, helped him work the crowd as Governor Clinton and I chatted in the corner. Clinton admired Deval, thought he was smooth. "He has a future as a politician," the future president cooed.

So, years later, on a soft Washington April day in 1993, I signed on, committed to "enforce the laws as passed by Congress." Framed by a beaming president and prompted by my emotional connections to a proud Attorney General, I had declared—some would later say pro- claimed—in the Justice Department courtyard, "I will enforce the laws as passed by Congress."

In the five weeks following the late April courtyard ceremony, I was no longer defending the importance of enforcing the laws; I was barely given the opportunity to defend myself. The I that I knew in "I will enforce the laws as passed by Congress" had been replaced by the *Wall Street Journal*'s "Quota Queen," the *New York Times*' "guerrilla warrior," the "strange name, strange hair, strange ideas" lead of *U.S. News & World Report*, the "Real America's Madwoman" of a Philadel- phia columnist.

Anna Quindlen, at that time the only female *New York Times* regular op-ed columnist, offered a simple explanation: no one actually read the articles, just the distorted reviews of them. Bruce Shapiro wrote in *The Nation* that should anyone have bothered to read the actual writings, they "amount to an eloquent plea against electoral quotas, against measuring black electoral success in terms of the number of minority officials holding office." Even the titles of my articles spoke of this, as in "Triumph of Tokenism." Yet, as Professor Patricia Williams of Columbia Law School observed in an article in the *Village Voice*, "the label stuck, taking on a life of its own to the extent that, by June, my attempts to refute it became further proof." "[S]he was evasive, shifty, sometimes arrogant and pompous," wrote Ray Kerrison of me in *The New York Post*.

Clint Bolick, hot on the case as early as April, seems to have been the source of almost all the other media opinion. In his *Journal* piece, Bolick took my express rejection of the "shorthand" of counting black bodies and, as Pat Williams observed, "twisted it into an assertion—can I say a lie?—that she wants more quotas, and, as the myth grew, not just quotas for 'authentic representation,' but for lots of 'authentic' black bodies."

Compare, Pat Williams suggested in her article on June 15, one of my law review footnotes with the characterizations it spawned:

In Virginia, where Douglas Wilder is the first black elected Governor since Reconstruction, some commentators have interpreted his victory as a "new black politics." *But cf.* Ayres, Virginia Governor Baffles Democrats With Crusade for "New Mainstream," *New York Times,* Oct. 14, 1990 at A22, col. 1 (Wilder considers himself "a governor who happens to be black not a black who happens to be governor.") . . . Others see Wilder's win as the triumph of a single-issue constituency in the wake of recent Supreme Court decisions on abortion. In either case, given the narrow margin of victory, Wilder's ability to govern on other issues important to the black community is considerably vitiated.

The editorial excerpts, supposedly derived from that one footnote, read as follows: "So even Virginia's African-American governor, Douglas Wilder, isn't 'authentic,' she says, because he was elected with votes of the white majority. He therefore must pursue a mainstream agenda that isn't 'important to the black community' " (Paul Gigot in the *Wall Street Journal*); "As for the notable and formerly impossible elections of black politicians like Gov. Douglas Wilder of Virginia, she questions whether he is an 'authentic' figure for blacks—because he owes his job to white voters as well" (Editorial, *The New York Times*); "She does not think whites can adequately represent blacks—which, if true, means we should unload Mayor Dinkins tomorrow because a black, by that logic, cannot adequately represent whites" (Ray Kerrison, *The New York Post*).

As Professor Williams wrote in the *Village Voice*, "For those familiar with her work, this [began] to resemble some drunken party game in which each person gossips a message to his neighbor, each embroidering 'the story' until no story is left, only inebriated malice. As if that weren't enough, the most corrupt part is that the message that began all the whispering was not Lani Guinier's, but Clint Bolick's."

The ignorance that Williams described was enabled and reinforced by the absence of competing narratives. The White House was silent when it could have been recruiting political scientists, legal academics, and political leaders to speak out. Given the dearth of opinion makers writing from the perspectives and about the concerns of blacks or women, the interpretations of a few conservative and neoconservative writers enjoyed enormous circulation at the prominent establishment organs.

I was simply remade. An elite group of opinion molders depersonalized and demonized me. With access to my real ideas withheld, my words and most especially my voice were suppressed.

"She," this media construction, spoke for me. "Her" thinking was telescoped and reduced into verbal pretzels, selective and twisted excerpts of my law review articles. "She" talked for me; "she" thought for me. "I" had disappeared.

Even in private, my friend, the president of the United States, began seeing "her," not me.

CHAPTER TWO

Virago

VI-RA'GO, vai-re'go or vi-ra go (xiii) n.
1) a bold, impudent, turbulent woman; termagant; vixen
2) [Archaic] a female warrior

—*A Standard Dictionary
of the English Language,*
Funk & Wagnalls (1908)

MY PICTURE, stern-faced and grim, confused even my mother, who called me from Boston to report, "Lani, someone is using your name. I see your picture in the paper but I don't recognize you." I didn't recognize myself.

I was being humiliated by words and condemned to wordless silence simultaneously. This passive spectre was not how my parents, Ewart and Eugenia Guinier, had raised me to be. But while my parents had managed wordlessly to make me understand just who I am, their message involved the use of words: Listen carefully to those who know more, whether simple folk or polished intellects, learn from rather than internalize criticism, develop allies, then speak truth to power. Those were the lessons of my childhood: passivity was not a good strategy for leadership unless it is tied to resistance and grounded in common struggle. Those who triumphed were those engaged in spirited action.

In my father's case, he never spelled out this strategy affirmatively. He used stories instead. My sisters and I would sit for hours while he regaled us with richly remembered vignettes. We begged him over and over again, "Tell us the story of when you were a little boy." These were our bedtime stories. He never read to us.

His stories, chockfull of details about scarcity and making do without enough money, were uplifting tales of triumph. Almost everyone in them, from his childhood in Linsted, Jamaica, to his coming of age during the depression after leaving Harvard College, was black. They were poor; they were decent; they were survivors.

We knew most of the stories by heart, but hearing his voice recount his own living was magical. My father was grateful for our rapt attention, even though we never hesitated to interrupt him when he strayed off course. He would not, however, be rushed. If his audience got too impatient, he knew how to slow us down. Whenever I or one of my sisters asked something he could not answer, or tried to push him too fast in his recitation, he would immediately chasten us with an old ditty from Jamaica. Especially if we were so rude as to question his most recent version by asking, "Why?" meaning, "Why aren't you telling us what you said last night?" he would quickly recite: "Y is a crooked letter, cut off the tail, leaves V." Gaining steam, with obvious gusto my father would continue the singsong, "V stands for Virago," and with his finger pointing at his interrogator, "just like you!"

As a child, I never heard anyone else use the term "Virago." Nor did I ask my father what it meant. I just knew that a Virago was some kind of rascal or rapscallion. I surmised that a Virago was a loving but nettlesome troublemaker. My father called us Virago—Virago must be wonderful! Yet, for some, I have since learned, Virago is a negative term, closer to churlish shrew than courageous combatant. But for me, a Virago was someone admirable, someone who would not let anyone get away with lazy or loose arguments.

Not all of my father's stories were uplifting.

My father's mother, my Nana, Marie-Louise Beresford Guinier French, had left the West Indies, and her three oldest children, including my father, who was raised by several different relatives, including his great-aunt Sarah. My father's father had been a timekeeper on the Panama Canal. He left his family to study to become a barrister in England; he died in London of pneumonia when my father was six. My father's mother remarried and emigrated to Boston with her second husband, with whom she had five more children. She left my father, his older brother, and a younger sister to live with relatives in Kingston. My father had not seen his mother in many years when, in 1925, alone, he emigrated to Boston to join her. He was fifteen years old.

After an exemplary record at Boston's English High, my father applied to college in 1929. In the early spring, he received a letter from Dartmouth, admitting him with a full scholarship—board, room, and tuition. A little later, he got a letter from Harvard, also admitting him, but without any scholarship at all. He was denied scholarship aid upon admission, he was told, because he had not submitted a photograph with his application. This, he later discovered, was a ruse to discourage his matriculation; Harvard had already admitted a black applicant from

Cambridge, inadvertently exceeding its informal quota of one black per class.

Harvard had a policy that all freshmen had to live in the dormitories on campus. This "house system" was designed to deepen the educational experience. The housemasters were generally scholars of some reknown; besides teaching, they had the responsibility of setting a tone for the house, encouraging those who did well to do better, and keeping an eye out for students who might have some problems adjusting to the particular Harvard atmosphere. You could only be excused from campus residence by making a written application and giving a good reason, such as poor health.

My father wanted to live on campus. As he told an interviewer later in his life:

> I thought that with the money I had saved from working on the boats, and the prize money I had won at [high school] graduation, and a loan from Harvard, that I could, with careful management, pay the full tuition and room and board for my freshman year, so I did not apply for a waiver of the residence requirement. Besides, I *wanted* to live in the dormitories with all other freshmen. But, in the middle of the summer, I got a letter from Harvard stating that I "had been granted permission to live at home."

> By this time I had refused the offer from Dartmouth, and had no way to locate my counselor to seek his advice. In fact, there was no one I could turn to—so I just accepted the situation, and planned to commute from Roxbury as a day student. Had I only known. In a residential college like Harvard, even the white day students were isolated, and the Black freshmen (all two of us) would become invisible.

He made no request to be excused from campus residence. Yet he was not permitted to reside in the Harvard dormitories because they were segregated in the 1920s. Only one or two blacks, including the son of a black U.S. senator, had ever been allowed to live in the campus residences at the time my father applied. According to the *Harvard Alumni Bulletin* of 1923, the official policy was one in which "men of white and colored races shall not be compelled to live and eat together, nor shall any man be excluded by reason of his color." Notwithstanding the official policy, at least six black men were in fact excluded from the dormitories before my father enrolled, including Roscoe Conkling Bruce, Jr., a grandson of Blanche K. Bruce, the U.S. senator from Mississippi in 1875–81. Roscoe Bruce, Sr. (Blanche K. Bruce's only child), had graduated from Harvard, Class of 1902, and twenty years later, in 1923, he wrote to Harvard president A. Lawrence Lowell complaining that his son, Roscoe Bruce, Jr., was not allowed to live in the freshman dorms where residence had recently been made compulsory.

During my father's enrollment in 1929–1931, much of his time on campus was spent alone. Few would speak to him, including upperclass Harvard students he had known previously as classmates in high school:

> During the first week of classes in September, I attended the freshman assembly at which Harvard President A. Lawrence Lowell spoke. There seemed to be a thousand people in the hall. I was the only Black. As we left the meeting I could hear conversations being started all around me,—but no one looked me in the eye; no one spoke to me. As I walked toward a group, they would move away.
>
> I went to the library that was designated for freshmen. The student from English High who, like me, had won the coveted Comstock Prize the previous year was at the desk. I remembered him, and proudly went up and told him that I had followed in his footsteps. He looked somewhere above my head, gave no response, and finally asked, "What books do you want?" He went and got the books, and then turned to the next person.

My father drew a sharp contrast with his other interracial interactions:

> There simply were no rewards [at Harvard] for working hard. No instructor ever called on me to speak in class; no student ever initiated a conversation about the course work, or anything else. Even though Roxbury was no model of integration in those days—or today, for that matter—still my life had included normal interactions with the white people around me. At English High, although I was certainly in a minority, there was no overt hostility on the part of either the white students or the teachers. To the contrary, I had been rewarded for working hard, and had been chosen for leadership positions.

The first person to welcome him to Harvard upon his arrival, and one of the only people to speak willingly, was a man he met at the Coop, the large bookstore where all the students bought their textbooks:

> When I went into the Coop and was looking for the right counter, I caught the eye of another Black man,—we were the only two Black people in a milling sea of white students crowding around the counters. This man, all dressed up and looking like a successful businessman, made his way over to me, and said, "Welcome to Harvard!" It was Ralph Bunche.
>
> Bunche was in his last year at the Graduate School, and was probably at least seven years older than I. He was the first person who

spoke to me voluntarily, and gave me some sense of community and connection with Harvard. We talked a little, and he suggested that I try to get a job waiting on tables at one of the private student eating clubs. At Harvard, these clubs take the place of fraternities. They were (and still are today) organized for the elite, and naturally did not admit Blacks as members, only as waiters and kitchen help.

These clubs usually had two older Black men in charge, a chef and chief steward who worked full time. The rest of us were all waiters, and all Black. There wasn't much money attached, although sometimes the white boys would give us a tip, but there were the meals which was almost the same as money, and some sense of companionship. Some of the other Black students, mostly students in one of the graduate schools, would stop around, and we would play cards. I didn't win a lot, but I didn't lose either, and whatever extra money I got was very helpful. But it is ironic, isn't it, that we had to create the only supportive mechanism to help Black students adjust to the university in the kitchens of the white boys' clubs.

These early experiences affected my father's entire life, and, as I was to learn in 1993, my life as well. They became the stock story of my youth; Try hard, aim high, but don't be surprised if the bogey of racism gets there first.

My FATHER did not save his stories for his daughters' bedtime ritual. He shared them publicly. They were his gift to an audience, and he was a generous man. He used his stories to engage his listeners in the intricacies of logical arguments that became absolutely compelling because of his own passionate commitment to them. He was energized by an audience. He never hesitated to speak out in support of his progressive agenda, even at moments when others, with less courage and more wisdom, might have opted for silence.

For example, during the 1949 elections for the Borough of Manhattan presidency, my father was chosen to run on behalf of the American Labor Party (ALP). The ALP picked him as a likely winner because of his wide constituency in the labor movement and among black civic and fraternal organizations. I believe that my father was chosen to run for Manhattan borough president, the first black candidate ever to compete for that office, for an additional reason. Ewart Guinier was a forceful and spirited public speaker. Soon after his candidacy, my father gave testimony to a U.S. Senate committee, as International Secretary of the United Public Workers CIO in New York City. On several occasions the senators conducting the hearing told him to calm down; he should not be quite so animated in answering questions. After being admonished to lower his voice by Senator Ferguson, my father responded:

... [I]f I may seem to be a bit moved about this, it is because of the hell I have been through because I am a Negro. . . .

In Washington, I could not sleep in the hotel because of the filthy Jim Crow system here. I came here Friday and could not find a place to stay. . . . I cannot even eat in this building in your cafeteria. Why not look into that?

Talk about clear and present danger. Congress is looking all over the world for clear and present danger, and the danger is right under Congress' nose. Is Congress going to want me to help go look over the world when dangers that I suffer burn the guts out of me every day?

I volunteered for the Infantry in the last war and I went to Alabama and I would like you to know that the first day that I went to Fort McClellan, I had to go to the United States Government post office to buy stamps to write home and I was fearful because I did not know the kind of reception I would get because I was Jim Crowed on my way there.

I had volunteered and I was ready to give my life for my country and yet I do not feel that I had the protection when I was in Alabama.

He then continued:

... I stand against lynching, I am against the poll tax, for the FEPC legislation, I stand against covenants, and for full equality for Negroes in every stand of life, and I want that, and I do not want to wait a thousand years for it.

I think Negroes are full-fledged American citizens and should have all the rights of American citizens and should have it today.

By his example, my father taught me to be dignified in the face of great adversity. He had become a U.S. citizen, fought a war on behalf of his adopted country, and yet never felt fully acknowledged or respected, as even a human being. He suffered so many more profound indignities than I, and yet managed to step above them. He was never bitter. I could not be bitter, either. My father was shunned by his classmates at Harvard. I was shunned by my law school friends in the White House. My father was unprepared for the overt hostility he confronted among his college peers, in part because his prior interracial contact had been relatively comfortable, if not rewarding. I too found myself shocked by the torrent of criticism and hostility that rained down on me in the spring of 1993. Just as my father, during his two years at Harvard College, felt invisible, I too found myself disappearing in Washington, D.C., in the spring of 1993. But having been "invisible" as a college undergraduate, Ewart Guinier never again let himself be silenced.

My mother, Eugenia, helped me in that lesson, too. My mother was not religious, but she conveyed a sense of the Jewish immigrant experience through vivid accounts of growing up in New York. Her parents started with a small delicatessen on the Grand Concourse in the Bronx that they eventually developed into a catering business and restaurant. As a young girl of five, my mother was often put in charge of her brother, two and a half years younger. Her parents worked fifteen- to eighteen-hour days. Her father would come home to fix his two children dinner and then to tell my mother and her younger brother bedtime stories. After tucking them in, he cautioned my mother not to leave the cramped apartment; if she needed something, she should knock on the dumbwaiter and a neighbor would come upstairs. My mother's parents were never home at the same time. Her family never sat down to dinner as a family unless they were eating at my grandparent's restaurant.

As a young girl, I adored the *All-of-a-Kind Family* books—the children's series about a New York Jewish family by Sidney Taylor—partly because they mirrored tales my mother told me about her own experiences.

I remember fondly the stories my mother would read to me about Jewish history. The story of Moses, in particular, always inspired me. I admired the fact that Jews were once slaves, resisted slavery, and became free. The story of Jewish resistance to oppression early on defined my narrative of justice. The terrors of Hitler and Nazi Germany were still quite real to a young girl in the 1950s. My parents had met during World War II, when my father was stationed in Hawaii and my mother was sent there as an American Red Cross volunteer.

My parents never let us forget Hitler's atrocities. My most intense memories of being nine years old came from a lazy summer afternoon when our sixteen-year-old cousin, Sheila, led my six-year-old sister and me into an empty cabin next door to ours, at the bungalow colony where my mother was day camp director. We sat on the floor in a spare room devoid even of furniture.

For several hours my cousin, who had just seen the movie of *The Diary of Anne Frank*, reconstructed, scene by scene, the awful agony of Anne's vigil. Thereafter, haunted by the harrowing images this graphic retelling had planted, I became consumed with the game of "tents." Over and over, under upside-down chairs draped with tablecloths or curtains that were handed down to us from our grandparents' restaurant, we constructed safe houses. We were hiding out from the Nazis. We were in fear of persecution—that was an ongoing dramatic narrative for us.

I could have easily been hiding from the Ku Klux Klan as well, but in our fantasies, we were never pursued by southern racists. No, it was always the Nazis who were on our trail.

My mother's stories taught me to endure slights without becoming enraged. She was often more direct, however, than her stories. When the white kids in Catholic school who lived across the street from us picked on me, my mother did not allow me to dwell on the insults. Instead, she told me, put yourself in their shoes, replay the situation through their eyes. Perhaps they were jealous, not merely prejudiced. They hadn't skipped a grade as I had, so they had to show me up on their terms. "Don't see yourself as a victim," she reminded me. "But maybe you should just not play with them."

When I was in elementary school, I would proudly display my report card to my parents. My father would delight with me in my achievement. He burst with pride, showing off my excellent report card to anyone who happened by. My mother would glance at my good grades and make a brief, casual comment: "That's nice, Lani." She would then turn to me and focus her gaze directly on mine. Certain she had my full attention, she would ask, "But how many friends do you have?" Having changed the subject, she would continue, "Let's talk about your friends."

For my father, it was enough for me to achieve in his image. To my mother, it was more important that I develop healthy relationships with my peers. She schooled me diligently in the lessons that nothing you do by yourself or to benefit only yourself really matters. Any achievements must be measured or balanced by their ability to enhance good deeds. I might be a Virago, but I must be one in pursuit of a larger agenda than my own accomplishments.

We lived in a neighborhood that changed with our arrival—Italians, Jews, Albanians, Armenians, and Portuguese had been living side by side when we moved to Hollis in 1956. Working-class, white ethnics lived in neat, tiny two-family attached houses on both sides of the street. By 1964, there were almost no whites still living on our block except my mother. As the demographics changed, so did our zip code. We were now St. Albans, part of the burgeoning black migration from Harlem and Bedford-Stuyvesant to southeast Queens.

We celebrated holidays with family on both sides, but never together. Each side of the family had their own traditions and customs. My mother's brother had become a successful entrepreneur, catapulting himself and his family into an exclusive cul-de-sac of upper-middle-class Long Island. He took advantage of his parents' eventual commercial success and became an even more successful real estate developer. Uncle Murray and his family lived in a huge, well-decorated house he built in Great Neck, a predominantly Jewish suburb of New York City.

They took winter vacations, played tennis all year round. I remember many wonderful times attending my cousins' bar and bat mitzvahs and family seders, where the sheer quantity of food never ceased to amaze me.

Uncle Murray and his children were always friendly. They welcomed my sisters and me when we came to visit. I don't remember, however, any intimate conversations with my cousins or spending extended periods of time together. We were accepted as family. Our presence made any gathering more colorful, even exotic. But we never pushed our way beyond the outer circle of blood relatives. We were definitely related, but something was held back on both sides.

My cousins on my mother's side visited us two or three times a year. They never said so directly, but within moments of their arrival, the carpeting in our tiny living room suddenly seemed especially frayed; in the few minutes after we greeted them, their presence dwarfed even the physical size of our house, which seemed to shrink, under their scrutiny, from a cottage to a cave. They were always amicable, but I secretly harbored the impression that my cousins felt sorry for us.

My mother's parents, both immigrants from Eastern Europe, were extraordinarily generous with their money. They bought my parents a car; they paid for braces on my teeth; a savings account they established helped support me in law school. When my parents went to purchase the car, a black Rambler station wagon, with money given to them by my mother's father, they could only go to one dealership—the one my grandfather had selected. My braces had to be fitted by an orthodontist they knew. We were grateful, of course, for the additional resources. But I was never quite comfortable enjoying their largesse; it felt too much like charity.

Sometimes their comments betrayed their profound confusion about having a darker-skinned grandchild. Even though he made his considerable living as a shopkeeper, a businessman, a man who worked with money rather than ideas, my maternal grandfather, Grandpa Phil, fancied himself an intellectual. His father had been a rabbi; he was much better educated than my grandmother, who had dropped out of elementary school. His Russian heritage was superior in his mind to her Polish roots. Grandpa Phil was well-read, even cosmopolitan. He always challenged me to recite the populations of California and New York, to show off what I had learned in school.

When I was little, Grandpa Phil, a funny, outgoing, and very proud man, would sometimes give me baths. He inevitably would end the bath by saying, "Lani, I don't know what it is; I scrub and scrub. You are still dirty. I scrub your elbows and knees, but I can never get them clean." He wasn't being malicious. He was making an observation from his limited perspective, but it hurt, nevertheless. I loved him, but his ignorance defined our relationship for me much more than his witty banter about statistics.

My maternal grandmother, Grandma Molly, a quietly assertive, dignified woman, would offer me fashion advice. She used to tell me that I should never wear black. "You are too dark, Lani, to wear dark colors," she would admonish me. Black, especially, would only accentuate my darkness.

The daughter of a Jewish mother and a black father, I was only about eight or nine at the time. I didn't call myself "black" then. I would say, if asked, "My mother is white and my father is Negro." Or, "I come from a 'mixed' family." My sisters and I were "bridge people," my mother would tell us. We were children who lived in two worlds, but came from no one place. We spanned the experiences of two families of immigrants—Eastern European Jews and West Indian blacks. We were neither black nor white back then: we were interracial.

My parents named me after the woman who had helped them get to know each other in Hawaii. Iwalani Smith Mottl was the eldest daughter of an African-American couple, Nolle R. Smith, a rancher's son who migrated to Hawaii from Wyoming in 1915, and Eva B. Jones, a classical music teacher from San Francisco. They raised three daughters and a son steeped in polyglot, multiracial Hawaii. The atmosphere there was so far ahead of its time that Nolle Smith was elected to the Hawaiian legislature in 1929 and eventually became a prominent black Hawaiian statesman and diplomat.

My mom worried that mainland Americans would butcher the name "Iwalani" (pronounced "Eva-Lonnie"), so she named me Carol Lani. But soon well-meaning friends were calling me Carol Loonie or Carolina. Determined to reinforce the romantic and multiracial possibilities she had seen in Hawaii, my mother quickly shortened my name to Lani. Little did she know that Lani, which in Hawaiian means "Heavenly" and signifies great dignity, would later become the object of so much public ridicule.

I may have been taught by my parents that I was interracial, but in junior high school, I became black. The interracial hedge no longer sufficed. The neighborhood of St. Albans that we lived in had long since "tipped," and was then almost entirely black. I took a school bus to a magnet school, Junior High 59, which also attracted a large number of Jewish students from Laurelton and Italian kids from Cambria Heights. The white students were friendly during the school day, but it was the black students who made me feel welcome, especially after classes let out in the afternoon. They considered me one of them. We shared secrets; nothing was held back. I rode the bus home with them to my increasingly segregated St. Albans neighborhood. The other black students and I not only boarded the school bus together; they invited me to their parties and to their homes.

We all ate lunch together, blacks and whites, Italians and Jews, Japanese and Chinese. But when we left school we walked our separate ways to go to our different buses; that was the end of the socializing. Some of the white kids did call me on the phone and we would talk about schoolwork. But they never invited me to visit them in their homes. That was the way it was. Nothing special was happening to me. It felt natural.

I may have looked strange or foreign. I may have had an unfamiliar name; but what was important was that I did not look white. A clean color line was drawn both because of where I lived and how I looked.

Even earlier, I had noticed the difference between being cherished with tight hugs and loving embraces by my father's family and being loved from a distance by my mother's relatives. I was special when I went to visit my father's family. All of us were. My sisters and I were fawned over and exclaimed upon. My father's mother and his sisters and brothers doted upon us. I drew emotionally close to my father's people; their culture became my identity. I wanted to be affirmed, not just acknowledged. I was also by then exhausted by the challenge of belonging nowhere in particular.

When asked, as I frequently am, "Why do you call yourself black?" I say, I am a black woman whose Jewish mother taught me about the Holocaust and about slavery. I am a black woman who grew up "black" because that was how others saw me and because it was black people who embraced my mother when she married my father in 1945. I am a black woman who grew up celebrating both Passover and Easter, and who still occasionally sprinkles Yiddish words in my speech.

I am a black woman whose parents—both parents—introduced me to my heroes, people who resisted injustice, people like Sojourner Truth and Harriet Tubman, Frederick Douglass and W. E. B. DuBois. Both my parents educated me and helped expose me to different cultures and perspectives, but it was my black father's experiences with discrimination that provided the organizing story of my life.

As a child, I lived in a small house on a narrow street in a working-class neighborhood in Queens. I went to integrated public schools on triple session and then became one of only twelve black women in the entering class at Radcliffe College. I grew up with little money, yet I have the benefit of an elite education at both Radcliffe College and Yale Law School.

I have an unusual perspective, I admit. I grew up learning to be both outsider and insider.

• • •

I WAS TWELVE YEARS OLD when I first thought about becoming a civil rights lawyer. It was September 1962. Constance Baker Motley was on the television news, escorting a black man named James Meredith into a building of the University of Mississippi. Meredith was about to become the first black to attend that school. The cameras looked out from the doors of the building as Motley and Meredith walked calmly up the stairs and through a howling white mob in order to register for classes. Or so I remember. I could be wrong, but what I did know was that Constance Baker Motley was a black woman lawyer working for the NAACP Legal Defense Fund.

I don't remember anything that Attorney Motley might have said. I don't know that I even watched her speak. It was her erect and imposing figure that caught my notice. Her proud image spoke to me. Her stately bearing said it all. She was a large-boned woman, but it was less her size than her manner. She did not flinch even as the crowd yelled epithets. She was flanked by U.S. Marshals, as I remember, but she could, for all I cared, have been alone. She was that determined.

I thought: I can do that. I can be a civil rights lawyer.

Ten years later, I was in law school. I rented an apartment on the third floor of a small frame house on Garden Street in New Haven, within walking distance of Yale Law School. It was an apartment passed down through the years from one black woman to another. I never wondered why this particular apartment, except that my friend Nancy had lived there and she got the apartment from another black woman who had lived there before her. It was a modest one-bedroom in which the kitchen was the only room that allowed me to stand tall next to any of the walls. The rest of the rooms were built under one sloping eave or another of the roof.

The landlords were a friendly black couple who arranged the lease to attract students; they did not charge rent during the summer months when they assumed the apartment would be unoccupied. One day the landlady pointed out a big, heavy metal hook on the back door. "That was what Constance Baker Motley's father used," she explained to me. "Used for what?" I asked. "When Connie or her sister came home after curfew, he would latch the door so they couldn't get in without waking him up."

Every time I saw that latch, it spoke to me. It made me just a little more certain about my destiny. After all, I was living in the third floor of the house where Constance Baker Motley grew up in New Haven as a young girl. On some small scale I was following in Connie Motley's footsteps. She had been a legal pioneer—the only woman lawyer to work for Thurgood Marshall when he was head of the NAACP Legal Defense Fund. I was not a pioneer like Constance Motley. But I was in law school to do what she did: I was going to be a civil rights lawyer.

Becoming a civil rights lawyer would require determination to pursue justice despite the names an angry mob might call you. It would require a passion, not just a mission. For me, that passion came from a belief in the merits of my arguments and in the humanity of my clients. It also stemmed from the abiding conviction that freedom for blacks would bring freedom to whites as well. If we ended the hypocrisy between what America said and what it did for blacks, it would ease the gap between what we said and did for everyone.

That peculiar hypocrisy had plagued me for a long time. I can remember asking Mrs. Buxton, my fourth-grade teacher, how Thomas Jefferson and George Washington could have owned slaves and also could have been true to the Declaration of Independence and the U.S. Constitution. Mrs. Buxton did not take my question very seriously, but when I repeated it that night to my parents, they did. I experienced the disconnection between what the founders said and what they did as an epiphany. My fourth-grade lesson was ultimately a lesson in democracy. I realized that, despite Mrs. Buxton's reticence, real democracy required thinking about questions that did not occur to others. Becoming a civil rights lawyer, in retrospect, was critical to bridging that early gap.

I had another, more personal reason. I became a civil rights lawyer to vindicate my father's life. I had witnessed the way that institutional power, often marshaled on behalf of elites, had been used to isolate and humiliate my own father. I had internalized his stories of discrimination, starting with his banishment because of his color from the freshman dorms at Harvard, and continuing with his humiliation, for the same reason, as an elevator operator for *The New York Times* who could not even show his face on certain floors.

Not all of my information arrived in second-hand bedtime stories. I had also personally witnessed some of the ways my father suffered because of his color. He lived through the mid- to late 1950s as an outcast, punished during the height of McCarthyism because his union had refused, on First Amendment and freedom of association grounds, to expel members who were Communists. As far as I knew, my father was not a Communist, but he taught me to respect the dignity and commitment to workingmen and -women of those who were. In order to support his family, he buried his intellectual gifts and fighting spirit, selling real estate and insurance to upwardly mobile working-class blacks in Queens. Thinking he might have more independence as a lawyer than a union official, he attended NYU Law School at night and easily passed the difficult New York state bar exam even as he worked full time; but the committee of the bar nevertheless denied him a license to practice law because, they said, he had "bad character."

My father was a brilliant man, who might have become a legendary lawyer. He had all the tools—intelligence, determination, a sparkling wit, a masterful capacity to hold an audience spellbound both as story-teller and orator, and a passion for justice. He also had one too many deficits. As a Harvard law professor, Derrick Bell, once said about him-self, he paid the price for being a black man who was not grateful enough. Like my father, Professor Bell was defiant. He demanded re-spect. He was given a few opportunities but never accorded real recogni-tion. Like Professor Bell, my father wanted both, not just for himself but for those who would come after.

As my father's daughter, I too was a fighter. I would vindicate my father and all the others like him who were not "grateful" enough.

But I was not just a fighter for blacks or other people of color. One of the first cases I ever tried as a young lawyer was a criminal case against several men accused of enslaving migrant workers on a North Carolina farm. As part of a team of Justice Department lawyers, I helped convict the defendants, including a black man, for holding white and Latino migrant farmworkers as "slaves."

After I graduated from law school, I clerked for two years in the mid-1970s for a federal judge in Detroit, Damon J. Keith. Judge Keith later told a reporter he liked the way I analyzed a case and he liked that I often went dancing. He said I seemed like such a well-rounded person, with both mental firepower and common sense, that he hired me on the spot during my job interview. One day—Judge Keith recalled in an interview—he was instructing jurors and told them to retire to the jury room to choose a foreman and a spokesman. Later, there was a note on his desk from his law clerk. I had asked him if he would kindly consider making that "foreperson" and "spokesperson" the next time because maybe that would help the jurors think about selecting a woman.

Judge Keith tried to teach all of his law clerks to respect the rule of law, "but to realize it is a changing thing." That's why he liked my note: it showed "sensitivity" and "awareness of the need for change, even in our most basic speaking." But Judge Keith also likes to tell the story about that note because he appreciated the discreet way I let him know.

In 1981, I found myself walking in Constance Baker Motley's shoes, this time as a civil rights lawyer, not a law student tenant. By then I had worked for four years as special assistant to Drew Days, the first black to head the Civil Rights Division of the Department of Justice. When I was trying to decide, before I knew the outcome of the 1980 presidential elections, whether to join the NAACP Legal Defense Fund staff or stay on as a career lawyer in the Justice Department's Civil Rights Division, Professor Bell had told me: "Lani, you need to get out and travel through the South. You will learn how to be a lawyer if you stay at Justice, but you won't learn how to be a civil rights advocate. Justice Department lawyers know their craft. They are superb techni-cians. But they are also anonymous bureaucrats who rarely learn from the people with whom they work. Get out there and mix it up. You won't regret it."

I followed Derrick Bell's advice and left Justice to join the Legal Defense Fund in April 1981. I was hired by Jack Greenberg, who was director-counsel of the LDF, to work on the extension of the 1965 Voting Rights Act. The act had been passed by Congress as a temporary measure to address the century-old legacy of black disenfranchisement. It was due to expire in 1982 unless Congress renewed it.

As a result of the act, blacks, for the very first time this century, began to register to vote in large numbers. But throughout the 1970s blacks were still not full participants in the political process. Those blacks who were registered now could vote; yet for the most part they could not elect candidates of their choice. In Selma, Alabama, a majority of the residents were black, but the same white man—who as mayor in 1965 had called Dr. King "Martin Luther Coon"—was still the mayor. In neighboring Mississippi, state NAACP president Aaron Henry declared in 1981 that for blacks it was still easier to buy a gun there than to register to vote.

First-generation problems in just getting blacks registered and voting persisted through the seventies and eighties. But now a second generation of problems came to the fore. Many southern states, in response to increases in black voting, instituted jurisdictionwide elections. In conventional terms, these are called "at-large" or "winner-take-all" voting. Because all voters got to vote on all candidates, a candidate sponsored by the black community could not win unless he or she appealed to at least some members of the white majority. But throughout the Black Belt of Alabama, voting was still extremely polarized— whites would simply not vote for a black candidate. As a result, in many of the Black Belt counties that had large black populations but not black voting majorities, there were still no black elected officials, even fifteen years after the Voting Rights Act was first passed. These second-generation problems were more subtle and difficult to grasp than direct denial of the franchise. But they were no less a threat to genuine democracy.

As the 1982 extension of the act loomed, Jack Greenberg assigned me to the D.C. office of LDF to work with Elaine Jones, the first black woman graduate of the University of Virginia Law School. Elaine, he knew, was a coalition builder and an experienced lobbyist/litigator. He didn't know much about me. When Greenberg hired me, he emphasized my credentials (Harvard, Yale, a federal clerkship with a distinguished black jurist, Damon Keith), but he was also persuaded by a political manner "as conservative and careful as the business suits" in which I often came to the office. I had worked at LDF as a summer intern for Elaine in 1973 while I was still in law school. He was reassured,

Greenberg said, because I was "tall, dignified, and always perfectly tailored, with a soft manner and passionate feelings about race."

I began my full-time career with LDF working out of its Washington office in a space too small to accommodate another lawyer. From the moment I joined LDF as a staff attorney in April 1981, my office was a desk in a corner of the room already occupied by Elaine. Sharing an office with Elaine was no small feat since Elaine's presence fills every inch of every room she's in. Whether she was on the phone or reading her mail, her booming voice animated our small space.

On the other hand, Elaine is a very private person. The fact that she welcomed me into her office and encouraged me to stay reflected our unique working relationship. I felt important, as if Elaine had bestowed on me a special honor. Moreover, whatever its physical disadvantages, sharing an office with Elaine permanently enhanced my powers of concentration. Despite the incredible level of activity, you learn to focus. Even more, the close proximity made it easier for Elaine to school me in the multiple ways to be an effective legislative advocate. Sometimes affectionately called by her friends "the one hundred and first Senator"—a compliment originally bestowed on the legendary Clarence Mitchell, onetime lobbyist for the NAACP—Elaine is a great communicator.

Although LDF policy required all new lawyers to work from New York headquarters, Elaine had convinced Jack to allow me to start in Washington. Elaine desperately needed help in waging the legislative fight to renew the 1965 act. She wanted me to work full time on the voting rights extension.

I was doing the Lord's work, I thought, when I became a voting rights lawyer. On the one hand, it was what my father would call a "fortuitous concatenation of circumstances" that I started working at LDF in 1981, the same year the fight to renew the 1965 act started. I was assigned to work on the renewal because I was at the right place at the right time. Originally, Congress thought the law would solve all the problems blacks faced within five years. Passed in 1965 as an extraordinary but temporary measure, it had been twice extended, and unless Congress took further action, key provisions of the law itself would expire in 1982.

What began somewhat serendipitously became an intellectual, professional, and spiritual cause. It was through my eventual mastery of the Voting Rights Act that I learned to love the law. I found in it a concrete opportunity to begin to bridge the dissonance I had discovered in the fourth grade between American promises and actions. For me, the 1965 Voting Rights Act became a sacred document that took us as a society closer to the fundamental truths of democracy. The Voting Rights Act meant that for the first time in American history, black men and women, Asians and Latinos, Native Americans and Alaskan natives, would all be granted the basic freedom of the vote. If the act were vigorously enforced, I believed that blacks and other people of color might even get to participate in the decisions that affected their lives. But the promise of the Voting Rights Act was not simply a pledge to blacks or other minorities. It was a way to make America live up to its democratic ideals for all Americans. What was happening to blacks was the most visible, but certainly not the exclusive, injustice that needed to be corrected before America could call itself a genuine democracy.

Moreover, I found the story of how the Voting Rights Act came into being as valuable as any lesson of American history, because of what it says about the role played outside the formal electoral process by organized movements for social change. I felt privileged to be part of the 1982 legislative fight to renew the law. I felt myself a witness to history, blessed to be participating in an ennobling synergy of organized outsiders working in tandem with sympathetic insiders. This was America at its finest.

Within a week of my arrival at LDF in April 1981, Elaine introduced me to the twenty-five-person steering committee, operating under the auspices of the Leadership Conference on Civil Rights to coordinate the coalition working on the extension of the act. One hundred and sixty-five organizations made up the Leadership Conference, ranging from groups representing disabled citizens, women, labor, and education to religious and civil rights groups. The NAACP was central to the lobbying arm of the coalition, as were a number of Jewish organizations, the League of Women Voters, and the AFL-CIO. The Leadership Conference had built a strong relationship with congressional leaders, it had a grass-roots network, and many of its officers had substantial expertise in formulating and implementing legislative strategy.

But the Leadership Conference steering committee, while dominated by Washington insiders, also included representatives of litigating organizations such as the Mexican American Legal Defense Fund, the NAACP Legal Defense Fund, the Lawyers Committee for Civil Rights Under Law, and lawyers working for the Joint Center for Political Studies. Most of the lawyers related more to their clients in the South and Southwest than they did to the members of Congress with whom they soon found themselves working. Some had relocated temporarily to Washington to work on the legislation; others came in frequently to lend support but psychologically their community was outside the Beltway.

Armand Derfner, a frumpled, legally blind (without his glasses) civil rights lawyer from South Carolina, was a crucial member of the steering committee. Armand, then with the Joint Center for Political Studies, and Frank Parker, then with the Lawyers Committee for Civil

Rights Under Law in Washington, but before that a civil rights lawyer in Jackson, Mississippi, had been trying voting cases since the 1960s. Both men were seasoned. They were veterans of "the movement." As white Harvard-trained lawyers and outstanding litigators, they nevertheless spent much of their adult lives living and working their principles on the ground. They knew the law inside out. They also knew the needs of black people in Mississippi, South Carolina, and other parts of the South. These were their clients and, even more, their neighbors.

Within a week, I was working full time on the Voting Rights Act extension, participating in all of the steering committee's internal deliberations. The committee met every Friday and sometimes every day in between while the extension was before Congress in 1981 and 1982. Although I attended the first steering committee meeting with Elaine in April, I still operated mostly in her shadow. I had a certain knowledge base, having worked in the Justice Department Civil Rights Division for four years and having helped AAG Drew Days restructure the Voting Rights Section, which exercised most of the responsibility in enforcing a key oversight provision of the act. Most of my recent experience was as a Washington bureaucrat, but in my heart I was an outsider.

In 1972, the summer between my first and second years in law school, I had worked for Julius Chambers. Chambers was senior partner in the first—and at that time the only—integrated law firm in North Carolina. The year before I worked there, the law offices were destroyed by a firebomb; the summer I was there, the firm had taken temporary residence in a local hotel. Though the temporary offices were a constant reminder that the firm had been firebombed by angry whites, it was Julius Chambers that I feared. His expression solemn, he rarely looked at me as he gave me an assignment. His dark brown hands were never still—they were either holding a cigarette or playing with a rubber band. He rarely smiled. He was a compact man, always preoccupied with the pile of papers on his desk.

I remember staying up several nights in the hotel room converted into a law library, pulling heavy volumes of law books off the shelf one by one, trying to respond to Mr. Chambers's request for a memorandum summarizing all employment discrimination cases ever decided. In the age before computers, local civil rights lawyers lacked the resources to network information and were often reinventing the wheel. I did not realize this at the time. I had thought it was probably a "test," a way of putting me, a young and eager law student, through my paces. I was sure someone, somewhere had already compiled all these cases and that an experienced lawyer like Julius Chambers certainly knew them. But I kept my doubts to myself. Despite Chambers's formality and the tediousness of the assignment, I felt lucky to be working there. In my mind, this was on-the-job training more valuable than any law school course. This was training to be a "movement" lawyer.

As I got to know him better, I asked Chambers whether he was ever scared doing the work he did. "I don't know about scared," Julius replied. "We were cautious about what we were doing and about our security. We had a bombing of my house, we had a bombing of my office, we had a bombing of my car. We all knew that these things were possible. But I don't think we were scared." He had been at a mass meeting the night his car was bombed. It was in the late 1960s, and Julius Chambers was addressing a meeting about a lawsuit challenging discrimination in the schools of Craven, Jones, Lenore, and Washington counties. Did he hear the explosion, I asked. "I was speaking at the time when we heard the explosion," Julius answered. He continued, "So we stopped and went outside to see what had happened and then we went back inside to finish up with the program." I was astonished. "You saw that your car had blown up and you went back inside?" I asked. "Yeah," Julius said matter-of-factly, drawing out the word into two syllables. "What could you do? I would not have been able to drive it, so, okay, let's just go on with the program." "Did anybody call the police?" "Yeah, we called the cops when we had finished the mass meeting."

My law student summer internships with Julius Chambers's law firm in North Carolina and the following summer at LDF with Elaine working on cases in Alabama had seared in me a connection to the power of local people changing their own lives. My hero was Julius Chambers—a man who saw his own car blown up outside the North Carolina church where he was speaking, and without skipping a beat continued the mass meeting. I was in Washington now, but like Armand Derfner and Frank Parker, my clients and the people I was fighting for were those who lived well beyond the Beltway.

Formally working as an LDF attorney, I aligned myself with people who also had witnessed firsthand the terrors of an angry white South. I admired the more experienced litigators whose judgment I trusted implicitly. Armand and Frank tutored me throughout the month of May when we worked closely with Democratic congressman Don Edwards of California on the House hearings that were essential to establish a public record as to why we still needed such a law and why, even more, the law itself needed to be strengthened. We burned the midnight oil helping prepare witnesses who traveled to Washington to tell their stories in ways that members of Congress would find most persuasive. Based on those local stories, we knew that many southern county school boards and local governments would try any strategy available to them to avoid complying with the law. Blacks in the rural South, just like Mexican Americans in South Texas, were still fighting an antebellum mentality. Armand and I also helped former Assistant Attorney General

Stan Pottinger (President Gerald Ford's Republican civil rights chief) with his testimony. Stan provided pizza, and from time to time even joined our drafting session in his swank law offices, where we worked until eleven o'clock the night before he was scheduled to appear before the committee.

When the extension was first considered by the House of Representatives in April 1981, Ronald Reagan had just been elected president. But the Reagan Justice Department could not formulate a position on the law, in part because the Assistant Attorney General for Civil Rights slot was still vacant. No one from Justice testified during the twenty days of House hearings that May. As a result, with only isolated dissents from conservative intellectuals, those hearings made a powerful case for why the law was still needed.

Vernon Jordan, then president of the National Urban League, was one of the first witnesses. Seated next to Elaine Jones at the witness table, Jordan appealed directly to Congressman Henry Hyde, Republican of Illinois, who was vigorously orchestrating opposition to the extension. "We are talking in good conscience, I believe, Mr. Hyde, about finding a midground. But I don't believe that for black people, given our history in this country, there is a midground when it comes to our voting rights. I don't believe that to do away with this act, to find a midground in this act, to find some political solution to this problem, is keeping the faith for those black people and white people who walked that forty-mile distance from Selma to Montgomery."

Jordan decided to remind Representative Hyde how hard blacks had to fight to gain the right just to vote. He read a passage from Pat Watters and Reese Cleghorn's *Climbing Jacob's Ladder,* about the courageous band of black people in Terrell, South Carolina, who sang Baptist hymns to corral their faith and bridle their fears so they would not back down when intimidated by white law enforcement. His voice booming but pitched just right, Jordan described how the old white sheriff of Terrell County and fifteen other white men burst into a voter registration meeting at the Mount Olive Church. The sheriff moved quickly to the front of the church, where the Reverend Charles Sherrod was leading the mass meeting. The sheriff explained how happy Negroes were in Terrell. "We want our colored people to live like they've been living," the sheriff said. "There was never any trouble before all this started."

" 'As he spoke,' " Jordan read, " 'the whites moved through the church, confronting little groups of Negroes. Finally, the whites left. A few nights later, three small Negro churches in Terrell County, one of them the Mount Olive Baptist, with Jesus and the American Presidents on its walls, were burned to the ground.' " Blacks had struggled and had paid the ultimate price to vote. It was too soon to turn back, Jordan concluded.

When Vernon Jordan finished speaking, Colorado state senator Polly Baca Barragan picked up the baton, describing more recent events that affected not just blacks but Mexican Americans. She talked about the May 3, 1980, primary in Frio County, Texas. Juan Pablo Navarro was a poll watcher who observed changes in his own ballot when it was counted after the election. He recognized his ballot because he had written in his own name for one of the offices and because he recognized his handwriting. Yet "his votes for the candidates on his ballot had been changed. He also noticed that many other ballots had been tampered with and, not coincidentally, it was those ballots which affected the race of the Chicano candidate, Mr. Adolpho Alvarez." Nothing, of course, was done about the ballots that had been changed after they had been cast. Nor did white election officials in Texas stop at blatant efforts to deny office to Mexican Americans; they also used more subtle kinds of gerrymandering and at-large elections to keep Mexican Americans from obtaining political power.

Republican Henry Hyde, who originally opposed any extension, had a change of heart immediately after attending a field hearing in Montgomery, Alabama, in mid-May. There Maggie Bozeman, a black schoolteacher, testified that in Aliceville, Alabama, white policemen were stationed inside polling places taking pictures of those who attempted to assist black voters. Mrs. Bozeman also talked about "open house voting." There was no secret ballot—no booths, no curtains; just an open table under the watchful eye of white officials. After hearing testimony about a burdensome reidentification procedure that required all voters to reregister—with registration hours limited to 9:00 A.M. to 4:00 P.M., Hyde said, "I just want to say that I have listened with great interest and concern and I will tell you, registration hours from nine to four are outrageous. It is absolutely designed to keep people who are working and who have difficulty traveling from voting. If that persists and exists, it is more than wrong. The lack of deputy registrars— only twelve Alabama counties have them—demonstrates a clear lack of enthusiasm for getting people registered, obviously."

Congressman Hyde's conversion was critical in convincing the litigators that all we needed to do was to give those simple stories greater visibility. Our most able advocates were local people such as Maggie Bozeman and Juan Pablo Navarro. Their stories were vivid reminders that many Americans still lived in only a partial democracy. Those who suffered daily the indignities of being silenced and excluded needed to tell their stories. It was the plain speech of ordinary people that would help the rest of America bear witness to a different vision.

Hyde's repositioning, however, soon provoked a crisis within the Leadership Conference. While Hyde now conceded the continued need for the act, he was also hard at work to weaken its major provisions. Hyde had been persuaded that the law should stay on the books; his approach was to extend the law in principle but create large loopholes so that each of the southern states could easily escape coverage. Hyde drafted a loosely worded proposal that "recalcitrant jurisdictions could have driven a Mack truck through," as Armand put it.

Some of the Washington-based lobbyists were tempted to endorse Hyde's bailout provisions. After all, Ronald Reagan was president; the Republicans controlled the Senate. What good would it do to stand on principle in the House (where Democrats still controlled majorities) and lose everything in the end?

People like Ralph Neas, the newly installed head of the Leadership Conference; the established civil rights advocate Bill Taylor; and a handful of other lobbyists on the Leadership Conference steering committee saw Hyde's move as an opportunity, not because they trusted Hyde but because they thought they knew him. Michael Pertschuk, in his book *The Giant Killers*, quotes Neas explaining the importance of distinguishing among adversaries:

> Now Henry Hyde was someone I had watched carefully over a long period of time. Philosophically, he was not uniformly against positions of the Leadership Conference. He had been very effective, for example, in support of the Legal Services Corporation fight, and on certain civil rights issues he prided himself on leaving the fold of the conservative Republican administration; he didn't want to be pigeon-holed solely in the extremist camp. . . . The Hyde [anti-abortion] amendment made him a national figure, and he wanted to compensate for that Far Right image by doing well on the Voting Rights Act. From the beginning, I think he perceived himself as the architect of some type of grand compromise. This was an historic bill. He was playing an historic role.

Lobbyists within the Leadership Conference were also keenly aware that they too were playing "an historic role." They were especially conscious of the changing political climate in Washington following the repudiation of the Carter presidency. In their minds, it was politically expedient to find language that might narrow the gap with Hyde. The principal Democratic Party House Judiciary Committee staffer was Alan Parker. Parker and other committee staff members also argued that we needed to forge a compromise, or else we would doom the entire Voting Rights Act. House staff thought negotiations with Hyde were essential to establish legitimacy in the Senate. In philosophical sync with the lobbyists, staff on the Hill kept looking for compromise language so that Henry Hyde, a conservative Republican, could be their stalking horse in the Republican-dominated Senate.

Moreover, we all knew that time was of the essence. Congress was getting ready to adjourn for the August recess. If we rejected Hyde's plan, we would really have to scramble to come up with something that the Judiciary Committee could vote on and then take home with them. It was crucial that we have a tangible bill during the August recess so we could energize a grass-roots lobby in the home district offices of individual members.

While there were no plans to stage a confrontation as dramatic as what had taken place in 1965 on the Edmund Pettus Bridge in Selma, we all knew the importance of bottom-up momentum. Unless members of Congress heard from their own constituents, they were less likely to vote the way we wanted. All civil rights laws were controversial at some level. The Voting Rights Act, as American as apple pie to some, was no exception. Even the more liberal members needed occasional bucking up.

Nevertheless, Armand and Frank opposed the formulation of the compromise. Those who knew the law best were skeptical of the fragile compromise the lobbyists and committee staff tried to hammer out. Why compromise, they argued, when we had the votes to pass the bill in the committee and on the House floor? There would be plenty of time and reason to compromise when the bill reached the Senate. There we would need the strongest possible language as a starting point, knowing that Republican Orrin Hatch of Utah was heading the crucial Senate subcommittee and Republican Strom Thurmond of South Carolina was in charge of the larger Judiciary Committee. With the Justice Department off "studying the legislation," we had the field to ourselves.

It was not just the Reagan Justice Department that was missing in action. The Leadership Conference faced no organized opposition anywhere. Although many of the well-funded conservative think tanks that now line the streets of Washington had opened offices, they were still new to the business of trying to influence public policy in a coordinated and well-heeled way. As Dianne Pinderhughes writes in a paper prepared while a guest scholar at the Brookings Institution, these groups had not yet created "a network of policy institutes, legal bodies and other organizations which actively monitor and aggressively participate in public including civil rights policy formation."

The neoconservatives had only begun to exploit the intellectual backlash to government intervention on behalf of disadvantaged "groups." Soon they would figure out how to tap into the country's weary view that the problem of civil rights had already been fixed by national legislation. But for the moment they were not yet on the ascendancy.

The litigators, with whom I identified, were also furious that the lobbyists—who knew next to nothing about enforcing the law—were controlling the process of negotiations, excluding the litigators who had the substantive knowledge. Frank, Armand, Barbara Phillips (a black woman who had tried voting cases in Mississippi and now worked for the Lawyers Committee) and others, such as Jose Garza and Joaquin Avila from the Mexican American Legal Defense Fund (MALDEF), who were in the business of trying voting cases, immediately went into action to challenge the escape hatch that Republican representative Hyde proposed. The litigators suspected Hyde was simply engineering the escape of the South from supervision through the loosely worded sieve of a bailout provision. Hispanic groups were also wary of any compromise. They doubted the commitment of the Leadership Conference to the bilingual provisions of the act, and feared they would be abandoned in the heat of negotiations. Few of the litigators trusted Republicans. Fewer still trusted Hyde.

By July 1981, Hyde's proposals had prompted an intense and painful breakdown within the Leadership Conference coalition. Principals accused the litigators of trying to torpedo the compromise they were crafting. Tempers were short. I agreed wholeheartedly with Frank, Armand, and the other litigators from the Lawyers Committee for Civil Rights and the Mexican American Legal Defense Fund. I also knew that Elaine, who had begun to defer to me as she worked on other matters, was skeptical about Hyde's larger agenda.

At one point toward the end of July, I was the only one present representing LDF on Capitol Hill. I was inclined to lend LDF's support to the opposition; but with Elaine out of town, I did not know the extent of my delegated authority. Within the hierarchy of LDF, as well as the Leadership Conference itself, I knew I was low on the totem pole. I had been on the job for less than three months, and with no one else from LDF present, I had to decide what position to take on a proposal that threatened the very integrity of our coalition. I remember trying to hide from Robert Pear, who was covering the extension fight for *The New York Times*. At one point, a recent black Wellesley graduate, Laura Murphy (whose family published the *Baltimore Afro-American*, the famed black newspaper) and I stayed behind in a stairwell so we would not have to speak to reporters, whose antennae had picked up the scent of a fight but whose coverage would only lock people into hardened positions.

I darted out of the congressional hearing room where Hyde's plan was being debated, found a pay phone, and dialed Jack Greenberg's number at the LDF offices in New York. He listened quietly as I described the competing perspectives. Then he asked me what I thought LDF should do. I told Jack I thought we should oppose the compromise.

But I was careful not to mislead him. I was very clear that there might be political costs to be paid within and by the civil rights coalition. From the other end of the phone I heard the words, "Lani, sometimes you just have to do what is right."

Jack Greenberg described this exchange in his book, *Crusaders in the Courts:*

> As one who had made some compromises and had refused to enter many a Quixotic fight, I was hardly an ideologue in backing Lani and Elaine. The law would have been weakened. Our resources might have been drained in needless litigation. Besides, I wasn't sure that if we stuck to our guns we would lose and in fact, we won. LDF's strength lay in large part in the energy and enthusiasm of its lawyers. More than once I said "no," but when I felt I could back the staff I did.

Although some of us stood firm on principle, it was not our principles alone that won the day. Representative Hyde overreached, refusing to change a key provision in his bailout plan. His stubbornness allowed the lobbyists safe cover for retreat. Once it was clear that the compromise did not command a consensus, the litigators and lobbyists on the steering committee stayed up half the night to forge an alternative. A group of us had already prepared what we thought would be the perfect bailout provision, what we would like in the best of all possible situations. We bunkered down to write a substitute bill using the ideal draft as the starting point, but we did so without the blessing of the House committee staff. They were fuming. By temperament and positioning, they were eager to continue to try dealing behind the scenes with Hyde. The subcommittee staff were so angry with us that they would not help in drafting an alternative. They did, however, let us use their offices while they went home.

As veteran Washington insider Bill Taylor noticed during one of our interminably long meetings on the Hill, each of us played a role much like the "types" or positions taken by countries at the United Nations. Armand Derfner was the Hamlet of our coalition—he could always see both sides. Frank Parker, his views honed on the battlefields of the Mississippi Delta, was the red-bearded principled warrior, adamant and vehement. Ralph Neas, executive director of the Leadership Conference and a former Republican staffer for Senator Ed Brooke, was the pragmatic politician—no one was better at counting votes. I also remember deferring to the nonlawyers on the steering committee when it came to speaking in the court of public opinion. People like Laura Murphy of the American Civil Liberties Union (ACLU) had a facility with plain English and a spirited delivery that always enlivened our joint radio interviews defending the extension.

I don't remember what role Bill Taylor assigned me. I was one of the youngest members of the coalition at thirty-one, and had not participated in the civil rights mass movement of the sixties. I had worked in Washington as a Justice Department insider for four years and knew the players. But by temperament and training, I was more like the litigators. I was never without a briefcase stuffed with all the versions of the compromise, our ideal draft substitute, our talking points, questions and answers, or Xeroxed copies of legal cases interpreting the prior law. My briefcase served as a portable office, overflowing with paper just like the cramped space Elaine and I shared. I focused my attention on documents and finding clear language that we could enforce in court. I was always taking notes, making a record of every meeting I attended. I loved the all-night brainstorming sessions, testing and reshaping our arguments. Sometimes I alienated our allies with my insistence that we get it right.

Ralph Neas, as a principal lobbyist who was not always on LDF's side, saw me as "a very determined person" who could be "fiercely independent, totally committed to whatever [she was] working on, and very aggressive about how [she went] after it." While my tenacity was ever present in Ralph's mind, he later acknowledged that I had other qualities as well, saying that I was "open-minded, a coalition builder, inclusive and effective."

Armand, too, saw me as a bridge person in the struggle between the litigators and the Washington people. In describing my role, Armand told a reporter, "[Lani] had a great deal of knowledge, and that and her hard work gave her credibility on both sides." Armand remembered my laugh most of all. Armand said. "She can talk to anybody, meaning anybody from presidents to railway conductors, white or black. And she has a terrific laugh; you can hear it from here to kingdom come."

By ten o'clock on the morning after my phone conversation with Jack Greenberg, the Leadership Conference had repudiated Hyde's compromise. A group of us had also produced a new bill. Everyone was in a celebratory mood. All the animosity of the last few days was gone. Nine members of the steering committee had stayed up until 3:00 A.M. and completely rewritten the bill in a way that was, in Michael Pertschuk's words, "so technically sound and carefully drafted" it remained essentially intact in its future passage through House and Senate. The Leadership Conference working group had also prepared a technical section-by-section analysis of the bill and summaries for the press, something that under normal time pressures would take three to four intensive weeks to produce. In place of the Hyde proposal, Congressmen Hamilton Fish (a liberal Republican) and James Sensenbrenner (a conservative Republican who we were told harbored deep personal antagonism toward Henry Hyde) sponsored a Leadership Conference—backed provision that did not include the dreaded compromise language. Briefed by Bill Taylor just fifteen minutes before the committee meeting, Congressman Fish defended the bill as if he had spent all night writing it. The Judiciary Committee sent it to the floor by an overwhelming vote and it passed the full House 389–24.

That experience crystalized my thinking about social change. I was elated. My judgment and my principles had been affirmed. I had been validated as a civil rights lawyer. I "kvelled," my mother would say, with the joys of a hard-won accomplishment. But, even more, I felt connected to a community of people, joined by common ideals and a common project. This was not a one-person or a single-strategy enterprise. Nor was it an alliance that walked in lockstep or shared a single set of experiences. We were a multiracial and multigenerational partnership that came together to attack a perceived injustice. We all worked hard, contributing different insights and perspectives. From this large, unwieldy coalition of "types" and roles, I discovered the importance of creative synergy. The tensions between the litigators and the lobbyists were essential in beating back the Reagan administration's attempt to dilute the House bill in the Senate. The line was held; with the help of compromise language offered by Senator Dole, but crafted essentially by our coalition, the final version of the act was very much like the strong House-passed bill.

The principled stand by the litigators forced the lobbyists to reconsider premature compromise; but the eventual legislation reflected the informed perspectives of a varied and broad-based coalition, one that began as individuals meeting every Friday morning and grew together as a community at heart. We were a community by virtue of our chosen, not biological, identity. We came together as blacks and Jews, litigators and lobbyists, experienced insiders and idealistic newcomers. We shared a common passion for social change, but we did not all share that passion to the same degree or with the same energy. Most of us enjoyed the privileges of an excellent education and good jobs, but we did not always agree either by ideology or temperament. Yet we functioned as a single, loosely coordinated organism, each one pulling his or her weight at different times and in different ways.

We were all experts in our own singular domain, yet our sustained collaboration reminded us that the whole was greater than the sum of its parts. The lawyers knew the law; the lobbyists knew the Hill. But neither the lawyers nor the lobbyists alone could tell the stories of exclusion and degradation experienced daily by blacks in small rural southern communities or Chicanos in the Southwest or recently naturalized Asian-American citizens. None of us could tell the stories of continued injustice as eloquently as the witnesses who traveled to

Washington to testify during the twenty days of House hearings. It was those stories and the participation by those ordinary witnesses that made what we were all doing real and important and fundamentally democratic. It was all made possible as well by the ability of organized labor, the League of Women Voters, and other groups with local constituencies who met during the recesses with their local members of Congress in their home offices. This was an inside-the-Beltway operation with legs.

We operated by consensus. Ralph was our leader and was authorized to speak for the group, but only after the group itself had signed on at least in principle to the position he was to take. Everyone who sat at our steering committee meetings was encouraged to participate, to speak up, to question the received wisdom. Some observers, like Judiciary Committee staffer Alan Parker, who did not participate in steering committee meetings but witnessed their results, dismissed us as the "civil rights circus." Ralph told Michael Pertschuk that he knew Parker well:

> Alan did not appreciate working with what appeared to be an excessively democratic group of people. To him, it looked leaderless, disorganized. To a degree there was some legitimacy to this point of view. It certainly did appear to be an unruly mob at times. This was our formative period; trust and relationships hadn't been established. We hadn't won anything really significant yet. And we were not speaking as one.

In a legislative battle for an inclusive and truly representative democracy, our ragtag group of lobbyists and litigators had practiced exactly what we tried to get Congress to enact. We explored the dynamic tension between different kinds of knowing, among different groups of people, and around different ways of mobilizing power— by those with local knowledge and outsider resources and those with individual access and insider expertise.

Everyone had a chance to speak; everyone's view was respected and considered. While we did not speak as one, we did succeed as a whole. Where others saw chaos, we saw democracy.

It seemed to me that our efforts in 1981 and 1982 had been guided by at least three crucial ideas. One was that direct communication from ordinary people can bring important members of the establishment to the table. Whether it was the determination of many citizens to march in the streets as in the 1960s or the plain-spoken eloquence of the witnesses at the field hearings in 1981, the actions and voices of real folk can inspire powerful people who otherwise do not want to talk or act to come to the table. Mobilizing ordinary people to march or speak gives their leadership the power to back up their demands. Second, a broad-based coalition is necessary. The black civil rights groups couldn't do it alone. Just as in 1965, when white clergy, Jewish leaders, business people all joined the movement as it marched for voting rights, a mammoth collaboration fueled our legislative efforts in 1981. Finally, the movement was not just a plea for special rights; it was a crusade for justice. This was about realizing the promises of democracy, not just gaining voting rights for blacks.

My experience in 1981–82 enabled me to see myself as a civil rights lawyer with a mission and a promise. My mission was to encourage ordinary people to make their own lives better. The promise, I thought at the time, was that by vigorously enforcing the Voting Rights Act, we could do just that. As a member of an itinerant band of lawyers marching throughout the courts of law of the American South, I would help fulfill Martin Luther King's legacy and complete the unfinished business of the civil rights movement. I would be a member of the legal bugle corps, playing the newly extended Voting Rights Act as my instrument. Having worked to strengthen the act, I now had to implement its terms.

The next step for me was to challenge directly the Reagan administration's civil rights policies, and especially its civil rights chief, Brad Reynolds, who seemed determined to subvert the promise of the Voting Rights Act, at least as I saw it. In an updated version of Nixon's "Southern strategy," the Reagan civil rights enforcers were seeking to abstract racial justice into a question of formal neutrality, detached from any historical or social context. Thus, Ronald Reagan announced his decision to run for a second term in 1984 in a small town in Mississippi, signaling a willingness to represent the "Old South" and all that it stood for. But they were also energetically repositioning the idea of civil rights itself. Whereas the civil rights movement of the sixties and seventies had engaged in protest and litigation to open up the society to more diverse groups of people, the Reagan idea of civil rights throughout the eighties was to break the backbone of group redress in favor of providing the appearance of individual opportunity.

The problem with the Reagan approach was simple: It ignored the reality in which we found ourselves. It denied the existence of disadvantaged groups who by virtue of historical, social, and economic circumstances were structurally positioned at the bottom, unable to take advantage of formal neutrality. Indeed, it transformed the reality of group oppression into a problem of individual pathology and bad character (and in its more virulent form, bad genes). Moreover, it coopted the rhetoric of formal equality to a principle of inaction. If we simply declared everyone equal, then that assertion spoke for itself. We had absolved society, and particularly its governmental agencies, from acting to remedy or interrupt anything but isolated acts of contemptible racial animus directed at single individuals. By limiting civil rights to discrimination against honorable victims, they individualized a systemic problem and justified doing nothing to help either black Americans or white working-class Americans as a group or a class. In the name of race, they buried increasing inequalities of class or group disadvantage generally.

My job was to take on these ideas in court. In 1983, I was part of an LDF team that fought Louisiana's racially biased redistricting plan, which Reagan civil rights chief Brad Reynolds had reviewed and approved as nondiscriminatory under the Voting Rights Act. The record was replete with racially bigoted statements from one local official who claimed that the plan was engineered by himself and other Louisiana politicians because they wanted desperately to avoid electing any more "nigger bigshots." Yet Reynolds had personally given his blessing to the discriminatory plan, over the unanimous protest of the people who knew the law best, the department's career staff. The Republican governor who engineered the plan admitted that it "looked funny," but testified that it was designed to ensure compliance with his ceiling of 44 percent black voters, a quota he imposed on all Louisiana congressional districts. To Reynolds, such reasoning was evidence of political, not racial, bias.

A three-judge court eventually threw out the Reynolds-approved plan. The following year, I gave a presentation about the case at an LDF luncheon in New York to which all the chiefs of the Civil Rights Division of the Justice Department, past and present, were invited. I had a big map which we had used during the court case to persuade the judges that the plan deliberately severed all the black wards and none of the white wards. On it I traced the Reynolds-approved plan, revealing how similar it was to a picture of Donald Duck superimposed on the city of New Orleans.

When I finished, Mr. Reynolds turned to the audience and tried to strike a note of polite irony laced with discomfort that he had been served up for the other luminaries to feast on: "Thank you for inviting me to lunch. I didn't know I was to be the main course. Lani Guinier is obviously an able advocate, but as you know every story has two sides. However, I have to leave to catch a plane so I don't have time to give my side."

During the early eighties, I also found myself representing clients such as Mrs. Maggie Bozeman, the fifty-five-year-old black schoolteacher from Pickens County, Alabama, who had been prosecuted by state authorities for assisting elderly blacks to vote by absentee ballot. Maggie Bozeman had taught school in Pickens County since 1947; in 1978 she was charged with voting fraud, with voting more than once, and with forging absentee ballots. She was convicted by an all-white jury in Pickens County in 1979 and sentenced to serve four years in the Alabama penal system. The prosecution was able to prove that some of the ballots cast by black voters, which were supposed to be signed in front of a notary, had in fact been signed out of his presence. Aside from the fact that Mrs. Bozeman knew many of these voters, there was no evidence to connect her to the improper signatures. Moreover, apart from the evidence that the ballots were improperly notarized, there was no evidence that they were fraudulent.

At her trial, the only testimony directly linking Mrs. Bozeman to the election came when a witness said that Mrs. Bozeman was in the same car as her friend, Mrs. Julia Wilder, parked outside the courthouse on election day, and that one of the ladies in the car walked into the courthouse carrying a brown paper bag. The lack of evidence, apparently, was no barrier to conviction.

"I didn't know I was in trouble," Mrs. Bozeman told the historian and journalist Roger Wilkins, explaining in a 1984 *Esquire* magazine profile what had happened the day she was arrested.

> I was doing exercises with the children in the playground when I saw all these cars coming up to the school. They weren't police cars, honey. They were sheriff's cars. I took the children back into the school, but I told them not to worry because the sheriff was supposed to help. I was going to get my tea from my thermos to relax myself.

But the sheriff's cars had not come to help Maggie Bozeman; they had come to collect her. Before she would have her tea the principal summoned her over the intercom system.

> One of the white children in my class began to cry and I told him not to worry, it would be all right. I thought the principal was joking with me, but he wasn't. When I got to the office, Louie Coleman, the sheriff —he's big and heavy—said, "Maggie, come with me. You have been charged with vote fraud." Then he read me a little card. And so I went back to the classroom and told the children that the sheriff had come for me. I left, and Louie Coleman walked me out like a criminal. But he let me drive my own car down to the courthouse, and all these sheriff's cars followed me right from school. It was like a funeral procession.

When asked what she had done to merit this attention, Mrs. Bozeman explained to Roger Wilkins:

> I was trying to educate people; trying to inform them about the political process and how they should be involved. My primary role was to

gather information and to put it in the people's heads and to inform them about what the law was.

I got my information from the Alabama Democratic conference that put out a memorandum written by Alabama Assistant Attorney General Walter Turner that gave, according to the law, the steps—one, two, three—on how you could assist people to register to vote. Before that, we didn't have the information to educate the people.

That's what bothers me also, I followed the law and still I got convicted.

Maggie Bozeman's real crime was that she was trying to get some political power for blacks in Pickens County. Forty percent of the population was black and yet the county had never had a black elected to anything. Upon hearing this, Roger Wilkins was incredulous. "Not to anything?" he asked. Mrs. Bozeman answered, "To no thing, honey. To NO thing!"

Blacks had run for office, but they were always unsuccessful because all county offices were elected at-large rather than by district. Thus the black vote, though a large minority, was swallowed up by the larger white majority. These were exactly the kinds of problems Mrs. Bozeman had testified to during the field hearings on the 1981 extension of the Voting Rights Acts. It was in part because of Mrs. Bozeman's forceful testimony that Congressman Hyde changed his mind and decided that a federal presence monitoring local voting practices was still needed.

Because voting was not only at-large but winner-take-all, the winning majority won all the seats. And because *whites as a voting majority tended to support the same white candidates* and still refused to vote for any blacks, the black minority was never able to elect anyone "To no thing, honey. To NO thing!"

Prosecuting Maggie Bozeman of Pickens County seemed part of a pattern by Alabama authorities to keep blacks from gaining office. Bozeman's convictions had a predictably chilling effect. Black absentee voting in Pickens dropped off sharply, as did black voting generally, especially when the Alabama Supreme Court upheld her convictions.

Several days after Maggie Bozeman and her seventy-year-old co-defendant, Julia Wilder, began serving their sentences Jack Greenberg read about their plight in *The New York Times*. He studied a picture of the two women serving time in Tutwiler state prison on a work release program under the sheriff of Macon County. Jack summoned me to his office and showed me the article. "I want you to do whatever it takes to help these women. If necessary get on the next plane, file a habeas petition, and argue the case in federal court. Just get these convictions overturned." With the help of Siegfried Knopf, a volunteer lawyer who had graduated earlier that year from Columbia; Anthony Amsterdam, a brilliant law professor with a photographic memory of legal opinions; and Vanzetta Penn Durant, a bright, energetic LDF cooperating attorney in Montgomery, Alabama, we did just that.

Buoyed by our victories in the Bozeman case and the Louisiana congressional redistricting, I told Roger Wilkins when he interviewed me in 1984 about my work, "Voting rights is an idea whose time has come. Black people have a lot of hope in it. I feel good as a trustee of that hope. It is the community choosing the agenda, not the lawyers running the show." My role as a voting rights attorney, I explained to Wilkins in 1984, is as "an energizer of movement. I want to encourage people to make their lives better—to activate their spirit and their concern."

I BECAME A LAW PROFESSOR in 1988 when I joined the faculty at the University of Pennsylvania Law School. Now I was a legal scholar and educator. I could help train and inspire the next generation of legal advocates. I also seized the opportunity to interpret and reflect on my own advocacy experiences. I began to see a need to change direction and momentum in the fight for civil rights.

My experiences fighting to amend, extend, and implement the Voting Rights Act became part of a larger battle to bring democracy to life. I saw participatory democracy as a system in which the people, all of the people, get to participate in making the decisions that affect their lives. I was convinced that genuine democracy was a prerequisite for genuine freedom. After all, democracy, "the rule of the people," in what the historian Arthur Schlesinger, Jr., terms its "unarguable sense," means that all of the people collectively decide the course of their own historical fate.

Participatory democracy was not just a racially inclusive version of government by and for elites. Participatory democracy meant giving ordinary people—those whose power depended on their willingness to struggle in association and relationship with others—the incentive and the opportunity to have a voice in public policy. It was not enough to vote, although universal suffrage was a precondition. People deserved the opportunity to cast a vote for someone who could get elected. But in addition to the vote, they also needed a voice.

A vote and a voice that mattered. This was, in my view, what the early civil rights movement had fought for. Many activists turned to electoral politics to awaken ordinary black folk to their humanity, their heritage, and their potential, as citizens, to participate in democratic self-government. As one activist observed in 1964:

I think one of the things that made [us] so hopeful, so expectant, was the fact that people had made a discovery that there is a way out of much that is wrong with our lives, there is a way to change it, and that is through the execution of this vote. . . . That's the way we [felt] —really excited about the fact that we were at long last going to be able to participate, to be represented.

Like other proponents of participatory democracy, civil rights activists Septima Clark (who organized citizenship schools to teach blacks to read so they could pass literacy tests) and Ella Jo Baker (an SCLC youth organizer) had faith in the ability of ordinary people to provide much of the leadership for their own struggle. For this reason, Clark once wrote a letter to Dr. Martin Luther King, Jr., asking him "not to lead all the marches himself" so that other leaders might develop who could lead their own marches. Dr. King read that letter before the SCLC staff, Clark remembered. "It just tickled them; they just laughed."

Black-elected officials, and white officials who were accountable to all voters, not just a narrow elite, would be the vanguard for a new social justice agenda. Indeed, civil rights activists sought the right to vote in part so they could elect more government officials who would be responsive to the needs and concerns of poor and working-class folk generally. But to people like Septima Clark and Ella Jo Baker, it was about much more than electing people to important jobs. Full political participation was necessary, not just universal suffrage. The aim was not just to teach blacks how to pass literacy tests; nor was the purpose of local organizing just about getting people registered to vote; the goal was to create involved citizens and to discover local community leaders.

I worried that the ideals that originally animated the civil rights movement were getting lost. We were all pushing to enforce the Voting Rights Act, but it was becoming primarily a vehicle to create geographic election districts in which blacks were the majority and thus could elect a candidate of their choice. I became concerned that majority black single-member districts were not necessarily the best tool for broad-based community empowerment. And I became critical of the single-minded devotion to a strategy that puts more black faces in high places rather than mobilizes ordinary people to get more involved.

The issues were changing and we needed to change our thinking to keep up. When I left LDF in 1988 for Penn, I continued to work with Dayna Cunningham, who clearly understood this new terrain. As Dayna explained in 1993 to *Washington Post* reporter David Von Drehle:

They're changing the rules so minority representatives can't function. I have a case in Shelby County, Tennessee, where redistricting required a two-thirds vote of the commission, but after an election they found they couldn't get two-thirds without winning some black members. So [to avoid having to reach out to the black representatives] they changed the requirement to a simple majority.

You see all this, and after a while you realize that simply creating a black district is not going to solve the racial problem in our government. We need mechanisms that will make people cooperate, build coalitions.

"I learned that from Lani Guinier," she told him.

I was not satisfied that any one of us had all the answers. I was not sanguine about simply recommitting the federal government and its resources to enforcing a 1960s vision of formal equality. I believed that new, innovative remedies were needed to address a different, more complex set of problems.

Blacks, as University of Texas Professor Gerald Torres taught me, function as the miner's canary—the fragile bird carried into coal mines to detect whether they harbor poisonous gases. The canary's death by suffocation signals the miners that it is time to beat a hasty retreat. By the mid-1980s, the New Democrats, with whom Bill Clinton had early on affiliated, wanted to reclaim a Democratic majority by downplaying "group rights." It was as if the canaries had banded together and made demands based primarily or exclusively on special interest or identity politics. We were all the same, the New Democrats responded to the canaries' plea for relief. But as a law professor in the 1990s, working with progressive scholars like Gerald Torres and my Penn Law School colleague Susan Sturm, I began to see the possibility of a different solution, which did not involve ignoring the canary's warning or the canary's special experience. Indeed, the canary's very visibility helped focus our attention in a way that could then be used to expose more systemic problems. I thought we should take note of the canary's admonition, not to fix the canary alone but indeed to improve the conditions of the mines so that neither the canaries nor humans risked asphyxiation.

In particular, I came to see in the voting rights context that the problems blacks had being represented by candidates of their choice was a problem experienced by many whites, too. Our conventional notions of democracy were entirely too passive as far as the role played by voters was concerned. In current election districts, representation was a function of living and breathing in the right district, even if the representative was chosen by others with whom you disagreed. I thought representation should be the result of community mobilizing and voter organization instead. Thus, cumulative voting, one of the alternative election systems I now began to explore, was a way of encouraging voters to mobilize and organize at the grassroots level consistent with the mission of the Voting Rights Act (if it were used to remedy proven violations) to better protect democracy for everyone. It would express a more active view of democracy generally. Groups would define themselves as political actors by their interests and by their ability to mobilize like-minded voters.

Cumulative voting (which I describe in more detail in chapter Nine) was a way of rethinking the role of voters and their representatives from the bottom up. It was a rather simple yet democratic vision: 51 percent of the people should not necessarily get 100 percent of the power, especially if they use that power to exclude a significant portion of the other 49 percent. If 30 percent of voters back a particular party or candidate for legislative office, I began to ask, why aren't those voters represented at all in a legislative body? Why should they sit empty-handed while 51 percent of voters gobble 100 percent of the seats?

Moreover, when the losers get nothing even though they represent a significant segment of the electorate, we are not necessarily acting in the best interest of the majority or the minority. When politics is "winner-take-all," the stakes are high. Politicians are encouraged to go negative, to drive up their opponents' negatives and drive away their opponents' supporters. A "winner-takes-all" culture suppresses voter participation. It reduces politics to a game in which voters become spectators rather than active citizens and it limits the ability of those with integrity and good intentions to remain so, if they want to continue to play ball.

By finding more inclusive and participatory electoral systems, I thought we could reinvigorate a new kind of politics in which all voters' votes count and in which all voters vote for someone who can get elected. Where everyone can win something, genuine collaboration is possible. These ideas of power sharing and "taking turns" were behind law review articles I began to write describing alternative election reforms like cumulative voting and other winner-take-only-some election and legislative rule changes.

Abbe Lowell worked with me in the Justice Department during the 1970s in the Carter administration. I understood "great concepts," Lowell said, but I never forgot Maggie Bozeman and the other LDF clients I had worked with. Even after I became a law professor, I still identified with "struggles on a human level." To Abbe Lowell, I became "a scholar with a heart."

But in 1993, neither the experience of my career, the many lessons it yielded, nor my actual views were important. For many people, what I did or what I believed did not establish my identity. "Who are you?" "What are you?" they demanded to know. Many of these people were white; but some were black. They were suspicious of me—was I really one of them? The questions were prompted by curiosity; they were also a plea for reassurance. A black waitress, London Sengale, was quite insistent as she served me lunch in a Hartford restaurant: "What is your ethnic background, going back to your grandparents? I know you're black, but who are you? I know you're black, but what are you?"

That was the sound bite in the spring of 1993. We know you are black, but what are you? And, without waiting for my answer, members of the establishment media supplied one. To my mother's great horror, I was once again "Looney Lani." I was also "Bill Clinton's Quota Queen."

What spoke was not how I looked to those who knew me. What spoke was not what I had done. What spoke was not what my mother had in mind when she named me after her Hawaiian matchmaker friend. What spoke was my "type," a black woman of the lunatic fringe. Too black was too crazy. Too black was the threatening Virago in my father's ditty—I was a troublemaker. I made white people feel uncomfortable. That made me not just black, but "too dark."

Too dark, too black, in other words, meant, in the eyes of my audience, that I was about giving blacks more than whites—I was "for" black people.

Too black meant too much of something unfamiliar and dangerous.

Too black meant someone too scary to let speak.

CHAPTER THREE

Nightline: A Lone Forum

IT WAS FIVE WEEKS since I had been nominated. On Wednesday morning, June 2, 1993, I was on the 8:00 A.M. Amtrak train to New York. I sat with Eddie Correia, who was traveling to the same meeting. Eddie was the first and only full-time staff person assigned to my nomination. He had been working with me for exactly one week. We were headed to New York to meet with the editorial board of *The New York Times*.

Eddie Correia, a Northeastern University law professor, had worked on Capitol Hill during the 1980s for Senator Howard Metzenbaum. We had been on the same side of various fights waged against the Reagan administration in the 1980s, but we did not know each other well.

Eddie had grown up in Oklahoma, in a small, religious family in a completely white community. There was not a person of color in his school from elementary to high school, except one Native American who happened to be the best athlete in the school. When Eddie was a kid, he went with his parents to the bus station to meet a relative. He wandered off and discovered to his absolute amazement that there was another, separate waiting room. Why were there two waiting rooms? he wondered. That's when he first witnessed segregation, "seeing a 'colored' waiting room," he later told me. He was six years old.

When Eddie was a senior in high school, his school was chosen as the site for the Oklahoma National Honor Society annual meeting. The teacher in charge convened an assembly to prepare the students for the event. While describing the logistics, the host teacher mentioned that there would be two "colored kids" coming from Tulsa. "Of course, the colored kids would be staying with colored families in Oklahoma City," she said. Eddie raised his hand; he spoke spontaneously. "We'll keep those kids at my house."

The teacher was stunned. The other kids in the auditorium were surprised by Eddie's boldness, but no one said anything. "It was as if everyone was intentionally silent," Eddie remembers, "because they knew this is what they should have done too. They almost were embarrassed that this thing had been set up so that these guys were going to have to be shipped off fifteen miles to Oklahoma City." Eddie went home to announce to his mother that two boys were coming to spend the night.

Eddie's mother was a Southern Baptist from Chickasaw, Oklahoma. Oklahoma, unlike much of Arkansas, is not the deep South, but both states shared common cultural influences, especially the religious values with which Eddie's mom and dad raised him. Eddie believed that he came from a background similar to Bill Clinton, probably learned about civil rights in the same way. In Eddie's case, he looked around the South and saw these battles going on and had parents who told him, "Black people are just like us and you don't have to use these terms that everybody is using." Thus, Eddie was not surprised how his mother responded to his announcement. She said, "Fine."

Eddie's religious upbringing had taught him race was a moral issue, not a policy question. He acted on a combination of faith and principle when Ricki Seidman called him on May 24, asking him to drop everything and come down for a few weeks to help coordinate my nomination. Eddie jumped on a plane and arrived in Washington the next day, May 25. Why did he drop everything when Ricki called? He vaguely knew the right wing was beating up on me. He later explained, "This was not a close call. This was not something that this is on the one hand, or on the other hand a real issue. Someone is getting beaten up unfairly in Washington and there are not enough people there that are standing up for her and I know how to do this. I know this process. I bet I could go and represent her." Once again, Eddie spontaneously offered his assistance to someone in need.

Ricki thought the hearing would be on June 9 or 10. She told Eddie that no one in the Justice Department or the White House was devoting much time to the nomination. They were relying on Carolyn, a high-octane, fast-talking, pull-no-punches, one-woman campaign machine. Carolyn Osolinik was an unpaid volunteer, working pro bono on my nomination while she maintained the full-time pace of counsel to a Washington law firm. She worked hard, but it was just Carolyn and voice mail and a secretary.

Carolyn was a fine lawyer. As such she was preoccupied with a litigation strategy. We were preparing for a trial. My confirmation hearings would be my trial. Carolyn told me to get a list of all the moderate jurists I knew who could counter the *Wall Street Journal* attacks by testifying to my credentials as a "within the mainstream" litigator. But she did not have a public relations strategy, in part because the White House was not letting me speak to the press, and in part because public relations was to be coordinated in conjunction with confirmation hearings. It was hard to generate a lot of outside support when I couldn't talk. We were in campaign mode, but until Eddie arrived, I had no full-time campaign manager.

Eddie knew Carolyn because they had served together as staff for senators on the Judiciary Committee. Carolyn had worked for Senator Edward Kennedy. Eddie called Carolyn the same evening Ricki called him. He told her, "I've read the *Michigan* article and it doesn't seem that bad." Carolyn said, "None of it is bad, Eddie. None of it's bad." Eddie later told me, "I said this is not bad, but I knew this was not going to win their hearts."

Eddie arrived Tuesday evening, was officially sworn in as a Department of Justice employee Wednesday morning. He met Carolyn at the Hay Adams Hotel for breakfast to talk strategy. They discussed the need for courtesy calls and for good press. Eddie knew from his experience on the Hill that many senators depend on personal relationships to make political judgments. Good press was important, but personal contact was critical. Eddie and Carolyn also discussed the pending "document request" submitted by Senator Hatch seeking copies of all my articles, speeches, and testimony, including unpublished drafts. Here, too, the department had not begun to help out.

Carolyn and Eddie agreed generally to divide up tasks, with Eddie taking the Justice Department and the Hill, and Carolyn working with outside groups. As they ate, they spotted Melanne Verveer (Hillary's deputy chief of staff), who came over to thank Eddie for coming down.

On May 26, two days after Eddie arrived, there were quotes in the morning newspapers from Senators Biden and Patrick Leahy and from an anonymous White House official, all negative. The worst was the White House quote that the nomination was in trouble and that there was little support in the White House. Eddie called Ricki to ask someone to say something positive and to disavow the quote; all we got was an equivocal statement from George Stephanopoulos at the afternoon briefing.

Things had definitely taken a turn for the worse just between the time Eddie got the first call and the time he showed up. In that forty-eight-hour period between May 23 and May 25, there was an internal debate raging within the White House in which some people were saying, "Let's get out of this," and others were saying, "No, you gotta stick up for her." As Eddie saw it, "With the president not having decided which camp to go with, which often happens, people within the White House began to get their side of the story out. And that's what was happening. So by that time, you've got warfare within the White House going on."

Eddie and I worked together on my "pitch" for a week. We continued on the train for the hastily scheduled meeting with the *New York Times* editorial board. Eddie kept hammering home the need to abandon my lawyering style. "You are not an advocate, Lani," he said. "You are not the law professor. You are the nominee. You have to sell yourself as a personality quickly. Get to the point. Don't meander on the nuances of your ideas. Remember, point, counterpoint." Eddie kept cutting my answers, shortening my presentation. "The press is in a feeding frenzy," Eddie reminded me. "The Republicans smell blood. The Democratic senators are gun shy. And no one has been on the other side; the story is not getting out on the other side."

This meeting with the *Times* editorial board was our first real opportunity to get the story out. Eddie had prepared a list of questions and answers. We went over his list methodically. We finished with time to spare. I now felt very prepared. Eddie was still a nervous wreck. His pent-up energy consumed all the cramped space between our seats. He tapped his fingers; he kept time with his legs. He could hardly sit still. If he were upright, he would have been pacing, but he was stuck in a train seat. He worried that we were going to be late. He worried that so much rested on making a good impression. He worried that we had waited too long to have this meeting in the first place.

Eddie never told me the real reason he was so worried. The night before, Tuesday, June 1, he and Carolyn Osolinik had a meeting at the White House. Elaine Jones, director-counsel of the NAACP Legal Defense Fund, had been invited, but she did not show up. Eddie and Carolyn were there alone representing "our side." They were told directly that the White House was getting cold feet. It was not clear how high up the White House decision-making chain the chills had reached, but this was not low-level staff grumbling. Things had escalated. Neither Eddie nor Carolyn let me know how bad things were. Instead I was left to glean whatever information I could from Dan Rather's cryptic news bulletin on CBS, suggesting the White House was backing off the nomination. I didn't hear Rather's report myself. It was announced in person by my friend Aretha Marshall, then working for the local CBS affiliate, as she walked into my kitchen in Philadelphia at eight o'clock that Tuesday night.

Eddie never laid out the facts behind Rather's story; I did not know the White House was being completely disingenuous when it denied the story later that evening. I was in the dark about the machinations within the administration. I was riding to New York to save my nomination.

Eddie and I arrived at the *Times* building on West Forty-third Street. Returning to *The New York Times* was emotionally taxing for me. The meeting took place in a conference room dominated by a picture of Adolph Ochs. Ochs had been the publisher of the *Times* until 1935, the person with whom my father must have met at Harvard when Ochs invited all the Harvard students who had been high school newspaper editors to come to New York if they ever wanted a newspaper job. My father had taken him up on the offer. However, my father was not allowed even to meet with Mr. Ochs in his office because blacks were not allowed above a certain floor at the *Times*. My father had nonetheless insisted and Ochs, to his credit, remembered his pledge. He met my father in the hall outside his office and gave him a job as an elevator operator.

During the meeting, most of the editors assembled around the table were very quiet. They let me speak for about fifteen minutes, uninterrupted. I talked about my father and his experiences at Harvard. I nearly broke down in tears when I started talking about my father's time as a freshman, when no one would speak to him except Ralph Bunche. I never even got to talk about my father's experience at the *Times* because when I started talking about Harvard, I got out the words, "No one would speak to him," and I lost it. I could feel the tears welling up inside. I had to stop and catch my breath and not say anything. It was a very long minute. After that, I changed the subject. I just couldn't finish talking about my father; it was too close to home. I felt as if I were being forced to replicate his experience, not on a college campus but in a national spotlight. Like the law professor I am, I resorted to a scholarly presentation about technical legal points. I was too vulnerable to do otherwise—too personally invested to make a personal pitch.

I left New York, traveling by shuttle back to D.C. for a meeting with the *Washington Post* editorial board. At LaGuardia airport en route to D.C., and again in the terminal in D.C., I was approached by representatives of the ABC television program *Nightline*. One of them handed me a letter, a formal letter inviting me on the show that night. The letter made a point of noting that when Bill Clinton was at the nadir of his campaign, in February 1992, he went on Ted Koppel's *Nightline* to vindicate himself on the draft-dodging issue. The *Nightline* producers were now offering me a similar opportunity.

Eddie called the White House and told Ricki Seidman about the invitation to do the show. Eddie could not get a yes or no out of Ricki and could not even get an answer as to when or whether the White House would come up with a response to the *Nightline* invitation. So finally he said, "Are you telling me that the White House has no position on this?" Ricki said, "That's right. The White House has no position on this." Apparently she couldn't get back to him in time to take a position on whether I went on *Nightline* because she couldn't get anybody to focus on it. Eddie told Webb Hubbell that the White House didn't have a position and Webb said he didn't object as long as the White House didn't object. Eddie then called *Nightline* to make the arrangements, and he and I headed off to meet the *Post* editorial board.

Meg Greenfield, a *Washington Post* editor, personally met me at the front door to try to avoid the stakeouts that were all around the office building. She was very sweet. The meeting with the *Post* was quite different from the one at the *Times*. The *Post* editors had read my work. The meeting was much less atmospheric and much more substantive. The table was smaller; there were fewer people sitting and studying me, although Kay Graham and her son Donald, the publisher of the *Post*, stopped by for much of the meeting. Colby King, a black editor whom I had never before met, had familiarized me with the people who would be at the meeting, and that helped. No one had bothered to do that at the *Times*. A friend, Diane Camper, who is on the *Times* board, did not say one word at the much stiffer *New York Times* meeting.

Eddie kept reminding me: Washington politics is hardball. People learn to become very, very tough and go to the press, and you need to work with the press and get your story out and make agreements on the terms of reporting. He reminded me of that lesson after I met with the editorial board, when he and I sat briefly with reporters Ruth Marcus and Mike Isikoff of *The Washington Post*. Mike Isikoff was trying to ask about where I stood with the White House. Eddie yelled across the room, "Don't answer that." Eddie told me when we left, "I know Mike and Ruth and consider them both sort of my friends. I mean, Ruth Marcus is getting married to Kohl's chief counsel; they are both nice people, but I'll tell you, when they do their jobs, they go for the jugular. They don't have your interest at heart, of course, one bit. They want a nice story. It's tough. But that's the game, so you must really play that game."

After the *Post* meeting, I returned to the Justice Department to prepare for my *Nightline* appearance. I was told the White House had weighed in and *Nightline* was off. I called Elaine Jones and told her that if I couldn't go on *Nightline*, maybe she could instead, and she could use the time to speak positively about the nomination. She agreed, but I later learned she sought to recruit two other LDF attorneys, Penda Hair and Dayna Cunningham, to speak in her stead. All I knew at the time was that Elaine called back to suggest that Jesse Jackson go on to replace me. Her view was that threatening to use Jesse would scare the White House into letting me do it. She believes that this is what ultimately happened.

It was now about 7:00 P.M. There was a knock on my office door on the fifth floor of the Justice Department. Solicitor General Drew Days asked if he could come in. He said, "Lani, I am here as your friend. I am not here as the Solicitor General. The Solicitor General does not do these kinds of things." He sat down at one end of the couch in my temporary office. I sat at the other end. Then he said, "Lani, I have bad news. They just don't have the votes for your confirmation." I said, "Drew, what are you telling me? How could they have the votes? I haven't met with very many senators. They haven't done anything except send one letter up. All that the senators know is what they have read in the newspaper. It doesn't matter whether they have the votes or not." I paused to see if he heard me. "It isn't a relevant time to be taking stock of the votes."

He responded, "If you proceed, do you think it might hurt the president's economic program?"

"I don't think so," I said.

Drew said, "If they have to focus on your nomination and it is very divisive, it won't give them the opportunity to focus on the president's economic program."

I countered, "Then have my hearing tomorrow. Or set my hearing for Monday, and then they don't have to worry about distractions because my hearing will go forward. If they don't have the votes after I testify, then we can have this conversation. At this point I think this conversation is premature."

Drew persisted, "Even if this is going to jeopardize the president's other programs?"

I sat upright. I looked at him directly. I met his gaze: "Drew, I am not withdrawing. So if you came to talk about whether I am going to withdraw, the answer is no."

Drew got up from the couch. He stood up straight. He walked to the door, opened it, and said, "I'll get back to you." He signaled no pleasantries. He had come as an announced friend but was serving as a messenger, "their" messenger. I later learned from LDF lawyers that other "friends" had also been dispatched to urge my withdrawal out of personal concern, that suggestions were made to explore a deal to ensure my personal comfort.

I had discussed the "withdrawal strategy" with Elaine Jones and separately with Carolyn and Eddie. They each said it was my decision but they all believed if I went to a hearing, I would be confirmed. As long as the administration remained firm, we would prevail ultimately. They had concluded that, as with many civil rights initiatives, most senators were cowardly. They didn't want to vote, but if they had to, they would vote *for* me, not *against* me. Even if the vote was negative, the hearing itself would provide an invaluable opportunity to further a civil rights agenda. I could use the press attention to educate the American people about real instances of discrimination and the need for continued vigilance.

After Drew left, I sat in stunned silence for a few minutes. I had my head in my hands when Carolyn Osolinik walked into the office. She came to tell me that White House congressional liaison Howard

Paster was in the Attorney General's office meeting with Webb Hubbell. Half an hour later, I received a telephone call, summoning me to the Attorney General's conference room on the fifth floor.

I walked with Carolyn and Eddie into the Attorney General's office. From the reception area, we went together into the conference room. The wood-paneled room loomed almost as large as a football field. It was dominated by a huge dark wooden conference table surrounded by black leather chairs lined up like soldiers. The room was grand, but except for the American flag, the Department of Justice seal on the wall, and the brocaded red carpet, devoid of ornamentation. Howard Paster and I were on one side of the table. Next to Paster was the Justice Department public information officer, former NBC reporter Carl Stern. At the head of the table was Webb Hubbell, who said nothing the entire meeting. To Webb's right were Ricki Seidman; Nancy McFadden, a Justice Department lawyer on Webb Hubbell's staff with close White House ties, who had worked on the campaign, and before that with the law firm of my Republican mentor, Bill Coleman, secretary of transportation in the Ford administration; and then Eddie Correia, Drew Days, Carolyn Osolinik, and all the way at the other end of the table the Attorney General, Janet Reno, who didn't speak during the meeting until the very end.

Howard Paster and I had met twice before. Once I met him one-on-one and once I had joined him in his office with the Attorney General, Carolyn Osolinik, Ricki Seidman, Sam Dubbin (the AG's special assistant from Florida), and Nancy McFadden. During the large meeting, Paster had said, "We're going to win this one," and Nancy McFadden, who knew Paster from the 1992 campaign, said that was a good sign because Paster doesn't say that unless he means it. Later I learned that what he basically meant was, I'll try to do what I can do but I am not going to try very hard and at the first sign that it is going to be tough I will back down. Paster was reluctant, he later told me, because he was put off by my observation that a number of senators seemed afraid to have another hearing in which they had to grill a black woman publicly. He didn't hold a grudge, he said. He was pleased I had "learned my lesson" that I couldn't be a black female advocate. I had to be a raceless, genderless supplicant. So I asked, "Who then is my advocate?"

Howard did not answer my question. He smiled at me. He offered his most engaging grin. He seemed satisfied that he had said what it was I was supposed to hear. I, however, was not satisfied. I told Paster that someone needed to represent me. At the very least, I said, the White House could be more affirmative in supporting me. He agreed, but he didn't know if he could deliver. He was very busy with the budget reconciliation—and getting Drew Days, Webb Hubbell, and Phil Heymann confirmed. I saw George Stephanopoulos right after I met with Paster the second time. This was several hours before Stephano-poulis was "demoted" from his job as press secretary. I told Stephano-poulis it would be nice if he could say something more affirmative, and he said, "Well, give me the facts." I told him about my few courtesy calls (which I thought went well) and he seemed interested but distracted. He was watching a televised report on Clinton's speech in Philadelphia at the time.

This meeting in the Attorney General's conference room on June 2 was the third time Howard Paster and I were face-to-face. It was about 8:00 P.M. when Paster began the meeting. Paster had a tenseness about him that was surprising, given his almost boyish demeanor. He was not a big man. He did not command a room. He was energetic and bouncy behind this thick glasses. It was not obvious, from his demeanor at least, how he had gotten as far as he had.

Paster launched right into his prepared speech about how they didn't have the votes. As far as I was concerned, he made a very weak case. He didn't say, "Lani, I have done X and I have done Y and I have done Z and we still don't have the votes." Instead, all I saw him doing was reporting self-evident and unsurprising information. What other outcome could you expect when the administration had yet to act affirmatively?

I did not immediately respond to Paster's declaration. His presentation seemed silly and beside the point: he was merely stating the obvious. In my eyes, Howard Paster had no credibility. Despite that fact, I knew I could not be dismissive. He was taking everything he said very seriously, and he obviously took everything I said just as seriously. He had chastised me the week before, disapproving of my reference to the way the senators on the Judiciary Committee handled Anita Hill.

I chose, therefore, to respond by repeating what I had said to Drew earlier that evening, "I am not prepared to withdraw."

Paster acknowledged my statement. "I am not asking you to with-draw," he said. "The president is not asking you to withdraw. We just want you to know that we don't have the votes, and that if we go forward, we have to take into account that the personal cost and the human cost is going to be terrible for you. It is going to be very divisive. The hearing is really going to be a wrenching experience."

I responded, "I understand you do not have the votes right now. I understand your position. If I get a say in this decision, however, my position is that I am not withdrawing."

We went back and forth this way several times, at which point Paster remarked, "I guess one thing you are very unambiguous about is that you are not going to withdraw." He continued, "Why don't we sleep on it and talk about it again in the morning?"

Eddie and Carolyn interjected to reinforce what I was saying: they argued that the absence of votes now didn't really mean anything. If you are saying it is up to Lani, she is saying she wants to go forward. Carolyn also reminded Howard that Democrats controlled the Senate. She told him that on civil rights issues the senators never want to vote, they are always looking for a way out, but whenever it comes down to voting they vote with us as long as we present the issues passionately and clearly. "Lani is her own best witness," she argued, "and if she testifies, we are convinced she will be confirmed."

Eddie chimed in: "Within the Senate behind closed doors you always get the moderate or the conservative Democrats saying, 'Get us out of this, get us out of this.' It's a strategic question, and on that I think we have a good strategy. Her articles are dense, no doubt about it; it is hard to understand some of her arguments and easy therefore to ignore her logic. But on the other hand, it is just as easy to come up with a good explanation of her position. And that's exactly what a hearing is all about. I have a clear vision of this hearing. I have heard nothing that changes it. There will be that initial volley of nasty opening statements and the initial round of tough questioning, followed by Lani's gracious, calm answers, then there will be two or three follow-up questions, but that will be the end of it, because there are answers for everything."

Eddie stopped to make sure Howard was still listening. Eddie had two more points to make, which he added quickly. "Now that it has come to the public's attention, this is also an issue of 'who's going to stand by her?' She's the president's friend. He has to stand by her." That was the first point. It led nicely to his second argument. "We need to make race a moral issue again. Race has become something lawyers argue about, and even though these legal cases all have a moral content, that gets lost in the lawyers' complexity. Lani is in a position, with her hearings, to reclaim the moral high ground. She has been beaten up on in the press; people will be listening when she testifies. She can really grab not only their attention but their hearts."

At one point Carolyn said, "Okay, now that she has heard that you don't have the votes, can she go on *Nightline*?"

Carl Stern suddenly piped up, "How can she go on *Nightline* if she has heard that you don't have the votes?"

Carolyn answered, "Look. I have been very careful and I have listened to what Howard said. Let me make sure I understand. You are not telling her to withdraw."

Howard said, "No."

"So," Carolyn asked, "what difference does it make if she goes on *Nightline*? She wants to make her case to the American people. You have denied her that ability and as a result you are now telling her you don't have the votes. Why can't she go on *Nightline*?"

Carolyn had directed her question to Howard Paster, but Carl Stern responded, "Well, you know at some point, I know everyone is very honorable, but at some point it will come out that we had this meeting and that she was present, and if she goes on *Nightline*, then it will be revealed that she was not being truthful."

Carolyn pressed the point. "Not being truthful about what? Howard just reiterated that he is not asking her to withdraw, the president is not asking her to withdraw, they are saying the decision has not yet been made but that they don't have the votes."

Until now, the Attorney General had not said a word. She looked sympathetically at me from time to time but she said nothing. She apparently saw her role as member of the audience. This was Howard Paster's show, not hers. But now she had something to say. She turned toward Carl Stern, who was directly opposite her, and said, "Carl, be quiet. You don't have to say anything further. This is between her and the White House. We don't have to be involved in this decision."

Carl quickly fell silent. Howard Paster got up. He said, "Well, I'll get back to you." He left the room to make some phone calls. Ricki followed him. Webb and Nancy also left.

The rest of us just sat around the table. No one was talking. I, too, was still. I felt that my fate was being decided by these other people in this other room and the Attorney General and I were just sort of looking at each other. Carolyn and Eddie and Drew were just sort of looking at each other. At least fifteen minutes passed, maybe twenty. Even though I was on the hot seat, I didn't notice how much time elapsed. I was numb. I was in shock. I felt imprisoned in that conference room. I was frightened by the isolation I felt. Here I was, surrounded by my "supporters," and except for Carolyn and Eddie, the troops were falling one by one.

This meeting was the most difficult of the three big meetings I had had that day. The cumulative effect of selling myself was wearying, especially since I was now selling myself to a group who already knew me. Unlike the *New York Times* or the *Washington Post* editorial boards, this was not a meeting among strangers in which I had ten minutes to make my "pitch." I was a known quantity. I had worked with many of the participants before, some of them over a period of several years. Yet all of these people, including an old and dear friend, Drew Days, were just sitting there not saying anything.

It was finally dawning on me. I knew Bill Clinton was smooth— "living-room charisma" was what I called it. But I believed in him, in his potential to be a great president, a historic figure, a twentieth-century healer. I began to see him differently, as a watcher, not a doer. It was now my reputation, my sense of self, my cause that was being chewed over, by a president who remained passive. His aides, thinking they were protecting him, merely encouraged his caution.

I would have to defend myself.

Howard Paster returned. He looked exhausted. He spoke quickly. "Okay. She can go on *Nightline*."

We breathed aloud in unison, taking in our moment of triumph. Carolyn quickly offered condolences to Howard, "She will be a team player. She is not going to criticize the White House." I said, "That is fine. I am not on there to criticize the White House. I am on there to defend myself and the cause of civil rights." It was about ten minutes to ten; the car from *Nightline* would pick me up from the Justice Department at ten minutes to eleven. I still hadn't eaten anything all day.

As we left the Attorney General's office, Drew hurried to my side. He was my friend again. Tears just started rolling down my face. I was thinking, What the hell am I doing? I am going to go on *Nightline*. The White House is backing down. These people are a bunch of cowards. I am sitting around a room and the only people who are defending me are Carolyn and Eddie, who are clearly partisan. Drew put his arm around me, which was comforting but somewhat awkward, because he is so much shorter than I am. "Well, what do you want me to do?" he asked.

I said nothing at first. I wasn't sure I still trusted him. I no longer knew whom to trust. As we walked down the hall in silence, I thought about the fights Drew and I had waged, together, when he was Assistant Attorney General for Civil Rights and I was his special assistant. Back then, we had walked these same halls, but in the opposite direction. We would be heading from the office of the Assistant Attorney General *to* the office of the Attorney General. We would be walking, talking, preparing to make our best case. Back then, it was clear we were on the same side. We had been a team. It had been my job to stay in the background putting out fires, to move into the foreground only when necessary to help prepare him for internal and external battles.

Those memories were both a stark contrast and a source of relief. They reminded me of a basic friendship we shared over time. They also suggested something about Drew that I had almost forgotten in the chaos of the last meeting. Drew was an organized, methodical thinker. I could certainly use his help now. I answered quietly, "I don't know. Maybe you could help me, moot me for my *Nightline* appearance."

He went to his office. I went to call home.

I called Nolan. I told him I was going on *Nightline* and that he should call my mother to tell her. I started crying on the telephone. I told Nolan, "All this emotion is getting to me. I feel like I am not being supported by the White House in the way they should. The only people in my corner are Carolyn and Eddie."

Nolan listened. He told me he loved me. He said he was proud of me. He said, "Whatever you do, don't withdraw. That would be dishonorable." And then he reminded me of my pledge. I was not, under any circumstances, to cry in public.

Nolan later explained why he had taken such an absolute position. He worried about how I would live with myself after all this was over. He explained why he thought I couldn't withdraw. "If you had withdrawn," he told me, "you would hate yourself for the rest of your life. And it is better that you hate him than you hate yourself."

Nolan's explanation resonated. Taking a strong position allowed me to channel my fear, my anger into something substantive. Unlike the courtesy calls on senators where I was supposed to play the role of supplicant, I was now back in familiar territory. This was a posture with which I was comfortable—I became an advocate, preparing for *Nightline* as I had prepared for many an appellate argument or trial. Lawyering was something over which I had control.

I hung up the phone and walked directly to the ladies room. The first thing I did was wash my face. I watched the water flow freely from the spigot for a few seconds before I let its coolness run down my puffy cheeks. The water diluted the saltiness of my tears. It also smeared my makeup, but I didn't care. At that point I was not worried about what I looked like in the bathroom mirror. I returned to the small conference room next door. It was sparsely furnished, with plain white walls. Compared to the grand, majestic aura of the Attorney General's conference room, this room felt almost comfortable, its understated furnishings in keeping with my sense of diminishing stature. As I walked in, I noticed all the pictures on the wall of the former Attorneys General for Civil Rights. Except for one—a picture of Drew looking fifteen years younger—the photographs were of white men, many of whom had meager qualifications for the job prior to being nominated. Yet, despite their thin "qualifications," none of them ran into confirmation trouble. Of course not, I thought.

Eddie and Carolyn were already in the room, waiting. We started eating the pizza that a thoughtful secretary had ordered earlier that evening. Then Nancy McFadden showed up. About fifteen minutes later, Drew showed up. The four of them prepped me. They helped me answer the inevitable question, "Is the White House fully behind your nomination?" I refused to lie and say yes, but on the other hand, I hadn't been told that the president was withdrawing my nomination. I had in fact been told the decision had not yet been made. I was told when they did decide, it would be made in consideration of my wishes and the "human" element. I had made it clear I wanted to go forward.

So we worked out three responses. If Koppel asks me once, I should say this. If he asks twice, I say that. And then the third time I just say, yes, the White House is still supporting my nomination as far as I know.

Nancy McFadden taught me my first media lesson about the "pivot." She coached me on the ways then Governor Bill Clinton had used *Nightline*'s public platform in February 1992 to change the subject away from draft-dodging to the issues he wanted to discuss. I now had to try to do the same thing—to reframe the conversation about my nomination. I remember watching that show and watching Clinton and thinking that he had acquitted himself well, given all the pressure he must have been under. Nancy told me that one of the things Clinton was able to do was "pivot." She stood up to emphasize the point. "When asked a question that has to do with process, which is what the media is always trying to deal with, you need at some point to say, 'Look, I don't think the American people really want to hear about the process. They want to hear about what I intend to do in this job or what my actual ideas are,' and just move forward."

Drew made a few helpful suggestions about substance. If they asked me about affirmative action or other issues, I should say that all of these decisions would be made in collaboration with the Attorney General, that it would be inappropriate to describe my views in great detail and prejudge the department's position.

Eddie had prepared a list of points that he thought I needed to be sure to make. I wrote them down on a small piece of paper so I could slip it into my pocket. We had about five minutes before the *Nightline* car arrived. I ate another piece of cold pizza and drank some warm Coke. Then Eddie, Carolyn, and I piled into the car. When we got to the ABC studios, a number of reporters and photographers were milling outside. Nina Totenberg was there. She told me she got out of bed to meet me. Could she have an interview afterwards? I smiled but kept walking. I didn't want to repeat a disastrous hug sequence at that April 29 press conference which was then used by several commentators to question her "objectivity."

I was directed toward the makeup room, but Cokie Roberts brushed past me. She was doing the intro to the setup piece and had to be made up first. She was whisked away by the makeup artist, leaving me to ponder my fate. But I was not alone. Ted Koppel was sitting there making himself up in the same room as I was. His humility was reassuring.

I eventually returned to the green room, where Eddie and Carolyn were waiting. There were trays of fruit, chocolate, and pastries. Maybe if I had eaten a regular dinner this might seem like dessert. But it was eleven-fifteen, and the food seemed too much on top of the pizza I had just wolfed down.

Then Ted Koppel came into the room. He remained standing as we sat. He said, "Lani, I just want you to know that I have *The Washington Post* and they are faxing tomorrow's *New York Times,* and both of them have on the front page a story that the White House is withdrawing your name. I want you to know that I am going to ask you about this on the show, and if you don't want to go on the show in light of this, I understand."

I said, "Let me talk to Carolyn and Eddie."

He said, "That's fine." He left us alone. This was about seven minutes until air time and Carolyn and Eddie both said, "What do you want to do?"

I thought for no more than ten seconds. I said, "Well, these days I don't believe anything I read in the papers, so I'm prepared to go forward."

I scanned the first paragraph of the *Post* and then said, "I want to go forward. They haven't said anything that I haven't already heard from Howard Paster about not having the votes. It just seems that White House staff people are leaking stories because they are unhappy with my nomination. The story doesn't say the president has decided to withdraw the nomination. So that is not information that I think should affect my decision." They agreed. I then asked, "Should I change any of my answers?" They said no.

When Koppel returned, I said I would proceed. I told him that I had never been on national television before and that I didn't know what to do. The cameramen instructed me to sit up straight and look into the lens of a particular camera. I focused hard on that camera. I thanked Koppel for letting me sit next to him. I thought that was very respectful and I thought he had behaved in a very dignified way, something I truly appreciated because I hadn't been treated with much dignity during the whole nomination process.

Koppel introduced me as a "distinguished law professor," nominated to one of the most important subcabinet posts at the Justice Department. Professor Guinier, Koppel said, is a "very opinionated woman and a prolific one," whose opponents were dissecting her law review articles "with public relish," "salivating" over the chance for payback for Robert Bork. There is "division within the Clinton administration itself," he told his audience, "on whether to let Professor Guinier's nomination go before the Senate Judiciary Committee or whether to get her to withdraw." Then Ted Koppel displayed the next morning's *New York Times* headline, AIDES SAY CLINTON WILL DROP NOMINEE FOR POST ON RIGHTS, and turned to ask me whether I was reeling from shock at this information.

I smiled and responded carefully, "I am here tonight to explain, I hope, who it is that the president nominated and who it is that Attorney

General Janet Reno would like to be Assistant Attorney General for Civil Rights."

"You are clearly talking like someone," Koppel acknowledged, "who believes however slim the hope and chance may be that you want to go forward with everything you've got in you."

"That's who I am," I quickly responded, with another big smile. I actually felt relieved. I was finally getting to speak in my own voice.

The camera turned to Cokie Roberts's setup piece, which reviewed chapter and verse the charges against me. It did not include my refutation of those charges because, of course, the administration had not permitted me before that evening to make any public statements. It stated the case against me and then turned to what it saw as the real issue: What would President Clinton do about this controversial nominee? The piece tried to document the president's shifting defenses by including a clip from his statement three weeks earlier at the May 11 Leadership Conference on Civil Rights Annual Dinner. I remembered that evening well. President Clinton's presence, along with that of the Vice President and the Attorney General, seemed to mark the event as the mainstreaming of the movement to bring full civil rights to all Americans. The president and I had been backstage before his remarks and my introduction to the Leadership Conference community as the administration's nominee. He commented on the necklace I was wearing; but despite this rather personal observation, he seemed remote. He lacked, somehow, the regal bearing he had had holding court two weeks earlier in the interior courtyard of the Justice Department. He seemed distracted.

To voice his support of me, the president reminded the audience that I had sued him when he was governor of the state of Arkansas and hadn't lost. He said that his graciousness in nominating someone who had been an adversary meant that the Senate "should put up with a little controversy, too, and go on and confirm her." I must say that at the time I did not experience his remarks as the unqualified endorsement I needed to shield me from the attacks that had already begun.

Now, three weeks later, as the statement was replayed on *Nightline*, it rang even more hollow. The *Nightline* piece also depicted Janet Reno, then "the most popular person" in Clinton's administration, saying, "I'm going to do everything I can to support her nomination and to get her confirmed." But again, Reno's strong support was included mainly as further evidence that Clinton was in an awkward position. There followed a head shot of President Clinton from earlier that day obviously responding to a question in midsentence "that a lot of what has been said is not accurate but on the other hand I have to take into account where the Senate is and I will be doing that and talking to them and until I do that I should have nothing else to say."

At this point I was not just someone carrying "a little controversy." I was a major problem for the administration. The *Nightline* setup piece suggested that this was because I actually believed in quotas and other out-of-the-mainstream ideas. The piece highlighted a sentence from a footnote in an article I had written, suggesting that the Senate Judiciary Committee should use its advice and consent power to ensure more people from underrepresented groups get judicial appointments. Koppel then picked up on the sentence and asked me, "Doesn't that amount to a quota?"

"I do not believe in quotas," I said. "I have never advocated quotas." That single sentence from one of my articles, I assured Koppel, referred to the effort to be more inclusive and racially diverse, the same thing President Clinton was doing in making his cabinet look like America. It was not a quota but an effort to respond "to the failure of the prior administrations to do any outreach not only to people of color but to women."

Well, Koppel continued, "when you talk about creating racial diversity, do you believe that should take priority over qualifications of individual candidates?"

"No," I said promptly. "And indeed if they had included either the sentence before or the sentence after that one" (referring to the way the single highlighted sentence had been taken completely out of context by the *Nightline* producers), "it said just that." I continued, "I am not talking about appointing anyone who is not qualified to any position, including myself." I then repeated my own qualifications as a litigator, as apprentice to the position's incumbent in the Carter administration, as a judge when I was a referee in Juvenile Court. I have been a teacher, a law professor for five years, I said. I have shown myself able to enforce the law.

Despite the pressure of being on national television, I found myself smiling a lot. It was a heady feeling finally to be able to defend myself. For the first time, someone was publicly speaking back to the unnamed White House aides leaking stories anonymously to undermine a nomination they didn't like. For the first time, I was given a forum in which to talk about my real ideas, implicitly challenging the cautious politicians whose inhibitions about tackling substantive issues are reinforced by just the kind of win/lose media frame the *Nightline* producers had used in the setup piece.

I'm not sure I said all the things I was supposed to say during that *Nightline* interview, but I certainly didn't say anything I wasn't supposed to say. The main point I remember emphasizing was that this television interview was *not* my confirmation hearings. I argued that I should have a chance to testify before the United States Senate. A half hour television show was not a Senate hearing.

After the show I said to Ted Koppel, "The only show I regularly watch on television is *Nightline*. This is a big deal for me to actually be on *Nightline*. No matter what happens, I just want you to know that I will be able to tell my grandchildren that I was on *Nightline*." And he said, "I hope you have something more to tell them than that." Then Jesse Jackson called and said a prayer over the telephone as I sat on a couch in the green room and actually, that was really nice.

After I went on *Nightline*, I discovered I had many new friends. Most everyone who saw me said I did a great job. Everyone except the White House. "The White House," whoever that entity is who personifies the edifice and the position. "They" were furious at the way I had conducted myself. "They" felt I should have used that forum to talk about my views, but that I shouldn't have asked for a hearing. I kept talking about the need for a hearing in order to express my views fully and that was inappropriate. That made them angry. They had concluded that I was not a team player. As a result, the next morning, I was forbidden to do more interviews. An AP reporter tried to hustle a story from me. I told her I could not speak with her, that the White House had changed the rules.

Carl Stern informed me that since I had gone on *Nightline*, obviously I was now on the record, so he had set up a meeting with Joe Davidson of the *Wall Street Journal* on the record. I had to cancel the *Journal* meeting. The White House overruled Stern. As far as I could tell, that was the most proactive Carl Stern had been since my nomination was announced.

About noon that next morning, June 3, Ricki Seidman came to the Justice Department to meet with me alone. She told me she came as "a friend." No one from "the White House" had sent her or knew she was there. She had played it every which way in her head. She now felt there was no way I could be confirmed.

I said, "Well, Ricki, I can't really play out the political game with you. That is not my area of expertise. But people who I have confidence in have told me that if I testify, they think I will be confirmed. And I think even if I am not confirmed that I should at least be given an opportunity to testify and then if you want to revisit this after my hearing and you tell me that despite every best effort I can't be confirmed, that is a different story. But I am not going to withdraw."

"Won't you even consider it?" she asked.

"No," I said. "I will not withdraw."

"You know something, Lani," she said. "I think maybe some of these people are right that you are not a team player and you weren't the right person for this job."

That made me furious. Loudly and with great passion I said, "You are being told this by people who never wanted me to have this job in the first place. These are people who never lifted a finger to help me get a hearing, much less a job. These are people who have virtually sabotaged my chance of ever getting a hearing and these are people whose judgment I don't respect. So to ask me to rely on the judgment and commentary of people who have been actively working to oppose the nomination I think is asking a little too much. At this point I feel I have to rely on my own inner confidence because I don't trust any of you to be acting in my best interest or in the interest of the administration or frankly in the interest of effective civil rights enforcement."

She retreated. "Lani, you are looking at this personally," she said.

"I *am* looking at it personally—I admit that," I said. "But I am also looking at it in terms of the president, because he has a reputation as a waffler. If he can't stand up for a friend, who will he stand up for? Why should people think he is going to stand up for them to fight for issues that they believe in?"

It was not just personal. I also wanted a hearing to flush out the administration's civil rights position. I was personally appalled by their lack of conviction in me as a human being, as a friend, as a partner. But I was incensed too by their apparent lack of commitment to the issue of civil rights. This was not merely a nomination; this was about a policy of social justice. Whatever our disagreements over particular forms of implementation or program, the larger issue remained unresolved. What were their civil rights principles? How did the administration intend to broaden the constituency for active enforcement of civil rights? Could they, would they actively assume moral leadership?

Ricki just gave me the same spiel about the economy and the president's initiative on health care I had heard from Drew the night before. I said, "If the issue is the economy and health care and you don't want to spend any more capital than what you have already spent, which is nothing, then have the hearing tomorrow. Or schedule the hearing Monday so you don't have to spend any more capital. Or just schedule the hearing for the fall and you can put it off. Then you can work on the budget or the economy." I paused, gulping in enough air to continue. "If the issue is the economy and the president's position on it, if he can't stick up for me in this little fight, he is going to be compromising and giving up the whole store on every other issue. In some ways, the position he takes on my nomination is going to set the agenda for the position he takes on more substantive issues. So I think that the position I am taking is not only a personally important position, but a *principled* position."

Ricki backed down. She knew that arguments about political capital were pretty pathetic when the White House hadn't lifted a finger in support of me, except for the one letter Howard Paster hand-delivered to Senate majority leader George Mitchell. That letter, in which Paster declared that I was "the victim of a big lie," was delivered to all of the senators the last week in May, right before the long Memorial Day weekend, and less than a week before this very conversation with Ricki at the Justice Department. Ricki knew that that letter was the only substantive effort taken by the White House to make the case for my nomination during this entire period. Yet I noticed subsequently in *Time* magazine that an unidentified White House staffer described my reaction as typical of civil rights advocates. My decision to become independent because the White House hadn't stood up for me was described thus: "Lani was practicing the m.o. [modus operandi] of the civil rights movement which is to stand their ground, declare defeat, and then go out and publicly seek sympathy."

I wanted and needed a hearing. I felt entitled to a hearing. I believed that everything the Democratic Party and this president stood for was reflected in my position. By fighting for a hearing I was pushing the administration to do what it was not then prepared to do—fight for principles of fairness now, and in the long term show its commitment to put social justice issues front and center before the American people.

I had an epiphany, right there with Ricki watching. I realized that my hearing stood for much more than my fundamental right to speak and define myself and have others defend me. This was not simply about due process or fundamental fairness. This was a test of presidential leadership, a window on the presidential soul. The manner in which the president of the United States would treat a friend was an insight into his character as a human being, but it was even more than that. It would become an unexpected peek into his character as a leader.

Columnist Russell Baker once called him "President Peek-a-boo Bill." That was the danger; the underside of this challenge. So far, I could look under every rock, but could not find him. He had found a safe spot and did not move. His silence alarmed me. He was good at playing hide-and-seek. But is that how he wanted history to know him?

After Ricki left, other than Eddie, I did not speak to anyone who worked within the administration about my nomination that day. I fielded many phone calls from Black Caucus chairperson Kweisi Mfume, Senator Carol Moseley-Braun, Jesse Jackson, Mary Frances Berry, all telling me to stand firm, not withdraw. That was the closest I got to a discussion of principles. I did not discuss strategy, a withdrawal strategy, with anyone, including the president of the United States.

CHAPTER FOUR

The Oval Office:
Death by a Thousand Cuts

O<small>N JUNE</small> 3, thirty-five days after the sun-splashed April court-yard ceremony, I was in a black government car headed for a meeting with the president. I imagined how this meeting could have been. We could be meeting to discuss the administration's vision for civil rights and how my testimony during confirmation would underline that vision with commitment. Instead, I was going to meet the president under circumstances where the president's lack of clear vision had created a vacuum that was quickly filled by characterizations provided by refugees from the Reagan administration who were now masquerading as thoughtful social critics. They had adroitly used caricatures of my views to put the administration on the defensive and to employ me as a bludgeon to damage the president and secure their own ends.

As we cruised past security, I realized the backseat of the car was not much of a camouflage. I tried to keep my eyes focused straight ahead, conscious of photographers using their lenses to invade the car's modest interior. The flashbulbs were punctuated by the insistent chattering of reporters hawking questions. Like fortunetellers at the circus, the press squad leered into the passenger window. Every gesture, every blink was scrutinized. Physical proximity to their subject only encouraged even closer inspection. They hugged the car, coming so close it seemed they might jimmy the lock with their badges and invade its private space. I kept looking straight ahead to avoid eye contact. I can't say that I was seeing anything clearly; my mind was occupied with the encounter that was about to take place. I was readying myself for a meeting with an old friend about the future of my nomination to be Assistant Attorney General for Civil Rights. I was determined to appear in control, knowing full well I had not been so for some time. In fact, this wasn't my meeting. In so many ways, it was no longer even my life, much less my nomination.

I had been summoned by the White House chief of staff, Thomas F. ("Mack") McLarty. Could I please be at the Southwest gate of the White House at six-fifteen? After I arrived, I was seated in a comfortable-looking room and asked if I wanted anything. I asked for water. I took a few sips and then sat on a sofa watching the water glass perspire onto the polished wood table in front of me. Mack McLarty entered the room and sat down opposite me. We had never met before; we had only spoken once—on the telephone earlier that day. But that didn't matter. Mack McLarty was an important face, a familiar visage made larger than life because of his close association with power. Mack McLarty as Mr. Magoo—a businessman with an unimpeachable pedigree (he and the president were best friends in kindergarten), but hapless and ineffective as a political adviser or presidential chief of staff.

McLarty smiled. The muscles around his small eyes never moved. I detected a hint of sadness, like the doctor sitting with the patient before an operation for a terminal condition. Or maybe he was the chaplain ministering to the death row inmate. I couldn't be sure. His demeanor was calm, tense, and utterly assured that justice would be done. He spoke about his son, who went to Georgetown. His main worry, he told me, was that the family was infringing on his son's space by moving from Arkansas to Washington. Under the circumstances, his chat gave new meaning to the term "small talk."

Then, without much fanfare, I was ushered into the Oval Office alone. It was smaller than I had imagined. The president came to the door, shook my hand, and said, "Hi." I said, "Hello."

I followed him around the head of a seated figure and toward the two straightback chairs that faced each other at the end of the couch. The president sat in one and motioned for me to sit next to him. Opposite us, I could now see her face, sat Ricki Seidman, the one White House aide who had been working to get me a hearing on my nomination. She sat at the very other end of the couch. The president said, "So you know Ricki Seidman?" "Yes," I replied. Indeed, Ricki and I had just talked that morning when she came to urge me as "a friend" to withdraw. Now, however, she was silent. She was not here to participate in the conversation.

I remember looking all around the room, trying to take the measure of my surroundings. I didn't notice the oval shape of the room; I was too taken by the lightness of the atmosphere. My surveillance was caught short by the sense of blinding brightness. There was something vaguely comforting about the way the late afternoon sunlight dimpled the room's formal facade. I felt oddly serene. I was struck by a light-headed, airy feeling almost like Alice in Wonderland. I felt swallowed up by the immense proportions of the windows, the physical space itself. I also felt larger than life: something big was about to happen.

I finally could confront the president directly. I no longer looked to Ricki for advice or assistance. Sitting at the edge of the sofa, Ricki almost disappeared. She was outside the circle of conversation. Even though she was no more than ten feet away, Ricki seemed detached, not simply beyond our lines of vision.

I settled into the chair. I sat somewhat stiffly, conscious that my lower back should not touch the chair's tight-woven fabric. The president immediately began to speak. He talked without interruption for about fifteen minutes. As he spoke, I noticed his hands. They were white; his knuckles particularly so. His face was ruddy. He talked at length and with great earnestness. He treated his presentation like a test for which he had recently studied.

He told me that he had heard from both Senator Joseph Biden and Senator George Mitchell (the Democratic chair of the Judiciary Committee and the majority leader, respectively) that they didn't have the votes—that the nomination was certain to be defeated. He told me that he had sat down and read my *Michigan Law Review* article on a brief helicopter ride, and that he agreed with some of what I was saying but that he basically did not agree with the arguments that I was making there.

I waited to be called on, unsure of the proper protocol. I sat in silence, listening and watching him. He sat upright, legs planted in place, almost rooted to the carpet. His body was stationary, his bearing erect. His words came fluently enough but without much conviction. Despite his verbal facility, he did not appear sure of himself. He appeared to me like a man self-consciously seeking to control a tremor. His eyes betrayed him: they hinted at a turbulence just under the surface of his skin, a tension between political intuition and personal instinct. He wanted to appear fair, formal, and decisive on short notice. But nothing he did disguised the inner ferment.

When he finally paused, the room was still. Neither Ricki nor I moved. The silence lasted for several moments. I watched him carefully to be sure he had finished speaking. He had. I took this to mean it was my turn to say something.

I spoke and was surprised how easily the words came. "Well, what argument am I making that you don't agree with?"

He answered quickly enough. "You talk in your article about this proportional interest representation and some of the criticisms of it, and I agree with the criticisms of it, that it is balkanizing. That it sees things as us against them."

I responded politely, "I think you are misunderstanding what I am proposing, certainly in the context of this particular job." I reminded him that the remedies I described were remedies that had been adopted or at least approved by the Reagan and Bush administrations, that all the remedies were already in use in counties in Alabama, and that the supermajority rules I discussed were common in the U.S. Senate. I told him that these remedies could be less polarizing than conventional race-conscious districting. I gave him examples where not only blacks and women but Republicans had been elected for the first time when Chilton County, Alabama, adopted cumulative voting, a strategy also used to elect corporate boards throughout America and one that I proposed as a remedy for a proven voting rights violation in certain local communities. I said that these were proposed responses in actual voting rights cases, such as one in Mobile, Alabama, that had gone all the way to the U.S. Supreme Court, and in which the local court found that prejudice had corrupted the Madisonian Bargain of shifting and transitory majorities looking out for the minority, because they too might become one. I explained that these remedies fostered cross-racial coalitions and gave election opportunity to minorities of all kinds, including women.

The president listened as I spoke. He seemed pleased by my earnestness. He told me he thought black districts had worked well, he saw no reason to abandon them. He was concerned with the way my article could be interpreted, and raised certain questions that suggested he too had misunderstood its format. The article discussed something I called "black electoral success theory," a set of assumptions I analyzed and then critiqued. But the president, like many others who were unfamiliar with the law review style, may have simply skimmed the text and failed to appreciate that I was describing a particular strategy (promoting black faces in high places), but not agreeing with many of the basic ideas behind the strategy (in fact, I was explicitly disagreeing that merely electing more blacks necessarily advances the interests of black voters). Once I clarified this distinction, he mentioned no other problems with what I was saying. Indeed, he specifically said that if what I was saying was my position, then he had no problem with it—but that's not how he read my article.

I told him that one of the most innovative ideas I described had been ruled on by the Supreme Court, again as a result of positions taken in the Court during the Bush administration. In the *Presley* case, for example, the Bush administration had tried to apply the Voting Rights Act to issues of legislative decision making, challenging white incumbent officials in a rural Alabama county who had changed the rules as soon as the first black was elected to the county commission. The white commissioners eliminated all the power of each individual commissioner, instead hoarding—really monopolizing—power within their own self-segregated group. When the Court decided the case, it said that the law applied only to elections, not to governance, thus rejecting the Bush administration's attempt to extend the act, as I had proposed, to discriminatory actions of elected officials. Given that recent decision, I told the president, it would now be an abuse of discretion to try unilaterally to implement at the legislative level some of these academic proposals, and in the context of the Civil Rights Division post I would not do that.

The president watched me intently. He said, "I don't have a problem with what you are saying."

I said, "That is what the article is about."

He repeated that he did not have any problem with what I was saying, but that my article was subject to a different interpretation.

I said, "I can't be responsible for the interpretation that other people may make of what I am writing, especially when they are making that interpretation without the benefit of talking to me. Your staff has prevented me from talking to most senators. Those people that I have talked to have been very receptive."

I told the president that the courtesy calls were crucial, yet the Justice Department people were thinking, who is first in line, not who is getting hit by the ball. They were thinking of pending confirmation hearings chronologically, not strategically. I thought about giving the president chapter and verse, rehearsing all of the details of my difficulty even scheduling courtesy calls with senators. Instead, I said that I felt I'd been unfairly maligned in the media, but when I actually met with senators they seemed to do a double take.

Not wanting to drown the president in too much detail, I did, however, specifically mention that I had met Wisconsin Democratic senator Herbert H. Kohl (who had used his prominence as the owner of a basketball franchise in Wisconsin to get elected as a U.S. senator). I told the president that Senator Kohl had urged me not to withdraw. One of my favorite Penn Law students had worked in Kohl's office and Kohl seemed to take a personal interest in my situation. When I met Kohl in his office on May 27, he told me I might not be confirmed but that I could not withdraw, as a matter of principle. Kohl had said, "There are people who have a withdrawal strategy, but you should not withdraw, you can't withdraw. You must proceed. You must have an opportunity to clear your name and testify. Your reputation is on the line. You cannot withdraw."

At this point the president interjected that Senator Kohl had come to him privately and said, "If you don't withdraw this nomination, I am not going to vote with you on the BTU tax," referring to part of the budget negotiations. The president repeated how Senators Biden and Mitchell had also said, "You have got to withdraw this."

I acknowledged the irony, even hypocrisy, in the advice the president was apparently getting from the Hill. But I tried to reemphasize the larger issue. This was an opportunity for a conversation on race, on racial justice, on where we as a nation must go from here. The remedies I had discussed were innovative. They were a useful guide, a way to get us to move beyond the polarizing rhetoric of race-based preferences and special interest legislation. These remedies were in fact race-neutral. If I had a chance to speak, I implored him, I could explain how these remedies would ultimately empower *all* voters, not just blacks or Latinos or Asian Americans. These remedies could be used by women, by Republicans in Democratic cities, by Democrats in Republican suburbs.

I told the president that this was a fight worth fighting—not only to redeem my reputation but to show his commitment to civil rights and racial justice. This was a fight to show how civil rights was everyone's fight. Talking about race would allow us to explore the real problems confronting Americans of all races. The civil rights nomination could help him reclaim America's moral high ground. On the other hand, if he wouldn't fight for a friend, if his administration would leave a friend twisting in the wind with no defense, what is the message? What does that say to ordinary Americans about this president's willingness to fight for them?

The president then offered his own assessment: the next three weeks during the period until my hearing would be extremely unpleasant. He warned me that the right-wing opposition would come after me in ways that would not be good for me. The president repeated what he had said earlier: Senator Biden wanted him to withdraw the nomination. If we went forward, against that advice, "it would be death by a thousand cuts."

I tried to respond to the president's concern about my welfare directly. I told him that I was willing to risk further assault, that I was committed to an open exchange at a public hearing. I told him that I deserved an opportunity to clear my name and to respond to the criticisms in a public forum. I told him that it was an uphill fight but I was willing to fight it. I felt I understood the basis for some of the initial resistance. I said that for the first three weeks after my nomination, there was no response to any of the criticism in the press, and that, finally, the fourth week, there were *two* favorable pieces.

The president probed further. Why, he asked, did I think I was being attacked? I told him that the adversary model has come to supplant balance in the media. I explained my view that an adversary model means there are two, and only two, competing sides to every issue. You give both sides their due by characterizing each position in the most extreme way. This is presented as a balanced story even if it fails to represent the full facts or fails to engage the audience.

In my case, because the administration had instructed me to remain silent, there had been only one side of the story. Given that I was not allowed to speak to the press, and combined with the fact that I was not permitted to meet with most senators, it was not surprising that many senators were upset. I told him even my own mother did not recognize me in the way I was being portrayed. I admitted that I myself wouldn't vote for me if all I knew about my record was what the press were saying. I ended by pointing out, "It is me who has been out there twisting in the wind without any support."

The president took note of all of this. He said, "We did respond." He spoke of White House congressional liaison Howard Paster's letter, the letter that Paster had personally written with attachments on my behalf. Howard Paster's letter went out on May 24 as a defensive gesture in response to criticisms. It was not an affirmative statement of the administration's commitment to vigorous civil rights enforcement and to pushing my nomination as a proven enforcer of the law.

Aloud, I said, "Yes, but that was one letter, it came just last week, and it was not in the press. The senators are forming their opinions about me in the press, not based on anything that I actually said." I added, "And I have not been given an opportunity to meet with most of the senators.

"I'm actually looking forward to the hearings, to being able to speak and possibly even being heard. In any event, I may not get confirmed but I can't withdraw," I explained. "Elaine Jones and others in the civil rights community seem to think that if we force them to take a vote that I'll be confirmed. They remind me all the time that senators never want to vote on civil rights issues but if pushed, they will, and will often do the right thing."

What I didn't say but thought to myself was, I may be so weakened that I wouldn't even want the job. My husband Nolan and I had talked about the possibility of going to Harvard. Despite the student protests challenging Harvard's failure to hire a woman of color, the controversy there seemed so restful and *quiet* compared to all of this. And yet a year ago, when the dean had called me to offer me a visit, I was panicked by the prospect of becoming a public martyr there. My worst nightmare had always been public humiliation. It just shows you, I concluded, that your worst fears *do* come true.

THE PRESIDENT never asked me to withdraw.

He never told me during our meeting that night, June 3, that he had decided to withdraw my nomination. He did say, "You know Lani, if this were about you, if this were a fight on your qualifications, or about your litigation, I would go to the mat. I wouldn't care how many votes we had. I wouldn't care if the only votes we had were Carol

Moseley-Braun and Ted Kennedy. But it is not about you, it is about your writing, and we can't seem to move the debate."

I told him that he hadn't tried. I had become emboldened by now and said, "The administration has not taken the leadership in trying to move the debate. No one has ever made the affirmative case as to why you nominated me." I repeated that this was why we needed to go forward with confirmation hearings.

I told the president I was the victim of benign neglect. I was hypervisible and yet I was treated in the same way as others who were for the most part invisible. I recalled the reception I had attended on May 16 in the White House for federal judges. Judge Richard Arnold, an old friend of Clinton's from Arkansas and a onetime contender for a Supreme Court opening, was there and said he would come and testify on my behalf. He told me that he thought I was a great lawyer. I had argued a case about the majority-vote requirement in Phillips County, Arkansas, before him. In fact, it was that very case that got me thinking about the relationship between majority voting and democracy.

Anyway, I used the reception for a bit of humor, to lighten the otherwise somber tone of this meeting. I told the president that several of the judges had offered me their condolences. One woman who had been on the bench only a few years commiserated, "I don't understand why you would put yourself through all of this. At least when we go through the confirmation ordeal, we get life tenure!"

The president sat quietly listening. Then he continued as if I had not spoken.

"If we could have the hearing Monday, then maybe that would be okay. But we won't be able to have the hearing, Biden tells me, for another three weeks. And that means we are going to have three weeks of them cutting us with thousands, a thousand cuts."

"Well, why not ask Biden at least to set the hearing. They can set it up next Thursday, which would be three weeks from the date they sent up the committee questionnaire, three weeks from May 20," I ventured.

And without realizing it, I then blurted out: "Ask Biden to schedule the hearing tomorrow."

The president looked at me sadly and said, "Biden can't do that."

More calmly this time, I said, "Then ask him to schedule it a week from today, because that is within the three-week period."

"Biden won't do that," Clinton responded.

"But you are the president," I said. "You can at least ask him to do these things and if you want to move on, and I can understand that, then have my hearing and you can move on. But I feel that the White House's inattention and White House policy barring press contact before hearings has left me in a very unfair position. I have been attacked in the press and the White House has not defended me except for one letter."

"I saw Howard Paster's letter," he countered. "That was a good letter."

I was not impressed. "One letter?" And then, in great detail, I recounted the three weeks after my nomination and all of the criticism in the media and the fact that there was not a single meaningful response from anybody in the White House. I turned my body, angling it to face the president directly. I said, "The irony here is that I am committed to dialogue and I am being silenced."

"I understand what you are saying," the president said. He then talked about how hard a decision this was and how divisive a hearing would be. "It won't be good for the country because it will be very polarizing."

Still I urged, "Then have the hearing in the fall, put it off. I just feel that these issues should be explored in public." He reiterated the line about death by a thousand cuts.

I told him, "I would never have accepted the nomination if I didn't think you and I had a similar vision for America. I didn't need the job. I am a tenured law professor. I love what I do. But I was the consensus candidate of the civil rights community. I was their choice and I am committed to follow through. Last fall you were accused of waffling on a lot of issues and I was very moved by your appearance when still a candidate on a show with Bill Moyers. Moyers asked, was there anything you were firmly committed to, that you would never waver on. You said without flinching, 'The one thing I would not back down on is racial equality.' This is your opportunity to show that you would not back down. At the Leadership Conference Dinner [May 11, 1993] you tried to talk about the need to have a conversation in which we are not shouting at each other. That we should be able to walk and chew gum at the same time. Well, those are all the kinds of things that I am committed to."

The president had no verbal response to any of this. He shifted slightly in his chair as if it was the placement of his body that was making him uncomfortable. I felt I was reaching him at some deeper level, but he was determined to keep to his game plan. He repeated in short form his initial statement that my articles were subject to this other interpretation that he couldn't go along with.

Then he conceded: "I don't have any problem with what you are saying, I don't have any problem with what you are representing your views to be; my problem is with your articles and what other people are saying about them, and it will be divisive to have this conversation and I need these senators' support on other things."

The president did not go much deeper into his political calculations. He did tell me, almost as an aside, that "if we could work something out, we would both come out of this okay." He suggested that I had it in my power to "be helpful." Then, as an afterthought, he whispered: "You will emerge in any event as a public voice."

We must have talked for about an hour and a half. It was a very long meeting. He was sitting there, especially at the beginning, with his knuckles defined and prominent, the skin on his hands drawn tight. His face was white, with big red splotches. His voice betrayed nervousness.

I later saw the same expression on his face on February 1, 1994, when he announced that Deval Patrick was his choice for Assistant Attorney General for Civil Rights. I watched a replay of the press conference on television after Elaine Jones had called to alert me, she said, to what she construed as "my vindication." The first question the president was asked at that February 1994 press conference was "Is Deval Patrick a stealth Guinier?" And the president's jaw moved quickly, he blanched and he spoke with some difficulty. He said something dismissive about those who are opposed to civil rights trying to hide their substantive opposition behind noisy confirmation battles. Then, once he answered, he regained composure. His face resumed its empathetic glaze.

But this evening, we were alone in the Oval Office. There were no television cameras to impress. No one was there except Ricki Seidman and me. Ricki never said anything. I almost forgot she was sitting on the couch. I never looked at her, not even once. My eyes, my attention were focused on him.

Toward the end of our meeting, the president said, "Is this the most painful meeting you ever had?"

"No," I replied truthfully.

In many ways the meeting the night before in the Attorney General's conference room had been more stressful. There I had been on the spot in front of an audience. There I was trying to rally a group of silent faces. There I was defending my honor while others whose judgment I valued watched. True, Ricki Seidman was physically present here too, but now she was merely eavesdropping. She was neither caretaker nor reporter, neither audience nor auditor. She was irrelevant to the conversation as it unfolded.

Here in the Oval Office I had a chance to be what I knew best, a teacher. I also saw this as my opportunity to be an advocate. I was not an unsuspecting guest on a television melodrama; I was a lawyer at oral argument. While I was alone in representing my cause, I at least did not suffer role confusion. I was now clear in my identity—I was the client who could finally advocate for herself. I could use my training to marshall the facts and analyze the arguments. I knew the "record." After all, I had written those articles myself. And I knew the judge and jury. He was my friend. I felt oddly at ease. The Oval Office was a comfortable space to have a conversation.

There was no small talk, no kibbitzing, however, in the Oval Office. This was strictly business. After over an hour the president said, "I guess we have each said what we have to say."

"I guess so," I replied. I got up from my chair. I took a few steps. I turned to look at him very closely, noticing that his eyes were a little wet.

I stood very still. Without moving any part of my body, I said, "I just want you to know, whatever you decide, I will still respect you."

Then he got visibly moist in the eyes. That made it very hard. I turned away and walked out.

Like buzzards hovering, a flock of White House staffers had positioned themselves by the closed door of the Oval Office. Once the door opened, they nearly fell in. I had to maneuver my way gingerly to avoid a collision with this infusion of humanity. George Stephanopoulos was there and Mack McLarty. Ricki walked me out into another room. She had said nothing until now. She escorted me out the crowded doorway, motioning me away from the traffic lane. Then she assumed her full height. She turned toward me and said, "Lani, did your mother tell you every day that you were wonderful?"

"No," I said.

"I could never have done what you just did. You have such confidence and poise."

"My mother didn't tell me that." I paused. "But my father did. Without uttering a word. He always conveyed his high expectations about who and what I should be and do."

Nancy McFadden, another Justice staffer who was waiting for me, told me she overheard the president say as I was leaving his office, "That woman has character. Her character is stout." Ricki and Nancy both hugged me and the tears started streaming down my face. It was just too much.

Earlier that very day, Ricki had come to my temporary office at Justice to tell me as a friend that I should withdraw. Ricki's presence in the Oval Office during my meeting with the president merely underlined the lack of credibility her protestations that day of independent judgment had. Now that she had seen me interact with the president, she was telling me I was incredible. It felt surreal, as if these people didn't allow themselves to have honest emotions. That I could sit with the president and be passionate, personal, and genuine in ways they could not dare seemed to leave them stunned.

• • •

I LEFT THE WHITE HOUSE in a car all by myself. My faith had been kept. The president had finally intervened. My situation was grave, but I was finally being treated with some measure of dignity.

It had started to rain. The light misting cast a dramatic shadow over the brightness of what I had just left. The driver took me the long way back to the Justice Department. It felt good to sit in the car, alone in the back seat. I let my mind wander aimlessly as we crossed the empty streets.

Maybe fifteen or twenty minutes after I arrived back in the temporary Assistant Attorney General–designate's office, the phone rang. It was the White House switchboard command center and they put me through. The president was calling.

He got right to the point: "Lani, I have decided to withdraw your nomination."

I said nothing.

He continued, "You made the best case I can imagine, but you didn't change my mind."

Still I said nothing.

The president went on, "I'm sorry. I will take full responsibility. I hope to make it up to you. I feel badly. You didn't do anything wrong, we did. I take full responsibility for it." He added something about spending the rest of his life making this up to me.

I finally found the words to say I was disappointed but that I "appreciated the opportunity to serve, brief as it was."

"You'll have another opportunity," he reassured me.

I thanked him for his call. I thought I heard him hang up, so I put down the receiver.

The phone rang. I picked it up. "Did you hang up on me?" the person on the other end asked. It was the president calling back.

"I thought you were finished, I'm sorry," I said.

Then he told me about his scheduled press conference. I had collected myself enough in the interim to ask when he called back, "What would you like me to do now?"

He responded that I should "coordinate a press statement."

That was my last conversation with the president. Since that second phone call I have not had any communication with President Clinton or the first lady, although I did get identical, machine-signed White House Christmas cards in December 1993, December 1994, December 1995, December 1996, and December 1997.

Instructed by Eddie, I turned on the television and watched from behind my desk. I looked closely to see how the president explained the decision. Other than his worry about "death by a thousand cuts," he had not given me any clue as to how he was weighing the problem during the meeting we had just had. I hadn't expected him to make a decision so soon, since he had said nothing to me in person. I can't say I was surprised by the outcome. I can't say I felt much of anything. I watched the president's face, only vaguely following his words. I looked carefully at his eyes. They were not quite tearful but seemed full of emotion. Despite his determination to look in control, once again his eyes betrayed him.

I was watching his eyes for what seemed like a long time when all of a sudden I heard the president use language that pierced the cocoon-like atmosphere of my office. I heard the president say out loud that my views were "antidemocratic."

My body jerked forward in the chair. It was an involuntary gesture. I stood up in disbelief. I could feel myself reeling, as if the president had physically assaulted me while the whole world was watching. The president was joining the chorus of attackers on national television. I was now officially branded. Disgraced by the president of the United States. My friend, the president, was humiliating me on national television. I could feel the raw emotion burning the skin of my face; I felt dizzy. The room did not spin, but my heart was beating erratically.

The phone calls started immediately. I found myself fielding other people's anger and outrage. I was more hurt than angry, but there was no time for self-pity. Several civil rights leaders told me they were having a press conference right then but that I should wait and see what I could arrange for the next morning. It was now about ten o'clock.

Feeling very sad and utterly bewildered, I walked the long, empty corridor between my office and that of the Attorney General. I had met with Janet Reno immediately before my trip to the Oval Office. She told me then that she did not know what the White House would do. Seated comfortably, in a solemn and straightforward manner, she repeated the advice she had given them: "If you stand on principle," she said, "you can't lose. Because even if you lose, you still have your principles."

During our meeting earlier that evening, Janet Reno had been sitting on the couch, opposite the portrait of Bobby Kennedy walking on the beach. That seemed to be her favorite spot in the office. Every time I met with her, from the day of my first interview, that's where she sat. From that same spot she had proudly pointed out the picture to me on her first day in office. This time, I found the Attorney General expressionless behind her desk. Her desk had neatly arranged piles of paper which she was reviewing. I sat down opposite her. We were separated by the desk, the paperwork, and the knowledge that the White House had not followed her advice. She told me how sorry she was that things had turned out the way they had. She asked me to think about names for possible replacements. She agreed, after I told her the president suggested I release a statement, that I should convene a press conference the following morning.

PRESIDENT CLINTON withdrew my nomination on the stated ground that the furor over my nomination had actually caused him to read my academic writings for the first time. If President Clinton is to be believed, he withdrew my nomination because my views were "antidemocratic"; my views were "difficult to defend"; my views were not consistent with his. On national television he tearfully protested, "It is not the fear of defeat that has prompted this decision. It is the certainty that the battle would be carried on a ground that I could not defend." That was the public explanation. In a June 6, 1993, letter to members of Congress, the president wrote: "Ms. Guinier is an extremely bright and distinguished civil rights lawyer whose background prepared her for the position for which she had been nominated." "I realized that Ms. Guinier had adopted positions in her legal writing with which I did not agree. . . . I concluded I could not ask for confirmation of a nominee with whom I disagreed." At the same time he wrote, "I regret the pain that has been caused to Ms. Guinier, who bears none of the responsibility for the situation in which we find ourselves."

Given the conversation I had had with the president in the Oval Office, it did not ring true. Had such a giant breach of faith occurred between his views and mine, there would have been no need to argue, as Howard Paster did, that they simply did not have the votes. Nor would it have been necessary to treat me as if I were the unsuspecting guest on what was the melodramatic equivalent of "The Howard Paster" daytime television talk show the night before in the Attorney General's conference room.

It did not ring true given the anguished, white-knuckled ordeal of our extended Oval Office meeting, the meeting he spoke of as brutal and heartbreaking, "one of the most painful" he'd ever attended. If I could not be trusted to do the job for which I had been nominated, I assumed he would have said so when we met face-to-face, if only out of respect for our friendship. After all, following an earlier May 14 news conference, the president himself had told reporters: "Based on my personal experience you will believe me when I say I am confident that she will follow the Constitution and the laws of the United States." He did not signal me when we met in person that we were not on the same side, that we actually had intellectual disagreements deeply threatening to his understanding of civil rights. Instead, he privately listened and then publicly called me names. Indeed, fifteen minutes after the president notified me by telephone of his decision, he appeared in the White House briefing room, *The New York Times* reported, "to read from a statement that had been prepared before the meeting with Ms. Guinier began, and that he had edited."

Maybe he figured he could reconcile the dissonance by retrospectively affirming his "great respect for Ms. Guinier," who has been "a constant champion" of the Voting Rights Act; a leader. Or by his dramatic post-withdrawal announcement at a White House dinner party, that "This was the hardest decision I've had to make since I became president." The guests in the green room included R. W. Apple, a *New York Times* reporter, who was struck by the star-crossed look on the president's face when he spoke "with ill-concealed bitterness" about the "campaign of right-wing distortion and vilification." The president then went on to explain, "I love her. I think she's wonderful. If she came to me and asked for $5,000 I'd go down to the bank and give it to her, no questions asked."

Perhaps he thought it was enough to acknowledge just how hard our earlier meeting was, a painful meeting "between two people who like and admire each other." He was shaken, near tears, visibly distressed, according to reporters who witnessed his withdrawal announcement. He complained that his nominee had been subject to "a vicious series of willful distortions on many issues, including the quota issue." And he noted that I was "surprised" he felt the way he did.

In our meeting, the president did say that he was disturbed by the interpretations others took of my views and that he initially shared some of those interpretations. But once I stated my actual position, he never elaborated further on our supposed disagreement. Even after our meeting, I could not tell Eddie Correia, who was waiting for me at the time back at the Justice Department, what the president might do. To this day I do not know which of the "positions" I had actually taken, if any, doomed my nomination.

It was "unfair," Reverend Jesse Jackson argued, when he accused the president of "capitulation." "She was never able to face her accusers or face the public." "The only injury [here]," Roger Wilkins declared in my defense, "is an injury inflicted by the ineptitude of the White House. They . . . left her out there by herself, then they themselves began to attack her in an anonymous and cowardly way."

I had been called to service, "down from the ivory tower," David Von Drehle wrote in *The Washington Post*, where "your job is simply to think . . . to think and write challenging things that press, probe, provoke, at the edge of understanding." No one, however, suggested that I was unwilling or unable to assume a new role; again in Von Drehle's words, "to ameliorate, to do the public will." Instead, Von Drehle concluded, "after a gruesome Washington spectacle of anonymous stiletto thrusts," I was sent to my "political death."

I was sent to my "political death" for proposing remedies that were highly technical, "growing as they do from the abstruse viscera of the dense Voting Rights Act," Von Drehle observed. But these remedies did not originate in academic speculation. I had learned about things like supermajority voting from the Reagan and Bush administrations, and "from us," Alabama attorney Jim Blacksher noted. Supermajority remedies are "things that have been achieved," he told *The New York Times,* "in the grand old fashion of southern politics of working out practical accommodations between the white community and the black community. Lani isn't hung up on them." Blacksher continued, "She refers to them because in specific particular situations, they've been useful for resolving conflict and empowering African-Americans and Latino minorities."

Indeed some of my ideas were actually quite familiar, "made incendiary by the introduction of race." Von Drehle pointed out that the idea of "minority vetoes" was common in the U.S. Senate. "Few trembled for the nation's future when a Republican minority 'vetoed' the Clinton stimulus package by use of a filibuster." The real problem: None of my ideas "translated well into sound bites."

Certainly, no one had prepared me for a sound bite litmus test for public service. Nor had I realized that accepting the nomination required 100 percent agreement on every issue. Or maybe that was just the public pose. After all, the president had never asked me, "Will you follow the administration policy?" He never worried aloud, at least in my presence, that I would sabotage his commitments to racial healing. He never intimated that I would advocate blacks do to whites what whites had done to them. Of course not. My whole academic project was about collective decision making and power sharing. I never said power sharing was zero-sum. I never advocated minority rule. I never proposed or supported quotas. I favored collaboration to avoid the problem of one winner and multiple losers.

I combed my memory for a hint, a sentence fragment lost in a larger conversation. Nothing surfaced that helped me understand his public pronouncements. What was missing was any evidence of leadership by moral conviction and explanation, by hard-in-the-trenches building of opinion and understanding.

I kept waiting for a phone call, a message, a signal that would explain all this. The president's June 6 letter merely reinforced rather than erased my confusion. I had left the Oval Office without a clue as to what the president was really thinking. He had hinted at but had been unable to state the "positions" in my legal writings "with which [he] did not agree."

Civil rights always involved a fight. Sometimes it was a fight worth having, especially if it served to educate and enlighten, not just demonize or divide. Republican senator Arlen Specter seemed to recognize this when he told *The New York Times,* "There are some fights you have to fight even if you may lose them. I think [the president] misreads the Senate and this is going to do him some harm as he faces a tough battle on the budget." Specter was giving the tactical argument for not retreating in the face of political pressure, but there was also an even more important principle at stake. Yale professor Harlon Dalton reminded us of that when he explained to a reporter, "Her Senate hearing would have been a conversation about what democracy looks like in a multicultural society in the 1990s, and I think that's a conversation we need to have. Instead, the Senate and the president ran away from it."

I did, of course, agree with the president that a confirmation hearing that was guaranteed to be nothing more than "a sustained and bitter debate over civil rights" was undesirable. But how could we predict the outcome without, in the president's own words, giving me "more ample opportunity to clarify" my views?

Abbe Lowell, Attorney General Ben Civiletti's assistant in the Carter administration, had suggested that my "true personality will come out in the hearings." "She's the kind of person who fills the room when she walks in," Dean Colin Diver of the University of Pennsylvania Law School once said of me, "You really notice her, not only because she's quite tall but she also has a kind of aura of self-confidence and she's very articulate." Eddie also said I was my best witness. I could tell, even as we talked that June night, that the president was having a hard time disagreeing with me in person. It was not that I was such a powerful arguer. It was that I am a different person from the one some had read into my articles. He knew that.

Pat Williams described it exactly right in her article in the *Village Voice* on June 15, 1993:

> The presidential decision to retreat is a disaster on many, many levels. On the simplest level, Clinton seems to have forgotten he has the power to craft a policy that will direct the course of remediation available under the Voting Rights Act. What got lost in the flurry of comparisons of Guinier to Robert Bork is that she was not up for a Supreme Court post, which is life-tenured and shielded from any review; she was nominated for a position that would have made her the servant, so to speak, of the president's pleasure. The job of assistant attorney general is one circumscribed by review and by the constraint of the commander-in-chief's direction; it is a position in which the appointee acts as a surrogate for the president. Even if she had written articles with which he disagreed, the test was whether or not she could follow the law and advance the president's policies, as she had done in her years at Justice under President Carter—a point Janet Reno kept making and which was pretty universally conceded, even by Guinier's enemies.

On a more abstract level, while everyone knows the attack on Lani Guinier was at heart a carefully engineered attack on Clinton, leaving him few politically popular options, it is also true that Clinton handled the whole thing so incredibly badly that you could hear the Republicans popping champagne corks for days. It was like watching some juvenile gang rough up the new guy with the fancy pants and expensive haircut. Robert Dole shouts wimp and Clinton flinches; buoyed, Dole resorts to the ancient schoolyard bully tactic of ranking him out: your momma is ugly and your policies are on fire; your nominees all have rocks in their heads and, furthermore, you're a sissy. Clinton says tearfully, I am so a man; if I'd seen those rocks I'd never have made her my nominee.

Meanwhile, the senators hear an accusation of rocks in the head, and leap to measure the public pulse. They don't bother to hear or look at the nominee. They don't even care that it's clearly a hyperbolic lie. They don't want to talk about it because she's already been marked, identified, and her image has a life of its own. She's been wired and anyone who touches her will be politically electrocuted. The winds of public opinion—as well as gang politics—are very intolerant of anyone who has been marked as feminist, liberal, civil rights, quota, black, academic, political, activist. They don't want the details or even the truth. Just get her out of here before the radiation consumes what's left of Clinton's mad, reckless tea party.

For all the ballyhoo, Guinier is a distinguished career civil-rights advocate, whose fairness and equanimity are celebrated, who has argued and won cases before the Supreme Court, and who holds tenure at one of the most conservative law schools in the country. If she is the radical crackpot fringe, one wonders if the Mainstream is really a mirage after all, a powerful fantasy concocted by that wacky fun-loving knucklehead Clint Bolick.

CHAPTER FIVE

Through the Looking Glass:
A Parable of Passive Leadership

DURING THE SPRING of 1993, after my nomination to be Assistant Attorney General for Civil Rights was in trouble, there was a corps of lawyers and friends, valiant and dedicated people who worked hard to bring the case before the American public. People like Eddie Correia and Carolyn Osolinik sacrificed in numerous ways to help me get the one thing that mattered most—a Senate confirmation hearing. Friends like Mary Berry, Barbara Arnwine, and Elaine Jones were loyal, even devoted. "Dayna and I and several others," Penda Hair of LDF told me, "were working all day, fifteen-hour days and more, mobilizing and attempting to talk some sense to the media. The problem is that we did not understand who should be the target of the mobilization." Remember, she tells me, all those at the grass roots who "were springing up from nowhere, calling to help, offering to bring buses to the hearings." People were mobilizing themselves, calling around the clock offering support. "We were directing them toward the Senate, not the White House. Obviously that was a strategic error," Penda admits, "but at the time we were less able to foresee a betrayal of the magnitude that occurred. We expected that the White House would not be much help in lobbying the Senate and getting the hearing together, but we did not expect it to pull the plug."

Other LDF cooperating attorneys who knew me tried to make the case for a hearing, signing petitions, writing letters, making phone calls. Academic colleagues like Susan Sturm circulated a petition signed by almost four hundred law professors in less than two weeks. On May 26, I attended the Washington Women's Dinner. Jamie Gorelick (then general counsel to the Department of Defense and subsequently Deputy Attorney General to Janet Reno), Ruth Bader Ginsburg (prior to her nomination to the Supreme Court), and Judge Pat Wald all came up to me urging me to let them know what they could do to be supportive. "Anything I can do," they each said. My friends were civil rights lawyers, judges, and law professors. Despite their commitment, they were not part of a movement that depended on or knew how to sustain ongoing mobilization or organization.

There were many people trying to be helpful. Yet there was no one person or coalition of organizations that I could send them to. Nor was there a vehicle for making the public aware of the letters of support, the petitions, the op-ed pieces that went unpublished. This was, in part, because our focus was on the Senate hearings. We were lawyers, after all, treating the nomination as pre-trial wheel spinning. It was as if we were awaiting an actual trial date to get organized. Once hearings were finally scheduled, I was told, the letters of support and the petitions would all become part of the record or read on the Senate floor. Until then, they should be collated and filed.

So we waited in silence for the hearings. We watched alliances form and dissolve. We were counseled to follow procedures that were the opposite of what I had been trained to expect as a civil rights lawyer. All the rules were invented or inverted. What we saw made me feel like Alice in Wonderland after she fell down the rabbit hole and found herself on trial before the Queen of Hearts: the sentence came first, the verdict afterward. When Alice protested, the Queen, purple with rage, told her, "Hold your tongue!" "I won't!" Alice proclaimed defiantly. "Off with her head!" the Queen then shouted at the top of her voice.

At a meeting of parents at Sidwell Friends School one weekend in the middle of May, a friend who teaches at a law school in D.C. saw Hillary Clinton and approached her to discuss the nomination. "The press is having a field day with Lani's nomination. What should we do?" my friend asked. Hillary mouthed the word "organize," but said little else. Hillary's admonition was not even whispered, much less spoken aloud. While her advice seemed sound, to read her lips meant openly challenging the rules that had been set by White House staff. As far as my friends knew, administration policy still required that we follow the rules set down earlier by the White House and Justice Department. The press was "off-limits" to me, while I was fair game to it.

Those rules undermined any efforts to organize. As soon as I was nominated, I was instructed to let first the Justice Department, then the White House, make key decisions. I had to behave in a manner consistent with my designated role, even as this distanced me from former civil rights clients, colleagues, and supporters. I was not allowed to speak to the public, whether through formal interviews or at public events held in local communities. When LDF cooperating attorney Jim Blacksher invited me in mid-May to speak to a group of politically active blacks in Alabama, I was told by my White House handlers to say no. I was an administration nominee and administration policy governed my decisions. I was off-limits not only to the press but also to the people.

The administration set the tone not only for my behavior but for sympathizers on the outside. Those who tried to be my advocate were encouraged to capitalize quietly upon existing relationships with important people in positions of authority, casually calling senators and administration officials they knew. They were instructed to follow the protocol of pre-confirmation hearing silence, which meant few were speaking out; fewer still were organizing; no one at all was successfully disrupting the chain of events that the right wing opposition had set in motion.

Vernon Jarrett, a columnist for the *Chicago Sun-Times,* wrote an opinion piece in late May 1993 entitled "Black Professionals Should Be Defending Lani Guinier" that began: "Brothers and Sisters, where are you? Paging all Brothers and Sisters. America needs to hear from you, too." Part of the reason Jarrett's plea went unheeded was that my friends and supporters had the expectation that the nomination would be handled properly within the political process. They assumed others would undertake the defense they knew was available. They also believed there would be time. Their eyes, like mine, were on the hearing we believed we could make happen. We trusted the administration's lines. The Justice Department press office urged, "Don't engage the opposition, that just keeps the story alive." Later they added, "Just wait. You'll get a hearing, and then you can respond." From within the White House, I heard, "We're gearing up. We'll get someone to read your articles and comment on them favorably. Just wait." And from close friends of the president like Vernon Jordan, I was told, "Remain calm. The president is behind you. He won't abandon you. I'll help too, when the time comes." The time to help, apparently, never came.

The civil rights community was trusting. After all, we felt as if we had won the presidential election of 1992. We now had a progressive southern governor back in the White House. Many of those newly in charge of various civil rights lobbying organizations therefore thought they were in a position to influence the agenda quietly, behind the scenes. I don't know all that they felt or all that they tried to do, but what many said to me was that they were finally in a position to tilt things their way. They had built up lines of access through friendship and networks of accomplishment. Some even agreed with the proposition that any conversation on race was politically dangerous, that the president's reelection was more important than a fight over political vision or a principled political strategy. Some were cowed by the right.

Others were cajoled by the administration. None questioned the instinctive reliance on an insider strategy.

The problem with trusting your instinct at a moment like this is that it caused those who should know better to put their compasses away. *Yet our experience had shown us that* the compass of the civil rights movement had been the lives of ordinary people. Not *the* people who had easy access to the White House, or the Congress, or the other corridors of power, but those whose daily lives were the reason for the civil rights movement itself.

The civil rights movement, as a movement of ordinary people, had in fact withered because of this instinct to insider politics. Those still involved were captured, in part, by our own success and our own expertise. We had achieved formal access. No one could be forced to sit at the back of the bus. The law would not permit it. Jim Crow, and its legally enforced system of separate water fountains and separate schools, was dead. We had at best leveled the playing field (at least as described in the law books), yet we acted as though because some blacks were now important insiders we had equalized the teams.

Some who now enjoyed formal power yielded faith to momentary opportunity and sacrificed moral courage for career. But many who still believed deeply and passionately in the necessity of change were nevertheless convinced that quiet, backroom dealing was the only way to proceed. Now in Washington, they played an inside-the-Beltway kind of politics, where access is the coin of the realm.

In my mind I see Elaine Jones, director-counsel of the Legal Defense Fund, and one of my most fervent backers. Elaine Jones and others in the civil rights and women's rights community had rallied around me; their unwavering support at that time convinced me that this was a job I wanted to do. People like Wade Henderson, Barbara Arnwine, and Mary Frances Berry prodded me to accept the nomination, once it was offered. They championed my nomination and sought to convince administration officials, despite some objections early on to my writings, that the right choice had been made.

Elaine knows how to reach people. She is a powerful, dramatic persona, whose impassioned oratory prompted me to walk up to her at a conference on blacks and the bar examination while I was still a law student. After I heard her speak, I volunteered to work for her on the spot. During the 1982 legislative battle to extend and amend the Voting Rights Act, Elaine was head of the LDF lobbying efforts in Washington. From Elaine I learned firsthand the value of outside agitation; she never backed down from holding accountable those lobbyists whose establishment ties tempted them to embrace a premature compromise.

Years later, Elaine told me that she saved some of the messages I left on her answering machine during the period when my nomination was pending. Elaine said she could hear in my voice the tension and the stress. Elaine felt personally responsible for some of that tension. After all, she and others in charge of the major civil rights organizations had been unanimous when they urged me to accept the nomination in the first place. I recall that on April 29, the morning of the nomination announcement, I had called Elaine and left a message on her machine: "I don't know whether to thank you or curse you."

Elaine had promoted me precisely because of the qualities that the right wing and the neoconservatives found so threatening. Clint Bolick described me as a bold thinker and a tenacious litigator even as he "crowned" me a Quota Queen. He warned his readers that I had the mental firepower and personal litigation experience to bring fresh ammunition to a progressive civil rights vision. As many people would later compliment me, the right-wing establishment was justifiably scared of me.

Even after the nomination was publicly controversial, the civil rights establishment valiantly pushed me forward. They telephoned me day and night, offering constant reinforcement. They encouraged me not to withdraw; they rallied to get the White House to insist that the Democratic-controlled Senate schedule confirmation hearings. Once the president pulled the nomination, the withdrawal became a lead item on the network news. Local grass-roots membership organizations were now "in the loop" and made their voices heard. Chapters of the NAACP from around the country hailed my stand.

William F. Gibson, the NAACP's chairman, said President Clinton had "kicked us in the teeth" by abandoning the nomination. When I spoke a month later, in July 1993, at the NAACP National Convention in Indianapolis to a packed house, an organist introduced me by playing key chords from "The Battle Hymn of the Republic." Encouraged by his fervor, thousands of delegates at the Hoosier Dome in Indianapolis began chanting: "Lani! Lani! Lani!" They applauded my observations that the withdrawal of the nomination without a public hearing demonstrated that racial issues have been swept under the rug by Democrats and Republicans alike. The audience interrupted with chants and amens throughout my address. That I was neither preaching nor singing didn't matter; we were making music together. The resonance of that call and response continued to echo for days thereafter. I felt connected to a powerful force.

Yet, my friends in the D.C.-based lobbying organizations failed to channel that untapped power into sustained support for their demands. Unable to cajole the administration into putting up a fight for the nomination, they were left to watch as the right wing slowly circumscribed the administration's options. The White House soon retreated, cowed by the noisome conflict. My interests and those of the people I represented and wrote about were now publicly portrayed, if at all, by ideological adversaries. As the same academic colleague who confronted Hillary at Sidwell Friends later reported to me after the president withdrew the nomination, "Clint Bolick should apply for the job. He has successfully defined the administration's civil rights policies."

While the nomination was still pending, the Washington-based civil rights lobbyists had wasted valuable time before trying to mobilize a grass-roots effort, trusting instead their access to key White House staff. But once the nomination became openly controversial, their influence within the administration waned. Pushed to continue working behind the scenes, they nevertheless tried to manipulate and shape events quietly, in ways that were invisible to a larger audience. As virtual insiders, their credibility as "team players" depended on *not* orchestrating a public outcry. Crippled by this habit-forming pattern, they could not take full advantage of an important outside force that might have moved the administration beyond its public silence.

Despite the individual willingness of civil rights leaders to speak out, the overall strategy was one of stealth. Acie Byrd was an organizer of the 1993 commemorative March on Washington marking the thirtieth anniversary of Dr. King's "I Have a Dream" speech. Byrd later took me aside to share his perspective on why I had not been invited to speak at that August 1993 forum.

At a meeting of the 1993 Program Committee in July, soon after President Clinton had pulled my nomination, Acie Byrd introduced my name as a potential speaker for the August rally. He and I had never met; we had never even spoken. Byrd was offended by the way my nomination had been handled, but buoyed by the way I responded. He saw me as a combat veteran on democracy's legal front. He gave the Program Committee another reason why I should be invited to speak: He was intrigued by the issues of political equality and representation that I had been trying to address.

Several of the black leaders of the march, including representatives from the Joint Center for Political and Economic Studies, whom Walter Fauntroy had brought in to craft the "March Call," opposed my speaking. As members of the Program Committee, they saw the invitation as "an unnecessary boat rocker." Why create a problem with the White House? My presence might disrupt the breakfast tradition established in 1963, when President Kennedy asked the March on Washington leadership and principal speakers, including Dr. King, to the White House on the morning of the march. Acie Byrd pursued his idea. He brought it up to Reverend Joseph Lowery, the head of the Southern Christian Leadership Council (SCLC), Dr. King's organization based in Atlanta. Lowery agreed that the Program Committee was creating the problem. They didn't know for sure that the White House had a problem with me in the first place; people were just assuming it would.

Minister Louis Farrakhan wanted to speak, but his name was never in consideration; Abe Saperstein and several Jewish organizations weighed in to oppose giving Farrakhan a platform, but it turned out their opposition was unnecessary. "Farrakhan was not in play. His name was not on the list. He was not the subject of controversy behind the scenes," Acie Byrd later informed me. "You were."

It was a hot, humid Washington afternoon in June 1996 when Acie Byrd and I had this conversation. Elbows resting on a thick, shellacked wood table at a neighborhood Tex-Mex restaurant, Byrd looked me straight in the eye, talking slowly in a rich baritone voice. It was air-conditioned inside, but beads of sweat bundled on his high, dark-skinned forehead. Though he had broached the subject, he knew he was talking out of school.

But Acie Byrd need not have worried. This was a strategy in which we all cooperated. It was a strategy that ultimately sealed my particular fate. But it also limited our approach to civil rights more generally. Without an organized constituency, even those with whom we did have long-term relationships, such as some of the black cabinet officers, stayed in the background, anonymous and disturbingly quiet. I remember discussing what happened at a dinner party attended by Bill Coleman, the prominent black Republican, a personal friend and champion who had extended himself mightily during the spring of 1993. Two weeks to the day after the president withdrew my nomination, Bill Coleman joined a group of us for dinner at a party hosted by Bill Cosby. Cosby, outraged by the president's retreat on my nomination, had abruptly canceled his master-of-ceremonies gig at the White House Jazz Festival. On the same June night at which he was to have hosted a party at the White House, Cosby instead sent his private plane to transport a group of my friends and family from Philadelphia so that we could attend a quiet protest dinner Cosby held for my supporters in Washington.

There, in the elegant surroundings of a posh restaurant at the Watergate Hotel, we all seethed—and cried. As we went around the room sharing our reflections about this episode, Bill Coleman said, "Where were the black cabinet officials?" During Republican administrations, blacks always came to Coleman to hold the black cabinet officers accountable. The "battle for the President's mind" was waged throughout Republican administrations by notable blacks with great establishment credentials. "Vernon Jordan is one of my best friends," Bill Coleman told us at that dinner. "Where was he?"

In May 1990, Vernon Jordan had publicly chided George Bush, whom he called "my friend, the President," not to veto "a bill that saves basic civil rights from the tender mercies of the Reagan Supreme Court." Jordan threatened "a firestorm of protest" that would "permanently rupture the administration's credibility" and damage Bush's opportunity, "the best opportunity in half a century to break the Democratic monopoly on the black vote." But no one thought to do the same in the Clinton administration. No one threatened "a firestorm of protest." Nor did anyone actively lobby the cabinet that looked like America to push hard for a public hearing.

It is true that after the withdrawal announcement, the Congressional Black Caucus declined to make immediate amends with the president, explaining that the president's "capitulation" was unprincipled. The president had sacrificed not just me, a job, and a hearing, but an opportunity, "a magic moment," Congressman Ron Dellums declared, to bring to national consciousness the continuing issues of racial injustice. How the administration responded to the controversy surrounding my nomination was a signal, after all, of how they would position themselves on future civil rights issues. We had expected the Clinton administration to usher in a new and long-anticipated era. They would lead the country, we thought, toward a more progressive understanding of the role that race plays in disabling the will for common cause among poor and working-class Americans. The hearings, had they come to pass, were an opportunity to use the media to convene a national conversation on race. They were a chance to organize a second round of national hearings on the continued need for a Voting Rights Act. They were a moment to challenge both the right wing's interpretation of my views and, more important, the right wing's increasing domination of so many public conversations on race.

"This was a magic moment," Dellums said. This was a moment when the country could take notice of the issues of racial discrimination and ongoing patterns of injustice. These hearings were a gift if used properly to draw the American people in, to confront the challenges of moving forward in the post–civil rights era. The president had needlessly put in jeopardy his commitment to vigorous civil rights enforcement, Representative Dellums charged.

The Black Caucus was angry. They refused to meet with the president for over a month, but they didn't pursue the opportunity to force the president to make solid commitments on civil rights. The Congressional Black Caucus didn't translate their own challenge to the president into an opportunity to hold hearings, as Congress did in 1981, on the need for strong civil rights enforcement efforts. They didn't marshall evidence or mobilize testimony about what the Voting Rights Act had and still needed to accomplish. No one played the role that Elaine and the group of insurgents had followed in getting Congress to amend the law ten years earlier. There was no bottom-up strategy in which civil rights organizations mobilized community pressure and demanded democratic accountability from elected officials within the national government. There was no public education campaign to explain to the American people why the Black Caucus had supported the nomination of someone like me in the first place or why vigorous civil rights enforcement efforts, including new and innovative remedies such as the ones I proposed, were needed now more than ever.

Instead of pushing for substantive issue-oriented hearings, even after the nomination was withdrawn, the civil rights establishment became entangled in a more specific, pragmatic goal. Public education was not the priority. After momentary eruptions of visible anger, they focused on using back channels to the White House to get someone else confirmed to the post of Assistant Attorney General for Civil Rights.

Throughout this period, I had many conversations with civil rights leaders inside the Beltway who kept trying to reassure me that they were simply working to ensure that the next nominee would be an excellent candidate. I kept telling them that it wasn't about positioning different individuals; it was about organizing to resist institutional and structural constraints. It was intervening to educate and transform public culture. I was beginning to realize that the policy script had been written and that the next nominee, whoever that person might be, would have to play within its limitations unless we first mounted a sustained campaign to educate and mobilize a constituency around civil rights enforcement. Without a mobilized constituency, I questioned how anyone could be effective in a skittish administration running a bureaucratic law enforcement organization that was always slow to act, but would now be fearful of acting at all, lest the hounds of the right set upon it.

Few, if any, within the Washington-based civil rights establishment seemed to agree with my assessment. Their initial anger gave way to concern with practical realities. They began to tell me that the president's decision to accept the right wing's version of my law review articles would not necessarily have a chilling effect on more general civil rights enforcement efforts. They were now justifiably preoccupied by the obvious need to fill the position with someone who would be energetic and sympathetic. They saw no other way, themselves, to take advantage of Ron Dellums's "magic moment." To many of them it became increasingly important to see the president's withdrawal in the most narrow way possible—as primarily a personal loss. That I felt hurt was a purely human reaction, one that disabled me from seeing the big picture. It meant that I misunderstood the policy portents. I had been knocked so far off balance that I couldn't see straight and reason well. The meaning of the Voting Rights Act would depend on how well intentioned or deeply committed the next nominee may be. The person would be the policy. After all, individuals could make a decisive difference.

My pragmatic friends were no longer convinced that we could effect major change. They did what they were now good at—creating openings for incremental change behind the scenes in legal briefs, in legislative drafts, in little nooks and crannies of influence and employment opportunity. I soon realized that the problem was, in fact, structural, not personal. We were all trapped. What I came to understand was that the problem was bigger than a timid president, a group of well-intentioned but pragmatic civil rights leaders, or a set of cautious politicians in Washington. The problem was that without a mobilized civil rights constituency, neither this administration on its own, nor even my civil rights friends and allies, could stand and deliver.

The story of how we abandoned bottom-up efforts to organize an oppositional mass movement in favor of top-down efforts to infiltrate established power is not just a critique of others. I too fell prey to believing in this world that I was hoping to join. I momentarily lost the perspective I had had in 1981 and 1982 when I worked with a creative and contentious group of litigators and lobbyists to extend and amend the Voting Rights Act. I forgot the strategic role outsiders played in creating synergy and holding insiders accountable. Instead, once I fell down Alice's rabbit hole, I wanted just to be another insider. Both logic and proportion were distorted.

In seeking the nomination for Assistant Attorney General, I too was at least partially seduced by the opportunity for short-term individual success. I knew that this job would be that of a legitimator, not a reformer. I was prepared to be used by powerful decision makers to legitimate safe choices, choices that offered short-term pragmatic advantages but sacrificed long-term principles. I remembered, but discounted its importance, that the insider response to the challenge of the civil rights movement was to *manage* the problems posed by our racial history. To manage rather than resolve had become the chief operating principle.

To some extent, simply by seeking this position, I had acquiesced in my own silencing. I was temporarily swept away by the promise of the "big job." The whole point of the Civil Rights Division, I thought, is its power to do good. That would eventually make it all worthwhile. Those on the outside, I thought at the time, are only as good as the people on the inside let them be.

Yet I knew I faced a paradox. I never forgot that real social transformation requires an organized constituency, not simply a cadre of well-groomed managers. I accepted the nomination, despite my reservations, because I believed that I would be working in a dynamic relationship with an administration committed to social change and with a mobilized civil rights community that would keep both me and the administration honest. As it turned out, I was wrong.

THE MOMENT OF EPIPHANY began the night I was to receive the Chairman's Award at the Congressional Black Caucus Dinner in September 1993. The Caucus Dinner is always a gala event and this year was no exception. Everyone seemed in a festive mood. Vernon Jordan, fresh from being showcased on the front page of *The New York Times* feet outstretched and sharing a golf cart with President Clinton, greeted me twice: first at the reception, second at my table. Both times he was more than cordial; he was performing a role, not just for me but for the world around us.

Vernon's overtures were meant to convey that though the president pulled the nomination, he would not leave me standing alone. I may have been abandoned by the president, but at that moment I was embraced by my community. The warmth and sense of solidarity was always important to me. It brought to mind the elation I and other lawyers experienced when we went South and mixed it up with people engaged in local movements for justice. It reminded me of the communion I felt with the organist and the audience at the NAACP Convention when, to the chords of "The Battle Hymn of the Republic," we made music together.

I knew that the president would be at the dinner. Two days earlier, I was taken aside and informed, in hushed tones, that the president would speak to the caucus on the same night I was to receive the award. I was told that the White House had requested that I receive my award privately; perhaps, they suggested, I might receive the award on a different day. Apparently, Kweisi Mfume, the chairman of the caucus, refused this request. Instead, last-minute negotiations had produced a compromise: the president would speak first, and then, as soon as he left the podium, he would leave the dinner. To avoid any potential surprises, the president would not have to witness the award presentation. Nor would I be allowed to speak after I received the award.

I talked about this later with my old Justice Department friend Charisse Lillie, now a partner in a major Philadelphia law firm, who told me that she was surprised the Black Caucus insisted on presenting me an award at the same time they invited President Clinton to speak. That they would have both of us in the same room at the same time to her represented an act of "courage" or commitment, a willingness to make a public statement that she found unexpected. In fact, to me it seemed just the opposite.

I suffered through their public statement that evening. It was an evening filled with many awkward moments, not least of which arose when I noticed Wade Henderson (then head of the Washington office of the NAACP and now head of the Leadership Conference for Civil Rights) and Elaine Jones escorting D.C. lawyer John Payton around the room, stopping to chat at the tables in the rear of the hall. As far as I could tell, they were circulating around the edge of the hall, stopping short of the table where I was seated. Payton, a brilliant, dedicated partner in a large D.C. law firm and former corporation counsel for the District of Columbia, was then Elaine and Wade's choice to be nominated as Assistant Attorney General for Civil Rights. Wade and Elaine were proudly introducing John to people they thought would be important for him to know. John was never nominated and never got to use those introductions. Watching them operate from my peripheral perspective, I had both a sense of déjà vu and a feeling that I had seen the future.

I was seated with my husband Nolan, among a group of strangers, as far from the president as was possible within the space roped off for awardees and honored guests. I was also seated away from my friends in the civil rights community, who were busy using the opportunity to move forward on the task of filling the still-vacant civil rights slot. In front of me, in the foreground, shielded from any embarrassment I might cause, was Bill Clinton, the obvious center of gravity. I looked behind me and there in the background were my old friends, otherwise preoccupied.

I was honored but hidden. I occupied a virtual island of untouchable space. I was at the Black Caucus Dinner in Washington because I had stood up for civil rights, Yet I felt very much alone. My friends in the D.C.-based civil rights community still acknowledged my presence, but they seemed determined to maintain some distance to protect their ability to continue to play in this field. They had a new mission: to confirm someone else. That person should not have to carry my baggage of controversy just to assume the seat I once sought to occupy. I remembered my friend and Georgetown law professor Pat King's wise advice to keep smiling, even if my lips felt like they were wrapped around a lemon.

I knew, of course, that someone had to fill the slot. Moreover, my friends in Washington could certainly point to examples of their personal influence within the insular world of Beltway politics, so it was not much of a stretch to assume that someone working from inside the Civil Rights Division could also assert leadership. As an intellectual matter, I could see that they did their best to produce the symbolic rewards that were within their reach. They could get a "big job" for the "right person" in the Justice Department, even if they otherwise had very little input on overall policy formulation. Still, I felt as if we were all missing an opportunity to teach and lead.

We were preoccupied with what was possible; we lost sight of what was needed. The magic moment had somehow passed without notice or regret. We were no longer engaged in a struggle to resist exclusionary and arbitrary power. We, myself included, were seeking instead to enlist power or, more to the point, to enlist ourselves within the circle of power. That evening I too tried to reenlist, partially to alleviate my own discomfort. My unsuccessful overture, of which I am not proud, helped me see even more clearly how tempting it is to compromise principle for access when framed as an individual choice between advancement and abandonment. Personal relationships were indeed the coin of the realm.

That night I tried to use Vernon Jordan, the president's friend, as an emissary. Vernon had come over to my table a second time to take his soundings of my situation. He seemed to enjoy shuttling back and forth between the president's table at the front of the VIP section, almost a football field's length away, and my seat, close to the ropes at the edge of the VIP section. We chatted briefly. Elaine had mentioned several weeks earlier that she had talked to Vernon Jordan soon after the president had pulled the nomination. Elaine had tried hard to explain to Vernon, who apparently supported the president's decision, the loss she felt in acutely personal terms. She talked to Vernon about his long-term friendship with Wiley Branton. Wiley Branton could have passed for white but was as "black" and feisty as they come. Branton was a civil rights attorney from Arkansas who represented the Little Rock students in 1957 when they tried to integrate Central High School. Wiley Branton had died prematurely, but he and Vernon had been close compatriots through many civil rights struggles, just as Elaine and I had been. Elaine said to Vernon, "Think how you would feel if this had happened to Wiley Branton."

Despite my knowledge that Vernon worked for the president and not for me, I asked Vernon to do me a favor. I said, "Vernon, I would like you to carry a message for me to the president. I am very uncomfortable right now. I don't like the position I am in with all these media intermediaries trying to force a relationship or to demonstrate the absence of one. We can agree to disagree, but it seems we could do so one-on-one. If we are estranged, I would like to know the terms. I would like to meet with the president. I would like to meet with him in person. I would like to meet with him privately, so we can begin to put the petty things behind us and move on to the important policy issues."

Neither Vernon nor I said anything about the widely circulated rumors in Washington that on the night of June 3 he had told the president that it was ten minutes to midnight, time to "dump me," or words to that effect. Instead, when I asked him to carry my message to the president, he looked at me in his comforting "I am there for you" way and took my hand in his. We both knew I was kissing the ring and he appreciated the gesture. He said, "That is not a favor. That is a duty. That is not a favor," he repeated, "and I am happy to do it." He patted my hand and winked as he left. At the time, I found comfort in Vernon's assurance about his "duty," but I never heard back either from him or the president. I learned years later that Vernon's explanation for not passing on the message was simple: it would never happen.

My plaintive request at the Black Caucus Dinner that Vernon broker a peace with the president, knowing all that I knew about Vernon's views and his relationship with the president, reflected both a degree of arrogance and a dose of self-pity. On some level, I enjoyed an inflated view of my own importance. That I still felt uncomfortable was a private sorrow, not a public crisis, yet I wanted to use back channels to the White House so I could feel better personally. Elaine Jones had told me a month earlier I was still mourning. She was right.

I was, at that moment, eager to connect, to get beyond the aching sense of abandonment I was feeling. I remembered the story Vernon had relayed to me early in the spring, when I had met with him for advice and coaching soon after the president had nominated me. Vernon recounted how gracious the president was the first time Zoë Baird returned to Washington, still reeling after "Nannygate." Vernon had invited Zoë Baird to lunch at a fine restaurant, then called the president to let him know where they would be. During lunch, the maître d' rushed over excitedly carrying a telephone. The president was on the line.

"I am so jealous," the voice on the other end began, when Vernon picked up the receiver. "Here I am working and you are having lunch with the beautiful Zoë Baird."

"You could have joined us," Vernon replied. "Would you like to speak with her?" And he handed the phone across the lunch table. He watched closely as his lunch companion sat almost motionless, listening. Her eyes began to water. She started to cry. "She was obviously moved," Vernon said. "That is just the kind of person he is," he assured me.

I realized that Zoë Baird and I had left Washington on very different terms. She had agreed to withdraw to save the president further embarrassment. I had not. Nevertheless, I wanted some closure.

What I was searching for more than anything was a place to land, a solid piece of earth on which to stand with others. I longed to be part of an organized constituency preparing to resist the administration's peace gestures. I had had the experience of being affirmed and connected to a community, and I desperately wanted to retrieve that good feeling. Instead, I found myself by myself, mourning the absence of a popular base or a group of allies organized to exert pressure and support demands. Inside the Beltway, there simply was no organized civil rights constituency behind me or beside me.

Dayna Cunningham, the young black LDF staff lawyer, helped me sort things out. Dayna was always in high gear, criticizing the socializing effects of opportunism and individualism on important black insiders. They had become insiders as a reward for their sepia-bronzed movement résumés. To them, justice for people like me—wrenched from the cusp of the kingdom of insiders—was simply a chore of finding appropriate, personalized rewards. Everything was measured in individual terms as notches on a career belt. "Blacks with their plaques" was how one friend described it. Dayna was adamant. "That's why it was okay that your reputation was destroyed as long as you could still get a six-figure job. Because, after all, what's a reputation if it's not earning power?"

Dayna told me that during my nomination, she fielded many telephone calls. "We were getting calls at LDF from friends inside the Washington establishment who were saying both that they were only concerned about your well-being and that they had heard this going on too long. For your sake, they were calling to suggest that you give up so a deal could be worked out. It was very clear that they were carrying messages directly from the administration. It was so gut-wrenching to hear these people say, 'But what about the president's economic plan? How dare she put her own self-interest above the president's economic plan!' " Dayna continued. "It was astonishing to see how deeply people bought into this . . . the extraordinary individual model of things: 'Don't we have to save the presidency because the president is an extraordinary individual?' And on this level they thought that you considered yourself an extraordinary individual and were putting your career above the president's and his economic plan. That it was you versus him. That's like the talk show material, not national policy.

"I just have to say this as an aside," Dayna had confided. "I didn't understand it. I didn't understand your loyalty throughout this whole thing. Your loyalty to the administration. Your loyalty to the civil rights movement. Us. It was just extraordinary to me." Dayna was a good friend. She was looking out for me as a person. She was also a committed activist who was troubled by the fissures she saw revealed in the civil rights infrastructure.

Dayna told me, "I can see how loyalty was just about all you have to hold on to in a sense. It's one expression of submitting yourself to a larger agenda than your own personal interest. On another level, the emotional weight of that loyalty was just breathtaking. You never struck out and said, 'Screw everybody, I'm just going out to save myself.' You never said, 'I'm not going to play by your rules anymore,' even after it was absolutely clear to you that the rules were being structured to screw you. You never said, even in the conversation with Ricki Seidman, you were still willing to play by their rules. That's not a criticism at all. It's just an astonishing revelation to me that even at that point you still on some level had respect for the process."

The question for Dayna's callers from inside the Beltway was a simple one: What does she want? It was all negotiable. "They misjudged you," Dayna says. "They don't understand anything other than careerism because they are immersed in it. So they cannot distinguish themselves from it. And they could not see you except as they see themselves."

People never got specific with Dayna about what "deal" might be worked out. Except for a brief allusion during my Oval Office meeting with President Clinton, I heard little about any "deal" either until a high administration official came to see me in February 1994, the day before Deval Patrick's nomination as Assistant Attorney General for Civil Rights was announced. This official had called from Washington to arrange a personal meeting. "This is something better said face-to-face," he suggested.

We had lunch in Philadelphia. The government emissary recounted stories of his recent exploits slaying political and legal dragons. He began to pour Perrier into his glass. He assured me that his inside-the-Beltway experience was immensely satisfying. He continued to pour the Perrier into the full glass. Even after he realized that the water had overflowed onto the table, he didn't skip a beat.

The administration flag-bearer was also an old and trusted friend. He interrupted his war stories at one point to ask me whether I had anything I wanted to say to him. I said, "Well, I think my friends let me down." That was all.

During our lunch he never mentioned the reason for his visit. After he paid the check and we were getting ready to leave, he remembered. "Is there anything you want, Lani? Vernon got Zoë Baird a seat on the Foreign Intelligence Advisory Board, which oversees the government's intelligence activities. Is there something you want?" I assured him there was not. He nodded. "I didn't think so, but I had to ask." We parted.

I went back to my office in tears. I had expected something more. On the one hand, I wanted something personal, something more human, something like, "I'm sorry," not, "I can do this for you." On the other hand, I wanted to hear about the policy issues, the lessons learned, the way things were now different, better even. About twenty minutes later I got a telephone call. I picked up the receiver not knowing what to expect. Without any fanfare this same administration official said, "I just wanted to tell you that I was one of those who let you down." I had gotten my apology.

THERE WAS no explanation of the administration's public policy fallout and there was no "deal." As Dayna had said to my "friends" at the time of the nomination, "It's not about a deal. The deal is that this is a matter of principle. That's really the end of the story. I mean—you know, this isn't a concern for Lani and her career."

Despite my "loyalty" to a cause and to the process, as Dayna terms it, I did exude a certain self-righteousnous. As much as I was loyal to the process, I was even more committed to principle. Some, like Vernon Jordan, apparently took my righteousness as a sign of mistaken entitlement—that I confused a privilege to be nominated with a right to serve. Vernon's view that I "had to go" was partly, it would seem, a function of the careerist model in which the nominee mistakes the next credential as a reward. But for me, what may have begun as a reward or a right to serve soon became a right to be heard. It was about a commitment to the idea of fair play—for me personally, I admit, but even more for my clients and the community on whose behalf I had litigated.

I was loyal to the cause of civil rights; I was loyal to the team I was hoping to join, just as I had been loyal to the team that had championed my nomination. I was loyal, but I was not always wise. I somehow convinced myself that I could play the game of insiderdom as an outsider. I, too, thought that individuals could serve two masters and survive, even though one master was weak of will and the other lacked a mobilized constituency. By sheer force of my own will, I would be both lawyer and client.

Starting with the Black Caucus Dinner, and continuing through my lunch in Philadelphia, I was confronted with an unhappy realization. I too occupied the space in those fuzzy borderlands between unaccountable insiders and marginalized outsiders. Occupying that space was disorienting. I discovered that the effects of that disorientation can be a loss of the vision that pushed you into that space to begin with. Even worse, the modern bureaucratic state—and this description applies to state and local government as well as the national government—pushes the forces of change and advocacy into the well-worn channels that characterize "the way things get done." Yet surrender to those bureaucratic impulses for the sake of efficacy, I came to see, risks a substitution of one kind of responsibility for another. Even those like me, devoted to change and reform, find ourselves being torn; the pressure to substitute individual access for community responsibility is ever present and intense.

We aspiring reformers are deeply honorable people. Yet personal integrity alone proved inadequate. Our private inclinations and public commitment to movement traditions were overcome by the world we had recently entered. We isolated ourselves from the people in the movement because we believed we could minister to and protect civil rights interests from within the federal bureaucracy and Washington-based lobbying organizations. We were wrong.

I eventually understood why the strategy my friends, supporters, and defenders undertook ultimately could not succeed. *An inside-the-Beltway operation that failed to connect to our real clients, those people who formed the body of the civil rights movement, could never generate the kind of political pressure that would force the powers in Washington to act.* In our intense focus on getting *me* this job we had turned our backs on the more important constituency of people outside of Washington, many of whom had no jobs at all.

Thirty years after the Voting Rights Act was passed, with strategies for direct action seemingly no longer viable, many of us were seduced into choosing incorporation over transformation. In the aftermath of my nomination, I began to see that decision as both understandable and complex. Progress has in fact been made through anonymous bureaucrats working behind the scenes. Yet in the moments of clarity that I experienced following the Black Caucus Dinner, a clear-headedness that eventually replaced the acute sense of loneliness, I began to understand my silencing as a proxy for the more important silencing of a civil rights struggle.

THINGS GOT CURIOUSER and curiouser. Some of it started even while the nomination was still pending. During the spring of 1993, a small, influential group of former allies had joined the attack. Early patrons of civil rights, some staff members working for these groups used me to give a name and a face to their criticisms and discomfort with the Voting Rights Act and its explicit race consciousness. Exploiting the polarizing instincts of our media culture, they moved quickly to heat up the discussion in the most visible way possible.

On May 5, one week after the nomination was announced, *The New York Times* reported a statement faxed to the paper by the legal director of the American Jewish Congress. The statement, dated May 3, 1993, not only questioned my advocacy of certain positions, but suggested that the American Jewish Congress "shall be forced to oppose [the] confirmation" if I didn't change some of my positions. Simultaneously, the Anti-Defamation League (ADL) mailed a letter to me requesting a meeting to "clarify" my views, and Myrna Sinbaum and Jess N. Hordes of the ADL sent out a press release under the headline: ADL SEEKS CLARIFICATION OF GUINIER'S POSITION ON VOTING RIGHTS. When the ADL wrote me requesting a meeting, they attached a brief they had filed in the Supreme Court opposing the Bush administration's enforcement of the Voting Rights Act. The ADL and the American Jewish Congress refused to join the Leadership Conference when it issued its endorsement of the nomination. A. M. Rosenthal declared in the *Times* that my nomination had caused "grief" and created "shock." I was worse than a "bad after-dinner joke."

The May 3, 1993, statement issued by the American Jewish Congress implied that I advocated proportional representation to promote a politics based solely "along racial lines." One of the directors of American Jewish Congress' commission on law and social action, Marc Stern, accused me of wanting to "purposefully design . . . an election system with campaigns based not on issues or common geographical lines but on race." He also suggested that I believed that "public benefits should be apportioned generally in proportion with racial and ethnic presence in the population." The statement condemned such approaches as "wrong" but never defined its sources. Where had I said this? And if, as I believed, I had never said those words, what *was* the idea that I had been trying to communicate that had so successfully eluded him?

To the staffers drafting these press releases, I was advocating something quite terrifying. But in no way did they understand what I really said. These staffers were unable to distinguish between drawing districts based on race (which I did not propose) and allowing *all* voters, including those for whom race is an important source of political identification, the opportunity to be represented by someone they did choose, someone who gained representation in proportion to the percentage of *actual votes cast* by a group of voters within the electorate. The group need not be a racial group. It was like-minded, not necessarily like-colored, voters. I never could make this distinction stick. Because of White House policy, I was not allowed to respond.

In mid-May one of my neighbors, a Norwegian Catholic who teaches special ed in a Philadelphia public high school, got into an argument about me with a few teachers at his school, several of whom were Jewish. His colleagues couldn't understand, he said, why he defended me. "Why would you like her?" they demanded. "She's a racist. We can tell." Then, one of my friends on my faculty, also in May 1993, alerted me that when he had attended a conference in Texas of a national Jewish organization, the "buzz" there was all about me. The word was out: she is a "racist."

IN THE NATION'S CAPITAL, appearance is everything. Words mean what their most vocal users say they mean, rather than what ordinary people might think. With no organized movement behind me and no presidential leadership in front of me, I quickly became a carefully crafted conservative apparition. I had a shadowy persona; a known name, but an unknown substance. A mask with no person behind it.

In the volatile atmosphere of Washington, its explosive potential fanned by media scrutiny, a few leaders of organized Jewish groups kept up the drumbeat. Although they were ostensibly demanding a high-profile meeting to "ascertain" my views, to see the person behind the mask, their public rush to judgment made the meeting itself an issue. On some level, in a time of growing hostility toward much-needed remedies for past and ongoing racial discrimination, the importance of the civil rights nomination became lost and instead it became a war of positions over a meeting.

The black civil rights leaders, many of them new to their official positions, agonized about the possible fallout from a private meeting with those Jewish groups whose opposition was already made public. Elaine Jones, who had just taken over in February as the first woman director-counsel at the Legal Defense Fund, was concerned that if I did meet with the leaders of the two or three organized Jewish groups who had been the most hostile, the best I could expect was neutrality. If after such a meeting some of them were still opposed, that would be even worse, because the press obviously would find out.

My friends in the D.C.-based civil rights community later showed themselves reluctant to sustain a tangible show of force taking on the White House; they worried it might scare our allies in Congress and maybe even in the foundation world. Now, although asked to deal with a different kind of challenge, their instincts remained the same. They wanted to keep things quiet.

That was impossible. Even if it were convened privately, efforts at genuine conversation would, they suspected, break down in the ensuing media spotlight. They distrusted the motives of the staff in key Jewish organizations who early on violated the first rule of negotiations—a few individuals had gone straight to the press with their criticisms of me rather than attempting any kind of quiet, behind-the-scenes communication. Indeed, on May 3, less than a week after the nomination was announced, and without contacting either me or LDF, a formal statement raising serious questions about my views had been given to *The New York Times*. As Dayna Cunningham later pointed out to me, "There was nothing in these statements that was an invitation to dialogue. This was—as they used to say in the seventies—mau-mauing." This breach of etiquette created a sense of indignation and a skepticism about the ability of other, well-intentioned Jewish leaders to keep an open mind. An agreement with those leaders was reached "to make no further comments to the press," yet the press continued to recycle quotes from earlier remarks that predated the agreement.

The black civil rights leaders were justifiably wary of any dialogue to which the press might be invited. Indeed, later, in July, when the American Jewish Congress invited representatives of LDF to come to a voting rights meeting to talk, LDF sent regrets with the following explanation: "We believe that recent events that have touched on our two organizations respectively counsel that prior to a dialogue such as the one to which you have invited us, it would be appropriate to have a smaller and more private meeting of the leadership of our respective organizations." Whereas the civil rights groups had lost sight of the need for a sustained outsider strategy during and after the nomination battle, they were quite alert to the protocols of insider negotiations. They implicitly remembered the advice Walter Reuther gave President Kennedy when they met, along with other civil rights leaders, on the day of the 1963 March on Washington. "You call a big meeting," said Reuther, "and [if] you haven't got a little group organized that will give it a sense of direction, a little push, nothing will happen."

Perhaps these old friends in the Jewish community went straight to the press because they were unfamiliar with the new generation of leadership who had just taken over two key black organizations, with Elaine Jones at the helm at LDF and Ben Chavis newly installed at the NAACP. There must have been some nervous concern about the old partnerships within the civil rights movement and what the status of our Jewish allies would be in the new regimes. Why else had no one been consulted before statements were released to the press raising "serious questions" about my nomination?

The atmosphere became openly hostile in both camps. One side felt its autonomy was being disrespected. The other side felt its concerns were being ignored. Instead of a meeting, we had an absurd but dramatic misunderstanding.

The problem, however, was not only that I had been misunderstood or that the leaders of these two important factions misunderstood each other. The problem was exacerbated by the rush to public judgment by those who, with little information and even less inclination to check their sources, sought to take advantage of the media's preoccupation with conflict. Instead of a series of informal and quiet meetings, what shaped up was a conspicuously public fight with some of my former colleagues at the NAACP LDF jockeying to be the "macher" or important person who would bring me to a meeting with Jewish leaders.

In politics, I discovered, friendships and alliances are like the Cheshire Cat, with its disquieting, ever present grin. Is it a smirk or a smile of genuine warmth? Does he know something I don't? Or are these alliances more like microwaved food? They heat up quickly, even to the point of boiling, but the taste is often bland and the texture like some barely edible cardboard. In the same way that microwave meals are serviceable, political friendships teach us to value convenience over much else. Like microwaved food, they sometimes assume the shape of the containers in which they are heated. Assuredly, political friendships have their own aesthetic; but such relationships are often more appealing on the package than on the plate.

Washington was as much a microwave oven as it was a Wonderland. Picking a fight or watching one was more important than exploring the nuances or underlying significance of the words being used. Getting something to heat up quickly was the primary object. Positioning was more important than positions. Who you know and how well you know them may represent personal power in Washington, D.C., but these were not necessarily trusting relationships.

The image was laced with irony. My former civil rights colleagues who knew me well were publicly silent; those who might have been allies—but knew me not at all—did not hesitate to speak.

It reminded me of Alice attending the Mad Hatter's tea party, with the Washington media invited to watch. No one would be listening, as "representatives" of various groups simply kept moving around the tea table. Some of the guests would make incomprehensible remarks; others, like the Dormouse, would be asleep; still others, seated at the right wing of the table, would goad everyone on with rude and personal comments. But none would communicate. I could almost imagine the large table, with three or four of the most hostile participants crowded together at one corner crying out: "No room! No room!"

Despite the furor, I had had a good meeting late in May with Senator Howard Metzenbaum, who had then called Abe Foxman of the Anti-Defamation League and said, "You shouldn't be opposing her, you would really like her." Senator Metzenbaum's telephone call could have been a useful bridge had anyone followed up on it.

Ricki Seidman had tried; just the week before she had summoned the White House counsel, Bernie Nussbaum, to her office. Nussbaum had casually suggested then that former Brooklyn congressman Stephen Solarz was seeking an appointment from the administration and might be willing to act as a go-between. But no one in the administration followed up. When we tried again to get Bernie Nussbaum involved, because he had a lot of contacts in the Jewish community, the word came back that the White House was not taking an official position on the growing opposition of some of the organized Jewish groups. No one was managing the White House relationship with the Jewish leadership except a woman I only knew as Sarah Ehrmann, who called periodically to say she was in charge of Jewish relations for the administration and was investigating our options. She clearly knew all the players, but she had no strategy, no plan of action. Although she had apparently spoken with some of the leadership within the Jewish community, she could not describe to me the basis for their growing opposition. She told me, "Oh, I can't deal with that. I am merely the messenger."

Here was yet another failure to assert leadership. The Beltway strategy emphasized that individuals can make a difference. Yet no one in the administration came forward to broker this meeting. Nor was there a single individual outside the administration whom both groups trusted. Instead, each used the telephone to replay and then distort messages from one side to another.

I had expressed this concern to Vernon Jordan when I met with him the same day the American Jewish Congress statement was published by *The New York Times* in early May. The atmosphere in Vernon's office then was cozy; he padded around the plush carpeted floor in stocking feet. His secretary was getting his shoes shined. He didn't hide behind his desk. He sat forward in a strategically placed armchair. He stretched his magnificent frame so he occupied the entire center of his large corner office. From this powerful perch, he reassured me in his deepest, warmest voice, "The president will stand by you. He is your friend. Don't worry. Unless they discover you are importing AK-47s, he will be there for you." Yet the momentum, in my case, was inexorably moving to disprove Vernon's prediction.

Not all Jewish organizations were hostile. The National Council of Jewish Women supported me; so did many of my students. One, Ari Burstein, Class of 1994, national co-president of the Jewish Law Students Association, a surrogate speaker for the Clinton/Gore ticket on Jewish student issues, told *The Jewish Forward* that I was "extremely well-respected among the students" for my "fairness." He said: "She imparts a sense . . . that reasonable people can disagree but it's important to find areas of agreement and build on them." He volunteered to testify that I "always try to find common ground." Sam Rabinove of the American Jewish Committee called LDF to say he was uncomfortable with my writings but was glad not to take a position. He was furious with the American Jewish Congress: "They've thrown down the gauntlet." My uncle, who is Jewish and a prominent supporter of many Jewish organizations, rallied to my defense.

Faculty colleagues, students, associates, many of whom were Jewish, all tried to get their voices heard above the din. It seemed to my supporters, however, that the press had shut down. They had no access to the organs of the free media to communicate to other supporters. The civil rights and women's groups had a press conference that got virtually no coverage. The National Council of Jewish Women endorsed my nomination, but unlike the initial, well-reported opposition of the American Jewish Congress, *The New York Times* was not interested.

Even without sympathetic and in-depth press coverage, there were enough open-minded people that we could have salvaged the debate. Indeed, had we had time to put together a series of meetings, we might have actually learned something important and useful on which we could then have built subsequent collaborations. That had been my experience both personally and as a classroom teacher, when I convened seminar discussions with people from different perspectives who struggled in good faith to give context to our differences. For example, as a result of conversations I had with Susan Sturm, a close friend, co-author, and academic collaborator at Penn, I finally began to understand what may have been animating some of the Jewish staffers. Susan is Jewish. Her father was a Dachau concentration camp survivor who later emigrated to the United States, and then as a soldier in the U.S. Army returned to Germany and to his hometown of Augsburg.

Susan and I struggled together to understand the disconnect and suspicions of the Jewish leadership. Sitting in a car one night outside the train station, Susan first gave a context for why the staffers at these organizations were so threatened by my views, which they assumed, without investigating, to be focused on getting the government involved in race-conscious decision making. She reminded me that the Holocaust, for many Jews, is the paradigmatic example of wanton cruelty and mass murder. Its ultimate meaning is that for many Jews, public recognition of difference will always be used to "justify deliberate exclusion and subordination." If the Holocaust defines the consequences of emphasizing difference, the state cannot be trusted to act benignly in allocating benefits or inflicting harm.

But while the prospect of state-sanctioned brutality is ever present and should not be underestimated, many black people, including my clients, have a different discrimination paradigm in mind when they picture explicit, first-generation racial oppression. Throughout American history, the national government has been the saviour, intervening to protect blacks from wanton cruelty at the hands of private individuals or local authorities. For many of my clients, it has been private discrimination—whether overtly sanctioned by the local authorities or covertly ignored by those in power—that defines their experience. Slavery and its sharecropping aftermath were private economic systems that were politically approved but not politically initiated. Freedom for blacks came only when the federal government intervened over the massive resistance of local and states' righters. Unlike those who legitimately view the Holocaust as the ever present reminder of first-generation cruelty and oppression, progress for many blacks was symbolized by President Lincoln's Emancipation Proclamation, the Supreme Court's *Brown* decision, and Congress' 1965 Voting Rights Act. None of these federal government initiatives was the result of private initiative, local tolerance, or coerced racial silence. They came about because of open, visible political and legal struggle at both the national and local level. Nor did they successfully accomplish all that they set out to do. For blacks, then, government recognition of racial injustice and a government-backed commitment to uproot its legacy completely is just the beginning; but it is a vital beginning.

Susan agreed that the experience of blacks in this country was different in important ways from the experience of Jews in Europe. Our conversations allowed me to understand why I was so misunderstood by others. I had described alternative remedies, such as cumulative voting, that allowed any self-defined minority group to vote strategically to gain representation. I saw these proposals as race-neutral. Women, environmentalists, Republicans in Democratic cities could all benefit from an election system like cumulative voting because it rewarded people who organized and voted strategically based on commonly held ideas or interests. From the perspective of those who abhorred any public distinctions acknowledging racial difference, however, this was seen as enforced ghettoization, not empowerment.

Susan and I helped each other see how the different experiences of blacks and Jews organized their world views around issues of race. We were able to stand side by side as we gazed into the Looking Glass. Our exposure to different perspectives enriched our view, rather than distorting it. But therein lies one of the missed lessons of my nomination—if you are going to have a dialogue, you have to have enough time to meet in person. One meeting would not have been sufficient. It is important to meet over the course of several weeks, to give people the opportunity to reflect, to talk outside the meeting, to become familiar with what each person means, not just what they are saying. In the polarized atmosphere that was created around the nomination, there was no such opportunity for common insights or shared understandings to emerge.

Instead, this quickly had become a fight between a prestigious band of black and Jewish players, each asserting some proprietary interest in the role of civil rights first moralist. Someone needed to assert leadership. Someone with vision, with courage, with faith. I was certain I could win over even the few Jewish leaders who were most adamant, given half a chance and assuming that they, and I, were acting in good faith. But there would have to be several meetings, not just a series of endless negotiations over where, when, and how a single meeting might or might not take place.

I told Peter Edelman in a conversation the weekend following my "dis-appointment" that I saw my experience in a much larger context. Peter had been in charge of the Justice Department transition for the new administration back in December 1992 and had invited me to work on the transition memo for the Civil Rights Division. At the time, I had written an extensive analysis of where the present civil rights agenda was stuck and how we needed to move forward in new, bold, and imaginative ways. I said in that memorandum that civil rights had to become more than special interest pleading. We had to reclaim the moral high ground and spend much more energy explaining to the American people what the stakes were for everyone in talking about and working through our racial problems. The memo concluded with a plea for more public education, for lawyers to advocate in the court of public opinion, not just the court of law.

I had sent a copy of that memorandum together with a letter to President Clinton after I received his thank-you note for hosting the post-inauguration party his law school friends had held on January 23. In my letter to President Clinton, I had proposed setting up a Racial Justice Summit or a Racial Justice Commission.

When I wrote to the president on February 1, before I had even heard from Bernie Nussbaum about a position in the Justice Department, I argued that his was a historic opportunity for courageous leadership. Bill Clinton could lead a national conversation on race:

> ... The party, and conversations in its afterglow, have sparked an idea that I would like to discuss further with you and Hillary. I read in Sunday's *New York Times* that black Americans are more optimistic about the future than at any time since the *Times* started keeping this particular record. I am not surprised. As I mentioned to Hillary, my students were very inspired by the Inauguration, including the fact that one of your first official acts as President was "to hug a black woman." The symbolism of that gesture, as well as many others, clearly is resonating. But, while racial peace is clearly important to you, given the other issues raised in the campaign, I do not suffer the illusion that it is a priority. The economy and health care are both important, and, no doubt currently all-consuming.

> Which brings me to my idea. Why not authorize a National Commission on Racial Justice as a prelude to a Presidential Summit two years from now? As part of its authority to engage in extensive fact-finding, the Commission would be empowered to hold hearings, take testimony, invite scholarly reports, and generally participate in a national conversation on the issue of racism in American society. This could be a combination 25 year reprise of the Kerner Commission and a Presidential Gunnar Myrdal report to respond, in a comprehensive way, to the Los Angeles riots of 1992. The point would be to keep a dialogue going on the subject of race and to develop specific policy recommendations, without crowding your immediate agenda or distracting from other campaign pledges.

> I have suggestions as to who should lead the Commission as well as ideas on its membership and format. . . . If the idea appeals to you, please give me a call or write me a note. I will respond promptly to any Presidential summons.

Thanks again for making the party an historic and personally memorable event. I am confident you are the first American President to venture forth from the White House in order to fraternize with such a racially mixed and diverse group of long term friends and peers.

Best wishes,

Now I came back to that idea in my postmortem with Peter Edelman. I told Peter why we needed to start a national conversation on race, or rather, a series of local conversations on race in which people came together over time to understand and then to work on common or shared problems. This was a chance for ordinary people to show the rest of us how to have a conversation about race—one that is connected to efforts to solve, not just discuss, real problems; one in which people seek to collaborate, not just communicate. I told him in June 1993, "What I'm hoping is that we can have some kind of fact-finding hearing where lots of people get to talk; where there's press coverage; where it doesn't have to be polarizing around the selection of an individual to head the Civil Rights Division, but where it can be a much broader and ongoing discussion about race in America."

In talking with Peter, who still worked for the administration then (but who subsequently lost out on a nomination to the federal appellate court because of his "writings," and then ultimately resigned to protest the president's signing of the so-called Welfare Reform Act), I was thinking that he might try to rationalize what the president did as "passive leadership," that he would defend the president's thoughtful willingness to cut his losses as pragmatic, even sensible. Or he might tell me that the president, through his rhetoric, recommitted himself to the cause of civil rights. He did neither. For Peter and for me, the rhetoric of "We Shall Overcome" was only redeemed by the action to overcome. It was morally redeemed through passive resistance to violence, but not by passive leadership.

Peter and I talked about what happened with some of the Jewish groups; with understatement that bordered on the colossal, Peter admitted there were people who didn't approach this with an open mind. But he reminded me, "You have a lot of friends in the Jewish community as well." To which I answered laughingly, "Well, I know that. I know that. I had some friends in the White House, too."

I FIRST SAW HER when she was almost a city block away, a small, distant figure. It was June 3, four days before my telephone postmortem with Peter. Her thin frame was purposeful; her gait even more determined than my own. Her head held high, her shoulders in a fighting stance, her face seemed frozen. Not a muscle moved above her neck. But despite the obvious stoicism, the overall effect was grand, even larger-than-life.

Unlike myself, who felt captured—even lost—within the enormity of the occasion, this young woman was in charge. Those twenty-foot-high walls almost seemed to part, as if they too sensed the importance of her mission. They too acknowledged the moment's claim.

I had left the Oval Office. An hour earlier I had listened to the president call me antidemocratic on national television and had gone to commiserate with Attorney General Janet Reno. As I stepped out of the Attorney General's office, I steadied myself for that long trek back to the office I was occupying during the nomination period. The ceilings on the fifth floor, with their polished aluminum leaf, seemed even higher than their twenty or so feet. I felt about four inches tall, just like Alice when she first falls down the rabbit hole. My physical stature and my reputation had been diminished in the same direction.

My heels clicked on the well-polished floor, the sound seeming to come from someplace else. I took long steps, determined not to lose my composure in this empty but very public space. I felt as if I were watching myself walk down the hall. I remembered my husband Nolan's admonition: I must not cry.

As that solitary figure continued toward me, the halls of Justice fell still. The only sounds now were the walls breathing in sync with the breaks in her stride. Her legs stretched forward in paradelike fashion.

It was ten o'clock at night on June 3. It had been raining earlier, but I could have been in the middle of a hurricane for all I knew. I still felt intimidated only now I was not afraid. I tried to smile. It was a weak effort, without much energy or enthusiasm. My eyes were wet, my mouth was dry. Smiling was hard, but I tried nevertheless. I wouldn't let myself cry. She came closer. My friend Penda Hair had come to fill up the lonely space.

In the vacuum of leadership surrounding my nomination, I had discovered that a woman I knew primarily as a professional colleague now marched to a different drummer. Penda Hair, a lawyer for the NAACP Legal Defense Fund, a civil rights lawyer, had come to reclaim her friend.

For those who have never met Penda, the first encounter can be deceiving. Her strawberry blond hair, pulled back and cascading over her shoulders, matched by the light softness of her Tennessee accent makes you think of the southern girl next door she undoubtedly was at one point in her life. But beneath that southern girl demeanor is a will of iron, backed by a formidable intellect and commitment to accomplishing the unfinished goals of the civil rights movement.

During the spring of 1993 I stayed with Penda, her husband, and their two small children while awaiting Senate confirmation hearings. In many ways, her reactions are both emblematic and instructive. They are emblematic of the highs and lows that were felt during this ordeal by members of the civil rights community who really believed that it was morning in America again. They are instructive because despite her affection and sympathy for me as a friend, she understood that my experience had a much larger message. My "dis-appointment" was a warning sign, a signal that friends were in charge in Washington, D.C., but that did not mean that the establishment had really changed hands. The people we cared about were still in jeopardy.

Penda had graduated from Harvard Law School, clerked for Supreme Court Justice Harry Blackmun, and was teaching at Columbia Law School when I first met her at the NAACP LDF. She had come to LDF intending to split her time with Columbia. After about two years doing both, she gave up the salary, the prestige, and the privileges of academia for the nitty-gritty, low-paid travails of litigating civil rights cases all over the country. Even when eight months pregnant, Penda was in court.

She did not shy away from the rural back roads of the Arkansas Delta, interviewing witnesses or preparing to cross-examine, in her disarming but determined manner, the defendant's witnesses, including the state's governor, Bill Clinton. Like me, Penda had successfully sued the president.

Litigating that case, Penda found herself spending time in a place where the farms were still called plantations, owned by whites and worked by blacks. According to Penda, "The system hadn't really changed very much since slavery. It had just assumed a different form. It wasn't slavery in the formal sense, but a lot of what happened in slavery was still carried forward in the way people interacted." Time seemed to stand still in eastern Arkansas, a reminder that the civil rights revolution of the sixties had not yet happened there.

Penda Hair was born in Knoxville, Tennessee, in 1954. Both her parents worked—her father as an electrical operator at Oak Ridge Nuclear facility and her mother as a secretary. This was the Bible Belt and her family went to church two or three times a week. Penda's parents, neither of whom had gone to college, very much wanted her to get an education; she would be a schoolteacher because that's what women who went to college could do. Career night in eighth grade, Penda went to hear about two occupations—airline stewardess and lawyer.

Like the rest of the South, Knoxville was segregated. Penda remembers clearly the colored and white bathrooms in places like Woolworth's. In elementary school, she learned about Martin Luther King when her school's safety patrol trip to Washington, D.C., was canceled "because of him." She was taught to view Martin Luther King, Jr., as a "troublemaker."

Segregation infected both the secular and the sacred. In church,

Penda was taught she was supposed to love other people, but that turned out to be a difficult lesson to follow in the tangled web of southern culture. Her mother believed that black people were different and should be separate. "Blacks want to be separate," her mother said. But, at the same time, her parents taught Penda that all people are valuable and deserving of respect. At eight or nine, Penda was directly confronted with the ambiguity of this complex moral lesson.

One hot summer day in Knoxville, the Euclid Avenue Baptist Church was abuzz. A black family had applied to join. Penda's parents wanted her to witness firsthand this important vote. They took her from the young people's class and had her sit in the church balcony so she could observe the congregation. Penda watched without comment as the church majority voted overwhelmingly against admitting the black family. Why would a black person even want to come to their church? Blacks had their own churches.

Some years later, when Penda was fifteen, her youth group raised money, bought a bus, and used the bus to ferry black kids in from the Knoxville projects to Sunday School. They had a full bus every Sunday. Inspired by the evangelical spirit, her group would go out on Saturday and knock on doors and hand out fliers, saying, "Tomorrow morning we will be by at nine o'clock; anybody who wants to ride the bus to church should be ready at nine A.M." And the next day, it seemed perfectly normal that a group of black kids would ride the bus to Penda's church in downtown Knoxville. Her group played basketball with these kids, tutored them after school. After they had established a genuine relationship, some of the parents of the kids approached the church about joining. This time, Penda said, it was a really big issue for her; she now knew enough to have an opinion.

It was 1969: Penda's church voted once again to deny membership to the black families.

Penda was outraged. Her life's work became defending the rights of those her church had excluded. She was an unlikely crusader, but this became her mission, her penance for what her church had done to those children. "It was unbelievable to me what they did to those children, little children, some of them were only five years old." Penda became a zealous civil rights lawyer.

As a litigator, Penda could identify with the victims of discrimination; after all, she had grown up on the mother's milk of racism. The first case she worked on when she came to LDF was a case against the Post Office in Jacksonville, Florida. Coming from the South, she quickly grew to understand what the legacy of discrimination really means. She could see how many more opportunities she had had as the daughter of a blue-collar worker than the children of black families where the parents had an even better education. She could see the difference in the educational system that the black children had compared to her training at the white schools in Knoxville.

Penda's father had come back from the war with no high school education; he got a job at Oak Ridge Nuclear Facility. It was a nice, unionized, blue-collar job and his family lived a very nice, middle-class lifestyle. The people Penda met at the Jacksonville Post Office had college degrees, were roughly the same age as her father, and yet they were working in the lowest-paying and most taxing jobs of carrying the heavy mail. They were not called "mail carriers" because they did not deliver mail; they were "mail handlers," because they handled the big, heavy bags.

To Penda, this was not fair. "When these black men came back from the war, they went to college, mostly to black colleges because those were the only ones open to them, and the best jobs that they could get were the mail handler jobs. Those were the black people who were lucky because they actually got a job that had some federal benefits to it." As Penda explained her deepening sense of injustice, "I thought they had been wronged. They *had* been wronged."

At LDF, Penda and I litigated many civil rights cases together on behalf of clients who "had been wronged." Clients who could not even apply for a job, much less defend their claim on one. Evangeline K. Brown, eighty-seven, one of Penda's clients, had testified in an LDF voting case in the 1980s. Evangeline Brown stated that she and other black residents felt intimidated in their basic exercise of the franchise. Like many black people in eastern Arkansas, Penda's clients lived in something that called itself a democracy, but it was not fully participatory.

Evangeline Brown explained, "We have a state representative named Gibson, a circuit judge named Gibson, a municipal judge named Gibson, a prosecutor named Gibson, and city attorney named Gibson. I think the Gibsons think we all ought to be back working on their farms." Ms. Brown was not surprised when she was told that the Gibsons were now challenging the voting changes Penda and our colleague Dayna Cunningham had negotiated to open up the political process. "It's the same old plantation mentality," she said.

Ms. Brown lived in Dermott, Arkansas, where 85 percent of the 7,500 residents are black, yet in 1990 they still could not elect a black judge. The judge, Don Glover, finally won in 1992, as a result of an LDF consent decree. The consent decree created a few judicial subdistricts in which the majority of voters were black. Mr. Glover ran in one of them and won, with 60 percent of the vote. "I attribute my win," the fifty-three-year-old judge said later in an interview, "to hard work and the consent decree, which leveled the playing field."

When LDF filed voting rights cases to open up the electoral process in Arkansas, Penda observed, "some members of the white community seemed to feel the whole system was at risk." Prominent white members of the local Dermott establishment, for example, said the problem for blacks and whites was not the election system. The problem was the civil rights lawyers. The old system worked just fine before the black voters challenged it, claimed people like Charles Sidney Gibson, the city attorney in Dermott and chairman of the Chicot County Democratic Party, and his cousin Bynum Gibson, the chairman of the state Democratic Party. Everyone could vote. Everything was fair. "The fact that a black judge *came close to winning* [in 1990] proves that," they argued.

As Penda later told me: "If African Americans organized and could fully exercise their political power, it would break the lock of white dominance in the community. This was very threatening." What was threatening was the challenge by Penda and her clients to become a real democracy.

It was Penda's steadfast belief that the Department of Justice should be the natural ally of her clients, rather than the enemy it had been for the previous twelve years that led her never to waver in support of my nomination. She was convinced that the fight over the nomination was as much a fight over the beliefs that motivated her life as it was over the fate of a friend. I also am confident the one thing that would have caused her to question her commitment to the fight would have been evidence from me that the issue was personal, and not the principle.

On May 11, thirteen days after I had been introduced by the president of the United States as the Civil Rights Division designate, Penda drove me to the Justice Department. I had been commuting to the department from Philadelphia on the train, but now it was obvious I needed to spend more time in D.C. than those daily roundtrip rides allowed. We came in through the auto entrance on Ninth Street to retrieve my suitcase and the other belongings I had brought for my sojourn at Penda's house. As the car bumped over the cobblestones in the inner courtyard, each bump seemed to magnify Penda's happiness at being welcomed in the Department of Justice after twelve years of exile. The people Congress once cared about would again have a voice. The bust of Robert Kennedy that stands in the courtyard would no longer have to stand mute witness to the dismantling of his brother's legacy and that of his brother's successor.

Penda accompanied me into the Justice Department building to pick up the suitcase I had left in my "new" office. As we went up to the fifth floor, I pointed out the depression-era murals on the hallway walls and remarked how they had captured a period in American life when, though the present was bleak, the future seemed limitless. That was a heroic time in American life, whose symbolism seemed current but whose reality was as dated as the social realist style in which they were painted. Then Penda and I returned to the empty courtyard, quietly absorbing its majesty and dignity. Penda's reaction was one of elation, unlike the edgy uncertainty I was already feeling.

Penda's fighting spirit never wavered, but soon she was no longer rejoicing. Four weeks later, the president of the United States told the world he could not fight this battle on a ground he could not defend. Once again Penda Hair was back in the Justice Department, walking through its empty halls. She had witnessed the president's withdrawal statement on television and had arrived to rescue me. This time, she had come to retrieve me—not just my suitcases. She held me, tightening her grip to make sure I remained upright. "Get your things right now," she commanded softly. "I'm taking you home."

Penda's presence was a tonic. I could see myself through Penda's eyes—like her civil rights clients in the deep South, I had been wronged. I was deeply, intensely wounded. But Penda's presence distracted me from my own tears. I could see her eyes were red, her skin even whiter than usual. Under some other circumstance, she might have lost composure. But here, in the halls of Justice, her presence was like a siren song.

It was not until the next morning that Penda cried. At 6:00 A.M. on the morning of June 4, we were settled in the deep leather comfort of the back seat of a black limousine, taking us to my first televised interview of the day. The NBC driver had come to fetch us in a style to which, as civil rights lawyers, we were very much unaccustomed. Perhaps it was the hour of the morning. Perhaps it was the dramatic contrast between the indignity of the night before and the trappings of the day after. Perhaps it was just time.

The tears came. Penda tried to talk through her sobs. I remained solemn. After all, in a very few minutes I would have to present myself in a sound bite as someone who was not an "antidemocratic" Quota Queen. After that I would hold my first solo press conference before national and world media. I had yet to write a press statement. I was distracted by the task at hand. I was still not nervous, only preoccupied. I was talking, but to myself. Penda insisted on talking aloud, despite the pain in her voice. "Lani, you are now in a position to lead," she said. "Now, you will be heard."

Penda had been keeping a stack of media clippings about my nomination. There were actually two stacks on a white, waist-high bookshelf. The negative pile was overflowing. Its very mass overwhelmed the so-called positive stack. At one point, Penda had only two clippings in the positive pile. I could see Penda starting to imagine the ways in which the positive stack might finally now grow. She paused, as if to reflect on the potential. She folded her hands in her lap. But then she continued speaking. "It is a burden, Lani, that you will shoulder." Suddenly, she laughed. Almost chuckling, she said, "I for one am happy that you have been chosen." She became sad again. "Lani," she whispered, "Your people need you. So does America."

I could not feel sorry for myself. I would not last long as a victim. As Roger Wilkins reminded me, "Americans don't like victims." I had to be a survivor, in the great American tradition of dusting oneself off, then moving forward. Nor could I be angry. Black people are not allowed to be angry in public. My legitimate anger would not be seen as such; it would simply confirm the original stereotype. If I was to break out of type, if I was to speak in my own voice and be heard, I needed to speak differently. All that Penda helped me to understand.

I remember feeling an inner calm descend as I worked with Penda to prepare my press statement. The words came easily. Finally I was getting a chance to fight back against the image others had carved out for me. This was a familiar role, one that I knew from having defended others in the past. I was still feeling unsettled, but suddenly, I was no longer shadow-boxing someone else's image of me. For the first time in months, I was given permission to have ideas and defend them simultaneously.

In the Justice Department press briefing room, I remembered my mother's advice: "Stand above the situation." Perhaps this is something Jewish mothers often teach their daughters. Years later I learned from a *New York Times* profile that Supreme Court justice Ruth Bader Ginsburg's mother had passed on to her very similar advice. In her mother's message I heard my own mother's voice: "Anger, resentment, indulgence in recriminations waste time and sap energy."

Heeding my mother's advice, I tried to be gracious, even as I asserted that the president had grossly misread my articles. "Although the President and I disagree about his decision to withdraw my nomination, I continue to respect the President. He believes in racial healing and so do I." I asked the American people to learn "some positive lessons" from my ordeal—"lessons about the importance of public dialogue on race in which no one viewpoint monopolizes, distorts, caricatures or shapes the outcome."

I had been humbled by the president. I felt humiliated by the president, my friend, not just because he had buckled in the face of pressure but because he justified his action by mischaracterizing who I am and what I have stood for. I had been comforted from across a desk filled with neatly arranged piles of paper, by someone I had known just briefly—the Attorney General, a woman who told me she believed in losing on principle over winning on tactics. I was saved by someone who would only cry when she thought we were alone. From that day forward, Penda never let me forget my mother's advice or Roger Wilkins's important admonition: I was now a woman with a cause, not a grievance.

Penda Hair also reminded me that it was not ties of blood that would liberate me. It was bonds formed in close pursuit of common interests. I, a child of Queens, the daughter of a black West Indian father and a Jewish mother from the Bronx, shared the bonds of community with a white Baptist woman from Knoxville, Tennessee.

Penda Hair, that strawberry blond from Tennessee, saved me on the night of June 3, 1993, and many times thereafter. She pushed me always to link up to our community—past, present, and future. By reconnecting me to the civil rights movement I once felt a part of, Penda Hair rescued me from the Washington rabbit hole and restored my sense of purpose and belonging.

From my moment of profound loneliness in the immediate aftermath of the withdrawal of my nomination, I retrieved this important lesson: my redemption would not come in Washington and it would not come if I remained either isolated or quiet. If I had to reinvent myself, it would be outside Wonderland.

In crisis there is opportunity. Leadership would mean seeing the opportunity and taking it, not dwelling on the minor unchangeables in the drama but taking advantage of the new opening that had not existed, not really, before. This action would not be at the level of the "inside game." To have the community act it must know what deals were being made in its name. They have to hear to be at the table. A quiet inside game, while useful, shut them out.

I had to make our case beyond Washington, not just on my own behalf but on behalf of others. I had to reconnect to the people on whose behalf I had sought the nomination in the first place. It was a painful awakening, but it brought me back to Martin Luther King's original truth. It is the people themselves who must "take hold of the laws and transform them into effective mandates." Only when people are organized to back up demands of their representatives can we meaningfully speak truth to power.

Bridges

CHAPTER SIX

The Bridge Toward Freedom: Fighting for a Vote

WHEN HOWARD PASTER, President Clinton's legislative liaison with Congress, confronted me with the news that "we don't have the votes," I was not particularly alarmed. After all, the history of the civil rights movement in general and the Voting Rights Act in particular was a struggle to *get* the votes. Civil rights was always controversial, and we never started a fight for justice with enough votes. We never abandoned a just cause simply because we did not have the votes. Indeed, one of the movement's most enduring battles, the one with which I was most closely associated, was the fight for the right to vote itself. But the right to vote was fundamentally about the right to participate and be heard, to give voice to a moral vision and a progressive agenda that would benefit everyone. It was never a plea, even when it was ostensibly about voting rights, just for votes.

Yet, as Penda Hair reminded me, few Americans knew, much less understood, the civil movement, its amazing struggles or its present challenges. Some of us were taught, as she was, that Martin Luther King was simply a "troublemaker." Others were schooled to believe that the issue of civil rights was a thing of the past. We had overcome, after all. Rosa Parks no longer had to sit at the back of the bus, whites and blacks could now drink from the same water fountains, and Dr. Martin Luther King had dreamed in a famous speech on the steps of the Lincoln Memorial.

As far as many Americans could tell, Congress passed and President Johnson signed the Civil Rights Act of 1964 and the Voting Rights Act of 1965 because it was the right thing to do, not because they were dragged kicking and screaming by a mass national movement to guarantee civil rights for all. For most Americans, unfortunately, those events are now just the stuff of history and the reason for national holidays and memorial services. Few realized what Penda and her clients knew all too well—that to awaken the national conscience and to create a national will to right present wrongs, the movement had had to fight to get the vote. Even more, it still had to fight for a hearing so its story could be told.

But that fight for justice had never been successfully waged in Washington alone. Chris Gates, head of the National Civil League in Denver, captured the need for connecting up to local initiatives when he recently noted, "If you study the history of social movement in the United States, the clear lesson you learn is that change doesn't occur in Washington. Change is codified in Washington." Nor could it be a fight just among articulate elites. The success of the civil rights movement depended on ordinary people speaking words with their feet. Or, as Dr. King had once observed, because blacks had such limited access to "television, publications and broad forums," the movement wrote its "most persuasive essays with the blunt pen of marching ranks."

Knowing this history, Penda reminded me that I, too, had to continue to argue for a voice—not just for myself but for the cause of racial justice. I now had an opportunity to share with others the stories of our civil rights clients, so that more Americans could understand why it was still necessary to fight for a hearing and votes that matter.

By telling this story, we could create our own hearing—a hearing we deserved because America deserved to hear the truth about the larger democratic vision, shared by many within the civil rights community, that was the foundation for my much-maligned law review articles. Our stories could also remind others of the need for an honest and forthright discussion of what years of civil rights backtracking had meant for the real people that Congress had intended to protect and empower with the laws it passed in the 1960s. We would not get past the racial polarization that had been fueled by the actions of politicians and others as long as we were afraid of speaking directly to the continuing problems that our racial history creates for the civic life of our country.

Even more, our stories could be the impetus for a conversation, a conversation about race to be sure, but not just about race. Our stories could form the narrative structure for a much-needed conversation about justice. The people I represented wrote this dramatic narrative as much with their own blood as with sweat or ink.

THIRTY YEARS AGO, when I was still in high school, the Voting Rights Act was merely a gleam in the eyes of J. L. Chestnut, then the only black lawyer practicing in Selma, Alabama. Acting on behalf of the Dallas County Voters League, Chestnut sought Martin Luther King's help. During the summer of 1964, Chestnut drove to Atlanta, to the

Southern Christian Leadership Council (SCLC)'s headquarters, to convince Dr. King to come to Selma and assist their local efforts to gain the vote for blacks.

Dr. King was no stranger to Selma; he had already visited several times to give a boost to the local voter registration campaign initiated there by Mrs. Amelia Boynton. Just a year prior to attorney Chestnut's journey, forty elderly black women were locked out of a rest home for protesting when one of them had been beaten in a voter registration line. Mrs. Boynton had then turned to Dr. King for financial help. She asked for money to purchase a sewing machine so that some of the women could find work in private homes. Now Chestnut and the activist community were asking for more than money. They were inviting Dr. King and SCLC to come to Selma to help them sustain a mass movement around a century-old problem of the suppression of the black vote. "Well, what the hell," Chestnut reasoned. "We've been meeting for years and only one hundred fifty black people are registered. What kind of a Voters League doesn't have any voters, anyway?"

Selma is in Dallas County, the heart of the Black Belt, so called because of its rich dark soil. But it was no accident that Dallas County, as well as the surrounding counties, was also majority black; the region was an agricultural society, which a hundred years before had been heavily dependent on slave labor. Though the Black Belt had a black voting majority, Dallas County had only a few registered black voters, and Lowndes County, just a fifteen-minute drive to the south, had no blacks registered to vote at all, although four out of five of the county's citizens were black.

For much of the twentieth century, the majority of the Black Belt counties' people were black, poor, and de facto disenfranchised. The Fourteenth Amendment had ostensibly given black men the franchise in 1870 (black women did not gain the ballot until 1920, with the passage of the Nineteenth Amendment), yet very few blacks could register, much less vote, throughout the South. With the official beginning of the "Redemption" of the South from Reconstructionists in 1876, blacks were denied the franchise by legal and illegal means— most notoriously terrorism by the infant Ku Klux Klan, the Knights of the White Camellia, and the Red Shirts. Redeemers used more long-lived, legal subterfuge as well, such as grandfather clauses and literacy tests. Indeed, the Alabama Constitution of 1901, for example, disenfranchised virtually all blacks, and many poor whites, through such mechanisms. In 1900, there were 9,871 black voters in Dallas County and 181,471 in all of Alabama. After the Alabama Constitution was enacted with its disenfranchising provisions, 52 black voters were left in Selma, the county seat of Dallas County, and 3,654 in the state.

In 1964, the summer that J. L. Chestnut drove from Selma to

Atlanta, blacks still could not register or vote. Whites controlled all ten county commissions, eleven boards of education, and about thirty-four towns, despite the black population majority. The Southern Organizing Committee for Social and Economic Justice described the way white politicians exploited poverty and fear in the Black Belt:

> The Black Belt has long served Alabama's demagogues as the South had often served our nation's misleaders: as a reservoir of enforced poverty, racism and oppression to be drawn upon at the will of politicians of great skill and little conscience. In many ways, geographically, politically, and economically, the Black Belt has been the South's "South."

In 1964, Albert Turner, the Alabama coordinator for SCLC, was living in Perry County, about twenty miles from Selma. Growing up on a farm amid grinding poverty, Albert Turner knew that white politicians wielded terrifyingly real, not just dramatically symbolic, power over black folk.

> You didn't go to the courthouse for nothing when you was black when I was a child, they just didn't let you in. You could go in there and pay your taxes, but that's all. You couldn't use the rest rooms or nothing in the courthouse then. The sheriff was *the* power. I mean, he was everything. Whatever he said, when you got arrested, that was it. There were no black lawyers. I mean, Chestnut probably was the first black man lawyer in this area and he was not there all the time. All of the judges was white. . . . It's hard to believe when you try to think about what it was like and this was in the sixties. When I started trying to get the right to vote in 'sixty-two, there hadn't been a black person in this whole area for ten years who had gotten registered to vote. There was not a black registered voter from 1955 to 1965 in Perry County. You just did not register.

When J. L. Chestnut and the Dallas County Voters League invited King and SCLC to Albert Turner's Alabama, they were not simply soliciting King to preach at a church, to send money, or to swoop in and out with the national press corps in tow to spotlight the reign of terror under which people like Albert Turner lived. White violence against blacks, by itself, was not enough to spark change. After all, blacks had been killed over the years for trying to vote or even register. Blacks routinely had close encounters with the raw power of local sheriffs like Dallas County sheriff Jim Clark, and there was no response from respectable members of the white community. What was needed was an organized movement response that made the injustice visible *and* unconscionable.

They needed more than just a leader who would help transmit the experience of local people to the rest of the nation. The idea was to have local activists organize daytime and even riskier night vigils outside the local courthouses to focus attention on the way symbols of justice were manipulated directly to exclude blacks. If Dr. King then participated in these demonstrations and mass meetings, that would shore up local support and assure the attention of journalists, especially if something visually dramatic occurred. By organizing the local community, they were also building a movement that would back up their leader's demands and be there after the leader left. They wanted to galvanize the national conscience, provoke federal intervention, and then have people in place to carry forward whatever the federal authorities might initiate.

The SCLC leadership learned these lessons gradually, beginning the year before Chestnut's trip to Atlanta when the federal authorities failed to react decisively to the brutal bombing of the Sixteenth Street Baptist Church in Birmingham, sixty miles from Selma. The blast ripped through the building in September 1963, killing four young black girls who were attending Sunday School. The night that Dr. King eulogized three of the four victims of the Birmingham church bombing, Diane Nash, a young civil rights organizer committed to nonviolence, was nevertheless consumed with desire for retaliation. The best revenge, Nash and other organizers finally decided, was to force the national government to act. Only the national government could stop the white southern terrorists, who operated in Alabama with the implicit sanction of both private and public authority.

In the wake of the church bombing, Nash and other local activists realized they had no choice but to focus on winning national legislation to enforce the right to vote, so that blacks and sympathetic whites could drive out the politicians whose rhetoric and personal animus made criminal acts like the church bombing not only possible but probable. Either they would "solve the crime and kill the bombers," writes Taylor Branch in *Parting the Waters*, or they would run out of office the segregationist politicians whose rhetoric and message lent implicit encouragement to the gruesome acts of the Birmingham terrorists. King, they urged, should command a local army of voting rights activists who would descend on Montgomery, the state capital. Nash's plan was to surround Governor George Wallace's government in Montgomery with "a sea of bodies, severing communication from [the] state capitol building. . . . Lying on railroad tracks, runways, and bus driveways."

Initially, Nash's plan to mobilize dramatically around the right to vote left King unimpressed. He did not take the idea seriously. At the time, in September 1963, King refused even to convene a special strategy session. Instead, he sought help by reaching out directly to the politicians in Washington. King left Diane Nash and other young activists in Alabama while he went to the capital to plead for federal assistance. His plea for aid, however, was not supported by an independent plan for action, such as a march or demonstrations toward specific demands. The Kennedy administration, forewarned by federal officials that King was arriving empty-handed, took advantage of King's failure to link his trip with organized reinforcements or publicly mobilized protesters.

Kennedy quickly dashed King's hopes for an aggressive federal response. Minutes before King arrived at the White House, the White House press secretary announced their very modest proposal: President Kennedy had appointed two personal emissaries to mediate the racial crisis in Birmingham: former Army Secretary Kenneth Royall and former West Point football coach Earl Blaik. By timing its public response to precede King's meeting with President Kennedy, the administration undermined any claim that King had influenced even this token gesture.

Unaccompanied by grass-roots protests or the threats of disruption that Diane Nash had in mind, King's options and his effectiveness were limited. He soon realized his mistake. A second round of empty meetings in Washington cemented King's decision to make Nash's plan the germ of a Selma-based campaign in 1965. In his memoir *An Easy Burden*, Andrew Young tells the story of two eye-opening back-to-back sessions in Washington, D.C., in December 1964, after Dr. King returned from Oslo and the Nobel Peace Prize ceremony. Received like royalty across Europe, only the private plane that New York governor Nelson Rockefeller offered to fly Dr. King and Andy Young to Washington suggested any elevation in their status back in the United States. King and Young arrived without fanfare at the Justice Department to meet with Attorney General Nicholas Katzenbach and Vice President Hubert Humphrey. His cause now endowed with worldwide prestige, King broached the subject of a voter rights bill.

King and Young had an agenda. They wanted to push the Johnson administration to pass a Voting Rights Act in 1965. The meeting was cordial enough, but the administration was unresponsive. "I'm sure we can't get a voting rights bill, not in 1965," Humphrey pleaded. "We passed the civil rights bill only a few months ago. It's too soon." Vice President Humphrey's message was simple: Back off. We don't have the votes. It was the same message delivered to me by Howard Paster, working for a different Democratic administration almost thirty years later: we don't have the votes.

After they talked with Humphrey for about an hour, Lyndon Johnson summoned them to the White House. King once again pressed forward, telling the president that they "desperately needed a voting rights act, and as soon as possible." King's pleas fell on deaf ears. President Johnson spent the entire session talking about what he was already doing, not deigning even to recognize the possibility that more needed to be done. As they left the White House, King remarked to Andy Young, "Kennedy asked questions for an hour; Johnson talks for an hour. That's the difference between them." The bottom line, King realized, was that whether they asked questions or talked, both presidents were cautious when it came to civil rights. Neither was prepared, on his own, to initiate bold new legislation.

By late December, after his uneventful meetings with both President Johnson and Vice President Humphrey, King decided that he would come to Selma on the first of the year. There, in Selma, King joined people already in motion. Younger activists had already begun to implement a version of the Nash plan themselves, supporting Mrs. Boynton and others in the area with locally based insurgency. The Student Nonviolent Coordinating Committee (SNCC), a group of college students formed in the wake of the first Greensboro Woolworth sit-ins, sent three organizers to press for voter registration, using Mrs. Boynton's office as their headquarters. Bernard Lafayette, a slender, self-confident young minister, recruited local teenagers to join SNCC's crusade. John Lewis, one of Lafayette's SNCC colleagues (now a congressman from Atlanta), was soon arrested for carrying a ONE MAN/ONE VOTE sign outside the Dallas County courthouse. Civil rights activists like Lafayette and Lewis were the seminal political campaign workers, with their unbounded enthusiasm for face-to-face persuasion. They followed an activist model of continuous political campaigning and community education. They organized "citizenship schools," conducted by people from the community who could read and write. As Dr. King acknowledged, they tried to make every barber shop a school.

David Garrow, in his comprehensive study, *Protest at Selma: Martin Luther King, Jr. and the Voting Rights Act of 1965*, argues that Selma was chosen because of its dramatic potential—a confrontation there was almost assured, and with it a national audience. J. L. Chestnut and others who wanted King to use Selma as the "hub" of a nationally credible, locally grounded voting rights campaign had a strong argument in the intemperate and volatile Dallas County sheriff, Jim Clark. Sheriff Clark was sure to provide the necessary dramatic symbol.

Sheriff Clark did not disappoint. Sheriff Clark made sure that King and several thousand demonstrators were soon arrested. When King was jailed early in February 1965 for parading without a permit and unlawful assembly, he wrote a letter to *The New York Times*: ". . . This is Selma, Alabama. There are more Negroes in jail with me than there are on the voting rolls." King again met with President Johnson to discuss voting rights legislation soon after he was released from jail.

But it was not King's visits to Washington or his meetings with Justice Department officials that finally convinced the president to introduce voting rights legislation. Nor did the defiant and wanton violence of Sheriff Jim Clark, alone, force President Johnson's hand. President Johnson finally acted when Alabama citizens, inspired by the activism and leadership of young local teenagers, put their lives on the line and in broad daylight marched across the Edmund Pettus Bridge. Johnson later admitted that they passed the 1965 Voting Rights Act on a bridge on March 7, 1965, heading from Selma to Montgomery. The dramatic high point of the Selma campaign came when ordinary people did extraordinary things.

It was a Sunday when, in full view of the television cameras, Alabama state troopers and white civilian volunteers deputized by Dallas County sheriff Jim Clark attacked with tear gas and clubs an unarmed group of blacks, including Mrs. Amelia Boynton and Perry County civil rights organizer Albert Turner. The group of people, which included children and senior citizens, was quietly marching across the Edmund Pettus Bridge en route to Montgomery, the state capital, to assert their right to vote. The idea for the march came on the heels of Jimmie Lee Jackson's murder in neighboring Perry County two weeks earlier. Jackson, a twenty-seven-year-old black pulpwood cutter, had been shot in the stomach by state troopers on February 18, after he tried to protect his mother from the clubs of troopers breaking up a night registration vigil. When Jackson died a few days later, Albert Turner and other young turks in Perry County threatened to take Jimmie Lee Jackson's coffin to Montgomery and present it to Governor George Wallace. At Jackson's funeral, J. L. Chestnut remembers people saying, "Goddamn it, we ought to carry his body over to George Wallace in Montgomery." These angry sentiments soon evolved into a plan to walk to Montgomery to petition Wallace for the right to vote.

As the marchers approached the bridge on March 7, the troopers sounded a "two-minute" warning. Then, without waiting more than a few seconds, they attacked. A state trooper's club hit Mrs. Boynton on the back of the neck and she fell to the ground. While she was regaining consciousness, she heard someone ordering her to get up and run or she would be tear-gassed. Former U.S. senator Harris Wofford, who came to Selma to join a subsequent march, describes Mrs. Boynton's eyewitness account of what came to be known as "Bloody Sunday": "Then the tear gas can was dropped next to her head. To a mounted posse, Sheriff Clark shouted, 'Get those goddamn niggers! Get those goddamn white niggers!' and the horsemen charged with bullwhips. 'Deputies' using the electric cattle prods, chased the marchers still on their feet all the way back to Brown's Chapel." Films of the event resembled a battle scene, with bombs, smoke, and mass chaos. There was widespread public concern after video clips were shown on national television, interrupting an ABC Sunday night special, *Judgment at Nuremberg.*

Yet for the White House and its occupant, it was still not clear what to do. Although Lyndon Johnson believed in civil rights, he dreaded being drawn into a showdown between federal and state authority. The scene in Selma represented a real threat to federal/state relations. On the other hand, it also presented opportunities for President Johnson to further the civil rights revolution in his native South. He now had the moral support and organized reinforcements he lacked when he met privately with Dr. King in December 1964.

Johnson, however, remained confused and somewhat hostile. Roger Wilkins, then assistant director of the Community Relations Service, remembers how angry President Johnson was at all the demonstrations that seemed to erupt spontaneously in response to the atrocious thing they had seen on the Edmund Pettus Bridge. Roger had been attending a conference at Michigan State University when he turned on the television that Sunday evening to see John Lewis and others getting beat up on the Edmund Pettus Bridge. He flew back to his office immediately and found the people who worked at the Justice Department deeply moved. All over the country, it was the same story. "The country just rose up in arms," Roger explained. Many of these protests were held in front of federal institutions.

Roger's uncle, Roy Wilkins, then head of the NAACP, was one of the national leaders whom President Johnson immediately summoned to the White House. Why are they demonstrating against me? Johnson demanded when he met the next day in the Cabinet Room with Roy Wilkins and other civil rights leaders. "I've passed all these civil rights bills. I've made speeches. I drafted an executive order." Why aren't they more grateful? Johnson seemed to ask. What more do they want from me? Johnson's subtext was clear. He was their protector. He was not the one who beat the marchers.

The U.S. government was floundering, Roger thought.

MEANWHILE, so was Martin Luther King. Dr. King had to continue the momentum established in the aftermath of Bloody Sunday without alienating one of his few local white allies. On March 7, King had been in Atlanta giving a sermon, and missed Bloody Sunday. His absence led more militant and younger organizers to challenge his political credibility. These younger civil rights activists were determined to follow up the march that had been aborted on Bloody Sunday. In part to reassert his leadership, King agreed to lead a second march the following Tuesday, March 9, but to do so would mean violating a federal court injunction.

Judge Frank Johnson, a usually sympathetic federal judge based in Montgomery, had surprised the lawyers. This time he had denied the NAACP LDF's motion for an injunction prohibiting Governor Wallace from interfering with the follow-up procession planned for Tuesday, March 9. As Jack Greenberg writes in *Crusaders in the Courts*, his book about the organization's role in the civil rights movement:

> Martin faced a terrible dilemma. If he disobeyed, [Judge Frank] Johnson would send him to jail. Moreover, Johnson had often ultimately upheld us, and as a consequence suffered ostracism, vilification and death threats. To flout his order might alienate him and cost us dearly in the future; I was sure that he would give us an injunction after a full hearing. On the other hand, if Martin did not march, he might be seen as a man who had been absent when John Lewis and Hosea Williams [another civil rights activist] risked death and was now buckling in the face of a white establishment court order.

Sometime during the evening of March 8, Jack Greenberg was on a conference call with Dr. King and Attorney General Nicholas Katzenbach, who was urging King to obey the court order. Greenberg told King what he had learned from an LDF cooperating attorney, Fred Gray—that Judge Johnson would put King "under the jail" if he defied the court order and went ahead the next day with a march to Montgomery. But Greenberg, acting as King's lawyer, did not tell King not to march. "As with other advice, I felt he had to make his decision knowing the legal situation as fully as I could explain it."

That Tuesday, with Judge Johnson's injunction still in effect, King staged a symbolic march, leading fifteen hundred people to the Edmund Pettus Bridge, where they kneeled in prayer and then turned around. According to Greenberg, "Martin had hit upon a brilliant solution, for while it puzzled both followers and opponents who had not expected the march to halt in the prayer, it focused world attention on Selma, avoided violence and did not defy [Judge] Johnson's injunction." King then cooperated with LDF lawyers to get Judge Johnson to lift the injunction.

Meanwhile, no one marched. But in Lowndes County, 80 percent black and just to the south of Selma, something profound was already happening. Lowndes County was the home of Thomas L. Coleman, "the good old boy," a June 1997 *New York Times* obituary would later read, "who killed an unarmed civil rights worker, then won a jury acquittal" before an all-white jury. "Nobody was much surprised," the obituary concluded thirty-two years later, even though Mr. Coleman, an unpaid special deputy sheriff with a pistol at his side and a twelve-gauge shotgun in his arms, murdered Jonathan Myrick Daniels, an Episcopal seminarian from Keene, New Hampshire, in cold blood in broad daylight, as Daniels and other civil rights workers tried to enter a small store to buy sodas. After all, black people, who outnumbered the white people of

Lowndes County by four to one, were kept in line by constant intimidation.

Yet, a week after Bloody Sunday, the first blacks ever were registered. On March 15, the all-white Lowndes County board announced it had started processing two blacks.

ALTHOUGH A REVOLUTION was taking place in Lowndes County, Alabama, President Johnson's course of action was still not settled. The president remained uncertain even after a white Unitarian minister who had traveled to Selma to support the demonstrators was clubbed to death leaving a local restaurant. Late that same week, the president called a meeting of the Council on Civil Rights, chaired by Vice President Humphrey and attended by Secretary of Labor Willard Wirtz, Attorney General Nicholas Katzenbach, and many other high-ranking federal officials, including Roger Wilkins, who was directing a special project for the vice president. Everyone at the meeting was solemn, very solemn. Seated at the head of a big rectangular table in the Indian Treaty Room, the vice president called the meeting to order. He spoke of his concern, shared by the president, that these demonstrations in Selma might be the work of outside agitators, maybe, Roger heard him say, even some Communists. "The President wants your advice," Humphrey announced. "I want to go around the room and have each of you tell us what you think the United States Government should do. I want you to be very candid and I will convey your advice to the President."

Secretary of Labor Wirtz was the first person to speak. Seated at the vice president's left, Wirtz was not intimidated by talk of outside agitators: "We should stop fooling around," he declared. "We should send up a Voting Rights bill." Wirtz was clear. It was time for action. But Wirtz was one of the few men in the room who spoke in favor of a dramatic federal initiative. Attorney General Nicholas Katzenbach, scholarly, almost dispassionate in his demeanor, came next. Katzenbach spoke at length of the draft voting rights bill on which the Justice Department lawyers were hard at work. He spoke what Roger termed "lawyer pettifoggery" about all the technical problems with the present bill. They couldn't send a bill to Congress. It was still too soon. Sitting to the left of the Attorney General was John Doar, chief of the Civil Rights Division in the Justice Department, who was working closely with the lawyers on the bill. Roger remembers Doar speaking in his careful way, echoing Katzenbach's reservations. "I agree with Nick," Doar said. Andrew Brimmer, the black assistant secretary of commerce, spoke shortly thereafter. "Well, Mr. Vice President," Brimmer began, "I love to watch Western movies. In those movies it is all disorder and lawlessness until the man rides in who is wearing a badge on his shirt.

That man is the law. That man is the U.S. Marshal. We should send in the United States Marshals."

Roger doesn't remember the actual words the others spoke. To him it all seemed like "more mush." Under his breath, Roger then said a personal mantra to himself to get up his courage. When it was his turn, Roger's voice rang out loud and clear.

> Mr. Vice President, I agree with Secretary Wirtz. The President needs to send up a voting rights bill to Congress. The Justice Department lawyers can sit there to make a perfect bill. They can spend the rest of their lives doing that. We don't need a perfect bill. We need a bill. Congress will change the bill anyway. The President should say this bill is necessary for democracy. He should say this in the most forceful way possible. I am disappointed, Mr. Vice President, that you see this as the work of outside agitators. These are American citizens demanding American rights. All of us sitting around this table would be fighting just like they are, if we were denied our birthright as Americans. Indeed, we would probably find it difficult to exercise as much restraint as they have. This is the central cause of justice—to enlarge our democracy."

Silence greeted Roger's declaration. The two other black men who had not yet spoken then each said something supportive of the need for action. They were the last to talk. Vice President Humphrey then spoke, compelled to clarify the record. "I did not say anything about outside agitators and Communist influence," Humphrey said. "Yes, you did, sir," Roger insisted. At which point Humphrey changed the subject. Turning to the White House counsel, Humphrey asked what advice he would give the president. "Well, I don't think there is anything more to say than what Roger Wilkins has already said and that is what I am going to tell the President."

Roger's outburst clearly changed the tone of the meeting. It probably also forestalled any more waffling by the White House. Two days later, Roger recalls, the president went to the Rose Garden and in language that borrowed liberally from the very words Roger had spoken in the Indian Treaty Room, told the American people that the time for action was upon us. "That day was probably the greatest service I ever rendered to my country," Roger Wilkins now says with quiet, almost restrained pride. But, Roger is quick to note, it was not his personal eloquence and passion that inspired a sympathetic presidential turnaround. "The reason what I said had resonance," Roger remembers, "is that there were all these people marching, demanding their rights. My responsibility was to bring the voice of ordinary people, regular black people into that room. My words worked because these other people were speaking those words with their feet. I simply brought those words into that room."

Despite his earlier ambivalence, Lyndon Johnson now moved eagerly. He immediately proceeded to introduce the voting legislation that King and Young had pleaded for privately to no avail back in December. Those marchers on that bridge, and the national reaction to the bloodbath that ensued, exploded the sense of paralysis that had led both President Johnson and Vice President Humphrey to discourage Dr. King when he pleaded personally for a voting rights bill. Johnson was finally willing to fight to extend federal authority in order to protect the mass of blacks who still could not vote throughout the region.

He wasted little time in announcing his plan of action to a joint session of Congress. He placed Selma alongside Lexington and Concord and Appomattox as turning points where "history and fate meet at a single time in a single place" to shape our "unending search for freedom." Speaking "as a man whose roots go deeply into Southern soil," Johnson said to a hushed chamber: "There is no Negro problem. There is no Southern problem. There is no Northern problem. There is only an American problem." Johnson told Congress that "the real hero of this struggle is the American Negro." After all, "who among us can say that we could have made the same progress" but for the protests of blacks "designed to call attention to injustice, designed to provoke change, designed to stir reform? . . . Their cause must be our cause too. Because it is not just Negroes, but really all of us who must overcome the crippling legacy of bigotry and injustice. And we shall—overcome!"

King, inspired by the soaring rhetoric and decisive action of the country's chief executive, dutifully waited until Judge Johnson lifted the injunction to command a full-scale march to Montgomery, protected this time by an Alabama National Guard who answered to federal rather than state authority, and following a logistics plan drawn up by Jack Greenberg and other LDF lawyers in a motel room sitting on the floor with a yellow pad. As Greenberg later admits, "We mostly made it up, writing that the march would begin on Friday, March 19," but as they were not entirely sure, they added " 'or any day thereafter.' " Once the injunction was lifted, King and 25,000 people marched the final leg of the 50-mile journey from Selma to Montgomery. It was a great day for the civil rights movement, a moment of victory applauded by a now responsive president.

President Johnson, a sympathetic southerner, presided over a joint session of Congress to put America on the side of ordinary black people, the real heroes of this struggle. Johnson was moved to act by valiant, anonymous Americans. Bernard Lafayette and other SNCC organizers had laid the groundwork, assisted by lawyers like J. L. Chestnut, by the voter registration campaigns of people like Amelia Boynton, and by the local efforts to make "every barbershop a school," schools where people could learn to read and write. He also was pushed to act by the courage of Americans around the country who reacted in horror to the bloodshed on the Edmund Pettus Bridge and whose actions were put into eloquent words by government insiders such as Roger Wilkins.

The grass-roots movement in Selma was successful because it embodied at least four crucial ideas. First, that direct action can bring people to the table. Civil disobedience, the determination of regular folk to march in the streets, can bring powerful people who otherwise do not want to talk or are slow to act to the table. Mobilizing ordinary people to march gives their leadership credibility and moral authority. It gives sympathetic insiders the courage to utter "words that work" and it pushes those in charge to fight for votes, not just complain about their absence. Second, a broad-based coalition is necessary. The preachers couldn't do it alone. Black preachers couldn't do it alone. White clergy, Jewish leaders, business people all eventually joined that march from Selma to Montgomery. Moreover, lawyers had to carry their weight in court, getting Judge Johnson to lift the injunction, showing up to release King and others from jail when necessary. Third, it was not enough to file legal cases or to pursue voting rights in court, if those cases were not linked to an organized, grass-roots mobilization. The role of the lawyers, while helpful, was secondary. The clients had to use the legal cases as organizing tools, as part of a monumental public education campaign. They needed young people who were willing to take risks and mobilize public support, giving the leadership the power to back up their demands. They needed a movement that would engage the media as its unpaid staff, drawing on the resources of these powerful storytellers to garner national support for a voting rights act. Finally, the movement was not just a plea for special rights; it was a crusade for justice. This was about realizing the promises of democracy, not just gaining voting rights for blacks.

On August 6, President Lyndon Johnson signed the Voting Rights Act of 1965, providing for registration by federal examiners in any state or county where less than half of the adults were registered to vote. The civil rights movement, at the zenith of its power, gained the national legislation it needed when it found leadership within a broad-based coalition of heroic hearts and joined those people in motion. By speaking words with their feet, ordinary black people found a way to tell their stories so all of America could understand.

CHAPTER SEVEN

Selma, Alabama, June 1985:
Building Bridges
from the Bottom Up

Watch out," Rose Sanders had warned me when she picked me
up from the airport in Montgomery in June 1985, a week prior to the
first day of trial. "Selma can change you," Rose whispered. "Selma
changes people's lives. It changed my life." Rose was reminding me of
the need to remain connected to the passion and indignation that gave
the civil rights movement its strength and its resilience. By the mid-
1980s, the civil rights movement was in danger of succumbing to empty
phrases and moral indifference in the White House and Congress,
where a few smooth phrases about voting rights resembled the obliga-
tory nondenominational prayer, a meaningless gesture in which the
words carry no substance.

"Watch out," Rose repeated, smiling this time despite the heat. It
was one of those sultry, heavy Alabama summer afternoons. I could
feel my forehead already glistening with sweat. As we drove from the
airport to Selma, Rose was explaining her decision to settle there. Rose
was guided by a romantic vision that paid tribute to Selma as a site of
historic struggle. But her life was hardly the stuff of fantasy. Her defi-
nition of a successful life meant continuing that struggle.

At five feet five, Rose Sanders is a dervish of energy and enthusiasm. One of her most striking characteristics is her voice. It sounds
perpetually hoarse, almost gravelly, as if driven by an inner urgency
and passion. She and her husband Hank have lived their entire professional lives in Selma. Compared to others in their Harvard Law School
class, they chose a hard life. For them, achievement would not be measured in a fast track to partnership in a prestigious law firm, or in the
number of awards or high-status "big jobs" they received, but by the

number of people they helped, and the number of local institutions they built.

That commitment to collective struggle is also what keeps them going. For Rose Sanders, "the fact is that struggling is as natural as air." Rose says to stop struggling is "like trying to stop breathing." When I asked her how she and her law partners had sustained three decades of resistance, she told me, "It takes faith." Rose said, "You have to believe that the mighty river is filled drop by drop. You just have to put your drop in the river, and somebody else will put in their drop, and then eventually one day those drops will make a river. And then faith— that's what keeps us going."

Rose was an acquaintance of mine from the early 1970s when she was in law school and I was in college. Rose and her husband Hank settled in Selma soon after they both passed the Alabama bar because, as Rose explained, "we have always been community-oriented. We always wanted to do community work with our law degree." Looking for a community in which to settle, Hank drove south. He was awed when he "came through Selma, came across the Edmund Pettus Bridge, with all of its symbolism of struggle and victory in the civil rights movement." He "made a right turn at the bridge and knew instantly that's where he wanted to be." They were home.

They subsequently discovered there was only one black lawyer in town, J. L. Chestnut, brilliant, but an alcoholic. Rose remembered how "Hank made contact with him and stepped out on faith. A lot of young people had said, 'Well, he's an alcoholic; I'm not gonna go into business with him.' It never crossed Hank's mind that Ches's alcoholism would be a problem. And Ches basically said, 'Give me time to straighten up a few things and I will join you.' "

Rose Sanders, Hank Sanders, and J. L. Chestnut were in Selma when, in the early 1980s, the Reagan administration "launched its assault on black leadership in the Black Belt," Rose says, "through using voter fraud as the tool to disenfranchise black people." Tipped off by several white politicians who had lost ground in the September 1984 Democratic Party primary elections in Alabama, the federal probe fastened on key black activists throughout the Black Belt, including Spiver Whitney Gordon, a former official of the Southern Christian Leadership Conference who was called the "black Moses" of neighboring Greene County, and Albert Turner, Alabama coordinator for SCLC during the 1960s, who was one of the marchers beaten on Bloody Sunday in 1965 and who subsequently led the mule train at Martin Luther King's funeral in Atlanta. Prominent politicians worked closely with FBI agents and Justice Department attorneys in the investigation of seven black activists and a white sympathizer. The Perry County Civic League was a particular target of the investigation. Headed by Turner, this community organization had helped black voters who could not get to polling places to vote by absentee ballot.

Rose explains, "Fortunately, we were here. Being the kind of law firm that we were, we instantly came to the defense of people without money. Never asked them for a penny. What we did do, because we realized it was too awesome, that the task was too great for us to handle, because it was coming from every direction and about eight different counties, [was] we called upon the NAACP LDF, the Center for Constitutional Rights, we called lawyers throughout the country to help us. And the response was overwhelming."

That's how Rose met me for the second time. She had not seen me since I was an undergraduate at Harvard and she was there in law school. This time, she got to know me as a person, when I came to Selma, as Rose remembers, "in response to our cry. In response to our human cry you came with Deval Patrick and other people from other parts of the country."

It was Hank Sanders, by then an Alabama state senator, who had first called me at LDF's offices in New York. Hank's manner was low-key and persuasive. I remembered Hank as a big man with smooth, dark brown skin. What I also knew was that behind that cherubic face is a razor-sharp intellect and a deep integrity. Hank told me that the federal government initially pursued seventeen people in Perry County alone, all of whom were black, but finally "decided to cut it down and get Albert Turner, his wife [Evelyn], and Spencer Hogue, who were the key leadership in most of Perry County." Hank told me that the Reagan administration zeroed in only on the absentee ballots cast by blacks and only on black voters who had received assistance from local black civil rights activists. The Reagan attorneys had issued a total of 212 felony indictments between Greene and Perry counties alone. This was not about the federal government upholding democracy or dispensing even-handed justice, Hank explained. This was about the federal authorities helping a few local whites hold on to power, the old-fashioned kind of power of the local planter class.

After the passage of the Voting Rights Act in 1965, the white South, terrified by the specter of black political power, fought back. With all that the act accomplished, one thing it could *not* do was change the minds of southern traditionalists determined that blacks would have no voice in political life.

As hard as voting was, voting effectively, that is to say, voting with the possibility of one's vote mattering, was even harder. J. L Chestnut recalled that after the federal registrars came in 1965, the number of blacks registered to vote shot up in Dallas County alone, from 150 registered voters to 10,000 in a matter of six weeks. Before 1965, Perry County had twelve registered black voters; by 1980, it had five thousand. Yet they still couldn't win any elections.

THE USE OF AT-LARGE, winner-take-all elections was only one of many schemes to dilute and disenfranchise the newly registered black voters. Many blacks continued to work on land owned by whites on whom they were economically dependent and to whom they felt socially beholden. Others worked for whites who would give blacks, but not whites, overtime on election day, even though they never gave overtime away during the rest of the year. Still others found themselves prohibited from leaving during their lunches, and watched while their white colleagues left to exercise their citizenship rights. Some voting places were only open from 1:00 to 5:00 P.M., making it very difficult for anyone who worked during those hours to vote, and all but impossible for the many blacks who worked out of the county. Deputy registrars who had been successful at registering blacks to vote were eliminated. Finally, a disproportionate percentage of the black population was over sixty-five years old. Though many were people who had marched on the Edmund Pettus Bridge, and many more witnessed Bloody Sunday, they were older now, and it was difficult for them to get to the polls in a rural county with no public transportation.

Black electoral success in the Black Belt was inhibited not only by efforts to chill the black vote but also by whites' effective use of the absentee ballot. By using the absentee ballot to register every possible white voter, white leaders maintained political control of many majority-black counties. Observers of the region were fond of noting that black politicians went to bed thinking they had won the election, but in the morning, after the absentee ballots had been counted, they would always learn they had lost. As Reverend Joseph Lowery of the SCLC complained in 1985, "They have given us our voting rights, but they are trying to take away our voting results."

Throughout the late 1970s, Chestnut and others complained to the Carter Justice Department about the way local white politicians were using absentee ballot boxes to manipulate elections to keep blacks from winning any office. As Chestnut explained to me:

Jimmy Carter has a relative named Chip Carter, and it was through Chip that we first began to complain to the White House that these people were cheating us; we always win at the polls but we never can win when they count the absentee ballots. Somebody in the White House directed us to the Justice Department and directed somebody down there at the Justice Department to hear us and we complained not directly to [Attorney General] Griffin Bell but we complained to officials at the Justice Department and we sent them letters directed to Griffin Bell and the first explanation we got back was that "you need to learn how to do that better; it's more y'all than them. You coming up here complaining to us; get out there and learn how to do that."

Chestnut spoke to several people and got back the same directive: "Get out there and learn how to do that." Every time he went to Washington, Chestnut kept lodging his complaint that whites in the Black Belt who could go to the polls were instead voting absentee. Every time he got back the same answer: This is a state matter, the federal authorities don't have any jurisdiction. Chestnut and others continued to complain, but they were simply told: Don't complain. Do it better. Chestnut remembers:

> We finally got word from the White House that, and this came from my uncle Preston Chestnut. Word came back through him that this is something that the Carter administration will address in its second term; we don't want to deal with that now. That was the last answer that we got on that.

Albert Turner also remembered specifically being told, "It's more of y'all than them. What are you up here complaining for? *They* ought to be up here complaining." Everyone they spoke with at Justice directed them to learn to use the absentee process themselves. And so, in the early 1980s, they did.

They were careful. Turner was "suspicious": "If we were catching all this hell from Jimmy Carter, the Democrat, and now we got Ronald Reagan, the Republican, I know things are gonna go from bad to worse." As a result, Alabama State Senator Hank Sanders testified to Congress, "blacks have gone out of their way to stay within the bounds of legality." As had always been his habit, Turner continued to pay close attention to the rules: "I know the law," he said.

The Perry County Civic League (PCCL), of which Turner was president, became very active in providing voter assistance in the form of sample ballots, published slates of endorsed candidates, door-to-door registration of voters, and door-to-door organizing to assist infirm or elderly voters in applying for and filling out absentee ballots. They had to ensure that the forms were properly filled out with birth dates, signatures, notarization, and the like. Certain forms of voter assistance could only be provided through absentee voting.

The absentee ballot and voter organizing made a difference in people's access to voting. Those who otherwise would not have been able to vote, either because they worked out of the county or could not get to the polls on election day, were now voting. As Mattie Brown, a

Perry County resident, observed, "People just wouldn't vote if they couldn't vote absentee."

The results were visible. Compared with the kind of near-complete political domination of whites immediately following the Voting Rights Act, gradually during the early 1980s blacks gained some representation in seven county commissions and nine towns. Before 1965, there were virtually no blacks registered to vote in the ten western Black Belt counties of Alabama; in 1982, there were now about 70,000 blacks registered and voting. The 138 black elected officials in these ten counties now constituted almost half of the total number of black state elected officials. In particular, blacks gained majorities in both the county government and the school boards in five counties: Greene, Sumter, Perry, Lowndes, and Wilcox.

The results in Perry County were particularly startling. According to Albert Turner, compared with Birmingham's voter turnout rate of 15 to 20 percent, and the state's average of 50 percent, Perry County often turned out 2,300 of its 2,600 black citizens. He boasts that on average, Perry County has a turnout rate of about 80 percent. "And that doesn't just happen," Turner reminded me. "We organize daily, down to the precinct level." Consequently, the Perry County Civic League and organizations in other counties mobilized to make black voters in the Black Belt a vote to be reckoned with, even at the state level.

In imitating others' success with absentee ballots, the Perry County Civic League was able to elect a few blacks to political office. This electoral success did not go unnoticed by some elected white officials in Perry County, including Clerk Mary Aubertin and District Attorney Roy Johnson, both of whom then initiated the federal investigation. Joined by a carefully selected handful of local politicians, Aubertin and Johnson identified for the federal authorities the key black leaders in each of these counties: Albert Turner and Spencer Hogue in Perry County; Spiver Gordon in Greene County. Albert Turner, his wife, Evelyn, and Spencer Hogue would become known as the Marion Three.

Aubertin and Johnson wrote to Assistant Attorney General Brad Reynolds, who told them to go to the FBI and to the U.S. Attorney for Alabama's Southern District. In the fall of 1984, U.S. Attorney for Alabama's Southern District Jefferson Beauregard Sessions III initiated an investigation of the PCCL. The local lawmen were now joined by federal agents, who hid with them in the bushes at the post office, watching as Albert Turner posted his mail. They then swooped inside and seized absentee ballots from the mail slot as if the ballots contained drug paraphernalia, making special marks on the envelopes.

Finding nothing criminal going on at the PCCL meetings, the federal agents began to harass the voters themselves. Dozens of FBI agents made repeated visits to scores of rural shacks on dirt roads with no indoor plumbing, interrogating Willie Lee and hundreds of other elderly citizens who resided in the Black Belt. The FBI showed their badges and flashed a copy of each voter's ballot. Still standing, the agents then asked how each voter had voted and if the voter had received voting assistance from the Perry County Civic League. Agents often returned to these rural residents two and three times to pursue their inquiries, demanding to know, "Can you read and write?" and, "Why did you vote by absentee ballot?" Department of Justice rules said that voter ballots could not be investigated to reveal the identity of the voter. The FBI agents investigating ballots cast by black voters in 1984 paid the rule little heed.

Whereas the Justice Department under President Carter had dismissed years of complaints from blacks about white use of the absentee process, under Ronald Reagan it seized the very first opportunity to investigate the absentee ballot process when called upon to do so by whites who had long held power. The FBI descended on precisely those five Black Belt counties where incumbent politicians lost support and where black newcomers were slowly gaining political ascendency— Greene, Sumter, Perry, Lowndes, and Wilcox counties. The agency conducted no investigations where local white politicians won. At the same time that the intensive federal investigation of Spiver Gordon in Greene County and Spencer Hogue and Albert Turner in Perry County was underway, blacks reported scores of substantial allegations of voter misconduct in ballots handled by white political organizations, but these violations went uninvestigated by the federal authorities. Whites continued to use the absentee ballot process in much higher proportions than blacks, but no white absentee ballots were investigated.

The geography of the prosecutions revealed the racially biased nature of the investigations. Senator Hank Sanders's testimony to Congress detailing the selective prosecution of black voting rights activists is worth quoting at length:

> Our concern is that the investigations are only going on in counties where blacks have achieved control of a government. If you look at a picture of a map there, you would see Lowndes which has a black county commissioner and blacks on the Board of Education; you would see them investigating there. Then you would go down to Wilcox. It has a black Board of Education, a black county commission; investigations were there.
>
> Then you would come to Dallas, where I live. We have no black elected officials on the county level. They skip over Dallas and they go to Perry. Perry has a black elected county commission and Board of Education. Investigations are going on there. Hale County, which is 63 percent black, but had only two county-elected officials, they skip over that and go to Greene. Greene has a black controlled government

—investigations there. They skip over Pickens because they have no black elected officials. They come back down to Sumter again where they have black officials controlling the government; investigations going on there.

If you look over the entire Black Belt, you see that pattern.

Clarence Mitchell, then a Maryland state senator, commented with exasperation, "The White Citizens' Council and the Ku Klux Klan can just close up shop these days because the Justice Department is doing their job with the taxpayers' money."

Despite a devastating record of black complaints about suspected misuse of the absentee ballots by white politicians, Reagan officials saw Turner as the charlatan, the PCCL as the vehicle by which he accumulated corrupt power, and black absentee voters as the victims to whose defense the federal government now came running. One official in the Reagan Justice Department's Public Affairs office defended the racially partial focus of these investigations as part of a "new policy," brought on by the "arrogance on the part of blacks" in these counties. Thus, by 1984 the federal government, twenty years earlier the main ally of Alabama's grass-roots voting rights movement, now became their prosecutor.

Not all the federal authorities were close-minded when confronted with the evidence of selection prosecution. The U.S. Magistrate who heard Spiver Gordon's selective prosecution claim in Greene County found that the federal investigation took place during a time of "an intense struggle between whites and blacks in the Alabama Black Belt with white persons seeking to retain political power and blacks seeking to share in it." After a hearing, the magistrate concluded that Spiver Gordon's evidence showed that "while others similarly situated have not been proceeded against," Gordon and his colleagues had "been singled out for prosecution."

It also did not take much to convince many local lawyers and civil rights activists in the Black Belt that the Reagan Justice Department had initiated these grand jury proceedings for political reasons solely to intimidate black voters. Alabama black attorneys J. L. Chestnut, Joe Reed, John England, and Fred Gray were alarmed at what was happening. With one or two others, these black lawyers went to Washington to meet Justice Department official Brad Reynolds and Attorney General Edwin Meese, to complain that black voters were being targeted for doing the same things that whites in the Black Belt had always done— vote by absentee ballot. These local lawyers brought evidence with them that blacks alone were being prosecuted. They presented absentee ballots cast by white voters that had not been investigated despite similar deficiencies.

Their suspicions were confirmed by the reputation of the leading prosecution attorney, Jefferson Beauregard Sessions III. U.S. Attorney Jeff Sessions had been quoted as saying that he "used to think" the Ku Klux Klan was "O.K." until he found out that some members were "pot smokers." Sessions was also reported to have made statements that he believed the NAACP was "un-American" and that the American Civil Liberties Union was "Communist-inspired." Sessions acknowledged many of the remarks but said they were taken out of context or were made by others in his presence, as, for example, when he agreed with the statement made by another person that a white civil rights attorney was a "disgrace to his race." But suddenly Chestnut had more than just U.S. Attorney Sessions to worry about. Chestnut was greeted by a level of ignorance and contempt for the facts that he found shocking when he met with Sessions's superiors at the Department of Justice in Washington, D.C.

Chestnut, who had by then been practicing law in Selma for thirty years, calls the session with Attorney General Meese "the strangest meeting" he had ever attended in his life. Chestnut met with Meese in the Attorney General's conference room, the same room in which eight years later Howard Paster delivered the Clinton administration message to me that "we don't have the votes." Given my own experience in that room, I could understand how eerie it must have felt for Chestnut, a small-town black lawyer, to be there. Certainly, the sheer size and cavernous dimensions overwhelmed many of its occupants. But Chestnut was just as disoriented by the rush of activity, then the two minutes of absolute silence that followed Meese's entrance.

The group of Justice lawyers who accompanied Meese "were like trained seals," Chestnut reported.

> I've never seen anything like that. They were sitting around this table with Ed Meese and when Ed Meese laughed they laughed, when Ed Meese had a cough in his throat they had one. It's just like trained seals. We sat around this long table and here we were five little black lawyers from Alabama, ushered into this huge room with this huge table and sat down at the far end and we were left cooling our heels there for at least forty minutes and finally in comes Edwin Meese like some grand potentate with his legal pad, and surrounded by an entourage of at least at least twelve Justice Department lawyers all dressed alike, all dressed in black, looked like they all going to a funeral, all in black. This is the truth. And they sit at one end of the table and we sit at another end and there was this big gap of space and I thought that was so symbolic.

Ed Meese sat at the head of the table, his arms folded. With his big legal pad laid out in front of him, Meese listened as Chestnut and his companions presented examples of some ballots that a number of white activists had handled in precisely the same manner as Albert and Spencer and the others were handling them. Chestnut reminded Meese that it was from whites in Alabama that Albert and the other defendants had learned how to use absentee ballots. The black lawyers pointed out all the similarities in the ballots to Mr. Meese. The black lawyers then said, "if it was wrong for Albert and Spencer, it was wrong for these other people and the government ought not to have singled out these black folks."

Meese looked at the people from Main Justice who were following his every gesture. He asked them whether this was so. They said they didn't know anything about it but they would look into it. According to Chestnut, Meese began "to write seriously on his legal pad and he promised us that he would look into it and we would hear from him shortly. We never did hear from him, never expected to."

Chestnut left the meeting with Attorney General Meese "unbelieving," convinced that those who testified before the grand jury were deliberately intimidated while federal officials in Washington looked on approvingly. His law partner, Rose Sanders, agreed, calling them "Voter Persecution Cases," whose "whole purpose was to chill the black vote." Rose saw the Reagan-initiated inquiry as playing into "the politics of race in the South—it's used to engender fear and apathy, because what it does is it leads black people to think, 'Well, it's no use,' and they give up, and what white people do is come to the polls en masse because of fear of black control." Jesse Harper, a member of the Perry County Civic League who was not investigated, said emphatically, "The people that are testifying . . . are doing so because they are scared."

Here was Willie Lee, ninety-two years old, disenfranchised for most of his life, facing a federal grand jury asking details about his voting practices during the 1984 season's primary election. Ninety-two years old and feeble, Willie Lee was hauled by federal agents to Mobile to testify before a federal grand jury. After interrogating almost two hundred voters in Perry County—and conducting hundreds more interviews in five Alabama Black Belt counties—the government had scraped together twenty people whom they bused to Mobile to testify before a grand jury. Some witnesses were led to believe that they would receive $300 for testifying, though in the end the money covered only lodging and expenses. Four state troopers, three FBI agents, two Marion, Alabama, police officers, and a state conservation officer gathered Lee and the other elderly black witnesses onto a Greyhound bus headed 160 miles for the trip from Perry County to Mobile.

Many witnesses were intimidated by an investigation focused, as it was, solely on local black civil rights leaders in Alabama's Black Belt and raising the specter once again that voting was absolutely dangerous.

For most of the lives of these grand jury witnesses, even trying to register had required great courage. As black people over the age of sixty in Perry County, they also did not assume that white people who came to their door were there to help them. Indeed, many concluded from the investigation that they had broken some law simply by voting absentee. Their natural inclination was to distance themselves from voting at all. Ninety-two-year-old Willie Lee, for example, whose absentee ballot was immaculately prepared, was so frightened by "the law" that he was afraid to admit he had even voted.

One grand juror joked with eighty-four-year-old Maggie Fuller when she was on the stand: "You didn't know you was going to get to come to Mobile when you was voting, did you?" Assistant U.S. Attorney General E. T. Rolison chimed in, "You made that X and got a ride all the way down to Mobile!"

But voting was not a joking matter for black people in Alabama. The government's witnesses had risked a great deal to register and then to vote. Now their worst fears had come true, and some took the experience as a lesson.

"Is this the first time you've voted absentee?" a grand juror asked another Perry County resident, Fannie Mae Williams. After having her ballot investigated by the FBI, and having her voting practices intensely scrutinized by a federal grand jury inquiry, Mrs. Williams could only murmur, "Uh-huh. First and the last."

Other elderly blacks in Perry County, Alabama, had already reached similar conclusions. They had believed deeply in democratic participation and acted accordingly; but the government-sponsored fracas in Mobile had convinced them that voting was a dangerous activity, one not worth the risk. Like Fannie Mae Williams, Zayda Gibbs declared that due to "all that had gone on with the investigation," she didn't want to vote any more at all. Mattie Perry said loudly that she "may be through with voting." Another elderly woman, wearied by all the activity, sighed, "If I'm able to get to the polls, I'll vote. But I ain't voting no more absentee."

Following the grand jury sessions in Mobile, the federal government charged Perry County activists Spencer Hogue, Albert Turner, and Albert's wife, Evelyn Turner, with mail fraud and conspiracy to vote more than once. The government indictments promised each defendant more than one hundred years in prison if convicted on all counts of federal criminal activity, including felony charges under the Voting Rights Act of 1965. I joined the defense team several months after the Mobile grand jury investigated and then indicted the three Perry County civil rights activists.

Hank Sanders believes that getting lawyers like me from out of town was crucial, not simply because of who but because of what we represented. LDF, in particular, "helped to give a legitimacy to the whole struggle that was very much needed. Because other civil rights organizations were diving away from it, that sent an unusual message. And because of the long history of the Legal Defense Fund in the whole civil rights arena, it gave a legitimacy that I can't tell you how much that meant. It was all out of proportion to the actual litigation role you played."

Sanders organized a team of lawyers, recruiting an experienced and impressive group. The most prominent were Oakland attorney Howard Moore, who had defended Angela Davis in the 1970s, and Morton Stavis, an experienced First Amendment and constitutional lawyer from the Center for Constitutional Rights, who celebrated his seventieth birthday during trial preparation. Also helping out were J. L. Chestnut; lawyer Robert Turner (Albert's brother) of Marion, Alabama; Dennis Balske, a young white criminal defense lawyer from Montgomery and the Southern Poverty Law Center; Margaret Carey, a young black woman then practicing civil rights law in Mississippi; and several LDF staff lawyers, including Deval Patrick (who replaced James Liebman mid-trial), and me.

Rose Sanders remembered fondly this national roundup of legal talent:

> Our law firm has been in the Black Belt up to about 15 to 16 years and we had carried so many of these struggles alone. We have responded to so many of these things without any resources other than the immediate resources that we had. We had taken a range of cases all without pay and it was clear to us that we could not do that, that we could not respond to this level of attack without help. And the fact that the help came so—I guess it was quick, I can't remember—but the people who came, they were just very dynamic, very caring, as well as confident. And that's what made it so exciting because they weren't just technicians, they were caring as well as confident people.

Hank also had to raise funds for those lawyers who were working free of charge. No lawyer got paid, but some lawyers were not with organizations, and Hank had to pay their expenses. Hank Sanders described what he did as a three-front effort. The first was "to get lawyers from all around the country to participate in this fight." The second was "to fight on a community organization basis." Within the Black Belt and in other places, it was Hank's job to organize "our communities so that whatever happened those communities would be able to go ahead and function politically afterward." This meant that Hank had to fight constantly "to try to define the issues so the community would be able to understand" what was at stake in the case and would rally in support of the defendants. He conducted a grass-roots appeal to educate the public in the face of a full-blown media effort to present only the criminalized image of the Marion Three. Finally, "we fought on a political basis. So we organized not just in Alabama, but we decided to nationalize it. We got help and support from lawyers from all over the country. We got help and support from community organizations all over the country."

The public relations battle was especially difficult. Hank recalls that the local press was very hostile. "They tried to publish anything negative and anything positive they simply wouldn't say." But despite initial resistance from the local media, Hank and Rose persisted.

> We first tried to organize it so that people other than us lawyers here would be able to speak. But the press would just shut them out. There would be no article at all. So at some point the lawyers—me and Rose and Ches—had to speak out a lot more. And we spoke out in ways that were strong and we had a lot of bar complaints filed against us to have our license taken on the basis of us speaking out on these issues. Ultimately, nothing came of those because they really were freedom of speech issues. Still, most folks would have slowed down, wouldn't have continued. Part of their theory was to weigh us so much down in our fight for ourselves that we couldn't fight for our clients and we could not fight for our community.

But the effort to intimidate the local lawyers, just like the effort to intimidate local residents, didn't work. For Hank Sanders, Rose Sanders, and J. L. Chestnut, "it was a political life-and-death situation." They saw the absentee ballot charges as the opening wedge in a full-fledged Republican battle to undermine black political power in the Black Belt. "If they had succeeded in that situation, we expected that they would be able to go to other places in the political spectrum. So, in light of that, we just simply said, 'Well, if they get us on that front, then they're gonna get us on every other front.' We really saw that as the beginning of an effort to roll back those gains—a second end of Reconstruction." Inspired by the determination of the local lawyers in Alabama, others joined the effort. Maryland State Senator Clarence Mitchell declared, "Vigilance is the price of liberty. We should never have left the streets. Now we're going to get back out there."

IN TRYING to take the measure of the effects of the investigation on blacks in Perry County, and in order to prepare for trial, a group of LDF lawyers and researchers rented a car and traveled the dusty dirt roads to meet the people the government had hauled down to Mobile. I also traveled the rural dirt roads to interview some of the people in Perry

County who had voted absentee but had not been hauled down to the grand jury in Mobile. We soon discovered that the government had pursued its case against the Perry County Civic League activists even though most of the FBI formal interview forms (called "302's") revealed nothing suspicious about the ballots in question. Our follow-up interviews uncovered nothing wrong from the voters' perspective in the way their absentee ballots had been prepared. Many residents told us that they had indeed received voting assistance, and that the ballots were precisely as they should be. Yet many of the FBI interviewers never addressed the content of the ballot at all, demanding to know instead why these elderly people needed assistance to vote, asking them to recall in minute detail the specific actions they took in checking off each name on the ballot. The FBI took the opportunity to investigate other matters as well. While interviewing eighty-four-year-old Maggie Fuller, the FBI "observed . . . in her front yard a 1965 Ford pickup truck." Whose was it, they wanted to know, writing down the license plate number. Who drove it?

A few of the people we met had refused to talk to the FBI altogether. Alma Price told the special agents who tried to interview her that "they have no business" at her home. Carrie Sewell wanted to know, "if the ballot is sealed, how do they know it's been changed?" Believing that the FBI had "done all of this dirty work" in order "to scare people," Mrs. Sewell challenged the special agents who came to see her: "The FBI came around to my house asking me a lot of questions. 'It's none of your business who I voted for. You better get out of my yard.' I got nasty with them because they made me mad. I told them, 'Don't you *ever* come around here.' No one had to tell me how to vote. I vote the way I want to vote. I've got a mind of my own."

These interviews helped confirm in my mind that I was on the side of justice fighting the Justice Department. But the sense of righteousness about my mission was incomplete until I met one of my clients, Spencer Hogue.

Spencer Hogue is a soft-spoken man. He and his wife Jane live in Marion, the largest town in Perry County. Although it was the county seat, Marion looked pretty much just like the rest of this rural county except that the roads were paved, some of the houses were brick, not just wooden shacks, and all of the houses were closer together. Spencer and Jane lived in a frame house with its own makeshift porch; it was a small house, with only two bedrooms. Their daughter and her family lived in a trailer at the rear of the house, so close it almost knocked up against the backroom wall.

During our strategy sessions, Spencer often sat at the dining-room table without speaking for long periods of time. He kept his hands folded in his lap; his back was erect. He wore his simple, freshly laundered shirt always buttoned up to the neck, no matter how hot the weather. Jane kept us all eating, with fresh tomatoes from her garden and delicious hot pies, still warm from the oven.

Spencer Hogue is a proud man. He has a few teeth missing in the front. To protect his dignity and sense of control, he preferred not to smile. But when he was genuinely amused, he could laugh with his whole body. His dark brown face would light up, his eyes twinkling with delight. When I first met him in 1985, however, Spencer did not laugh often. He was facing multiple felony charges; if convicted, he could spend the rest of his life in jail.

I asked Spencer why he joined the Perry County Civic League and why he worked with Albert Turner, knowing all that was at risk. "I guess a lot of things happened to me coming up," he explained. "My great-grandmother had been a slave. She used to tell me how they were treated and everything, and I guess that had a lot to do with it. It had a lot of effect on me and I didn't want to come up that way."

Not all of Spencer's activism reflected his great-grandmother's stories. Spencer had a few stories of his own. When he was five years old, in the 1930s, he and his great-grandmother and grandfather were living on a plantation. Cotton was the staple. The overseer had come over to his great-grandfather's house.

> That afternoon, my grandfather had a little plot of corn that he was plowing and I took him some water up there and I guess the overseer got there just about the time I did and when I carried the water to my grandfather, the overseer was right there. And when my grandfather finished drinking, he handed me the jar. The overseer was angry that my grandfather was working on his own plot. He cussed at him, calling him boy and everything else that he could think of. And I never did forget that. That followed me. I can remember having that jar in my hand and I didn't know whether he was gonna hit Grandfather or not, but I made up my mind that if he did I was gonna break that jar on him. And that followed me a long way. I didn't hate white people but that always stayed with me and it's still with me. I never did forget that.

Spencer Hogue also remembered how inspired he had been working with the Civic League during the 1960s. Throughout the South, Septima Clark of South Carolina had spread the idea of "Citizenship Schools," which were held "in people's kitchens, beauty parlors, and under trees in the summertime" to teach adults directly from voter registration forms how to write their names in cursive. Spencer and Jane Hogue turned their living room in Perry County into one such school. As Spencer explained to me, "We ran a school in our home to teach people how to read and write. People would come sit in the living room or we would move everything from the dining room into the kitchen and people would sit there. And a lot of people came to love us from that.

"My wife even taught her daddy how to read," he boasted quietly. In their small wooden bungalow, the Hogues, with help from SCLC, ran the school about two months without stopping, and then on and off for a number of years. People from the community would talk about whatever they had done that day; their stories would be written down, becoming the text for the reading lesson. Discussion deliberately emphasized "big" ideas—citizenship, democracy, the powers of elected officials. Local adults were taught to read newspaper stories critically and to be skeptical of politicians' promises. Neither Spencer nor Jane Hogue had finished high school, but they were the best teachers in these "schools." As respected members of the community who could project well, they could teach. People, they discovered, learn best from their peers, from people whose own status was not so different than theirs. Spencer and Jane became local leaders, just waiting to be discovered and further developed.

Spencer Hogue, a quiet, slow-moving man who wouldn't forget the indignities of growing up black in Alabama, soon associated himself with Albert Turner. Turner, who had also lived all his life in the same community, is an enthusiastic talker. Albert Turner has a story for every occasion, a fighting spirit, and a reservoir of energy that would keep two men going. Albert laughs easily; he is gregarious and full of life. He enjoys the sound and feel of his own words. When Albert speaks, he holds the words in his mouth while his tongue slides over the fullness of his message the way a connoisseur might sip wine, allowing it to linger on his palate to savor the texture.

Turner explained why the activities of the Perry County Civic League were so threatening to some of the people in the county. We had been standing in front of the courthouse facing a row of stores, a drug store across the street, and a fairly narrow sidewalk. I asked Albert what his life had been like.

When I first started with the Civil Rights Movement, we couldn't even walk the streets, I mean a black man had to tip his hat to a white lady, and walk off the street when he met her. Uh, they put you in jail and you would never get out. Now, this is in *my* lifetime, this is in the early sixties.

Probably 80 or 90 percent of all the blacks [in this area] worked the land. And you grew crops for them and you didn't get no money, you know. Hm! You picked cotton and they just buy you some shoes, something, or some groceries, but no money. You could make a hundred bales of cotton and there was no cash. It was like South Africa. That's a fact. And this, I'm talking about some thirty years ago. And this is what people did. It seems like for years [we've] just been their property, someone to make a living off of, to use for their economic purposes.

Now, suddenly, blacks were talking about sharing power. That idea frightened many whites, who figured blacks would simply use their newly acquired seat at the table to do to whites what had been done to them. What those whites didn't realize was that Albert Turner did not consider himself a regular politician. He was a man of big ideas. "I'm the kind of person," Albert said, "I consider myself as being one of those that make deep-seated changes. I'm called the 'root doctor' sometimes, and it's because I like to deal with the roots of a situation, I like to plow it out, to go down to deal with what really makes a situation work."

This was not about revenge. This was about justice. This was about a government that represented all the people.

Against the advice of their lawyers, Evelyn Turner, Spencer Hogue, and Albert Turner went to Mobile prior to trial and voluntarily testified before the federal grand jury. Albert Turner insisted on telling his story to the grand jury even though grand jury proceedings are secret: the only people present are the jurors and government attorneys. Turner and Hogue would not be permitted defense counsel in the grand jury. Nor would they be able to ask questions. But Albert Turner knew that he was innocent. He wanted to begin his defense early. He wanted to tell the local people in Perry County he was not afraid. He wanted to show his supporters that they had nothing to fear either. Albert Turner also knew that by testifying freely, he might begin to turn around the public perception that had been created by the local media.

Turner began his testimony to the grand jury by saying, "I felt that probably the grand jury ought to know the real truth about this. And I came today to answer whatever questions you want to ask." Albert Turner explained why he went to testify before the grand jury. "I'm simply doing this to try to prove that I'm not a person who walks around with a gun trying to intimidate people to make them vote absentee." Instead, he said, he helped people cast an informed ballot, telling them who the candidates are, what they stand for, and what the PCCL thought about their political agendas.

Turner explained to the grand jury how, in 1962, he, Spencer Hogue, and others formed the PCCL to mobilize for the right to vote. Turner was inspired to create the organization when he returned from college with a bachelor of science degree and found he was prevented from voting. He remembered, "I graduated from college, and I thought I knew something. And I couldn't register to vote. That set me off so I started by trying to get myself registered. That took about two years."

In the interim, he joined and was elected the second president of the PCCL. Over the years, the PCCL broadened its reach to include voter registration and voter education. The latter entailed the production of voting slates—lists of endorsed candidates such as those produced by many political organizations and such as were published by other political groups in Perry County. In more recent years, the PCCL turned its attention to serving the community's everyday needs, such as getting groceries to the elderly, helping the homebound get to the doctor, providing scholarships to students, sponsoring a radio program. Albert Turner told the grand jury, "the main goal of the Perry County Civic League now is to try to make life better for people who are oppressed, whatever we have to. For instance, we help people get food stamps and we . . . haul commodities to people. We try to encourage education and try to improve education." Turner explained that the Perry County Civic League was not just concerned about winning elections. "I mean, we went to the whole community, wherever the problem was. If they had a problem with the school, we worked on it; if they had a problem with food stamps, we worked on it. It was not just what you called electoral politics."

For Spencer Hogue and Albert Turner, this was what the civil rights movement meant by participatory democracy. As Albert later told me, "This government doesn't believe poor people should run government. They think people who own property and are wealthy—only the elites should vote and run government. I think everybody ought to run the government." Whereas some people had felt in the past that "we were just interested in what you call the *right* to vote," they weren't aware that more was at stake than the outcome of an election. It was about getting people involved in making decisions that affected their lives. "That's what it was all about all along," Albert said. "Everybody ought to run the government."

Government attorney E. T. Rolison completely ignored the subtleties of Turner's philosophy. He simply asked Turner at the grand jury:

> How do you do it? Do you say, "Who do you want to vote for?" Or do you say, "We're voting for this"—How do you actually handle it when you get to a person that's got the ballot? How do you help them vote? Tell me how you do that.
>
> A. In incidents where people don't know who the candidates are or nothing, we let them know who the candidates are.
> Q. That you're supporting?

A. And most times we also carry with us a sample ballot and let them know who we're supporting. And we let them make that choice *after they know who we are supporting, after they know who the candidates are.* And once the people say we want to vote such and such a way, then we vote that way. (italics added)

Spencer Hogue, though much less gregarious and outspoken than Albert Turner, also testified to the ongoing work that the Perry County Civic League performed. "The voter looks to us for more than just voting. They look to us for other services. . . . Well, in some cases I have to take some of my people to the doctor. I have to help them with other necessary business papers that they have. And a lot of them is on the food stamp program. I have to help them there." Spencer continued: "We've been working with these people ourselves since 'sixty-two for various things. And we have never deceived them. So whenever we make a representation, they almost always go with us. Ain't no doubt about it. The people in my community do." The people "almost always go with us" because of the work that Spencer and Jane Hogue did starting in the 1960s to hold citizenship schools in their dining room. "They loved us for that," Hogue said.

Flouting the recommendations of their lawyers, Turner and Hogue talked freely and voluntarily. They were, in this sense, their own lawyers, or at least insistent on advocating for themselves, speaking in their own voice. It was a commitment to speaking up, despite the risks, that in 1993 inspired me to struggle to go public on *Nightline* despite repeated administration warnings against defending myself and my ideas. It was my own exposure to Albert's and Spencer's experiences and their belief that everybody ought to run the government that later influenced my law review articles and my search for a more democratic way to include all of the people in making the decisions that affected their lives.

Just as administration staff kept counseling me before the confirmation hearings to remain silent, Albert and Spencer's lawyers worried that the defendants' stance before the grand jury was courageous but risky. As attorney Rose Sanders later explained: "Albert just wanted to talk because in his mind, he had nothing to hide. He actually testified before the grand jury and he didn't have to. That was a part of his right and in his mind, 'because I am right, I don't have nothing to hide.' But what Albert was not recognizing is that righteous behaviors are all right for righteous people but if you are dealing with the unrighteous, it often doesn't matter if you are right."

In Albert's case, the sense that he was entitled to be heard turned out to be a useful strategy. At trial, the prosecution presented the jury with copies of Albert and Spencer's grand jury testimony. Both had done such a good job of explaining themselves to the grand jury that we decided not to put them on the witness stand at trial, where they might have been tricked up by clever cross-examination.

Although Albert and Spencer never stopped believing that their cause was just, some of the defense attorneys early on looked for a way to avoid a lengthy trial, knowing that a conviction, even on a weak evidentiary record, was a distinct possibility. At one point, a couple of lawyers tried to negotiate a plea bargain. It had become clear to J. L. Chestnut, for example, that in all of the massive documents the government had collected, they could find some technical violations of the law. Since no one had any intent to do anything wrong, the question for Chestnut was whether U.S. Attorney Sessions "would be interested in some sort of misdemeanor which somebody could plead to, not have any permanent record, not serve any time, send some message that we want to be careful about voting." As Chestnut later explained to me: "I don't think you know about this, there was a discussion of whether or not to meet with Jeff Sessions and to see whether or not anything could be worked out. And we met with Jeff Sessions along those lines. Mort Stavis, deep down in his heart, I think did not want any compromise. Mort wanted it tried out and the government put on trial so the rest of the country could see it." Although Chestnut pursued the plea negotiations, he "didn't think we had a prayer of working anything out." Chestnut went down to meet with Jeff Sessions, but he didn't have any high expectations.

J. L. Chestnut told me, "I had no doubt in my mind about how ambitious Jeff Sessions was and is, and we met with him and I said to him: 'Jeff, what possibility is there, if any, of trying to work something out on a misdemeanor basis? I suspect that from what we have seen from this evidence, you may be able to establish some technical violation of the law.' And Jeff said there was no way that he was going to agree to any kind of misdemeanor plea.

"And I said, 'You're gonna fall flat on your face because you can't win.' And I'd tried cases before him, and Jeff was not then or now what I would call a number one trial lawyer by anybody's standards, and here he was in this case talking about no way. But that also confirmed that he had an agenda with me. I had made deals with him, plea bargains with criminals and all that, and here he was with these people saying no. It didn't even make sense, except I understood that he had this larger agenda far beyond convicting Albert and Spencer."

Albert also realized that the trial was not about punishing him "in terms of incarceration." "I was offered a bargaining chip, and Spencer was, too," Albert explained. "I was given the option, through a plea bargain situation, to be set free, one hundred and forty-five years dropped completely for a five-year probation which would have been, in reality, two election cycles, and all I had to do was tell them that I was not involving myself in politics." At that point there was absolutely no question in Albert's mind that the issue was "the deep-seated, deep-rooted kind of politics I was involved in."

Since Albert was not going to agree to change his "deep-seated, deep-rooted" politics, there was no deal. In response, the government's most important strategy was to criminalize the Marion Three. They indicted them each on twenty-nine counts, including conspiracy, mail fraud, voting more than once, furnishing false information to election officials, marking absentee ballots of elderly voters, vote dilution, "defrauding the citizens of Perry County and the State of Alabama of a fair and impartial primary election," and "causing the casting and tabulation of false, ficticious, spurious and fraudulently altered absentee ballots." Together, Albert Turner, Evelyn Turner, and Spencer Hogue were looking at 180 years in prison if convicted on all the charges.

The tactic worked at first: many people in the community were frightened by the number and the weight of the indictments. Senator Sanders remembered how hard it was to gather support for the Marion Three at the beginning of the trial:

> We tried to get help from SCLC and from ADC [Alabama Democratic Conference], and other places. We didn't get much help from the traditional places, even though Albert Turner had been state director for SCLC back in the '60s and early '70s, and led the mule train at Martin Luther King's funeral. But the reason we didn't get support is because people say, "Well, if they got that many charges against 'em, they must've done something! And they're going to get a conviction, and if I get too close to them I'll get dragged down in the process." A lot of individuals will desert you because they think, "They wouldn't have indicted them if they hadn't done something wrong."

The civil rights leadership were not the only ones initially wary of associating with the Marion Three. Community members were also afraid of getting involved. Though Perry County residents knew the PCCL well, the number and weight of the charges made them "nervous" and "self-conscious."

DAYNA CUNNINGHAM was a law student working for LDF that summer. She came down to help us get ready to cross-examine the government's witnesses. During the trial, she and LDF staff lawyer Deval Patrick traveled throughout the county interviewing people about the PCCL, about Albert Turner and Spencer Hogue, gathering information about the PCCL's practices and its activists' relationship to the community. The task was difficult because people were scared. Initially, they resisted talking to Dayna and Deval at all: "People were so afraid. The sense of fear was palpable. Nobody trusted us in the beginning, the law had been through there so many times." Dayna remembered one woman in particular:

> I'll never forget, we went to this one house and there was a woman on the front porch sweeping the front porch. We had learned by now that we couldn't just walk right up to the house, and so we were standing about twenty feet back, and Deval said, "I guess you know what's going on in the county and we just wanted to talk to you some about what's going on." And this woman had this broom, and she was holding this broom and sweeping the porch, and as she was sweeping it she said, "No! No! No! I ain't talkin' to nobody! Not nobody! Now you just get off my porch!" This broom was her weapon, and she was sweeping us off the porch with all the dust, you know?

> And Deval said, "Please, ma'am, we really need to talk to you. We are trying to help Spencer and Albert and we just want to spend a few minutes talking to you."

> The woman did not look up. "How do I know you are here to help Albert and Spencer?" The whole time she's sweeping. She did not stop sweeping once. She's not going to let us onto the porch and this broom is going to ensure that we don't get onto the porch. And so finally Deval, who is a master at this, said to her with this angelic smile, "Ah, now why are you being so mean to me?" And the woman could not help herself. She cracked a smile and said, "I ain't that mean, am I?" The next thing we were sitting in her living room drinking lemonade and she was complaining about her no-good husband.

Historical memory may also have solidified community fear of and for the Marion Three. In addition to the illicit and dangerous quality inherent in black voting in the South for so much of the lives of all but Perry County's young people, there were some very recent prosecutions of voting activists, including the well-publicized case of Mrs. Maggie Bozeman, the fifty-five-year-old black schoolteacher from neighboring Pickens County. Although her conviction was ultimately overturned after I filed a habeas petition in federal court, the case had a lingering effect in reducing black voter turnout in Pickens County, and an instructive and depressing effect for blacks in neighboring counties like Perry and Greene.

That local Alabama authorities might come after blacks for voting was one thing. But, presumably, the federal government should have been something entirely different. After all, it was a federal judge in Montgomery who ruled in Mrs. Bozeman's favor and threw out her state conviction for insufficient evidence. Even the blue suits in Washington had played an apparently sympathetic role, certainly for the last third of the century. Indeed, not until the federal examiners came down in 1965 after the U.S. Congress passed the Voting Rights Act did most blacks in the Black Belt of Alabama join the voting rolls.

Yet here we were being summoned once again to Alabama to defend voting rights activists, this time from federal, not state, prosecution.

EMMETT COX was the presiding judge at the trial. As Deval Patrick said: "He looked like what you would expect a judge to look. He looked older than he was. He wore a perpetual scowl on his face. He was impatient and crotchety. He had whitish hair. He seemed bigger than he was. Particularly in criminal cases, judges often convey they are giving the defense its time but not its due. The more vigorous the defense, the more impatient they seem. That was Judge Cox."

Dayna Cunningham remembered Judge Cox literally stepping down to do whatever he could to bend the stick toward the prosecution. During the testimony of a white law enforcement officer, "the judge actually got down off the bench and poured the witness a glass of water." By contrast, Dayna recalled the judge's demeanor with an eighty-five-year-old black prosecution witness. "The witness was sort of bent over and spoke very quietly, and the microphone was far from his mouth and so he was not very well heard by the jury, and the judge at one point just kind of leaned over and barked at him and said, 'Sit up straight and talk into the microphone! The jury can't hear you!' And it was just such a striking contrast to the judge getting off the bench and going to fill the water glass of a white witness."

The prosecution team, although not outresourced, was certainly outnumbered. Our defense team—seven blacks and three whites—took up two long tables. During most of the trial, U.S. Attorney Jeff Sessions was not present, leaving only two young white attorneys at the government table. Perhaps the judge was just trying to level the playing field in his own way.

Both Robert Turner (Albert's younger brother and a lawyer in Marion) and J. L. Chestnut thought Judge Cox was one of the fairest judges in the area. Robert in particular remembers how Judge Cox let him pull the numbers from the master wheel to select the jurors who would be seated in the box for questioning by the lawyers. Robert thought Judge Cox did this because he had already denied all of our defense motions challenging the discriminatory way in which the jury was empaneled in Mobile to hear a case from another part of the state that was dramatically different geographically and demographically. Robert Turner assumed that Judge Cox, given his jury rulings, was so confident the defendants would be convicted that he could appear to give them a little boost. Robert memorized the jury numbers of the black prospective jurors. After Robert finished pulling the numbers and both sides finished voir dire, we had a jury of seven blacks and five whites.

For J. L. Chestnut, the case was almost over once the jury sat in the box. "Black jurors," he told me later, "will convict blacks, Chinese, Eskimos, anybody else, they do it all day every day. If they would not convict in these counties which are seventy percent and seventy-five percent black, you wouldn't have anybody going to the penitentiary and there are no less people being sentenced in a county in Alabama that's seventy-five percent black than in a county that is fifteen percent black. There is no appreciable difference. What occurred is that because of the black experience, when the judge charges a black juror about the state's burden to prove beyond a reasonable doubt, they're glad to hear that and probably would hold the state to that standard even if it were not the law. Because they have had somebody in their family, somebody in their neighborhood that has had experiences which cause them to be suspicious of all authority and in particular of all authority that's closest to them— the police. Jeff Sessions never understood that, and his arrogance and the arrogance of the people working for him who selected that jury when they put all of those blacks in the jury box with this circumstantial case and they were not going to get close to proving any criminal intent, and once I saw the jury I knew that that case was over with."

Chestnut found Jeff Sessions's miscalculation understandable: "They figured they were the government; all they had to do was prove that these people had violated the letter of the law, and the jury would give the government the benefit of the doubt and assume intent. That's what they did and that's a crucial mistake. These blacks were not going to give the government the benefit of the doubt."

Early in the trial, the judge seemed to rule against every defense motion. He seemed particularly overwhelmed by the amount of legal papers the LDF lawyers filed. We motioned him to death. Most of our experience was as appellate lawyers. As in Maggie Bozeman's case, we were often the ones called in to salvage a case on appeal that had been lost at trial. Our strategy, therefore, was to protect the record in the event the defendants were convicted. Fortunately, the other defense lawyers, particularly Howard Moore and J. L. Chestnut, were more single-minded; they were interested in convincing the jury seated in the jury box to vote to acquit.

Judge Cox infuriated the defense team when he ruled that we could not even mention the word "race" in court. He had already denied our pretrial motion to dismiss the entire case on the grounds that the government was selectively prosecuting our clients because they were black. Now, the judge was afraid that, given the composition of the jury, he would lose control of the courtroom or the case if witnesses were even racially identified. He was not content merely to scold us at every mention of the racial undercurrents. At one point, Judge Cox went so far as to hold defense attorney Howard Moore in contempt with the promise of a later fine (the citation was later thrown out by the Eleventh Circuit) when, on cross-examination, Howard Moore simply asked Clerk Mary Aubertin, a government witness and one of the primary forces behind the federal investigation, to state for the record the race of two white voters whose absentee ballots she had handled personally although the voters had long since moved out of Perry County.

The government's case hinged on twisting constitutionally protected voter assistance into a criminal activity. They employed a novel theory to make federal criminals out of Alabama civil rights activists. The government claimed that marking a ballot *with the consent* of a voter, what Judge Cox called "proxy voting," was illegal. In the government's eyes, Turner and Hogue, by helping illiterate voters to fill out their ballots—with the voter's specific and voluntary consent—were themselves voting more than once. Assistant Attorney General E. T. Rolison told the court that

> It is our position that if a person obtains a ballot from an individual and the voter says, "All I did was make my X on this ballot where my name was to go" and that voter says, "I didn't make any of these marks" [in the candidate boxes], [then the voter] did not exercise any of these choices for these candidates. [T]hat is voting more than once and if a voter just hands over to a member of the Perry County Civic League without knowing anything [about] the slate or who they are supporting and they vote that ballot, that is also voting more than once.

Judge Cox immediately saw the extraordinary implications of the government's theory for any kind of political slate or public endorsements, or for spousal communication in which one spouse deferred to the political judgment of the other. Many people vote without being personally knowledgeable about every candidate. People vote with lists in their hands given them by neighbors or with sample ballots provided by advocacy organizations they trust. And, perhaps most commonly, they pull the lever in the voting machine for a political party sometimes without even knowing what offices they are voting for, let alone which candidates they are supporting. The court, comprehending the disjuncture of the government's theory with standard American practices, asked:

> Even if the voter authorizes someone to complete the ballot?
> *Mr. Rolison:* That is correct . . .

The Court: Even if the voter authorizes someone else to fill out the ballot?

Mr. Rolison: If the voter has no idea who is going to be voted for on that ballot that is voting more than once, because that person is exercising their will and control over that ballot and are making a choice that that person had nothing to do with.

In other words, the act of writing and marking a ballot was necessary to forming a political judgment. For the Reagan U.S. attorneys, voting was a profoundly solitary act, to be performed under circumstances in which the voter acts without connection to any other members of his or her family or community and without availing him/herself of trusted sources of information.

Judge Cox found that proxy voting was a legal and constitutionally protected activity in Alabama, yet the U.S. Attorney's office presented witness after witness to show that Spencer Hogue or Albert Turner had helped a person to vote with that person's consent. When the voter was illiterate, Hogue and Turner marked the ballot for them, calling out the names of the candidates. When the voter was confused, they informed the voter of the merits of various candidates.

There had been an unusual amount of confusion during the primary elections of 1984 in Perry County because the PCCL, for tactical reasons, decided not to put out a sample ballot or announce their preferences on the radio. Much of the voter education, therefore, took place in face-to-face encounters with the voters themselves. Of course, the opportunity for overreaching was certainly present. Had Albert Turner and Spencer Hogue been strangers to the community, or political hired guns, or even conventional political operators, they might have misused this moment of intimacy. But Albert and Spencer were a different kind of political activist: voting for them was about community empowerment, not individual advancement.

Perhaps Albert and Spencer could have spent more time with each voter educating them about the political process generally, not just advising them on the merits of individual candidates. Perhaps they should have insisted that the voters attend public meetings to make their voices heard. But these were elderly, impoverished people living in the countryside, with no means to get around. If voting was important, voting had to come to them.

One witness, a Mrs. Sanders, testified she told Hogue that she wanted "the man *we* all want." For Mrs. Sanders and others, voting was an expression of solidarity, based on relationships of mutual trust and common understandings of a collective plight. Other government witnesses also testified that they wanted to vote the PCCL slate, the "way the crowd was voting." They trusted Spencer Hogue and Albert Turner and wanted to vote the Perry County Civic League slate. "I been knowin' Albert all my life. I know his daddy. I know his mama and that's his little brother sittin' there beside him. Albert's been pickin' my ballot for sixteen years," one witness said.

Far from the picture of exploitative activists using unknown elderly people for their voting power that the prosecution needed, the witnesses expressed affection for the defendants, describing their relationships with Albert and Spencer sometimes from birth, but always characterized by cooperation and goodwill. Spencer and Albert helped them to the doctor when they were sick; they brought them food when they were hungry. Witness after witness testified to the longstanding bonds of community that held them together. They depended on the Perry County Civic League to gather information about the candidates, some of whom were running statewide and about whom the witnesses knew little or nothing. As Mrs. Sanders testified, she "didn't know none of the folks" running, and the PCCL slate was *itself* her choice. She, and others, deferred to the expertise and informed judgment of the Perry County Civic League in general, and in particular its members Albert Turner and Spencer Hogue.

LDF defense attorney James Liebman, who is now a Columbia Law School professor, told the court, "I don't see how that is any different from that situation where they have made a choice and that choice is I want to go with you or the PCCL slate." Judge Cox agreed: "I am not inclined to think that a situation where a voter gives someone else his ballot with the authority to mark the candidate he wants to mark and vote it is a criminal offense." He instructed the government's lawyers not to argue in court that such activity was a violation of the law. Judge Cox recognized that voting, for the government witnesses, was not an isolated act by a lone individual. Nor was it merely an autonomous expression of unmeditated, individual will. The witnesses' vision of voting—the one they insisted upon in court even when it provoked badgering by government lawyers, and the one upheld by Judge Cox as legal proxy voting—was an expression of community power. It did not take much cross-examination for the government's evidence to collapse under the weight of its own estrangement from common, democratic, and perfectly legal practices.

Still, this was only the beginning of the prosecution's problems. Judge Cox may have been initially sympathetic to the prosecution. He could not, however, resuscitate the government's case once it started to fall apart. The Reagan-appointed U.S. Attorney had delegated most of the dirty work to two junior attorneys, who based their case on the testimony of seventeen witnesses out of two hundred people interrogated by the FBI in Perry County. These witnesses turned out to be the prosecution's biggest liability.

A few of the witnesses were clearly disoriented to find themselves in a wood-paneled and physically imposing courtroom, testifying about something that did not stand out in their mind at the time, and that moved ever further into the past as the months passed between the September 1984 primary and the June 1985 trial. A few days into the trial, local papers, hardly sympathetic to the defense, were reporting that witnesses "could not remember voting at all," and that they "appeared frightened during the questioning process" or "confused and their testimony has been confusing." For example, Renear Green's testimony on direct examination by the government did little to further E. T. Rolison's theory:

> Q. Okay. And who marked the ballot for you?
> A. I marked it for him to sign.
> Q. So you—
> A. I done some scratching, but I don't know whether that is the paper or which one. It has been more than that and that. . . .
> Q. Did you tell the FBI that you did not know why Spencer Hogue marked the ballot for a candidate other than Reese Billingslea. Now, the answer is yes or no?
> A. I told him no, I didn't know none of them but him. I told him, yes or no.

The government attorney, getting frustrated, pressured another witness, Robert White, to name whom he voted for. "I can't remember what did I do because I had him fill it for me. I couldn't do it." White, like many other government witnesses, was corroborating the defense theory, what the judge called perfectly legal proxy voting.

Some witnesses gave contradictory testimony. Others revealed, on cross-examination, that they couldn't read or write, and therefore could not identify the ballots being waved in their faces by the government attorneys. Others could barely see. Some had no long-term memory of voting at all, but admitted that the problem was their memory, not their voting. Each in their own way actively undermined the government's case that they had been coerced or intimidated into voting against their will. Most of the government witnesses went even further, giving endorsements for Albert and Spencer. Their stories did not help the government. Had the government lawyers or agents ever listened to them, really listened, they would have known that.

Judge Cox tried to alert the government. "You should be on notice by now," he said, "that you have witnesses that are saying one thing in court that is different from the way the FBI understood it." But the government agents failed to pay attention to such details; they projected their own views onto their rural, community-oriented witnesses.

Mrs. Price's trial testimony, for example, revealed that she needed voting assistance because she "had arthritis in my hand and my eyes were bad." She had marked the candidates she did *not* want to vote for and she was "nervous [about voting] and couldn't write." Albert Turner provided the assistance that she needed. Frustrated and indignant that its witnesses were not making its case, the government badgered Mrs. Price, as it had every other witness, about the ostensible inconsistency between the FBI's 302s and the witnesses' court testimony.

Q. Do you remember telling Mr. Bodman [a special agent] that you don't know Evelyn Turner?
A. I remember that.
Q. Is that a true statement or were you mistaken?
A. Well, I meant that I knew her but I didn't know her as well as I knew her husband.

What the white FBI agents did not realize is that many black people in the rural South, confronted with their own powerlessness in the face of overwhelming white domination, often developed a way to soft-pedal bad news. They cleverly coded their messages so white folks could hear exactly what the white folks wanted, at the same time carefully maintaining the integrity of their own version of the truth. Some scholars call it "signifying"; Dayna Cunningham calls it "classic dissembling. Where you can't confront anybody, but you just want to go on your own way the best you can—steadfastly, you know? And 'Yeah, that's right, sir, that's exactly what I said'—never disagree with the man, but clarify and tell the whole story exactly the way you see it."

This is apparently what happened with Mrs. Price, when the government pressed on in questioning her as if she were not their own witness.

Q. When you talked to Mr. Bodman, do you remember telling him that you did not authorize anybody to make any changes?
A. No more than what I told them to make.
Q. Let me try to rephrase it [the prosecuting attorney insisted]. It really calls for a yes or a no, if you can answer it that way. Do you remember telling Mr. Bodman that you did not authorize anybody to make any change, either yes or no?
A. No, I didn't tell them to make no changes.
Q. Do you remember telling Mr. Bodman that you did not authorize telling anybody to make any changes? I am trying to get at what you told Mr. Bodman? [The prosecution leaned in toward Mrs. Price]
A. Yes.

Q. Do you remember telling Mr. Bodman that you did not authorize anybody to make any changes for you? [leaning in even closer]
A. The only changes were made—no more than the changes—

As the prosecution's voice got louder and the government attorney moved in closer to the witness, Howard Moore objected: "This witness has problems, but hearing does not seem to be one of the problems."

"Where would you like me to stand?" The prosecution sneered.

"Wherever you like, but not in the witness's ear," Mr. Moore shot back.

The government's aggression toward their own witnesses startled the jury. Albert's brother Robert observed during the trial that the jury appeared to be thinking, " 'You ought to be ashamed for asking something like that question. Why are you being like that, why are you picking on them?' " The prosecution's overzealousness and hostility toward its own witnesses even led Judge Cox to interrupt the prosecutors:

> You know, I can understand it once or twice, but you folks are on notice that we have witnesses coming in here saying things differently from what they said on a 302. We have to waste all of this time and that is what it amounts to, calling these witnesses to say one thing and proving that they told the F.B.I. something else, you know, and it doesn't accomplish anything.

One of Dayna Cunningham's jobs was to make a note of what moved the jury, what failed with them, what they paid attention to, and the like. She was watching the jury during Willie Anderson's testimony. Mr. Anderson, a man who seemed afraid of his own shadow, testified for the government that he didn't support the defendants because black people had never done anything for him. "To tell you the truth," Anderson said on cross-examination, "if it wasn't for the white people, I don't believe we would get them [Social] Security checks."

Once again, the government had failed to anticipate the effects of its witnesses and their testimony on community members—and though they were sequestered, that is what some of the black members of the jury remained: peers of the defendants and members of the Black Belt community. As Dayna recalled:

> I remember there were a couple of black women in the jury, and they looked like good, upstanding, churchgoing, solid Sunday-dinner-cookin' sisters. You know, they were matronly looking, with very large breasts, and you just knew when they left the courtroom they were wearing their hats. And I will never forget, they were sitting there, and when this man started to talk, they looked like my husband Phil's

Aunt Pearl. They had their arms wrapped around their massive chests and they just went, "Um um um." I mean, their faces were just dripping with contempt and pity. Their faces looked as if they smelled something really bad in the jury or had a memory of something that was really disturbing.

Despite the many moments of high drama in the trial, for Dayna Cunningham, whose job it was to observe the jury closely during the trial, the sad testimony of this quiet, beleaguered witness was memorable precisely because of the effect it had on the jury. His testimony also inadvertently bore witness to a nuanced black economic dependency that persisted in the Black Belt. Though blacks no longer lived in large numbers on white land, nor shopped at plantation commissaries, economic tethers continued to constrain black political expression.

By the seventh day of the trial, local newspaper headlines read: PROSECUTION WITNESSES FAIL TO ADVANCE GOVERNMENT'S CASE and WITNESSES SAY THEY AUTHORIZED AMENDMENTS TO ABSENTEE BALLOTS. On July 3, Judge Cox dropped the number of charges against the Marion Three from twenty-nine to sixteen against Albert Turner; fifteen against Evelyn Turner; and seven against Spencer Hogue—due to insufficient evidence. Only one witness (and a family which harbored a grudge against Albert Turner but couldn't seem to work out the inconsistencies in their own story) performed as the government wanted.

For its part, the defense did its homework. Its homework, however, was not just limited to making well-honed legal arguments. Its homework meant getting to know the witnesses, the community, learning the facts, not just the law. Deval Patrick and Dayna Cunningham's interviews with voters and with witnesses were part of the defense's research strategy. As Deval put it, the legwork in the community "paid off in spades." Because Deval had visited Robert White at his home and knew that Mr. White was living on his own quite independently, when a nurse appeared out of the blue in court, Deval felt "outdone." Deval immediately suspected that the prosecution had deliberately staged the entrance of a nurse in white dress uniform to send a message to the jury that Robert White was not only feeble but incompetent. Deval gently cross-examined Mr. White to show he did not need, nor had he asked for a nurse to be present.

Deval Patrick then asked that "the government dispense with the theatrics of having a nurse in full dress and stethoscope." "The judge scolded me," Deval remembered. "The Assistant U.S. Attorney threw her pad down. But the nurse did not come back."

As a result of the community organizing that Rose Sanders and Hank Sanders did, and as people heard what was happening in the courtroom, more and more local people rallied around the Marion

Three, attending court in greater numbers, until the courtroom was full on a daily basis. Community support was never more evident than after the fire at the Turners' house.

Judge Cox prohibited any mention of the fire in court—or defense suspicions that it was deliberately set on a night when Albert, Evelyn, and their lawyers were sitting in the kitchen. Howard Moore, who was helping the Turners prepare for court the next day, remembered it was late in the evening when he heard what he thought was a thunderclap and then saw the fire as it "just bolted through the house," accelerating rapidly and searing half the Turners' house. Dayna Cunningham remembered that though there was no mention of the fire in court, its effects permeated the courtroom. Attorneys Morton Stavis and Howard Moore, both of whom had been staying at the Turners' home, sent their clothes to the cleaners, but the smell of fire could not be gotten out and "every day there was a smell of smoke in that trial."

Evelyn Turner lost all of her clothes in the fire. But her family was determined that the fire not affect her appearance in court. "Every day," Dayna remembered, "she came to court with a beautiful new dress on. Because her aunt and her family and her supporters felt so strongly that she should maintain her pride and her dignity." Evelyn Turner remembered quietly how "different women in the community gave my aunt material and my aunt stayed up late into the night to make me clothes so that I could be decent in court during the trial."

If anything, the fire simply reinforced the extraordinary outpouring of community support for the defendants. Evelyn Turner remembers, "Oh, they were behind us, if there is such a thing, three thousand percent. During the trial we couldn't pay some of our bills: light, gas. People helped us pay the utility bills. We had one outstanding note where we had borrowed money and the church paid it for us. We got donations from as far away as Africa, and that money went to our defense fund."

At the conclusion of its reading of the defendants' grand jury testimony, the prosecution rested. The defense brought in character witnesses, including Andrew Young, then mayor of Atlanta. Andy Young had been pastor of a church in Marion. His wife grew up there. They were connected both to Albert Turner and to Marion, Alabama. Indeed, one day several weeks before trial, as I was leaving my apartment building in New York City headed to Alabama, suitcases and briefcases slung over both arms, a woman who lived several floors below me stopped to chat. She wanted to know where I was headed. This was an unusual request anywhere, but particularly from a stranger in New York, where anonymity is treasured, even among neighbors. I told her, "Alabama." Where in Alabama, she asked me. "Near Selma," I volunteered, thinking that was enough to satisfy her curiosity. "Where near Selma?" she persisted. "Marion, Alabama," I blurted out, worried now that I might miss my plane. "Oh," she answered with great delight. "I'm from Marion. My sister is married to Andy Young."

My neighbor had heard about the federal investigations in the Black Belt and was hoping, since she knew I worked for the NAACP LDF, that I might be involved. What seemed to be serendipity, however, turned out to reveal an important historical lesson about Marion, Alabama. I learned that Coretta Scott King also grew up in Marion, along with many others who eventually became prominent in the civil rights movement. Apparently, nineteenth-century missionaries had made Marion an educational center of the Black Belt.

At trial, my neighbor's brother-in-law testified about working with Albert Turner when Turner was the Alabama director for SCLC. Andy Young knew Albert Turner "as an independent person," who kept the staff on course in Alabama during the height of the civil rights demonstrations during the 1960s. "Dr. King was very much impressed with Albert Turner," Andy Young said. "I have trusted Mr. Turner in many difficult situations over the last twenty-five years." I asked Albert Turner why, when other local civil rights leaders waited quietly on the sidelines not eager to get involved, Andy Young was so willing to testify on his behalf. Albert Turner answered simply, "Andy and I were comrades. We slept and ate and we went to demonstrations in the streets. When we were being shouted at and beaten up and put in jail, Andy and I would sit side-by-side. Andy, I'd say really knew who I was, not what somebody said about me."

Before the case went to the jury, the attorneys had a chance to make their closing arguments. It was July 4, 1985. The jury had been sequestered for more than two weeks and the judge was eager to get back to Mobile, where he, the court staff, and the prosecutors all lived. All the lawyers made some reference to the Edmund Pettus Bridge. E. T. Rolison, the Assistant U.S. Attorney with the unique view that proxy voting was per se illegal, said no man was above the law, no matter who his friends were or who he marched with. Albert Turner, Rolison declared, had lost sight of his purpose and his civil rights dreams, pursuing naked power instead. Defense attorney Morton Stavis said the jurors would have a big impact on democracy in the region. "What happens to the democratic process if the people who win elections and have control of law enforcement can routinely go into court and kill off the opposition by criminal prosecution?"

When my turn came to speak, I carefully rebutted in detail the government's evidence against Spencer Hogue, demonstrating all the inconsistencies and contradictions. What was more important, in some ways, was my demeanor; the close attention I paid to every nuance in the government's case gave substantive reinforcement to the more powerful courtroom orators.

I also have a vivid recollection of what I did during the lunch break just before I was due to speak. In the front seat of a car parked outside the courthouse, I rehearsed my closing. I was not talking to myself. Deval sat in the seat next to me, prompting me, helping me revise for different emphasis, closely following every word. Like everything else about that trial, those moments of quiet collaboration meant so much more than the subsequent performance. I do, however, remember, as does Deval, J. L. Chestnut's closing. Now that was a performance. Indeed, when Chestnut finished, Deval had to wipe the tears from his eyes.

Chestnut is a great courtroom orator. He is not a big man, but he has an enormous, almost operatic command of his voice. When he speaks, he uses his entire body to punctuate his sentences. He knows how to reach an audience. Sometimes, Chestnut explains, "I'm speaking beyond the courtroom. I may be speaking to the public at large. If this is a case in which there are significant public issues and there is an opportunity within the vortex of representing my client that I can also educate the public, I will gladly yield and do that." This was such a time. He developed a refrain: "Who is this Albert Turner? . . . The government has singled out this black man in Alabama. I ask, 'Who is this Albert Turner?' He is a man who risked his life so blacks in Alabama could vote; a man who faced police dogs and armed state troopers when the government would not come. It did not come then. Now a scant twenty years after blacks fought, marched, bled and died to gain the vote, the government comes to criminal court to prosecute three black people."

On July 5, the jury deliberated for approximately three hours. They returned a verdict of not guilty on all counts for all three defendants.

WE HAD PREVAILED. All of us, from the government witnesses to the sequestered jury, had spoken truth back to power. The courtroom erupted in singing. It was not merely a victory—it was a triumph. We sang many of the old civil rights songs on the steps of the courthouse, the same steps we had climbed for the last few days, steps then crowded with community folk waiting to get into the trial, steps that almost parted in half as the lawyers approached. "Make room, the lawyers are coming," and the people who had taken off time from work, the people who had gotten up early in the morning, made a pathway for us to cross. Now we were leaving the courthouse, all of us, jubilant. We celebrated together right there on the steps of the courthouse.

Spencer Hogue had awaited the jury verdict calmly. He had been angry when they first brought the charges—experiencing the false accusations as "something that goes real deep"—but now he felt a sense of peace. For Evelyn, the anxiety kept mounting. The lowest point for Evelyn Turner had been the day she was fingerprinted. "They said I had been indicted and I just blurted out 'For *what?*' And Hank and Rose, they talked to me and told me that it was just a part of the procedure that they had to go through, that I had to go through. But I just didn't want to do it. It made me feel like I was a criminal, and I hadn't done anything, so I didn't want to be fingerprinted for nothing." Yet, here she was, moments after the jury verdict. "Words cannot describe how I felt," Evelyn said. "No words can describe how I felt—none. I had made up my mind that, well, what will be, will be. And when they came back with a 'not guilty,' I was overwhelmed with joy." We all were.

As the people spilled outside, the brooding image of the Edmund Pettus Bridge loomed in the background. We had labored throughout the trial in its shadow. With the memory of the marchers who passed the 1965 Voting Rights Act on that bridge, we had carried on a noble tradition. That is how powerful we felt: we had history on our side. Buoyed by the converging streams of historical memory and contemporary struggle, we spoke truth to power in the most meaningful way in a democracy—from the bottom up.

That bridge and the Selma trial reinforced for me so many of the things my father had taught me as a little girl. I always believed that ordinary people with little education still had a lot to teach. That belief, which my father's stories certainly planted, was cemented during the trial. I was my father's Virago—to some, a troublemaker, but to others a persistent questioner with big ideas, enormous curiosity, and an appetite for collective struggle. We pursued a dual strategy in the courtroom: some of us did the meticulous, well-researched preparation that provided the foundation for the more fiery performers. We were engaged in a series of collaborations, among the lawyers, between the lawyers and the clients, with the lawyers and the community witnesses. We showed that civil rights lawyers did their best advocacy partnering with a community. All of us worked in tandem to represent our clients and to locate that representation in the context that really mattered to Albert Turner, Evelyn Turner, and Spencer Hogue—their community. In representing Albert, Evelyn, and Spencer, we were also representing their neighbors and their friends. Those with whom they lived and worked were not technically our clients, but they came to see us as their advocates, too.

The trial also reinforced the idea that while lawyers often focus too much only on the legal aspects of a case, this case was an example of a different model. It was a different model because Hank Sanders pursued a public education strategy alongside the defense team in court. It was a different model because the lawyers were working not for fame or fortune or because we knew what was best but because we were willing to support local leadership in a community struggle against the more powerful forces of federal authority. We were lawyering to empower Albert Turner and Spencer Hogue to be able to return to their local community and do their important work as community organizers.

I saw firsthand the importance of "motherwit," the wisdom of common folk that Albert Turner and Spencer Hogue displayed, when they sought out opportunities to defy publicly both the government's and the media's characterizations of them and their ideas. This was an early lesson that ordinary people can prevail, even when up against the enormous resources of a government bureaucracy.

All of us eventually realized we had to speak beyond the courtroom. As was evident in Chestnut's closing argument, we had to speak to the public at large, trying, as Albert Turner did, to change the way people think. We saw an opportunity within "the vortex" of representing our clients to educate the jury and the public, both. We were architects of a legal bridge anchored in history but designed to allow the forces of change to meet the forces of tradition.

Our clients assumed enormous leadership within the trial strategy itself. They bridged the role between lawyer and client, sometimes advocating for themselves and their community against the advice of counsel, but always speaking out not from the elevated perch of technical expertise but from the more humble yet secure ground of their communities.

The elderly black voters, who were summoned by the federal government to testify against our clients, in effect testified as witnesses for the defense. These black citizens spoke with the greatest eloquence and the utmost dignity in their own voice and their own way. They were citizens of a community, they told the court and the jury. They were part of a communal "we" who sought to gain real power by harnessing their individual voting rights to a community agenda. They said, by the way they exercised their vote, that their power came from the power of collective action, the power of "their people." They said, by the way they spoke up in court, they had power because they did not see themselves as isolated and lonely individuals.

They may have been old. They may have been feeble. But they too were building bridges. They refused to back down from a community-based vision, even when badgered or provoked. It was their vision and their courage that stayed with me when I later became a legal academic. When I began writing about the importance of giving a voice—and a choice—to ordinary people, it was the witnesses in the Selma trial who often came to mind. They were mostly uneducated in a formal way, but they were schooled in the more important lesson of joining hands and standing their ground.

At that moment, rejoicing on the steps of the federal courthouse in Selma, Alabama, I realized how central Derrick Bell's advice to me had been four years earlier to go south, to mix it up, to become a civil rights advocate, not just a civil rights technician. I should not be content, in Professor Bell's words, to remain an "anonymous bureaucrat" who brings expertise but "rarely learns from the people with whom they work."

Dayna Cunningham captured the almost mystical power of Professor Bell's advice when she explained the significance of her law student experience working on the trial:

> That summer [1985] in Alabama just put the whole thing into focus for me. It made me realize that there was actually something immediate, and useful, and fulfilling that you could do with law school. And that was it. From that day on, the only thing I ever wanted to do was —in terms of the law—was to practice voting rights law at the Legal Defense Fund. That's the only thing I ever wanted to do. . . . I have absolutely no interest in the law or being a lawyer. Except to the extent that I could be a voting rights lawyer at the Legal Defense Fund.

That day in the shadow of the Edmund Pettus Bridge, I felt personally connected to the forces of nature Derrick Bell told me I would find if I went south. It was the kind of natural struggle Rose lived by. As individuals fighting to challenge false accusations, we each put small waterdrops of faith in the river. One by one those small drops became the river of a different truth as the lawyers, the clients, the formal witnesses, and the ordinary people who came to court every day to bear witness spoke out in unison for a change.

Rose Sanders was right. Selma changed me because it joined me to the force of the "ancient, dusky rivers" that were Langston Hughes's metaphor for a common oppression, a collective struggle, and an uncommon faith. I came to know Selma—its history, its bridges, and its underground streams of resistance.

Drawing strength from all that Selma represented, we built our own bridges to truths that were anchored in Albert Turner and Spencer Hogue's deep sense of underlying justice, fortified by Rose and Hank Sanders's grass-roots organizing to build community support.

Even in the face of intense and powerful opposition, we would not be moved.

CHAPTER EIGHT

Lawyers as Bridge People: Architects of a New Public Space

Ⓘ T WAS IN SELMA, Alabama, and throughout the South that I first saw how lawyers can bear public witness to injustice. To be a lawyer is to be part of a historic tradition of resistance to overreaching by private and public power. Lawyers in our tradition have been the guardians of the rights of unpopular minorities and dissenters. Rose Sanders, Hank Sanders, and J. L. Chestnut in Selma, Alabama, are black lawyers who enjoy enormous status because of just such independence and courageous advocacy within communities of color.

Working with each of these lawyers reminded me that the best use of the legal resources of national organizations was often to reinforce local energy and leadership. When national civil rights organizations came to help out in the Marion Three case, for example, we reinforced not only Chestnut's advocacy but his hopefulness. "You don't know how happy I was to see you," Chestnut later told me. "This was a desperate situation for us. By y'all showing up it said 'we care,' 'you are not alone.' " Chestnut had been worried "to death" about the possibility that everything they had sacrificed for would be gone if they lost the first trial. They would have had "one hell of a time trying to persuade people that it's not only safe but it's right to vote." Chestnut knew it was "all about to go down the drain" if they lost the first trial.

When we lost one of the first civil rights trials of the Clinton administration, I realized how I and other lawyers affiliated with national litigating organizations had lost sight of the need to maintain an open and dynamic relationship with the larger civil rights community. It was, after all, the ordinary people beyond the Beltway who had played such an empowering role in both my own life and in the life of the movement itself. Yet, by the early 1990s, litigators like me had become like the Washington insiders we were so suspicious of during the 1981–

82 fight for the extension of the Voting Rights Act. We reflexively distanced ourselves from the very people on whose behalf we brought the cases in the first place.

There were reasons for this reflex. We had become quite comfortable relying on personal relationships and quiet diplomacy because we had been successful during the 1970s and 1980s using back channels within the federal bureaucracy to fill in loopholes left by vague legislative or judicial opinions. During the Carter administration and the early Reagan years, we were also successful in litigating cases to enforce laws we had, after all, helped craft. Those strategies worked in part because no one else was looking. Even some members of our own community were unaware of all we were doing. We were caught off-guard, however, once strong undercurrents of resistance arose to the changes won by the civil rights movement. Those of us whose influence had been built up through years of insider operating found ourselves in increasingly hostile territory. Judges appointed by Presidents Ronald Reagan and George Bush began systematically dismantling the legal architecture on which our strategy depended. Yet in relying on back channels or lonely court proceedings to make our points, we missed important changes as the public grew restless and unconvinced that the remedies of the 1960s and 1970s made sense in the 1990s. This public included some of our clients.

We had forgotten the lessons of the voter persecution cases described in the last chapter. It was there that we learned to play a weak hand well. Though cowed by zealous agents of the FBI, frail and aging black voters in Perry County, Alabama, still spoke the truth as they knew it. And the truth did set us free. Through the simple act of testifying, these private people gained dignity and safeguarded their status as members of a community. In the singular, however, whether as voters or witnesses, they did not have power. Only by bringing people together and allowing them to speak their stories to the court and the world at large did their status generate power. Indeed it was the community bonds forged in the citizenship schools and the meetings of the Perry County Civic League that later came to haunt the Reagan Justice Department career lawyers when their prosecution of the Marion Three fell apart.

Gradually, more and more lawyers began working behind the scenes. Working exclusively behind the scenes or litigating increasingly technical issues in empty courtrooms didn't even make sense. We forgot what Barbara Major, former LDF client in New Orleans, told LDF cooperating attorney Bill Quigley, "lawyers have to learn how, with all of their skills, to journey with the community," to involve the community in "really getting a sense of who they are . . . to understand their own power."

In charge, we channeled a passion for change into legal negotiations and lawsuits. We defined the issues in terms of developing legal doctrine and establishing legal precedent; our clients became important, but secondary, players in a formal arena that required lawyers to translate lay claims into technical speech. We then disembodied the plaintiffs' claims in judicially manageable or judicially enforceable terms, unenforceable without more lawyers.

Simultaneously, the movement's center of gravity shifted to Washington, D.C. As lawyers and national pundits became more prominent than clients and citizens, we isolated ourselves from the people who were our anchor and on whose behalf we had labored. We not only left people behind; we also lost touch with the moral force at the heart of the movement itself. As *New York Times* national correspondent Isabel Wilkerson observes, the civil rights movement became increasingly ceremonial, "spoken of in the low whispers or the high eulogies reserved for the dead." We forgot the role of ordinary people, the faceless others in the grainy footage of "fedora-topped now-famous men marching across Southern bridges."

J. L. CHESTNUT, still practicing law in Selma, took time recently to reflect back thirty years ago when Lyndon Johnson, the president of the United States, called blacks "the real heroes" and told the American people that the cause of American blacks "must be our cause, too." The 1965 march from Selma to Montgomery marked for many the time when the civil rights movement had its greatest impact on the nation. Chestnut reminisced about the role of a few brave white lawyers from the North, people like Jack Greenberg. Then, with his arms describing great circles in the air, his palms cupped to reinforce his phrasing, Chestnut said: "Most people know what Martin Luther King's role was, Ralph Abernathy's role, Andrew Young, and later on Jesse's role. What they don't realize is that *before* the marches, *during* the marches, and *after* the marches, a monumental legal struggle went on by unpaid, underpaid, dedicated, quiet African-American lawyers."

Civil rights lawyers had played a critical, but supporting, role in helping ordinary people march to freedom. For me, the role of lawyers was embodied in the person of Constance Baker Motley as she escorted James Meredith to the University of Mississippi in 1962. At age twelve I admired this strong black woman lawyer.

Chestnut reminded me, however, that as important as Thurgood Marshall, Constance Baker Motley, and other prominent LDF lawyers were, they depended in turn on the staying power of courageous local cooperating attorneys in southern communities. The local black lawyers were people who had some independence as a result of their professional status within a segregated community. They made their living from other black people and could therefore afford to challenge the racism their clients encountered. Their cases were about many things, but mostly they were about being treated with respect. Lawyers were powerful because they were self-employed. More truthfully, they were employed by the black community.

Local black lawyers were still insiders though independent of the white-dominated southern establishment. J. L. Chestnut, the only black lawyer practicing full time in Selma in 1965, was an LDF cooperating attorney during the movement's apogee. Outspoken and courageous, he nevertheless often felt exasperated by his complicated working relationship with his even more outspoken client, Dr. Martin Luther King. Chestnut was provided expense money by the Legal Defense Fund, which worked through litigation, not street demonstrations. Its strategy was test cases: "Send four or five obviously qualified people to the registration office. If their constitutional rights are denied, file a lawsuit. King, by sending five hundred, was repudiating this concept—then calling on the organization to provide legal services and bail money." One time King said to Chestnut, "We're trying to win the right to vote and we have to focus the attention of the world on that. We can't do that making legal cases. We have to make the case in the court of public opinion."

Chestnut was often unsettled by King's message because it destabilized his role as a member of the legal establishment. He was an insider, trained to be cautious, not to disrupt. Chestnut writes in his memoir, *Black in Selma:* "As a lawyer representing the NAACP Legal Defense Fund in the midst of a street protest movement, I was stretched between competing philosophies and egos, and my own beliefs were challenged. King's philosophy that we had a moral right to disobey unjust laws ran counter to my legal training."

Chestnut's "role confusion" was understandable. He recognized the limitations of the judicial system; as he put it, "white men in black robes had upheld Jim Crow for almost a century." But he was trained to believe that you changed the system through the system. "You didn't go out and break the law. You went to court." King ultimately persuaded him that they had no better choice. "If the movement were to follow the legalistic view I was advancing, it would be reduced to the whims of [United States District] Judge [Daniel H.] Thomas and [Selma Circuit Court] Judge Hare and whether we could find some white judge a few years later willing to overrule them. You couldn't take a people's movement and reduce it to that. I had to agree. Hell, that's right. But as a lawyer, I still worried over the fact that we were deciding on our own which laws were just or unjust."

Despite Chestnut's qualms, he ultimately agreed with King that this was a moral crusade that could change America; this was not about marching in the streets from time to time or winning an isolated or even crucial legal victory. Nor could they be satisfied by short-term triumphs over local white law enforcement. They had to tell their story in such a way that the rest of America would listen and eventually understand. Chestnut understood this. He knew that as the lawyer, he was hired for a specific purpose: he should not confuse the tools of litigation with all that the movement could achieve.

Remaining connected to the struggle was the only way to negotiate his dual roles as a civil rights movement lawyer and local insider. For Chestnut, it was very important to attend mass meetings, even when he wasn't giving a speech or a report.

Mass meetings connected him to his clients. At those meetings, Chestnut heard stories of brutality by Sheriff Jim Clark or his posse —"slapping a woman, chasing a group of children with cattle prods." He was inspired by hearing "a mother describe how she'd lost her job, and knew she would lose it, but considered marching worth the sacrifice." The Constitution's promise gained real meaning for him when he saw young students "willing to get their heads whipped." But it was the sermons, the speeches, and the singing, most of all, that inspired him.

Many hundreds of miles north and east of Selma, another LDF cooperating attorney also witnessed the difficulties of a formal and legalistic ideal in which bad laws were the problem and changing them to good laws was the main solution. Like Chestnut in the 1960s, G. K. Butterfield in the 1980s believed that by changing and enforcing the law, lawyers would help open up opportunities for community organizers and local leaders to become elected officials. Positioning good people, integrating elite decision-making groups, would empower all people. But like Chestnut, Butterfield also came to discover the limitations of a strategy that seeks to make social change without a social movement.

G. K. Butterfield is sitting in chambers on the second floor of the courthouse in Wilson, North Carolina, overlooking the giant white marble steps that he and other demonstrators once climbed as staging grounds for protest. Now an elected state judge from a majority black district, Butterfield as a civil rights attorney had been at the forefront of movement activity in this rural community. Butterfield's hair is jet-black, neatly combed away from his face; his face is olive-skinned. He looks very much like a member of the working-class Italian family who lived across the street from me in St. Albans, Queens, where I grew up. Had Butterfield grown up somewhere else, he might have been mistaken for white. But not in Wilson, where the lines between blacks and whites are heavily policed. What Butterfield looks like is irrelevant. Where he comes from, everyone knows who his people are. G. K. Butterfield has always been black in this southern community.

Elegant in his judicial robes, Butterfield often thinks about his transformation from demonstrator to adjudicator. Looking out onto those courthouse steps, he likes to remind himself how far we've come. After all, he told me, that's why we went to court in the first place: to show our clients that "the system" does work.

Judge Butterfield describes himself as the "facilitator" for NAACP LDF voting cases. Attorney Butterfield, Leslie Winner (a young white lawyer who did many voting cases for Julius Chambers's law firm in Charlotte), and I had filed several cases throughout central and eastern North Carolina, challenging the use of at-large election systems, and ultimately producing single-member district plans, including the one from which Butterfield was elected a North Carolina Superior Court judge. "I delivered the case to LDF," he acknowledges, deliberately downplaying his important role as a cooperating attorney in generating local support for the legal action. His modesty established, Judge Butterfield admits that his neighbors give him all the credit: "We're local heroes. They think my former law partner Toby Fitch paved the streets. They think I brought three black commissioners to Wilson."

Relaxed and feeling introspective, G. K. Butterfield tells me a story about the unintended consequences of such hero worship. As a civil rights lawyer in Wilson, North Carolina, Butterfield had a reputation as a fighter; he was willing to take on the system. A group of local teachers and parents came to him, upset that as a result of a decision to consolidate the school system, no school in this 40 percent black county would bear the name of a black person. The powers-that-be had closed Charles H. Darden High School, the black school, sending all students to three other schools, two of which were newly constructed. The black community felt strongly that since one of the three schools was going to be a black high school, it should be named after a black person. The white folks said no; it was important to get away from naming schools after personalities. They proposed naming one Southeast and the other Southwest.

At first, the black community was mollified by the fact that neither school would bear a racially distinct name: all the schools would be named after geographic directions. But then a very prominent white member of Wilson died suddenly of a heart attack, and some of the whites in the county came to the board of education and said they now wanted to name one of the new schools after the deceased citizen. The policy against naming schools after individuals was about to change.

Black people from all over Wilson crowded into G. K.'s small law office. School teachers, administrators, and parents pleaded with him to make the case for naming one school after someone black. They all agreed to meet at seven o'clock the next night to attend the board of education meeting. G. K. stayed up all night. He drafted a press release and outlined his remarks, developing the argument that at least one of the high schools in this 40 percent black county should recognize, through its name, the contributions of the black residents.

The next night, Butterfield arrived as planned. The parking lot was filled; people were milling around. Butterfield had a hard time finding the entrance to the auditorium where the meeting was being held. He made his way through the crowd, clutching his briefcase. There were five hundred people at the meeting—all white. They were there to support naming the two new schools after two white men.

As he approached the building, the people who had solicited him to confront the issue were nowhere to be found. He saw only one black person, a gentleman who was supporting the board of education's new proposal. Butterfield stopped in his tracks. "I had to have a little prayer meeting with myself," he explained, as he contemplated going forward in the absence of his clients. After a few moments of quiet reflection, Butterfield decided he had nothing to say. He turned around and quickly left.

Ron Chisom, an LDF client in a number of voting cases, explains the phenomenon that Butterfield confronted:

> A lawyer steps in, in what is essentially a technical role, and shows some real authority and expertise by even simple things like taking notes which most people in the community do not do. People in the organization look up to the lawyer because of their writing skills, their reading skills, their education, their speaking skills and it really makes the lawyer look like they are doing something. People then tend to transfer their interest in the issue and the problem to the lawyer to have the lawyer solve it and this creates dependency. Total dependence on a lawyer by an organization is not good because most lawyers are "career-oriented." They will usually help the community, but they also later hurt the community by making money off the contacts in the community, by political aspirations and by leaving the community stranded. In many cases, they actually leave the community in a worse condition had they never been involved. Most lawyers do not understand about organizing. Lawyers do not understand that the legal piece is only one tactic of organizing. It is not the goal.

Chisom, who is an African-American community organizer and was the lead plaintiff in the Supreme Court voting rights case *Chisom* v. *Roemer*, was interviewed by William Quigley, now assistant professor and director of Gillis Long Poverty Law Center at Loyola University School of Law. When Bill Quigley interviewed him, Ron Chisom was not speaking specifically of G. K. Butterfield, but he could have been.

After all, Butterfield had been delegated to represent the views of a large number of black constituents, who then apparently felt relieved of their own responsibility to attend the meeting. As Butterfield tells it, their view was, " 'Let G. K. take care of it. G. K. will go up there. And even if he doesn't go up there, he will tell them. He will tell them what they need to know.' Meanwhile, they were home cooking dinner."

For local movement organizers, civil rights was about community participation in shaping a common destiny. It was the idea of unity, "sticking together, pooling our resources," that motivated a few local activists to pour their hearts and souls into these cases. They did so, not for any self-aggrandizement; no one got rich or even got monetary damages. Indeed, some paid significant personal prices—harassment, ostracism, loss of valuable time from their jobs.

The idea that black people had to fight back (" 'cause once they get you down, they'll ride you," Evelyn Turner told me) had inspired a mass movement. The idea behind fighting back, however, was that black people had to fight back together. Black lawyers like Butterfield and Chestnut often played key roles in that fight. But, as Ron Chisom warned, their status and training often led lawyers to channel political movements into legal cases. When lawyers took notes and assumed authority, their clients stayed home.

Indeed, after the whirlwind of activity in the 1960s, the mass movement, with its rhetoric of the beloved community and its passion for broad-based participatory democracy, died because it didn't completely understand the truth it was revealing. Instead of a moral crusade led by the people, the civil rights movement became an almost purely legal crusade. Because the law became, essentially, what the lawyers and the lobbyists said it was, no one listened to what it was the demonstrators and the marchers had to say.

The remedies pursued in these cases showed that lawyers favored standards of manageability even if they failed to provide the foundations for either mass movement or fundamental social change. We were advocates, not agitators. We pursued those options that we knew best: formal, technical strategies that often seemed mysterious even to clients most invested in our success.

Spencer Hogue's experience is instructive. Hogue was an LDF client in a 1985 obstruction-of-justice case the Reagan U.S. Attorney had brought contemporaneously with the Marion Three conspiracy case. As with the voting fraud charges, the case was part of an effort to intimidate; but unlike the voting fraud charges, the obstruction-of-justice case never went to trial.

What did he think happened, I asked Hogue, ten years after the charges were first lodged against him. He sat erect in his favorite chair in his living room in Marion, Alabama, and looked at me unblinkingly. "I don't know," he answered. "It went up to the appeals court and it just disappeared." Spencer Hogue didn't give the case too much thought after it "just disappeared." He was certainly grateful that his lawyers took care of it for him. But we never explained what was happening and he never really knew. Framing social change within a legal system remote from the people meant that those with the most at stake were left to wonder and hope, but not necessarily *do* for themselves. We had lost sight of the lessons we were teaching and of those we had learned.

We were no longer explaining to regular black folk what it meant to vote. Even more, we stopped talking about why it was important to participate beyond just voting. Instead, we were occupied with filing cases and launching inside-the-Beltway legislative or regulatory fights. We had forgotten Dr. King's admonition to J. L. Chestnut: we were no longer making our case to and with the people. Instead, courts were our venue; there we reinforced the learned expertise of some, like Pam Karlan (then an LDF staff attorney, now professor at University of Virginia Law School) and me, to the detriment of the lived wisdom of others. Though these others knew more about local politics, had to endure the consequences of local wrath, and had more at stake, they nevertheless had less input.

"I DON'T THINK they had ever seen anyone who is white and from outside of Phillips County take their claims seriously before." Pamela Karlan was sitting in her office at Harvard Law School, where she was a visiting professor, explaining her role in the *Whitfield* case that she and I had filed in Arkansas in 1987. As staff lawyers for LDF, we had jointly challenged Arkansas' majority vote runoff law. Pam was still shocked by the absence of *any* cross-racial politics in eastern Arkansas when I interviewed her seven years later.

We were reminiscing. Pam's bicycle was propped against the wall of her Harvard office. Dressed casually in beige khaki slacks and a pink open-collar polo shirt, she looked most unlike the popular image of a Harvard law professor. But she also did not look like the crusading attorney who regularly flew from New York to Memphis en route to Helena, Arkansas, a small town on the Mississippi River that was "one time zone and twenty years behind the East Coast."

Helena, in Phillips County, was a large, amazingly poor rural community in the Mississippi Delta region. The per capita income for blacks was less than $3,000 per year; for whites it was about $5,000. Forty percent of black households did not have access to a car, truck, or van; 30 percent did not even have a telephone. Pam recalls the rundown shacks: "They were not painted. Everything was old and shabby, as if no one had the time or the resources to take good care." When she thinks back to Phillips County, Pam tells me, "I think in black and white. I don't think in color, even though I can remember how incredibly green the soybean fields were or how incredibly thick and rich the dirt was. When I think about the town, I don't recall any colors."

During her many trips to eastern Arkansas, Pam never had a social encounter of any kind with anyone who was white. Indeed, none of the lawyers we worked with in eastern Arkansas socialized with white people. As Pam remembers, "When I was down in New Orleans or Birmingham working on cases, most of the people I socialized with were the local lawyers, some of whom were white. But in Phillips County and throughout eastern Arkansas, there wasn't a progressive biracial community. If there was, I didn't have any access to it. I never came in contact with anybody who was white, except for Martha, who worked behind the desk at the Old Edwardian Inn, and the man behind the counter at Burger King. And, of course, the white officials whose depositions I took.

"It would really be hard to be hopeful," Pam concluded, "if I lived in Phillips County, Arkansas. It just didn't seem hopeful. I wasn't in any town called Hope. I was in a place called Resignation."

Pam had never been south before she came to the Legal Defense Fund, and here she was in a part of the United States that was light-years away from anything she had ever experienced. As Pam remembers, "I really wanted to touch the Mississippi River. I wanted to experience it. I had never been there before. Phillips County was right up against the Mississippi River, but nobody seemed to know how to get there."

In this "place called Resignation," Pam and I, two eager young lawyers, thought we could use the Voting Rights Act, as it was amended in 1982, to bring back hope, to fix things for people like Reverend Julious Magruder. Magruder was a black preacher and radio repairman who had run unsuccessfully for his local school board. Magruder explained that the repeated defeats of black candidates caused many potential voters to lose hope that their votes would make a difference. "Well, just the heart and soul went out of us," Magruder testified.

Sam Whitfield, a thirty-two-year-old black attorney, told us that he ran several times without success for public office in Phillips County. He described the time he ran in a three-person race. In the primary, Whitfield came in first but with less than 51 percent of the vote. However, the majority-vote requirement commanded that he get 51 percent in order to win the seat. A runoff was called because none of the candidates got "a majority." Before the second runoff election, the losing candidate—the person who came in third in the first primary—came up to Whitfield and said, "You know, Sam, I believe you are the most qualified candidate, but I cannot support a black man. I live in this town. I am a farmer and my wife teaches school here. There is just no way I can support a black candidate."

Blacks like Sam Whitfield were unsuccessful in county elections because of the racially polarized voting. Whites tended to vote for whites and blacks, when they had the choice of a black candidate, would tend to vote for blacks. Voting in Phillips County was *extremely* polarized. In some precincts, not even one white person could bring himself or herself to vote for *any* black running for office.

In Helena, whites who ran the local shops along the one main street would not put up posters or campaign literature for Sam Whitfield, especially when Whitfield was running in the second primary, poised to defeat someone white. Several white residents testified that they privately supported the aspirations of some black politicians they knew and respected, but felt constrained by the culture of Phillips County from saying so out loud. When they supported a black candidate, they had to do so secretly, donating cash in plain white envelopes so none of their neighbors would know.

Racially polarized voting was not the only obstacle in democracy's way. Between elections the white county clerks frequently changed polling places without notice. In one heavily black precinct, the clerks relocated the polling places eleven times in a two-year period. Once, they completely confused voters in the largest black precinct, moving the polling place to a location outside the district. This, of course, reinforcd the image that voting was something very difficult and beyond the capacity of ordinary citizens.

The legal barrier that Pam and I were challenging was the winner-take-all majority-vote requirement. Winner-take-all majority rule, in itself, may seem the essence of democracy, but in a community that tolerates no cross-racial interaction and knows nothing of biracial progressive politics, it functions as a traffic cop enforcing racial divisions. It structures competition to police racial boundaries and assures that blacks, 44 percent of the electorate, have no formal electoral power.

The majority-vote runoff required a candidate to get more than 50 percent of the vote. If a candidate came in first but didn't get the crucial 51 percent, a runoff election was held. Since the second election was always held two weeks after the first, candidates had little time to mobilize their voters. Those seeking to campaign in rural black churches that did not meet every Sunday were severely disadvantaged.

Many blacks saw no reason to turn out a second time. By their reckoning if their candidate had polled the most votes in the first election, they had already won. They saw the majority-vote runoff simply as a ploy by white folks to "steal" the election. "Well, they're going to do what they want to do," Sam Whitfield's supporters told him. Overall, fewer people turned out to vote the second time, since many of the issues or races they cared about had already been resolved in the first election. Thus, the so-called majority runoff actually produced an artificial majority—51 percent of a much smaller pool of voters.

Whatever the abstract merit might be in holding two elections within a two-week period to select the most "popular" candidate, the reality proved itself at odds with basic ideas of participatory democracy. Indeed, the runoff primary had become, for the most part, an empty ritual few people practiced. Yet it was a ritual that served an important function in disciplining race relations in the county.

No black in Phillips County had ever gained a majority of the vote, since a black candidate's support came entirely from within the 44 percent black electorate. The majority-vote runoff allowed whites to fight among themselves in a primary election, and still win, despite internal squabbles within a politically fractured white electorate. Because they had the safety valve of a second up/down vote, whites, who were a voting majority, had the opportunity to work through their differences as if the only election that mattered took place within an entirely white electorate.

Blacks might consolidate their votes on the black candidate, and some blacks, such as Sam Whitfield, might gain the "most" votes. But the majority runoff, in which the only issue seemed to be will a white person or a black person prevail, prevented successful blacks from winning because they still fell short of a majority.

So, Pam and I stood up in court and argued that in Phillips County, Arkansas, a self-conscious, racially constituted, monolithic *group* was hoarding all power. We said that blacks in Phillips County believed in democracy. They turned out to vote. They fielded candidates. Yet they were not represented because a racially defined majority had created rules that kept out one group of people and kept in another. The election rules encouraged whites to run freely in the first primary and then gang up on any successful black candidates in the second runoff election.

The week before trial in early March 1988, Pam rented a car and drove to Helena with Terry, a young black LDF paralegal. As they approached Helena, driving up a hill and around the corner, she pointed out two landmarks where the concrete embankment met the road. On one retaining wall there was a sign for the King Biscuit Blues Festival. On another billboard, Pam remembers a big sign right as you came into Phillips County: HOME OF KEN HATFIELD, COACH OF THE ARKANSAS FOOTBALL TEAM. The Arkansas Razorbacks were popular. Terry could pick up a souvenir—one of the little red tractor caps with red felt ears, red felt snouts, and little eyes that bobbed up and down. But Terry would not be distracted by funny souvenir caps. He was preoccupied. He was from California and "had never been south before, but his grandparents were from the South, and when he first saw the cotton fields, it was in the early spring, the cotton was just starting to come out." Pam remembers that Terry started crying "when we drove past the little cotton museum and I pointed out the cotton ball in the window and he got all upset and started thinking about his family."

Pam, who is Jewish, had grown up in an upper-middle-class suburb in Connecticut. She decided to become a civil rights lawyer when she was twelve or thirteen and read about the *Brown* v. *Board of Education* case in Richard Kluger's classic work, *Simple Justice*. But even before that, her parents made sure she was aware of the dramatic struggle being waged in another region of the country. "I was in third grade when Martin Luther King was killed. They closed our school for a day. I lived in an all-white suburban community. All these other kids were outside playing and my mother insisted I stay inside and watch the funeral on TV. I remember thinking this must be very important for me to be home watching TV during the day."

After a prestigious Supreme Court clerkship, Pam turned down a faculty position at Yale Law School to come work at LDF. There was a part of Pam that found LDF attractive because of its reputation for having the best, smartest civil rights lawyers in the country. But Pam was also attracted to civil rights work because she "would be doing something really important with people who are different from me."

The Yale Law School dean believed that Pam "had just ruined" her career; but Pam was undeterred. She loved her work. "At LDF I really felt a part of things, I felt I was an integral member of the team. LDF was incredibly collegial, a very internally supportive place. In dealing with the clients, I always felt comfortable. We were on the same side and they always seemed delighted that someone would take their issues seriously."

Phillips County was one of Pam's first cases. There Pam was exposed to a poverty that is very close to the earth. Two of the local lawyers we worked with were farmers. Pam explains, "I had never met anyone who was a lawyer and something else on the side. They were country lawyers. Real country lawyers. Not like Sam Ervin."

Pam remembers that one of the local black attorneys who farmed was Jimmy Lee Wilson, a flamboyant man who would get a kick out of standing with her out in the parking lot in front of his office and seeing the uncomfortable reactions of the white people who passed. Helena, after all, was just one sleepy street where, in Pam's mind, "all the restaurants closed at five and all the vegetables were fried in fat." We would drive across the river to Mississippi every night to eat, except when Olly Neal, the other lawyer/farmer, would take us to eat barbecue at a local juke joint, the Forty Four Club. One night, at the Moon Lake restaurant in Mississippi, we caused quite a stir. The restaurant staff was stiff. They greeted us without enthusiasm but invited us in. Pam,

Terry (the black paralegal from California), and I sat down. "They say they are from New York," the waitress said standing in the kitchen, but talking loudly enough for us to overhear. Our little interracial dinner showcased the complete disconnection between blacks and whites in that part of the South.

We may have been eating out in 1988, but this was still the Old South. Our experiences resonated with that of our trial witnesses. One very independent-minded gentleman, Bankston Waters, was chairman of the County Republican Central Committee. Waters told the court he lived in Phillips County sixty-four years and knew of no other whites of his economic or leadership status who publicly supported black candidates running for office. When Mr. Waters broke that tradition, making a financial contribution to L. T. Simes, one of his tenants, Waters became a social pariah.

"When a white person contributes to a black person's campaign funds," Waters testified, "it is somehow or another known rather rapidly." No one threatened him directly but they "let him know" that "they did not approve."

Waters was invited to attend a banquet for Jesse Jackson, who was then running for president. This Republican iconoclast was the only white person present, except for the press and one other guest. He went simply because he was curious. "I've always been interested in what politicians said," Mr. Waters explained. After the event, he returned home. There he found his neighbors buzzing around his house, demanding to know, what he—a white man—was doing at a Jesse Jackson rally in 1984!

For Pam, the social distance and the shocking poverty reinforced an eerie psychological distance. "You were seventy miles from Memphis. You could watch Memphis PBS but FedEx wouldn't guarantee next-day delivery. This was when FedEx flew every single package through Memphis for delivery." That she couldn't receive or send packages using a company whose hub was only seventy miles away really made Pam feel she was outside of time.

We both prepared for trial in Jimmy Wilson's storefront offices, in what had been the old State Farm Insurance building. The office was dark and gloomy; for a law office, it did not have many books. But in a storage room in the back we would talk to the people Jimmy Wilson and Olly Neal brought in from around the county. Pam had dragged a huge computer from New York to take notes as she interviewed the local witnesses. But neither the bulky computer, the awkward work space, nor the slow-talking local witnesses were the problem. What really irritated her was the defense lawyer for the state of Arkansas.

Pam hated negotiating with opposing counsel. It bothered her that the state's attorney, Tim Humphries, was "smug and cocky and absolutely convinced he was going to win the case, and it didn't matter what we argued or what the evidence was." Humphries refused to cooperate with the most basic requests for information. He refused, for example, to admit that Arkansas had ever segregated its schools. Every interrogatory we posed was too burdensome to answer, so he simply objected to all of them. He didn't bother to find his own expert witnesses to analyze the voting returns. Instead, he arranged to take the deposition of our expert in New Orleans and made certain the deposition took place during Mardi Gras. At the deposition, Humphries zeroed in on one issue: could he use our expert's network of social scientists to help identify someone the state of Arkansas could hire to take the opposite view? Our expert, Professor Richard Engstrom of the University of New Orleans, who analyzed the county election returns for us, provided Humphries with the name of Harold Stanley, a professor and political consultant. Tim then tried to hire Stanley, less than a month before trial. Stanley pleaded unavailability because the trial was scheduled to overlap with the Democratic presidential primary, scheduled for Super Tuesday.

Though he had no expert, Humphries was not worried. He simply photocopied some of Harold Stanley's articles and handed them to the judge in lieu of his witness's testimony. To our shock, the judge accepted these reproductions as if Harold Stanley had been qualified as an expert witness, had been under oath, and we had had an opportunity to cross-examine him. Tim Humphries did little to advance his case and still he won.

Humphries was defending a system in which blacks, who were dirt-poor, had never in this century been able to elect a candidate of their choice to any of the seven countywide governing positions. His role was simple: defend the status quo, backed as it was by seemingly neutral, democratic rules that nevertheless skewed the results so blacks never won anything.

Our role was complicated. We faced a double paradox. First, we were challenging something called "majority" runoff elections. Because majority rule is so closely associated in the minds of Americans with the very essence of democracy, it seemed to some, including the judge, that we were in fact challenging democracy itself. Indeed, the judge's reaction should have forewarned me that winner-take-all majority rule, despite flagrant examples of its basic unfairness in Phillips County, had assumed a sacred role in American democratic mythology. At least in the abstract, I should have known then that no one with public service ambitions could touch it. Of course, in practice Americans don't strictly adhere to the preferences of a simple majority. Consider, for example, the U.S. Senate: To ensure that those in the political minority party can play a meaningful role debating and voting on key issues, a simple majority is not allowed to cut off internal debate among senators, and the thirty least populous states essentially enjoy minority rule since they get sixty senators although they contain less than half the country's population.

Our second dilemma was that even if the court should intervene to protect a minority that has been excluded, and excluded primarily because of radical prejudice, it was not clear exactly how that exclusion should be remedied. This is precisely where the issue is still joined. Indeed, the Supreme Court in cases like *Shaw* v. *Reno* and its progency seems determined to eliminate efforts to group black voters into single-member congressional districts in which the minority can become the majority.

It was in asking both these questions—how can a minority share power with a hostile majority and how do you remedy the violation?— that I eventually proposed winner-take-only-some remedies, like cumulative voting that later got me into so much trouble. I seized upon these alternative remedies because they seemed plausible ways to open up the political process, not just to racial minorities but to broad-based participation by citizens generally. The alternatives I considered involved rules to restructure political competition so that a hostile majority would begin to share power and to include a minority within the governing coalition. (I return to cumulative voting in chapter Nine.)

Pam was a powerful oral advocate, a brilliant, sharp-tongued, Yale-trained lawyer, who answered each and every one of the Arkansas federal judge's questions during three and a half hours of closing argument. Pam finally stopped talking only when she got so hungry she needed to ask for a lunch break. She pointed out the relevant circumstances, including uncontested witness testimony from both blacks and whites about voting along racial lines in Phillips County. Based on the law as passed by Congress in 1982, our case was not only textbook-perfect, it was basically unopposed. (Indeed, then governor Clinton, one of the original defendants, had offered in conversation with me—after he was dismissed from the case—to come testify for plaintiffs. Maybe, in retrospect, we should have called him as a witness. But even then we were not quite sure what he would say.)

To our great surprise, at the end of the trial into which Pam and I had poured everything we had, we lost. Pam just "felt outraged. We did everything right in that case. Great lay witnesses. All the facts in the world on our side. The law should have been on our side. And we lost."

Eventually, she grew more philosophical about the outcome, saying, "In some sense we lost because this was precisely a case about politics and the political philosophy of the judges." We lost, Pam believes, because "in a place like Phillips County, there is no 'liberal' solution when the system is designed to ensure the people have no power." For many whites in the South, "it is not about sharing power; it is about legitimating established power. They are open to a system that allows in a couple of blacks. Then, if a few blacks can get elected, their presence legitimates the status quo. But no one has to share real power." There is a worry about electing too many blacks. After all, Pam reminds me, "many politicians believe that you are not just trading one-for-one, but for every black person who gets elected, two white Democrats lose."

On the other hand, Pam refused to accept defeat. "I can't believe eventually we are not going to win. I think the law is on our side. The facts are on our side. In fact, there is a lot of racism, prejudice, and unfairness, and the system we have right now isn't working so well. I keep thinking eventually people will understand this. Call me an optimist."

We lost that case in Phillips County, even though the state defendants (who started with Governor Clinton and ended with the Democratic Party of the state of Arkansas) put up only one witness—a young man, he looked no older than twenty-three—who had been working for the state Democratic Party in Little Rock for about a year. His testimony consumed a total of twenty minutes. Our evidence took four days to present. The state's only witness had never set foot before in Phillips County. He, alone, testified for the defendants that whatever the unfair outcome, the Democratic Party was not intentionally discriminating when it held runoff elections.

But while Pam and I argued the law, we too were alone in the courtroom. Except for one day when a local teacher brought his high school class to court, a couple of the clients would come by, but otherwise the courtroom was empty. It was not that we hadn't done our homework. We had most of the community leaders involved in the case. All of the people who had been candidates for office, the people who had been involved in desegregating the schools, and all of the local black lawyers supported our legal claims. But unlike the Marion Three case, our courtroom was not a mass meeting. Nor had we been to a mass meeting to explain the case to the black folk in Phillips County on whose behalf we were fighting.

We learned, too late, that the courtroom is not democracy's forum; it is too hierarchical, too formalistic, too solemn. The judge was hostile to our claims. By challenging the use of a majority runoff by the Democratic Party in Arkansas, Pam, Olly Neal, and I were challenging his narrow conception of democracy. Next, he accused, we would question the constitutionality of holding elections!

We appealed his decision. After winning on the law before a panel of three appellate judges, we lost again when the appellate court convened as a whole. Meanwhile, nothing changed in the lives of the people of eastern Arkansas. We had pursued a legal strategy, directed by lawyers and other professionals, which by its nature left ordinary people in the community little role in the development of policy and program, except raising funds and cheerleading when victories came.

It was a mistake, I came to believe, to rely only on lawyers and politicians to frame the argument. It was a mistake because the people, encouraged by the fact that lawyers took notes and politicians made good speeches, stopped marching or doing much more than walking to the ballot box once every few years. It was also a mistake because as lawyers we focused on enforcing the law but then lost sight of the real problem: opening up the democratic process so that the citizens rather than the politicians could exercise real power. We forgot that the issue of civil rights depends on seizing the moral high ground. In the case of democracy, the moral high ground was not claimed with the mere presence of a few more black politicians. The moral high ground required that we find ways to give back the power to the people—all of the people.

The danger of our expert-driven strategy is both the obvious one of losing in court, as we eventually did, and, more important, of demobilizing our community base, which put great faith in our efforts and did not organize in other ways. This was the real loss—the subtle long-term demobilization of a social movement.

Our initial legal victories in places like Pickens County, Alabama, and Wilson, North Carolina, led some of us simply to celebrate the "illusion of change." We played the role of social reformers parachuting into a community, hoping to put our expertise and knowledge to work quickly to make things better. As a result, as Gerald Rosenberg writes in *The Hollow Hope: Can Courts Bring About Social Change*, "Social reformers, with limited resources, forgo other options when they elect to litigate. Those options are mainly political and involve mobilizing citizens to participate more effectively."

Despite our early successes, we had forgotten the four lessons of the civil rights movement: we had little grass-roots organizing effort behind us; we lacked a broad-based coalition anchored in local struggles; we did minimal public education; and we failed to seize the moral high ground. Voting and running for office were about a right to belong as a full-fledged member of society *and* a corresponding capacity to mobilize collectively to make a difference. By helping each other, pooling resources so you "don't ever let 'em get you down," blacks, in Albert and Evelyn Turner's vision, would be part of a community in which "everybody ought to run the government." But "everybody" did not mean just a few black people acting on behalf of everyone else. Unity was a valuable idea for mobilizing; yet it soon became a hollow notion when sticking together only meant mobilizing to elect somebody who looked like you and who then acted on your behalf, but without your input and active say-so.

Everybody, as in "everybody ought to run the government," meant that ordinary folk had important roles to play. Everybody also included other disenfranchised and underrepresented groups such as women, poor people, and the disabled. We lacked a vocabulary to show that everybody meant ordinary black people and white allies, too. My efforts to create that vocabulary would later get me in big trouble.

There were two problems with our approach. One was process— we were preoccupied with an elite-driven model of litigation for social change. The other was substantive—we were trying to incorporate a few more blacks into a political system that was itself bankrupt.

The danger came when, by shifting from protest to politics, leaders of the civil rights movement were absorbed as individuals into mainstream electoral activity, but ordinary black folk enjoyed little real power sharing. As a result, as Peter Applebome writes in his book, *Dixie Rising,*

> Many of the civil rights leaders of the 1960s are now the entrenched political class, but the state-mandated tax code still protects the interests of the white landowners who preceded them, and virtually all the major employers—businesses, stores, banks—are owned by whites. Lumber has replaced cotton as the region's main crop, but is controlled by either the whites who owned the land then or giant lumber companies that own it now, and the lumber business had no more need than cotton farming did for most of the blacks rendered obsolete by mechanized agriculture.

Throughout the 1980s, civil rights lawyers remained independent and principled. We challenged the established power structure, but we failed to articulate why others should care that black people in Phillips County had a vote but no voice. We talked the language of voting rights, of "Senate Report factors," of section two "equal opportunity to participate and elect." We knew that the experience of blacks in Phillips County could not be fully described in race-neutral terms. We had to talk directly about the black/white divide so that those who lived in "a place called Resignation" could speak aloud about why they had lost hope. But we forgot the importance of explaining how the fight against winner-take-all majority rule in Phillips County was an effort to bring in *more* democracy, not undermine it.

We should have used our race-specific grievance to open up a big conversation about democracy itself, a conversation in which others could identify and participate. We should have demonstrated that the solution to the problems of poor black communities in eastern Arkansas could have led to a richer and more fruitful politics for everyone. With an infusion of poor people who feel empowered to speak to their own experience, we could reinvigorate participatory democracy.

Mobilizing groups of people is not just important so that a black minority can gain representation: it is crucial to save democracy for everyone. After all, democracy means the people shall rule. Changing polling places and running two elections within two weeks demobilized *everyone* in Phillips County. Those who won the runoff did so only because the powers-that-be had artificially reduced the electorate to create a phony majority. We forgot what King often preached: that by freeing ourselves, black people free white people, too.

JAMES FERGUSON still considers himself a movement lawyer. Fergie (as everyone calls him) decided to go into law while still in high school in Asheville, North Carolina, in 1960:

> When we formed our group to engage in direct action and to desegre-gate public facilities in Asheville, one of the first things that we did was to seek some of the adults in the community to give us some advice. Two of the individuals that we talked to were the only two black lawyers in Asheville—Rubin Daley and Charles Epps. I know that is his last name, Epps. I'm not too sure about the first name. But we met with them truly expecting that they would give us these very carefully laid out legal guidelines, lay out the law to us of what we could or couldn't do and kind of tell us that, but they didn't. They didn't do that. Instead, both of them first of all agreed to consult with us free of charge throughout everything we did. They said, "We will be there to support you." Secondly, they said, "We don't need to try to tell you what the law is. You do what you feel you have to do and we will be there to support you." And they were. Throughout the entire movement in Asheville. These two black lawyers made them-selves available to be involved with social change. So that's when I decided that I would go into law because I wanted to be able to help people who were engaged in social change.

Today, Fergie is putting his ideas into action, making himself "available to be involved with social change." In 1996, he represented a group of ministers in Greensboro, North Carolina. One of those minis-ters, Reverend Nelson Johnson, was Fergie's client. Reverend Johnson is a former community organizer who went to the seminary and re-turned to Greensboro to pastor All Faith Church and to join with other black ministers to form the Pulpit Forum.

Reverend Johnson is soft-spoken; sometimes it seems almost as if he is whispering. I warmed to Reverend Johnson immediately upon meeting him because his style evoked my mother's lessons about the importance of listening, of leading by actively hearing what people's needs are and where they want to go. Reverend Johnson reminded me in fact of lessons learned from both my parents: lead with justice in mind, speak truth to power (but do not become seduced by power yourself), and listen. Because Reverend Johnson speaks so gently, you really have to listen hard.

Reverend Johnson and the Pulpit Forum turned to Fergie following a vigil they conducted in support of the predominantly black workforce at a Kmart distribution center in Greensboro. Workers at the Kmart distribution center, one of the few in the country that was majority-black, were receiving on average $5.10 less than any other comparable center, doing exactly the same work.

Every Sunday for several weeks members of the Pulpit Forum went to pray in front of the distribution center, prepared each time to get arrested. Reverend Johnson and the other ministers kneeled in front of the Kmart distribution center to support the predominantly black workforce, but they were fighting to build a community for all who lived and worked in Greensboro: the workers' families, the grocers they buy food from, the farmers who supply the food for the grocers, everyone who relies on a living wage given for an honest day's work. The Pulpit Forum supported the predominantly black workforce because it was being mistreated, but they never discussed the cause as simply a racial issue or a labor-management dispute. Instead, they described what Kmart was doing in not paying a living wage as a threat to all in Greensboro who want to build a "sustainable community."

Reverend Johnson concluded that "race and racism was the major factor in the assumption that you could set up this distribution center in a right-to-work state, hire a lot of black people, and pay them essentially nothing, and treat them any way you wanted to treat them." Reverend Johnson recognized, however, that if they framed the issue as one of race, many white people would hear it and say, That does not concern me, or even worse, I disagree. But if they framed the issue without discussing race, many blacks would hear it and say, That is not responsive to my concerns.

Reverend Johnson therefore talks about race in order to "get through race." But you don't get through race just by talking. "You have to walk through race; you have to work through race," he says. In Reverend Johnson's ecology of justice, race plays a key role, but everyone must struggle together to ensure that no one is left behind.

To highlight the importance of opening up a big conversation within the community, at first the Pulpit Forum members stood outside the Kmart distribution center alone. They intentionally limited to clergy those who first sat down in front on the distribution site to get arrested, "as a way of framing this as a discussion about this community." It was our way, Reverend Johnson says, "of giving our explanation as to why we would stand not just with the workers but instead of them." Anyone can stand for themselves, Reverend Johnson declared, his emphasis coming not from the tone of his voice but from the focus in his eyes. "We, as ministers, just walked in the door first. That gave us a week of public attention and discussion. The next week, the workers joined us."

Before the ministers would leave for the plant on Sundays, "we held church." They had a mass meeting each Sunday at church services, preparing the congregation spiritually to go forward. Soon, white workers from Kmart joined the black clergy and the black workers at the site on Sunday. The white workers would meet at their union hall; the black workers would meet first at church. Reverend Johnson also reached out to the local business community and to white and black politicians. Eventually some white ministers, a few white college professors, and others joined in. Many white merchants "didn't start getting arrested until way down the road, but they did join," Reverend Johnson tells me. "A college professor at Guilford College, his whole class went with him to jail. He went, and they went with him." Reverend Johnson laughed. "And they were discussing their grades in jail."

The ministers, including Reverend Johnson, were also arrested and sent to jail. One of the pastors who was arrested had been at his church for ten years. When they had a celebration for pastors in the community, "most of what his congregation talked about was how proud they were because he went to jail." Reverend Johnson continued, obviously amused. "From the children to the church elders, they didn't say much about his preaching. But everybody got up and said, 'We're so proud of you because you went to jail.'"

The governor's aide stood behind them when they prayed in front of the Kmart plant, and she got arrested, too. They were also charged in a civil suit in which Kmart sought an injunction to prevent them from going back on Kmart property. Some of them would be banned from Kmart property in the United States and beyond.

After several ministers and workers were arrested on criminal charges and also sued in civil court, Reverend Johnson's first thought was to hire a lawyer to defend them. But he also determined "to tell the world" about the legal issues in a way that made plain what was really at stake. It turned out that Kmart had only sued the black ministers and black workers. Rather than complain that this was further proof of racially discriminatory practices, Reverend Johnson conferred with the white ministers and white workers who were part of their struggle. Going to jail, or getting sued, is "the opportunity to really help share the faith," Reverend Johnson explained. The white workers then held a news conference, asking why their names were not on the complaint.

Why weren't they sued? they demanded to know. After all, they had done everything the black workers had!

Even in court, Reverend Johnson didn't want his attorney, James Ferguson, simply to win a legal case. Ferguson cooperated with Reverend Johnson's broad public education strategy. "I didn't know he could get so much common thinking into a legal argument," Reverend Johnson said. "We could actually understand what he was talking about, in the court." Fergie used his argument to educate not only the judge but his clients and their congregation. As Reverend Johnson observed, "He did it in such a way that whether the judge ruled this way or that way, it was helpful to all of us who were sitting there. And I don't know if that's a comment on his particular way of lawyering. He pretty much discussed with us what we wanted, and we wanted to tell the story. That's what we wanted, and we wanted the judge not to rule against us."

For Reverend Johnson and the Pulpit Forum, the challenge was not to let the lawyers or politicians take over. After all, the courtroom is "just another staging area" in their effort to build community. They wanted to use the experience of going to court to educate people about their rights and their responsibilities. They were as intent on building just relationships within and among the people in the community as they were on winning the case.

The Pulpit Forum resists foundation funding for its social action work. Its members want to build community rather than merely to win cases or buy resources. In 1996, when they held a conference of five hundred people at one of the local churches, the church had to provide food for the participants. They wanted the church members to be involved in more than just a spiritual way. Had Reverend Johnson simply applied to a foundation to cater the meals, they would have lost the opportunity to involve the twenty-five parishioners in the church basement who cooked dinner and connected, through their hands-on preparation of the meals, to the nurturing of the conference participants and the conference message.

Sometimes, with lawyers such as James Ferguson and clients like Reverend Johnson, courtrooms can still be transformed into places for collective struggle, almost literally a mass meeting, with ordinary people singing their way to courage. Reverend Johnson tells the story of going to court:

> The court was just full of people, and an old black woman stood up and started singing in this judge's court, "Ain't going to put my religion down," and the judge left the court. He came outside and asked us to ask her to stop, and she did. When she finished the song.
>
> After that, somebody stood up and prayed.

Reverend Johnson explains that "this lady was not asked to sing. She just did because she felt safe doing it, and my own view was the judge felt unsafe, actually. What do you do with an eighty-year-old lady who doesn't quite know she's even in court? She's just with the people she usually sings with, and expressing her desire about all of this." James Blacksher, another LDF cooperating attorney, a former Marine and a native white southerner, heard Reverend Johnson tell about the woman singing in court. "When that woman stood up and started singing in that courtroom," it became a different place, Blacksher declared. She literally transformed that room, because she was so moved.

Blacksher was impressed because Reverend Johnson and James Ferguson had presented the issues in a way "that moves the people, that mobilizes people." Reverend Johnson had inspired the elderly to go to jail to support the idea of "sustainable community." That fight aroused other folk to come show support. A lot of people also came simply because their ministers asked them to. The white ministers and workers were willing to cooperate with black leadership because they saw that leadership acting in their interests and in the interests of the community of Greensboro.

The goal was not simply to win a case, an argument, or a job. The goal was to tell their stories, and even if the judge ruled against them, "we don't really care that much" because "it's not that big of a deal, of ten, fifteen days in jail," Reverend Johnson declares. "It pales by comparison to what's going to happen in the lives of some people."

Indeed, losing would still be winning in Reverend Johnson's way of thinking. It is the fight that counts. The individual who struggles with others retains a sense of self with honor. Enduring bonds are forged. Even if they lost, they could learn the value of ongoing struggle both as a matter of personal integrity and interpersonal friendship. That, for Reverend Johnson, is the essense of justice—building and sustaining just relationships.

Bill Quigley has not met Reverend Johnson, but he agrees that there is "no big fee, no precedent-setting case, no pro bono award" that can ever substitute for the lifelong camaraderie and sense of purpose that energizes those who struggle together over the long term. Even when the short-term outcome looks bleak, Quigley notes, civil rights lawyers and clients, like the church members cooking for the Pulpit Forum conference or the woman singing in court, all gain a healthy sense of their potential power and dignity.

I had experienced that awesome feeling the day we sang civil rights anthems in 1985 on the steps of the Selma courthouse, after the jury found Albert and Evelyn Turner and Spencer Hogue not guilty. It was a joy that came from a sense of common struggle in the face of injustice. The woman singing in the courtroom also reminded me why J. L.

Chestnut insisted on attending mass meetings during the 1960s even when he did not have a report to deliver or a speech to make. There was an amazing power in the mass meetings during the height of the civil rights movement, when ordinary black folk sang and prayed their way to courage.

In the prologue to Watters and Cleghorn's *Climbing Jacob's Ladder,* the singing of spirituals emboldens the participants at a mass meeting in Georgia, when a group of white men, including the rough-looking white sheriff of Terrell County, suddenly appear:

> Car doors slammed outside on a hot July night in 1962 as the Rever-end Charles Sherrod, young, thin-faced, led the people who had braved the night to talk about voting in a county where even talk about it was dangerous. . . . Fifteen white men, four of them local law enforcement officers, came through the door and stood in a grim-faced row. "If God be for us," Sherrod intoned in prayer as they stood there, "who will be against us?"

> The Negroes began to sing. Voices that were weak at first, gained strength as they moved up the scale with the old, familiar words: "We are climbing Jacob's Ladder . . . Every round goes higher, higher."

> The Negroes began to sing the strains of another old Baptist hymn, one with some new words and some old, the rising anthem now of the whole movement: "We shall overcome . . . We shall overcome . . . Oh, ohhh, deep . . . in my heart . . . I do believe . . . we shall overcome . . . some day . . ."

The intruders finally left as the black people, still singing loudly, gathered their courage to go out into the night. That was the hallmark of the movement: ordinary folk singing and praying their way to cour-age. With a song in their collective hearts, ordinary people marched to freedom. Freedom did not come to them.

THE MOVEMENT looks different in Greensboro today than it did in Ter-rell, Georgia, in the 1960s or even in Selma, Alabama, in 1985. What Reverend Johnson is creating may generate a flurry of activity that moves the collective hearts of people in Greensboro only momentarily. Yet civil rights lawyers and clients who participate in social justice campaigns that "move people," even temporarily, are doing important work, especially if they don't try to "save" a community but to work with it.

Lawyers still have a central role to play. "We will use our skills and our training," James Ferguson, one of Julius Chambers's original law partners in Charlotte, North Carolina, told me, "to come to your aid when you need the help of a lawyer." But the role of the lawyer is different now. "It may not be taking the case" and sticking to it "until you get a ruling from the Supreme Court. It may be representing a citizens' group that needs to be given a voice in the local county commission or the local school board or City Hall. It may be educating people as to how the system works against them. It may need revealing to people how the prison system in America, being overwhelmingly black in its population, is not purely incidental. . . . It is up to us to educate people how the so-called drug war has had an impact on the black community."

But how do you educate lawyers to this new model? He answered, "It's using the same skills, a lawyer's skill to bring about change through persuasion, to bring about change through education, to bring about change through educating those in power. And those same skills have to be brought to bear in some extrajudicial ways, such as helping people to organize, helping educate people about issues, helping people to get involved in fighting the system, helping people understand what it is that causes them to be unable to get food or a job."

Using their clients' voices and perspective, lawyers can educate rather than simply notify the court of a legal violation. They can draft legal complaints not merely to plead a technical rule or invoke a legal principle but to give their clients' stories credibility and visibility. They can help bring important people to the negotiating table by grabbing the attention of the judge and the press, using their clients' words to highlight a sense of larger unfairness. They can also check the impulse to transform everything, including what might be better realized as political demands, into claims for judicially enforceable legal rights. Even excellent trial lawyers like Fergie, aggressively representing civil rights clients, will often fail to sustain victories in court unless their clients participate simultaneously in a bigger, more public conversation where ordinary people can sing or march their way to freedom.

As a counselor and adviser to this mini-movement, James Ferguson did all of those things. He helped his clients broaden the public debate to engage a different audience in an ongoing conversation. He offered options. He negotiated on behalf of his clients when the woman began singing in court. He met with the judge who had walked out on his own courtroom, and was able to help resolve the minor crisis without experiencing an immediate sense of betrayal in simply talking with or meeting with "the opposition" or the forces that put the clients in jeopardy in the first place. In response, a new vice president of Kmart showed up and said, "It's time to end the war. Let's get this thing settled." For the first time in two and a half years there was more than a one-day negotiation.

Peter M. Cicchino is the founder and director of the Lesbian and Gay Youth Project of the Urban Justice Center in New York City.

On November 18, 1995, Cicchino addressed the plenary session of the Political Lawyering Conference held at Harvard Law School. A former member of a Roman Catholic religious order and an openly gay man, Cicchino challenged lawyers to follow James Ferguson's advice and example. Cicchino did not speak directly about the new civil rights campaign as it is evolving in Greensboro, North Carolina. Instead, he galvanized the audience with two religious metaphors that capture the important role progressive lawyers like Fergie are now playing.

Like Fergie, Cicchino stressed that this is precisely the time when we most need a clearcut explanation by lawyers as to why existing relationships between management and workers, between politicians and voters, between those who make decisions and those who are expected to follow them are unfair and unjust. Indeed, lawyers

> need to do two things that all viable religious movements have— certainly the two things [America's] religious right has. First, we need a faith story, an account of a rational hope that provides people with an image of and principles for realizing the sort of lives they ought to live, lives that will make them happy. It is not enough to say that it is wrong to have children who are in the streets and hungry. We should tell people clearly, because it is true, that you cannot be happy in your Mercedes-Benz passing children begging in the streets. We need good news, what the Christian tradition calls "gospel" and what many religious traditions have in the sense of a canonical story, an "encyclopedic compendium" that explains and inspires.

> The second thing we need is called, in religious terms, "church"—a better term for this might be "community." We need a sense of union, not only among ourselves, but with all people of good will. That union, however, must be more than sentimental. We need structures of organization that allow us to witness effectively to the sort of world we are trying to create—one that is egalitarian, respecting the human rights of all people, and in which the operative principle of social reality is not violence or greed, but love.

Peter Cicchino's religious metaphors aptly describe the secular role of civil rights lawyers James Ferguson and J. L. Chestnut. We had done our best work when we gave people a rational hope and were supported at mass meetings by people in black churches singing their way to courage. Cicchino is right: we not only needed a church; we needed a faith story. We needed to find a public way to explain why all people should care, and we needed to design a public space that sustained the capacity for people, once they did care, to hope and to struggle together.

As lawyers, we were trained not to try our cases in the media. We tried them in court, where throughout the 1970s and 1980s we often prevailed. We had prevailed in court, however, when, as in the Marion

Three case, we let ordinary people speak about their own lives, when we used their stories to tell a larger story that other ordinary people could also understand.

Increasingly, however, the courts of law seem inadequate for the task at hand. With changes in the judiciary and with legal issues becoming more complex, we have to move to a bigger church, and preach a bolder, yet much older, faith: to witness injustice in public squares, whether real or electronic; to explain how the experience of black people reveals the possibility of transformation for all people.

Lawyers, in other words, are bridge people who can help fill the space between the courtroom and the public square. More such lawyers need to speak out, but it is also important that they engage others in speaking their truth. When they do so, they "directly interfere with the life of a community," so that it has to respond. If the powers-that-be do not respond in the court of law to moral suasion, they cannot afford to ignore lawyers who encourage their clients and their community as well to speak out for a change, and the people respond and produce a clamor for that change.

Peter Cicchino reminds us we need a faith story and a church. Lawyers such as James Ferguson and ministers such as Nelson Johnson have been equally eloquent in practice. But no one was more clear than Dr. King when he told J. L. Chestnut back in 1965: "We're trying to win the right to vote and we have to focus the attention of the world on that. We can't do that making legal cases. We have to make the case in the court of public opinion."

Because I once was part of a *people*-based strategy, my own experience became a personal, not just academic, reminder of what was increasingly missing from our movement. Now I hoped others would reacquaint themselves, as I had, with Dr. King's advice and would join me in the public square, in a large public conversation, because, after all, in a democracy, the true "powers-that-be" has to be the power of *all* of the people.

Hearings

CHAPTER NINE

The Task Ahead:
Breathing New Life
into American Democracy

As A CIVIL RIGHTS LAWYER I had often argued in court that participation matters. I had fought for the right of everyone to participate
in making the important decisions that affected their lives. Having
represented civil rights clients in court, and then reflected on the significance of that representation in academic articles, I began a process of
self-reflection and criticism. As a legal academic, I wrote that merely
casting an empty ballot is not the kind of participation we as a civil
rights movement and civil rights lawyers had in mind. I wrote that
winner-take-all decision making unfairly excludes those in the minority
from having a useful voice.

I soon discovered that the problem blacks had in gaining a meaningful vote or a real voice signaled a more fundamental failure in our
democracy. I began to realize that even though we promote ourselves as
the world's premier democracy, what we have in this country is partial
democracy. If democracy is about having a government "of," "by," and
"for" the people, we are failing. Although we do hold periodic elections,
the majority of the population doesn't turn out to vote. The level of
satisfaction among citizens with "the way democracy works" is low,
especially among the "losers," meaning those who did not vote or those
who did not vote for the governing party.

This has consequences not only for citizen satisfaction with the
electoral process. It also affects the quality of our daily life. A 1989
study, for example, found that those democracies with lower voter turnout levels have higher amounts of citizen turmoil and violence.

That said, let me add that voting is a rather trivial measure of
democracy. We should be careful not to make the mistake of placing

exaggerated emphasis on voter turnout. We could have very high levels of voter turnout—as some countries like Indonesia and Albania do—and still not have a very full democracy. Democracy is about participation in the process of public decision making 365 days a year, not just on a single day in a voting booth.

In my view, getting more people to participate fully in the political process is what democracy is really about. As my clients told me time and again, we want more than a representative democracy. We want a participatory democracy.

For my civil rights clients, politics is not a game. It exists to resolve the largest questions in this society. My clients rightfully felt they had a role to play in thinking about and discussing those big questions. Especially in a multiracial, polyethnic society, they saw democracy as essential, to help them engage with these issues and each other in a public space or a public way.

As political theorist Michael Walzer observes, such constructive engagement leads to "toleration," or the capacity for mutual understanding, collective deliberation, and ongoing accommodation. For Walzer, toleration is easier to achieve where people have a way to organize to express and fulfill themselves both as individuals and as members of groups. People, whatever their race, ethnicity, or religion, should enjoy their rights as individuals. Yet, we also need to acknowledge, as Walzer reminds us in his book *On Toleration*, that individuals live in groups and that each group, especially minorities, has a right to "a voice, a place, and a politics of its own." Thus, democratic rules that facilitate organized political parties and encourage citizens' groups are a good thing.

Walzer's conclusions and my clients' aspirations are supported by studies of the causes of crime and delinquency that find lower rates of violence in neighborhoods, even those poor and urban, with a strong sense of community. Strong communities enjoy a shared vision and social trust, a sense of ownership of public space. But, most of all, a sustainable or effective community depends on the willingness of adults to intervene, to get involved.

As individuals, we need opportunities for advancement; as members of social groups, we need strong intermediate associations—family, ethnic, union, and political. Thus, political organizations, parties, and citizens' groups like Albert Turner's Perry County Civic League and Nelson Johnson's Pulpit Forum are essential if we want adults to intervene and get involved. They enable citizens to join with others to express their opinions, not just to vote.

Similarly, in focus groups held by the Commission on Presidential Debates, the participants lauded the sheer experience of post-debate discussion as much as the debates, bonding like jurors with other panel members and compounding their appetites for politics. "We didn't intend this; it just happened," said Diana Carlin, a political scientist who ran the focus groups. The traditional American inhibitions against discussing politics fade and confidence grows with the investment of time and understanding in organized citizen groups.

Voting, therefore, is only one way for citizens to participate in a democracy. As Hannah Arendt once said, the voting booth cannot be the ultimate symbol of a democracy since it has room enough for only one. But if our current system discourages the majority of Americans even from voting, it is surely not a good sign.

Indeed, in the most important national elections we hold in this country—the presidential election—less than 49 percent of voters participated in 1996. That's the lowest it's been since 1924. Over 76 percent of eligible voters did not support President Clinton's reelection, either because they did not vote or they did not vote for him.

The effect of our partial democracy is particularly egregious on poor people. In 1990, 13.8 percent of American voters came from families with incomes under $15,000; in 1992, those low-income voters declined to 11.0 percent of voters; in 1994, they were just 7.7 percent. Why? "The basic cause is essentially that neither party is speaking to the interests of the lower-income brackets of Americans," explains Curtis Gans, director of the Committee for the Study of the American Electorate in Washington, D.C.

Part of the reason for this dismal level of participation is a historical artifact called winner-take-all elections. Whoever wins the most votes from a geographic unit called an election district goes to Congress. Essentially, whoever wins the most votes gets all the power. This makes sense if you think that democracy in America began as a revolution against the king. Winner-take-all elections took power from the monarchy and presumably gave it to the people. Of course, that's better than letting the king have all the power. But it still leaves many questions open. How many people should have a chance to exercise power? How do we resolve issues when we don't all agree?

In America, we settled early on for a simple system in which only one candidate wins the right to represent all the voters—even those who voted against him or her. Many of those who vote are thus assured of voting for a loser. Sometimes more people end up voting for the many losers than for the actual winner, yet the single winner still gets "all" the power. Even those who do vote are not necessarily represented by a candidate or political party of their choice. Indeed, in 1996, those who did vote for Bob Dole, Ross Perot, or Ralph Nader were "equally" represented as those who did *not* vote at all: none were represented by someone they actively chose.

Winner-take-all elections may make sense for the election of a single executive, such as a president, governor, or mayor, since chief executives often need to act decisively and with broad support. However, it is much harder to justify a straight winner-gets-all, loser-gets-none system for the election of "representatives" to a collective decision-making body such as a Congress, city council, or local school board.

Indeed, the more representative such a body, the more it can perform its deliberative function. A legislator or council member needs to consider a full range of views before he or she deliberates to reach consensus or to participate in a public conversation about important policy issues. A legislative body that is truly representative is also more likely to channel dissenting voices into constructive public policy debates. When a legislature or council simply excludes minority viewpoints, it leaves them no formal options within which to express their grievances. Moreover, groups of citizens are more likely to participate and organize when they have a chance to influence the composition of a legislative body and then enjoy a meaningful way to hold those representatives accountable.

This is a simple idea of taking turns or sharing power. It is an idea we often teach children. When asked which game a group of six children should play—four preferred tag and two wanted to play hide-and-seek —my then four-year-old son Nikolas got it right away. "They'll play both," Niko advised. "First they'll play tag and then they'll play hide-and-seek."

By contrast, the winner-take-all system limits who can play. It awards all the power to those with the most votes who then play "tag" over and over. It also limits the role of citizens' groups because the only real contest is between the two major political parties. One of only two political options or opinions "can win." This stifles political debate because it encourages centrism but not necessarily consensus. In other words, the winner has to move to the middle of the spectrum where most of the votes are. But the winner need not recognize or take into account legitimate, dissenting views of those in the minority.

Nor does the winner necessarily consider a good number of those who actually make up the winning majority. The winning majority is rarely monolithic. In 1996, for example, many progressives voted for Bill Clinton, a New Democratic candidate that they associated with a range of policies they didn't like. A good politician like Clinton then plays one part of his constituency against the other—signing the Republican Congress' welfare bill, giving lip service to affirmative action but not aggressively championing it in a timely way, when directly threatened by Proposition 209 in California. He knows that many members of his coalition have nowhere else to go.

Winner-take-all systems are also responsible for at least part of the problem with the way campaigns are conducted in America. When all that counts is winning, it's not surprising that candidates who fall behind resort to negative campaigns. If the point is to win more votes than your opponent—not to win as many votes as you can—then it makes just as much tactical sense to suppress the votes for your opponent as to raise your own vote totals. So candidates try to discourage at least some people from voting.

Most of all, in a winner-take-all system of geographic districts, voters don't choose their representative. Representatives choose their voters. This means that candidates are reelected not because they mobilized supporters to go to the polls but because they used the power of incumbency to draw the election district lines around those supporters. Representation, in other words, is often constructed rather than won. In too many instances, the election actually takes place when the districts are drawn, not when the voters go to the polls.

Thus, Americans distort democracy because we overuse winner-take-all elections that allow a single group to monopolize power. The composition of the group—partisan affiliation, race, economic status—is usually fixed in advance by those who draw the districts. Because the outcome of the election is predetermined from the configuration of the geographic districts to which citizens have been arbitrarily assigned, people are discouraged from even showing up to vote. Their perception, that their votes don't count, is unfortunately accurate. Indeed, although we hold congressional elections in this country every two years, the over 90 percent reelection rate of congressional incumbents shows that the only decisions that tend to matter were those already made when the district lines were drawn.

Congressional districts are presently drawn not by voters but by incumbent politicians and other partisans. They are drawn not to give voters maximum choice but the opposite: They are drawn to give elected officials maximum protection from the voters. Indeed, the reason so few congressional districts "turn over," meaning switch party affiliation, is that the districts are drawn consciously to collect like-minded voters into geographic units. Those who dissent, who support a different candidate, are free to vote. But their dissenting votes simply don't count. The outcome is stacked every ten years when the districts are drawn in light of new census figures.

While there is nothing unconstitutional about drawing such non-competitive districts to maximize a politician's tenure or to advantage a district majority, such practices do discourage voters from participating. Less than 40 percent of eligible voters turned out in the midterm elections of 1994; in 1996, less than 45 percent voted for members of Congress. The Republican so-called Contract with America landslide was approved in 1994 by less than one out of every five Americans. Yet, because Republicans won the most votes in districts that suppressed or minimized Democratic voting strength, they claimed an "illusory mandate," or false majority. For example, in 1996, the Republicans again controlled the House, and the House delegations from Kansas, Nebraska, and Oklahoma are *all* Republican. Yet Democratic candidates averaged 37 percent of the vote in these states' thirteen districts, leaving more than a third of the population in those three states unrepresented.

George Pillsbury and Rob Richie, in their work for the Center for Voting and Democracy, characterize our system as a fossil, an outdated historical legacy. Mount Holyoke professor Doug Amy calls it "the museum" of democracy. It has survived in their view not because it encourages participation in elections or even in a robust debate about ideas and issues. It has survived because it promotes a two-party system that, accompanied by the high costs of campaigning, gives incumbents enormous power to retain their seats. Thus, Pillsbury and Richie conclude that in the United States we are left with a system that might have satisfied the needs of a homogeneous (white, male, property-owning) electorate over two hundred years ago. But winner-take-all elections are ill-suited to the multiracial and polyethnic society of today because they are unable to fill the need for diverse debate and broad representation. Minorities and women are underrepresented, and campaigns focus on personalities and slick media images rather than substantive issues.

Although winner-take-all districts undermine democracy and discourage voter participation generally, the Voting Rights Act focuses on the tendency of such practices to foster minority-vote dilution. Minority-vote dilution occurs when black or Latino voters can never elect a candidate of their choice because the majority electorate is hostile and votes as a racial bloc. The majority monopolizes all the seats, and the minority feels shut out.

One remedy to this problem, adopted in Voting Rights Act cases during the 1980s and 1990s, is to carve out "majority-minority" voting districts. In North Carolina, for example, blacks, who formed 22 percent of the state's population, had not been able to elect a representative to one of the state's twelve congressional seats in this century. Armed with the threat of a Voting Rights Act challenge, civil rights groups and the U.S. Department of Justice forced the legislature to draw two majority black districts. The previously excluded minority was therefore able to elect representatives of its own choosing.

This is exactly the remedy that Leslie Winner and I had successfully pursued in the first Supreme Court case to interpret the 1982 amendments to the Voting Rights Act, *Thornburg* v. *Gingles.* And the remedy was eventually followed once Maggie Bozeman got out of jail in Pickens County, Alabama, and Albert Turner and Spencer Hogue were acquitted in the Marion Three case. Blacks in Pickens County as well as Perry County joined a lawsuit that yielded several majority black districts from which some of the first blacks ever were eventually elected.

Gradually, however, I began to see some limits to the strategy. I had already discovered, through cases in rural Alabama, that even when blacks get elected to office through single-member districts drawn to empower the black community and to enable it to elect candidates of choice, those elected officials may be outvoted within the still-majority white city council, school board, or state legislature. Indeed, because the black officials were elected from essentially isolated constituencies, they may not have the ability to influence their white colleagues, who also hail from now homogeneous, mostly white districts.

Another problem was that those blacks elected from single-member districts often became well-meaning but self-perpetuating incumbents, whose goals gradually narrowed both because of the culture of winning that governed their political options and because they became convinced, with our support, that their continued presence was central to our continued power. The "black faces in high places" litigation strategy failed to realize that the color of the advocate alone does not determine political efficacy. We confused presence with power in ways that often led to the demobilization of our real sources of strength and voice—an organized constituency that backed up our demands and allowed our elected officials to speak and be heard.

In the *Gingles* legislative districting case Judge Dixon Phillips had asked whether drawing homogeneous black districts would lead to diminished competition among black candidates. Judge Phillips's question had touched on the very important issue of incumbent power within single-member districts. After all, incumbents get to draw the districts, and they do so by protecting their electoral base first. But my reaction to his question had been right as well. This was not a problem limited to black incumbents. As with any individual vested with power, incumbent politicians of all races tried to draw safe districts to limit competition and thus decrease the role of voter turnout and mobilization, even on election day.

I began to see how, on some level, all districting is gerrymandering, meaning that the lines of voting districts are drawn by politicians to advantage those likely to support a particular viewpoint or to be sympathetic to the overtures of an individual candidate. The consequence is not just that each geographically designed district has a distinct political character or identity. The result is inevitably to disadvantage those in the minority—whether racial, political, cultural, or occupational—who have a different perspective or political identity. The district configuration may be compact or it may be irregular, but whatever the design, the people in the minority have virtually no chance of being represented by someone they actually vote *for*.

I began as a lawyer, and then as a law professor, to consider alternatives that do not involve winner-take-all districts. I learned that democracies formed more recently than our own have developed more nuanced systems, most adopting some form of proportional representation (PR). In 1994, in the negotiated transition to democracy in South Africa, the leadership rejected winner-take-all elections in favor of proportional voting that would enable the white minority there to have some representation in the legislature. South Africa used proportional representation to assure seats in the national assembly for political parties in proportion to the percentage of votes cast for that party. The National Party (white Afrikaners) received 20.39 percent of the votes cast and got 20.5 percent of the seats in the national assembly. The African National Congress (Nelson Mandela's party) received 62.65 percent of the votes and 63.0 percent of the seats. The Inkatha Freedom Party (Chief Buthelezi) polled 10.54 percent of the votes and got 10.75 percent of the seats. A total of seven parties qualified for representation in the national assembly. In addition, the three parties with more than 5 percent of the national assembly seats were each awarded a number of cabinet portfolios.

As a result of the negotiated transition to multiracial democracy, South Africa uses a party list system. Voters vote for a political party. The party fields a list of potential candidates. Not all of the party's candidates will win, unless the party gets 100 percent of the total number of votes cast. The candidates on the party list are only elected in direct proportion to the number of votes cast for the party they represent.

Another PR option is preference voting. Voters cast ballots that list their first, second, and third choice candidates. The first choice ballots are counted first. When a candidate is elected by a sufficient number of those who picked him or her as first choice, the remaining ballots are counted toward their second or third choice, thus minimizing potentially wasted votes. This system is still in use in Cambridge, Massachusetts, and was used for more than a decade to elect members of the New York City Council earlier this century.

Yet another system is cumulative voting. Cumulative voting allows voting city- or countywide, with each voter in the city or county getting the same number of votes as there are seats up for election. Chilton County, a very rural county in central Alabama with an 11 percent black population, adopted cumulative voting in response to a lawsuit brought by black residents. After a federal court found that voting was racially polarized, the county decided to implement cumulative voting to settle the lawsuit. As a result, groups that previously had not been represented—blacks, Republicans, and women—have been elected in significant numbers to both the county commission and the board of education.

The Chilton County school board and the county commission each now has seven members. Every voter therefore gets seven votes, to vote any way the voter chooses. Rather than being confined to geographic units, the voters "district" themselves (meaning align themselves politically) by the way they cast their ballots. If they want to put all seven of their votes on one candidate because that person reflects their most important, most deeply held preferences, they can. If they want to put six on one candidate and one on another, they can. If they want to put one each on seven different candidates, they can. It is up to the voter to district him- or herself by the way he or she casts or distributes the seven ballots.

In a study of cumulative voting in Chilton County that included field interviews with political figures and local journalists, professors Richard Pildes and Kristen Donoghue concluded that cumulative voting has some cultural and political costs, but the "worst fears" about it have not been realized. The elected leaders and party leaders were initially opposed when John Hollis Jackson, the county's attorney, brought the idea of cumulative voting to them. Yet, once they concluded that cumulative voting was their best option, they stood behind the decision in order to sell it to the public. The political leadership, as well as the editor of the major newspaper, put aside their earlier resistance and made "a concerted effort to explain how the new system would work and the reason for its adoption."

The first election under cumulative voting occurred in 1988, and Bobby Agee became the first black commissioner to the Chilton County Commission since Reconstruction. He was the only black candidate out of a total of fourteen candidates, and because of the ability of black voters to plump or "cumulate" their votes, he received more votes than any other candidate. About 1.5 percent of white voters cast a vote for Agee, and nearly all black voters voted for him. Most black voters gave him multiple votes. In 1988, two Republican women were also elected to the board of education. A third Democratic woman finished eighth, nearly winning. One of the Republican women, Sue Smith, noted that more women were considering running now that the new system was in place, because they felt they had a better chance of winning.

Pildes and Donoghue observed a local consensus "that cumulative voting was effective, necessary to achieve minority representation, and therefore begrudgingly accepted even while being disliked" by white voters, who would have preferred the creation of a single black majority district. With regard to public policy, Pildes and Donoghue also noted three improvements. One, road-paving decisions were now determined more equitably. Two, Agee's presence had led to the appointment of more minorities to administrative boards (although a majority of the commission must approve such appointments). The third benefit was intangible but perhaps even more significant: black residents now "felt more connected to local government."

Sue Smith, the former GOP chair and member of the board of education, felt that voter understanding about how cumulative voting worked grew over time. Moreover, the initial incredulity that voters had more than one vote each had an unanticipated benefit: the confusion made people inquire what was going on, and then they got more involved. There was "a resurgence of interest in the political process."

Likewise, cumulative voting was a critical factor in elections in 1990 of members of the Sisseton-Wahpeton Sioux tribe to the board of the Sisseton Independent School District No. 54-5 in northeastern South Dakota. Professor Richard Engstrom, the political scientist, participated as an expert witness in the voting rights lawsuit that was settled there by adopting cumulative voting. According to Professor Engstrom, 34 percent of the population in the school district was Native American, virtually all members of the Sisseton-Wahpeton tribe, yet tribal members had rarely been elected to the nine-member board. Numerous tribal members had sought seats, but lost because white voters failed to support their candidacy. In 1984, only one member of the board was Native American, "a member of another tribe," who was "handpicked," according to plaintiffs in the voting rights suit, by white board members and was supported by white, not Native American, voters. After the lawsuit was settled and the school district in Sisseton joined a smaller, mostly white school district, nine members were elected to the new school board using cumulative voting. As a result of the 1990 elections, tribal members formed one-third of the school board's membership.

In a completely proportionate election system, such as South Africa uses for national assembly elections, those who get 51 percent of the vote get 51 percent of the seats in the legislature; others who mobilize 20 percent of the vote, get 20 percent of the seats. Cumulative voting, however, is a semiproportionate system due to the way votes translate into seats. A politically cohesive group of voters is not guaranteed representation. Even where voters participate in sufficient numbers and vote strategically, there are imbalances due to the way votes get spread on candidates. No one is assured victory. Nor is anyone violating one-person/one-vote constitutional rules, since all voters get exactly the same number of votes.

It was an effort to reenergize democracy that initially led me to suggest cumulative voting as a compromise system of representation— not as proportional as the party list system of South Africa, but not as wasteful of minority votes as our winner-take-all system in the United States. It was my view that even a modified proportional system such as cumulative voting had the potential to encourage grass-roots organizing by rewarding local political groups with political power proportionate to the number of actual people they mobilized. For similar reasons, I described legislative rule changes (including supermajority voting) that would disperse power to include minority and dissenting voices, on the theory that progressive change occurs when diverse groups of people must deliberate and share information over time rather than when homogeneous groups of people are encouraged to hoard power or simply achieve enough support to be declared "the winner."

Cumulative voting is a semiproportional voting system that could increase voter choice, by giving voters more votes to cast in support of their preferred candidates. Since numerically weak but politically intense groups can gain electoral representation, proportional and semiproportional systems provide incentives for local, grass-roots organizations to educate voters and sustain voter mobilization. These other groups are not necessarily geographically concentrated, nor is their political potential enhanced or even recognized by contemporary patterns of incumbent-controlled, winner-take-all districting. Such groups include women, gays and lesbians, Latinos who live in dispersed but segregated barrios, environmentalists, Democrats living in Newt Gingrich's district, and rural poor people.

Not surprisingly, given the profound implications of my ideas for shifting power from individual politicians to mobilized voters and grass-roots organizations, I paid a personal price for my views. When Georgia congresswoman Cynthia McKinney, a former political science professor, introduced legislation in Congress in 1995 and again in 1997 to allow states to adopt proportionate and semiproportionate voting systems for congressional elections, she too discovered just how resistant her colleagues were. According to McKinney, "the political establishment in Washington has a difficult time with proportional voting, which requires that they earn their power, not inherit it."

In addition to their potential to encourage more voter turnout and a more diverse constituency, proportional and semiproportional systems respond to those, including the current Supreme Court majority, who criticize minority districts for making stereotyped assumptions about minority political views and interests based on racial identity alone. Proportional representation systems can strengthen the role of diverse minorities without dividing the electorate along racial lines or along the lines of winners and losers. No voter is coerced into voting based on race or any other affiliation simply because of where they live or what they look like. Voters are free to choose candidates who best represent their interests. They can forge multiracial coalitions; indeed, local grass-roots organizations might finally have sufficient incentives to do just that, since they would be rewarded politically based on the number of people who actually turned out to vote.

Neither politicians nor judges would choose who was a group or which group would gain power. The people themselves, by their voting behavior at each election, would make that choice. It is a choice among like-minded, not necessarily like-bodied, individuals. Moreover, voters are also free at each election to choose differently. They are not locked into geographic voting units that stay the same for the ten years between census enumerations.

The real value in exploring alternative election systems is that engaging with and trying to remedy the experience of racial underrepresentation can provide useful lessons about democracy for all groups, not just blacks. When we look specifically at district-based, winner-take-all elections for representatives in collective decision-making bodies, access for minority voters is a problem, to be sure. But access for all voters is also a problem, especially for anyone who, because of accidents of geography, cannot vote for the candidate they feel best represents their interests.

University of Texas law professor Gerald Torres came up with exactly the right metaphor for this process, based on his familiarity with both environmental rights and Indian law. Race, he told me, was the miner's canary, a fragile bird whose sensitivity to methane alerted the miners when the atmosphere in the coal mines became dangerous for them too. Like the canary, race was an environmental sponge that absorbed the toxins in our political culture and allowed us to see their visible and pathological effects more clearly.

The experience of voters of color—who can see how they are underrepresented in a system that protects incumbents rather than voters—acts the same way as the miner's canary. Race is the fragile canary who signals a more general phenomenon. We see "race": both the voters' color and the shape of districts drawn to protect racial minorities from hostile majorities seem to give the district a distinct, and in the words of Justice Sandra Day O'Connor, a "bizarre" appearance. For Justice O'Connor, that distinct identity is antithetical to her notion of elections in which voters are represented as individuals and not as members of a racial or political group.

But it is not just majority black or Latino districts that have a distinct identity. Almost all congressional districts have a particular political identity, which even money cannot reverse. They have a party preference, a regional or local majority, which usually determines the outcome of every election. This is quite predictable since the very configuration of the district was chosen by incumbent politicians looking to retain their seats.

Thus, the canary is warning us that many voters, not just racial minorities, do not feel represented by winner-take-all elections. Issues of minority inclusion become an opportunity to think about issues of voter inclusion across lines of race, class, and gender. The alienation that many blacks feel signals destabilizing declines in voter turnout and voter trust in politicians and government across the spectrum.

On some level, the citizens know this. That is why less than half of those eligible to vote even bothered to turn out on election day in 1996. This is also why the movement for term limits has generated so much citizen support. People want to take power from incumbents and return it to the voters. The ideas of proportional representation have much in common with term limits; both seek to ensure political accountability and to rotate and disperse power more broadly. The problem with term limits is that their solution is to limit voter choice. Term limits deny voter choice in the name of indirectly promoting a "people's" choice. But proportional representation seeks to return power to the people directly by giving "the people" (the voters) not just more choice, but more meaningful choices.

THERE ARE LEGITIMATE ARGUMENTS for making the election of a chief executive (governor, mayor, president) decisive and oriented toward the majority. Executives may need a mandate or at least sufficient support to govern effectively. Similarly, in a parliamentary government, election of the national legislature determines the composition of the executive branch. Thus, proponents of winner-take-all elections defend them against proportional representation, which in a parliamentary system may lead to a proliferation of minor parties that then hold the national government hostage. Fragile coalition governments, in the view of these critics of proportional representation, diminish legislative effectiveness. The big fear of proportional representation, therefore, is balkanization of the electorate and fragmentation of authority.

This fear may have some currency in designing an election system for president or governor. It is at least relevant in a parliamentary system in which the elections to the national legislature determine the composition of the executive branch. But the specter of balkanization is much less persuasive when considering elections whose only purpose is to determine the membership of an exclusively legislative body such as our Congress, state legislatures, and local city councils. Those bodies are already broken down into geographic districts designed to fragment and separate voters by region, local viewpoint, or party affiliation. Even winner-take-all proponents acknowledge that diversity of viewpoint is what legitimates those bodies and helps them to function effectively. So, the only real sticking point is whether diversity of viewpoint should include more political parties than one of the two established political parties and more perspectives associated with traditionally underrepresented groups, including women, gays and lesbians, environmentalists, working-class and poor people, and racial or ethnic minorities.

The "golden age" of the city council of New York City in the 1930s and 1940s, says Henry Stern, former head of the nonpartisan Citizens Union, illustrates the benefits and liabilities of a more politically diverse legislature. Council members were selected not from individual districts but through a system of proportional elections. Voters overwhelmingly approved the system of preference voting in 1936. Candidates were thereafter elected in proportion to their total boroughwide vote. The results were those expected of a proportional representation (PR) system. The Democrats' one-party monopoly was broken; the political spectrum was opened to new, able politicians; their diverse viewpoints enabled substantive and lively debate on public policy issues. Former president of the city council Newbold Morris told *The New York Times* that proportional representation had forced the two major parties to nominate "more articulate, more industrious candidates."

Professors Hugh Bone of the University of Washington and Belle Zeller of Brooklyn College found that the involvement of PR council members was greater than that of the pre-PR members, who were frequently absent from important committee meetings and often rubber-stamped legislation with little debate. By contrast, PR council meetings were now well attended and there was vigorous, *substantive* discussion in both committee and council meetings. The level of debate in council meetings was so high that the meetings themselves drew people interested in witnessing and following the issues.

After New York City adopted a proportional representation system for election of its city council, more people in some boroughs cast PR votes for city council than for the ostensibly more important races of mayor or borough president. Not only did turnout among voters increase in some places, but the number of energetic and public-spirited candidates also rose. The Democratic Party still controlled most of the seats on the council, but it no longer had a near monopoly of all the seats. Even more, those elected were a different breed of Democrat. Insurgents, beholden to the voters rather than to party bosses, won. While ethnic and religious identity did play a role in voting preferences, they were secondary in importance to party affiliation. Voters could "support candidates of their choice," Henry Stern says, "without worrying which side of a line" they were living on.

On the other hand, the Democratic Party machine soon resented its loss of control over the nomination process and the fact that formidable third-party candidates—including Michael Quill, later head of the local Transport Workers Union, and Benjamin Davis, a black Communist councilman from Harlem—were elected from areas that in a winner-take-all district system would have been Democratic strongholds. Within no time the traditional party leaders raised thousands of dollars to try to overturn the proportional election system, outspending those who supported it, $33,000 to $4,000.

Not all Democrats favored repeal. Key members of the New York City mayoral administration were divided. Those who rallied to support retention of proportional representation included the League of Women Voters, the City Club of New York, the Commerce and Industry Association of New York, the Federation of Jewish Women's Organizations, the International Ladies Garment Workers Union, the Women's City Club of New York, and the NAACP. The secretary of the Commerce and Industry Association argued that those favoring repeal wanted "to re-establish totalitarian, one-party rule in New York City." Others accused the Democratic Party of trying to protect its political patronage against proportional representation, the "strongest bulwark against machine politics and predatory special interests."

The *Amsterdam News*, the Harlem-based weekly, strongly supported retention of proportional representation, as did the Republican Club in Harlem's 11th Assembly District, which believed that anti-PR groups were attempting to exclude African Americans from the city council. The Harlem's Citizens Committee in Support of Proportional Representation hailed the system for "freeing Harlem from the ghetto system. . . . The electorate of Harlem became part of the borough [of Manhattan's] progressive electorate. . . . If PR is repealed, there will not be a single Negro on the Council. . . ."

What finally nailed proportional representation in New York City was that the party bosses capitalized on fear of communism. They called PR "un-American," undemocratic, and a threat to the two-party system, "to which," Republican chairman Thomas J. Curran said, "we owe the success of representative government in this country."

But democratic stability in this country does not depend on a two-party oligopoly. Justice John Paul Stevens noted this point recently in his dissent in *Timmons* v. *Twin Cities Area New Party*, a 1997 Supreme Court decision to uphold a state ban on fusion parties in Minnesota. According to Justice Stevens, the ban was not justified by arguments that political stability depends upon limiting the number of political parties. Stevens pointed to the experience in New York politics, where he found "considerable evidence that neither political stability nor the ultimate strength of the two major parties is truly risked by the existence of successful minor parties." Indeed, others who studied the role of significant third parties in New York found that it did not lead to "a proliferation of parties, nor to the destruction of basic democratic institutions." Citing a *Harvard Law Review* study, Justice Stevens concludes that historical experience in this country demonstrates that minor parties and independent candidacies are "compatible with long term political stability."

Especially in a body that is supposed to deliberate, minor parties with different viewpoints expand the range of the debate. A majority of the Supreme Court recognized in 1983 that minor parties promote "competition in the marketplace of ideas." Alexander Bickel, the constitutional scholar, agreed that minor parties are valuable to a democracy because they provide "an outlet for frustration," operate "often as a creative force and a sort of conscience," other times "as a technique for strengthening a group's bargaining position for the future." Indeed, in Bickel's view, minor parties would have to be "invented" if they did not come into existence regularly enough.

Nevertheless, the opponents of proportional voting in New York City successfully caricatured it as "un-American" and undemocratic. Fifty years later, I found myself also caricatured in the national media and by politicians of both major political parties for discussing similar ideas.

But what could be more American than a system used in the heartland itself? Had those who fear proportional representation looked to the Midwest, they would have seen that a form of proportional voting system—cumulative voting—was used for over 110 years in Illinois to elect members of the state House. The state was divided into multimember districts of three representatives. Voters in each district got three votes; they either voted for one, two, or three candidates, and their three votes were evenly spread among those they voted for.

Illinois' system of cumulative voting was proposed by a Republican in 1870; and because it protects minority parties, not just minority individuals, it succeeded in maintaining Republican representation throughout the state, including in heavily Democratic Chicago. This, however, was not just a boon to Republicans. Democrats in Chicago report that they were able to construct statewide majorities for Chicago-based reforms, for example, because Republicans could not isolate or write off Chicago since some Republicans represented districts within the city.

Emil Jones is a black Democrat from the South Side of Chicago. He thinks cumulative voting was good for the state and for the city of Chicago "simply because you had Republican legislators who shared the same interests" and who "carried influence in the Republican caucus." "If we had cumulative voting," Jones says, "there would have been enough Republicans to support school funding reform." Indeed, in his opinion, "they would have been the strong supporters."

By contrast, since cumulative voting was repealed in 1980 (as part of a budget-cutting proposal to eliminate fifty-nine state representatives), "Chicago has been cut off regionally." Chicago, in Mr. Jones's view, "got isolated because it's so predominantly Democratic." Also, the change to winner-take-all, single-member districts "caused legislators to be more political based on their district rather than being a legislator doing what's in the best interest of the state of Illinois." Legislators, both Democrats and Republicans, naturally preoccupied with reelection, were beholden to special interests so they could raise enough money to scare off challengers. The "individuals who got elected, they became more conservative, be it Democrat or Republican, they went with what- ever the majority of the people were in that district."

Senator Arthur Berman, a white Democrat associated in the past with the machine wing of the Chicago Democrats, concurs, saying, "When Republicans, for example, were in control of the Illinois House during cumulative voting, because a number of their members repre- sented Chicago communities, their approach was not as greatly anti- Chicago as it might be today where virtually no Republicans represent Chicago." Berman was elected to the Illinois House under cumulative voting in 1968 and served eight years, until 1976, when he won election to the Illinois Senate. Because "all you needed was one-third of the voters to support you . . . you didn't need as many votes." This allowed some "articulate" spokespersons for "a different point of view" to get elected. "That brought a flavor on the floor of the House. And they added something to the debate and added something to the discussions that I thought was very helpful."

Berman emphasized that he doesn't want to suggest "that cumula- tive voting is the answer to campaign funding reform, but it certainly doesn't require the kind of expenditure when you have four people or more running for three elective positions." Berman also noticed that more independents got elected. There was typically "one spokesman, so to speak, for the machine, one spokesman for the independents, both of whom are Democrats, and one representative of the Republicans. So that regardless of how you would describe yourself politically, you had 'your' legislator, who you could pick up the phone and say, 'Senator Berman, you know, I've been a precinct captain for many years and I want you to know my position on such-and-such.' " In Berman's view, "there was a greater identification with the legislators by knowledgeable voters than there is today."

A recent commentary by Dennis Byrne, a conservative member of the *Chicago Sun-Times* editorial board, also praised cumulative voting for promoting better lawmakers. He pointed out that a candidate for Senate in Illinois "was the leader years ago of the effort to rid Illinois of its unique cumulative voting system for electing state lawmakers, to save a few bucks. The old system produced such independent, smart and honest lawmakers as Abner Mikva and Anthony Scariano from both parties. No more. The 'great builder of democracy' instead has given us a Legislature, while smaller (but not necessarily less expensive), that's dominated by compliant party hacks, afraid to debate the issues and controlled by the party leadership."

Cumulative voting also helped propel Illinois to the forefront of women's representation. During the period of cumulative voting, women were 40 percent more likely to be represented in the Illinois House than in the national legislature. Even though the United States has a well-developed women's movement, at least compared to many European countries, it still has one of the poorest records for women's representation. Women have only increased their number of U.S. House seats from 47 (11 percent) in 1992 to 51 (12 percent) in 1996, despite the fact that 163 new members were elected during that period. In the Inter-Parliamentary Union survey of sixteen Western democracies, cited by Douglas Amy in his book *Real Choices, New Voices*, three of the four democracies with the lowest percentage of women in the lower houses of the national legislatures are the winner-take-all districting systems of Canada, Great Britain, and the United States. Moreover, even in countries such as Germany, which only uses PR to elect some members of its national assembly, women win three times as many seats in the PR elections as in the winner-take-all elections (39 percent to 13 percent).

The way proportional representation works is often a product of local political organization; where minor political parties are organized (as in New York City in the 1930s and 1940s) or where independents associated with the major political parties are common (as in Illinois from 1870 through 1980), PR systems often yield much more variation in results (and may lead to the election of candidates representing minor political parties). On the other hand, Chilton County, Alabama, found that Republicans, blacks, and women fared better than under the previous at-large system. Even under cumulative voting, however, the political leaders in local elections in Chilton County tend to be pragmatic individualists rather than strong partisans. Indeed, Pildes and Donoghue's study identified local people who criticized cumulative voting precisely because it led to the election of more "moderate" minority candidates.

It is important therefore to remember that while proportional representation does open up the political process to more parties and more viewpoints, it is not one monolithic system. Its variations and complexities are manifest when looking at all democracies in the world and in history.

Israel's system, for example, has an extraordinarily low threshold for inclusion. Any party with the support of 1 percent of the voters nationwide can get elected to the Knesset. Those who criticize the Israeli system on the grounds that minor political parties hold the larger parties hostage to their demands, need to understand that it is not PR that is responsible for the role of minor parties, it is the very low threshold for inclusion that the Israeli people adopted.

Similarly, those who blame Germany's PR system for the initial election and rise of the Nazis emphasize the possibility that higher turnout (perhaps due to PR) may have helped bring the Nazis to power. This argument neglects other important considerations, including the abdication of responsibility by many institutions, among them the courts during pre-Hitler Germany. But, most important, the political scientist Arend Lijphart argues that the rise of Hitler shows exactly why turnout levels need to be *maintained* via proportional representation and other mechanisms that increase participation. According to Lijphart, what allowed Hitler to come to power was the rapid mobilization of previously disengaged citizens.

As a solution to the criticism of pre-Hitler Germany and contemporary Israel, some advocate the use of PR with a relatively high threshold for representation. This is exactly what was done in West Germany (and now Germany), which adopted a 5 percent threshold to preclude a fringe party from gaining power. Present-day Germany, which still uses proportional representation to elect half the legislature and district constituencies to elect the other half, is now often held up as one of the most stable governments in Europe.

The bottom line is that proportional representation alone is not going to change the caliber of candidates or the nature of public debate. All forms of proportional representation have peculiar defects, depending on the historical and local conditions in which they are adopted. The "best" PR system depends on making trade-offs between representativeness (inclusiveness) and stability/keeping out extreme parties (exclusion).

On the whole, however, I support European-style proportional representation. I particularly like the mixed system now used in Germany. Prior to my nomination, I had only considered proportional representation as a remedy for proven voting rights violations. Since then, and in part because of my own encounter with winner-take-all politics, I have come to consider alternatives even more favorably. I believe it is much better to hear from the people with whom you disagree in a formal, legislative system than to leave them no options but extralegal means of self-expression. In my view, the legitimacy of a legislative body depends on answering your critics, not excluding them.

SHERYL McCARTHY, a reporter for *New York Newsday*, was present as I gave a speech at Columbia Law School in March 1994 defending the ideas about proportional representation that had gotten me into trouble. McCarthy was not surprised that I was greeted warmly on the Upper

West Side of Manhattan, but she was surprised that my "words echoed loudest in a most unlikely spot—the city's most conservative borough, Staten Island." The same week I spoke at Columbia Law School, the Staten Island Charter Commission submitted a bill that would, McCarthy wrote, "create a Staten Island Board of Education, to be elected by . . . could it be? . . . cumulative voting."

Joseph Viteritti, who headed the commission staff that did the research for the bill, most of which concerned proposals for secession, told McCarthy, "I personally think it's the most creative and most imaginative thing we did in the whole process." Viteritti said the thirteen commissioners were concerned about giving the island's minorities (8 percent black, 8 percent Latino, and 4 percent Asian and others) at least some input in the running of an independent Staten Island.

Why, McCarthy asked, is Staten Island, which is 80 percent white and the most conservative of the five New York City boroughs, "adopting the voting plan of a whacko Quota Queen?" "It's unfortunate that Lani Guinier was so misunderstood," Viteritti replied. "I'm really a supporter of hers. If you read her stuff, it is first-rate and it is not provocative. Her work is good and innovative, and it gets results." He said he had researched the concept of cumulative voting thoroughly, seeing how it helped Chicanos in Alamogordo, New Mexico, and Native Americans in Sisseton, South Dakota, to get representation and not be swallowed up by the majority. When "we presented the idea to the commissioners, they were very receptive," Viteritti said. How ironic, McCarthy concluded, "that Staten Island, the most conservative of places, has now found wisdom in the ideas of a madwoman."

Rob Richie, who founded the Center for Voting and Democracy in Washington, D.C., is inspired by the stories that he hears from places like Staten Island, and from San Francisco, where a referendum to adopt proportional voting was narrowly defeated in 1996. Richie believes a movement for proportional voting is now taking shape. People realize that proportional representation "is not a crazy idea," says Richie. "Just in the last year, we have made inroads in Congress, in cities, and in more and more public interest organizations. If we can get PR adopted in the next few years for city elections, and then perhaps in states, we will be ready for the next congressional redistricting in 2000 and 2001. Then we will hit away at gerrymandering. It is particularly vulnerable now, in that gerrymanders are getting worse and worse. It is a long haul, but we are starting to see things happening."

Arthur Berman, the white Democrat from Chicago who was elected for eight years under the Illinois cumulative voting system, was asked whether he would want to return to cumulative voting. Cumulative voting, Berman says, would give "a voice to the people that today don't have that voice." Thus, "If I was the King of Illinois," Berman admits, he would support PR if he were a "good liberal" king. As "a more conservative King I might give second thoughts to it but I think that the principle of cumulative voting, multimember districts, served democracy in a very good strong way."

As a House member elected by cumulative voting, Berman concluded that he witnessed "true" democracy with a small d, because "you had different points of view from the same areas of the state and you had a different voice." He observed liberal Democrats elected from a majority Republican stronghold. He also saw more representatives "concentrate on the people they wanted to have vote for them" because they didn't have to go and get "big money from the leadership." They could campaign "primarily through their own resources to reach their constituents that would help them get elected with the necessary one-third of the vote."

Taking our lead from people like Joseph Viteritti in Staten Island and Arthur Berman in Chicago, those of us outside the Beltway might reconsider many useful reforms to promote a more *people-based* vision of democracy. We could push for conducting simultaneous national and local elections; for eliminating runoff elections (which contribute to voter fatigue); for allowing weekend voting and extended voting periods; for voting by mail; for campaign finance reform; for reinforcing the obligation of television broadcasters as public trustees to grant free air time to all viable candidates and political parties; and for strengthening political parties and encouraging new ones through PR.

After all, what America needs is a system that disperses power more broadly. Ultimately, proportional and semiproportional election systems (reinforced by public financing of elections and free television time for all viable candidates and legitimate political parties) reflect ideas of cooperation and rotation—the importance of public access to power. Thus, reforms are useful that would undermine the culture of negative campaigning and candidate-centered politics. Such reforms might also encourage more voter participation and citizen involvement by enabling organized citizens' groups to gain political power commensurate with their effort.

Election reform, including proportional representation, is not, however, primarily about electoral rules. It is not simply about getting more people of color and women into office, although that would be an important incidental benefit. It is about learning how to *enlist* and *resist* power simultaneously. It is about transforming how power itself is exercised and shared. It is about opening up a different kind of conversation, during and following elections, because elections become a forum for voters choosing their representatives and expressing their ideas. It is about giving people in motion an incentive to stay in motion. It is about giving citizens their due.

Progressive change, in other words, does not emanate from those with big jobs in Washington, D.C. Things will happen when unanointed citizens take it upon themselves to do something. Right now, even active citizens hold a very weak hand. But support for reforms that draw people together in relationships is what can lead to real change. Many others have learned the same lesson: We cannot rely on change being initiated by those already in power or by those whose dominant operating strategy is public silence and private access.

That, in the end, is what happened to me. As a result of my own first-person encounter with the consequences of operating within a winner-take-all political culture, I began to understand in an entirely new way what was wrong with the zero-sum approach I had challenged. I saw how overrepresenting and inflating the power of the winners discourages and marginalizes the losers. I saw how the culture of winning justifies everything in its name. I saw that none of us who are committed to social justice in the name of community can succeed without changing that culture.

I discovered—in a personal, not just an academic way—that no movement committed to long-term transformation and justice can afford to become overly dependent on a single strategy, and especially not a strategy in which so very few can participate.

After all, democracy takes place when the silenced find a voice, and when we begin to listen to what they have to say.

CHAPTER TEN

Lift Every Voice

INITIALLY, I THOUGHT my strength came primarily from the people with whom I had worked in the South. They, like the witnesses in Selma, Alabama, showed me that dignity is strength in the face of powerful obstacles and determined enemies. I soon discovered, however, a larger community that buoyed me like a cork on the waves, riding from public humiliation to a greater sense of connection and possibility. I also realized that, despite the acclamation that followed my rejection, my role was not as a leader but as a facilitator of ideas and critical appraisals. I had always seen myself as an intellectual crusader, who, if effective, would prompt people to mobilize to reclaim their power. Now I had a chance to reach out to more people than I had ever previously imagined. Gratifyingly, I discovered many people who believe in the importance of democratic institutions that are worthy of the name only if they spread power rather than hoard it.

I did not know at the time that all the experiences, good and bad, that flowed from the nomination debacle would ultimately provide concrete evidence of the very ideas that had gotten me into so much trouble in the first place. Nor did I realize then that the nomination fiasco would lead me back to an earlier intuition about the need for a public conversation considerably different from the one that had just taken place. It did not take long, however, after the nomination was withdrawn to confirm that idea as well.

I discovered as a direct result of my own experience that what we need is an open-ended conversation on race, a conversation that starts with race but then links race to issues of fairness, justice, and the distribution of scarce resources in a democracy. I had urged President Clinton to engage the country in such a conversation before he nominated me. Now, I renewed my resolve to put the issue of racial justice back onto the national agenda. The very nature of the controversy surrounding the nomination suggested that issues of racial justice needed airing, not silencing. But I began to understand that we had to do more than simply change the subject matter of the conversation. As the dust settled on the nomination imbroglio, it became clear that while we need to talk about race, we also need to think and talk about race differently and in light of a new vision of social justice.

This was a circuitous realization, but one that came from meeting and working with, talking and listening to many people across the country—working people, journalists, civil rights activists, lawyers, local politicians, friends, and antagonists. In their voices I heard a plea for racial reconciliation, a call to people who are hurting, people who care, and people who are motivated to improve the lives of themselves and their neighbors. It was a call to people who have confidence in the capacity of the average person to make a contribution when given the incentive to engage in an interactive learning process. Most of all, it was a call to recommit to the language of justice and the passion of participatory democracy.

A conversation on race, they told me, cannot be dominated by the usual voices of opinion. The people with whom I met and spoke were not interested in more jabbering by national politicians or pundits. What they wanted was a chance for greater participation by plain-speaking Americans like themselves. Their involvement would come, they said, if we found public spaces for multiracial collaboration, forums in churches and union halls in which people could come together to solve racially charged problems within their local communities. I realized that such efforts would set loose a variety of responses, some good, some malign, but each important to understanding without illusion the path to justice that a country truly committed to democracy must follow.

One of the people who helped me to move forward was Eddie Correia. At three o'clock on a cold January afternoon in 1995, with cool, thin sunlight angling in sharply, I interviewed Eddie in his office at Northeastern University Law School. When Ricki Seidman summoned him to Washington the last week in May 1993, Eddie had dropped everything and come. Within twenty-four hours he had flown to D.C. from his law professor's office in Boston to become the only full-time Justice Department person assigned to work on the nomination. Now, a few years after that one lone week we had worked so closely together, I asked Eddie to look back and analyze what had happened that spring.

I asked Eddie if he agreed that announcing a civil rights nomination without a simultaneous plan for public education or a willingness to fight once the nomination became controversial was an early window into the president's problems. Penda Hair, Dayna Cunningham, and others had stressed that the president should have fought hard for the nomination or at minimum for a Senate hearing. They thought this not because I was so important, or that the position was the equivalent to a

Supreme Court nomination, but rather because it would have allowed the president to stake out a clear position on civil rights early enough in his administration to make a difference. They had assumed that the administration would pay more attention to the nomination precisely *because* it was controversial. What they didn't understand was that the controversy arose out of fundamental differences in public policy, both outside and within the administration.

Eddie was too diplomatic to answer questions directly about whether the withdrawal of the nomination was a window on the president's integrity or motivations. He admitted that what had happened to me showed that Democrats have a problem articulating any vision—let alone sticking up for it. They were preoccupied with winning the next day's news cycle, an obsession with tactics that was further exacerbated when the Democrats lost control of the Senate and the House in 1994. "You expect that from Congress because they're all out for their own interests," he observed. "That just makes it even more important to have the moral vision from the White House. If the White House is always sort of mixed up about it, then there's no moral leader."

On that January afternoon in 1995 he went on to explain: "I still think to this day that the Republicans probably were going to try to score points in this nomination process and you were eventually going to be confirmed. I always kind of thought that. I would guess that's the way the Republicans do that. What was absolutely shocking was that the Democrats started to bail out. And that's what was the eventual problem. Not the Republicans. They were just being true to form. If [the president had] stuck by you, I think you probably would have won, for one thing. But even if you lost, you'd have gotten a hearing and he'd have gained stature."

Intellectually, I understood what Eddie was telling me. The failed nomination had yielded profound lessons, not because it focused attention on the president's soul, but because it offered a moment of public insight into the decadence of American politics writ large. Like Eddie, more Americans were beginning to see just how vacuous politics-as-usual can be, and to recognize the need to do more than engage in what former head of the National Endowment for the Humanities Sheldon Hackney so aptly characterized as our "drive-by" political conversation.

I learned from the nomination debacle that speaking up is important, indeed critical, to democracy. I had written about the issue abstractly. I had stated the proposition differently, but the meaning was the same: coerced silence, whether it is the silence of permanent losers in the electoral process or the silence of someone who points out that flaw, is antithetical to democratic self-governance. Second, it became clear to me that democracy is protected by the electorate, not the elected leaders. The practice of democracy can only be protected by the people. Without a firm connection to communities, claims of leadership ring hollow. In a system where insiders manipulate power behind the scenes, those on the outside are kept both ignorant and disengaged. We become seduced by the mistaken notion that democratic power is best exercised by giving authority to the right individuals. Ordinary people then become conditioned to remain silent, which reinforces the power of the chosen few. Third, I found out how very hard it is to speak out. It often takes backing or affirmation by others before many of us find the courage to speak at all.

So, for me, an experience of rejection reaffirmed the need for greater power sharing and more participatory democracy both within the society as a whole and within those organizations committed to social justice. The entire episode became a personal, political, and intellectual revelation.

WHAT HAD SILENCED me as a Clinton nominee now gave me a chance, and even more a reason, to speak out. I now understand, both as a personal and as an intellectual matter, why civil rights lawyers and advocates need to do more than just defend ourselves or laws passed thirty years ago. We need to go forward by reclaiming the energy and the vision that directly led to the passage of those laws in the first place. The Voting Rights Act passed in 1965 because knowledgeable insiders like Roger Wilkins had worked with and were reinforced by passionate outsiders like Dr. Martin Luther King, Jr. It passed in 1965 because of the eloquence of uncommonly courageous people, writing our most persuasive essays with their feet and sometimes with their own blood. That same act was successfully amended seventeen years later because we were able to muster creative synergy between the litigators and the lobbyists. It was not the laws per se that would save us; it was the dynamic struggle of people working inside and outside the system simultaneously. Now, we needed to get more people involved in different, perhaps untried ways that would give those working on the inside new power to back up their demands. To do so could help us move from the important job of enforcing existing civil rights laws to the vital task of emboldening the struggle for social justice.

Even before the nomination, I had tried to speak out in law review articles about innovative ways to rethink old laws to share power more broadly. Because I wrote in dense prose about abstract ideas, it was easy to isolate and caricature me as "out of the mainstream"—a label the *Wall Street Journal* still uses to refer to my views. But while the controversy surrounding my views was enough in the short run to deny me a particular government job, in the long run it offered me a larger platform and, even more, a better sense of what is necessary to produce the kinds of fundamental change that as a civil rights lawyer I always believed we needed.

My "dis-appointment" ultimately freed me to function differently, outside the purview of conventional politics. It helped me clear out the underbrush of my own careerism, and changed my focus from individual advancement to the creation of a more democratic, participatory space for personal and intellectual growth. I began lecturing at colleges and talking to civic associations. I collected the "controversial" articles that had previously reached a limited academic audience and published them in a book, *Tyranny of the Majority*. I took maximum advantage of the opportunity that writing a book gives to fly around the country, speaking to audiences in bookstores and local media outlets about my ideas. Gradually, I learned to translate the academic jargon of law review articles into tangible stories for a lay audience.

I found that one trap I had to avoid, however, was converting people's interest in my notoriety into mere celebrity. I discovered that when given the opportunity, most people really did want to know the whole story. They knew intuitively that the news stories were not enough. *The New Yorker* had called me an "Idea Woman." I tried to live up to that appellation, inviting the curious as well as the skeptical into a conversation about issues and policy. Keeping a sense of humor helped.

For some, I was still merely a well-known name, one in a long list of aggrieved Clinton nominees. For others, I looked familiar but they could not supply the right name. I remember trying to hail a taxi cab in September 1993, in Philadelphia, en route to the airport. I was running late, trying to make a flight to Hartford, where I would then be driven to the University of Massachusetts. This was to be my first college lecture since the nomination was withdrawn and I was nervous.

It was raining hard. I stood with other people waiting my turn at a taxi stand near the law school. Despite the fact that several people were ahead of me in line, a cab with a passenger already inside pulled up to the corner and stopped right in front of me. The driver got out and came toward me, announcing, "The man inside says he knows you." I was soaking wet, so I eagerly looked to see who it was summoning me, but did not recognize the businessman in the rear seat. As the driver began lifting my bags to put them in the trunk, he tried to reassure me. "The man inside says he wants to take you to the airport." I felt relieved that the passenger knew my destination, but nothing about this middle-aged businessman refreshed my memory of ever having seen him before. I stared at him, waiting for a hint of recognition. The man in the cab grinned back at me. He broke out into a huge smile. "Zoë Baird," he exclaimed, greeting me warmly. "No," I replied. "But I'd still like a ride to the airport."

By the time we arrived at the airport, my traveling companion knew not only who I was but what I stood for. He asked for my card. He couldn't wait to tell the members of his bridge club back in Minnesota about our encounter.

One day, a year later, I was en route to New York City for the annual political science convention. I was traveling by train from New Haven. A political scientist from Yale introduced himself and told me he assigned my work to his students. Then a twenty-something woman across from me told me I had made her day. She beamed. She was overjoyed to meet me in person to tell me how naive she had once been; after my nomination, however, she no longer trusted politics and politicians. She was so angry at President Clinton back then that she had cried.

That these people were white did not surprise me. I had learned that there is a progressive community waiting to be energized. I discovered in their support an urgent need for a more truly democratic politics in which we all can fully participate and one that is consistent with the active consent of the governed.

At the political science convention, many blacks stopped me, and in Philadelphia as I waited at the train station for my husband Nolan to pick me up, a young black man waved to me from his car. His mother and sister had just gotten out of the car. They were members of the black sorority, Alpha Kappa Alpha, he informed me, and I had spoken at their convention. But that wasn't why he made contact with me from across the paved thoroughfare. It was to tell me I should have gotten that job.

For many blacks, my public ostracism was theirs, too. They identified in personal terms with what they saw as my repudiation. "Uprising from a Downfall," an elderly black woman at a bookstore in Philadelphia proposed to name this story because, as she saw it, my experience inspired others. In my public humiliation, she saw the human cost of a competitive political culture in which everything is zero-sum: my gain is inevitably your loss. I should use the opportunity, she said, the opportunity of getting right back up to speak my mind. "You spoke truth to power," she announced, her voice much stronger than her lean, frail body. "You refused to back down, and now, you have inspired others to lift themselves up, too." She leaned closer to me from across the table where I was signing books and spoke in a conspiratorial stage whisper. "Every time God closes a window, He opens a door," she told me.

In my willingness to fight back, she retrieved a lesson of redemption from betrayal: that betrayal, as Christopher Lasch has observed in another context, is the betrayal of American democracy by America's elites. The redemption, as Cornel West reminds us, is in the heroic energy of the men and women whose commitment to participatory democracy makes everything else possible. By speaking out, I might inspire more people to join me in the public square. By fighting back, others might struggle too to redeem their democracy.

Eddie was right. I now had a chance to talk in a clear voice about needed political reforms. Americans of all races began to "get it." A middle-class white man at the Global Ministry of the Methodist Church told me that what I was saying in those "controversial" law review articles challenging winners-who-take-all revealed the truth of what his wife had said over the course of thirty years of marriage: He fought to win; she fought to resolve. If more of us fought to resolve, no one would win it all. Yet everyone might win something.

Although my experience did not have the same spiritual dimension for him as it had for the elderly black woman in the bookstore, the middle-aged man at the Global Ministry echoed her advice. In voicing my ideas, I was giving voice to their ideas too. From my experience they saw an opportunity to reconstruct our broken civic life. The message was simple: If more people got back in motion, they would draw sustenance from each other and from the power of collective action to resolve problems, not just to win.

A FEW POLITICIANS also got it. I had first met Cynthia McKinney in the aftermath of my nomination, during the month-long showdown between the Congressional Black Caucus and the president. To protest his decision to withdraw the nomination, the Black Caucus had refused to meet with the president. During that period, they invited me to discuss my ideas—those ideas about cumulative voting and proportional representation that had gotten me into trouble—at their July 1993 monthly meeting. Afterwards, we sat around informally, chatting, taking pictures. We did not strategize about next steps as a group.

Two years later, I received a visit from Democratic representative McKinney of Georgia in the wake of her decision to introduce legislation that would permit the election of members of Congress using cumulative or preference voting. She and Democratic representative Chaka Fattah of Philadelphia were sitting quietly in my living room when I finally came down, my hair still dripping wet. I had been in the shower when they arrived, fifteen minutes earlier than our scheduled appointment. It was a Sunday afternoon, July 30, 1995. McKinney had her hair pulled back, caught in a big, bright yellow bow. She wore a yellow linen jacket over a dark, tastefully flowered blouse and a brown skirt. She looked very professional. Yet her large eyes and the eagerness in her face belied the attacks she too had weathered. Her dignified bearing brought to mind the Norman Rockwell painting of the young black girl being escorted by federal marshals to school: The little girl was dressed in her Sunday best. Her beautiful white dress somehow remained immaculate as she walked tall amid the hail of sloppy red tomatoes thrown at her by unseen tormentors.

McKinney, a forty-one-year-old single mother, had spent her first four years in Congress as a striking contrast to many fellow Democratic incumbents: she had stood firmly on principle to defend the interests of those beaten down by the 1994 Gingrich Revolution. The bill she came to discuss would open up the political process to new voices and grass-roots organizing efforts. Her bill would allow voters to elect members of Congress statewide, using proportional representation and some of the other alternative electoral arrangements I discussed in my articles.

We talked sound bites like winner-take-only-some as opposed to winner-take-all, about finding metaphors to show that racial justice is a necessary precursor to social justice. She agreed that we needed to reclaim the moral authority of the original civil rights movement, re-trieving our goal of multiracial collaboration from behind the curtain of color blindness that was being used to hide existing power relations. We talked about making coalitions with other electoral reform groups—in particular, the term limits people—and with environmentalists, Asians, Latinos, and women.

She took extensive notes on the back of my husband Nolan's "Blacks and the Mass Media" article. She only used the empty back sheet, and by the end of the meeting it was filled with names, ideas, and strategies written every which way across the paper. She was respectful and enthusiastic. What a contrast to the courtesy calls I had had two years earlier in the spring of 1993. I was once again a teacher, a collabo-rator, an advocate, and not a supplicant. It was exhilarating.

It was also revealing of an important but thus far missed opportu-nity. McKinney was eager to gain support for her bill on behalf of the silent voices she had come to Congress to represent in the first place. She recognized that election reform was necessary to make space for more people to speak, to organize, and to be heard. But our conversation was not just a conversation about electoral reform. We were discussing progressive, even transformative, social change.

We both knew that we would have to build on Dr. King's prophetic idea that the command post for any social justice movement lay in "the bursting hearts" of the people themselves. If we could begin to imagine a vision of social justice that others might embrace, we had the makings of a vibrant force. Each of us alone could become more powerful if we connected up with other people just as hungry as we are for new ways of thinking and doing. In *Why We Can't Wait* (1964), King had written:

> It was the people who moved their leaders, not the leaders who moved the people. Of course, there were generals, as there must be in every

army. But the command post was in the bursting hearts of millions of Negroes. When such a people begin to move, they create their own theories, shape their own destinies, and choose the leaders who share their own philosophy.

The energy for any effort worth pursuing needed to bubble up from grass-roots mobilization, from people ready to band together to solve community problems. But we could get and keep more people in motion if those in positions of power, people like Representative McKinney, were prepared for this bottom-up rising.

"It's a trip, Lani. It's a trip. They, too, are beginning to hear what you have to say." This was the conclusion of my old friend Charisse Lillie, former city solicitor of Philadelphia, when I told her about the meeting.

Gradually, the trauma of living a public life became less a burden and more a salvation. Both the pain and the healing occurred before an audience. That people were watching gave me a sense of theater. It made me appreciate that my dramatic engagement with Washington could also be a vehicle for political struggle. That people were also listening gave me a sense of purpose. My now-public voice endowed me with a mission, a faith, a vision.

Roger Wilkins had given me the best advice. "Lani," he told me within a month after the withdrawal of my nomination, "you must see yourself as a woman with an issue, not a grievance. People feel sorry for victims, but they don't listen to them. Victims whine; others soon tire of hearing the relentless complaints. You, by contrast, have an issue, which you must take to the American people. And when you speak, this time, they will listen."

My mother set me straight as well. "Who are you speaking to?" she would ask insistently. "If you think you are speaking to Bill Clinton," she reminded me, "you are wasting your breath. He isn't listening."

SOME OF THE PEOPLE who were listening surprised me. I had been characterized as a lieutenant of the radical fringe. Yet former president Gerald Ford sent me a handwritten note to say I should have had a hearing. After he expressed interest in knowing more about my ideas, I sent him several of the law review articles I had written. President Ford then wrote me again. He apologized for the delay in responding. He said he and Betty had taken a cruise. While she read John Grisham's *The Firm*, he read my law review articles!

I also discovered that if I spent time not just speaking out but listening myself, I could be even more pleasantly surprised.

In April 1995, I was in D.C. to speak at the Smithsonian Associates.

So many people had responded to the initial announcement that they had had to relocate the event to a larger auditorium. The public relations person there had been hounding me to do more publicity for the event now that she had to fill an even larger place. I had agreed to do the *Cathy Hughes Show* (WOL), a black radio call-in show, which was being simulcast that afternoon on C-Span. I was at a small D.C. hotel waiting for my ride to the radio station when an envelope was delivered.

It was a plain manila envelope. Inside was a heavy cardboard note; on the cover was a picture of the hotel building. The note read:

4/12/95

Dear Ms. Guinier, [an "a" in place of the first "i" had been crossed out and the "i" handwritten in]
    As a cook here, I am thrilled and honored that you are staying here at the Inn. Please let us know if there is anything we can prepare for you tonight—just call the kitchen and ask for Gillian. We'd love to meet you and talk politics, etc. So if you have a minute after your engagement come on down, tour the kitchen and have a bite to eat.
                                                                    —Gill Clark

I came in at 10:20 P.M. that night. The dining room was only open from six to nine. But when I returned, the clerk at the front desk said, "They are waiting for you. Just go on down." They were. They had fixed salmon with a "drizzle of chives and hollandaise sauce," tomato chutney, basmati rice, broccoli. The other cook—Gill's colleague—sat down, too. She told me had she been in charge, she would have doubled my portion. Truth be told, I would have easily devoured two servings of dessert—a truly extraordinary pecan pie. I ate. They watched, thrilled, because they don't usually get to see anyone eat their food.

Gillian was black, her colleague white; the waiter who served me a glass of Merlot was also white. They were all extremely kind, even solicitous. Gillian said she still had the *New York Times Magazine* article I had written about the nomination experience in February 1994. She was so proud. She was surprised they had let me write my own story, rather than being interviewed; "mediated," she called it. She insisted I sign something so she could prove to her husband where she had been this night, proof that she was not out Having an Affair.

Gillian told me that she had been excited that I had answered her note earlier, but when ten o'clock came and went without a sign of me, she began to worry. She paced. She went to the bathroom. She had asked the desk clerk how she should approach me. The clerk suggested getting a key to my room and sitting quietly until I came back. Gillian rejected that idea at first, but now she wondered, had she blown it? She kept saying to herself, like a mantra, "She is busy; she is busy; she is probably tired." Then there I was—exhilarated by the attention, by the delicious food, the kindness of strangers who felt like kinfolk and treated me the way my grandmother greeted my father, with pride and motherly care and a plateful of wonderful food.

We sat up talking. We talked politics—and quickly understood each other. Two of the four of us were black women. But we all spoke freely, including the white male waiter who joined us. We agreed on a lot of things. We began with small matters. They led to larger questions. I was with people who cared, people who were genuinely curious and unpretentious about what they did not know or understand. I felt renewed in my belief in the democratic capacity of ordinary citizens.

I became a real person to Gill and her co-workers and they to me. We sat as equals listening to each other's thoughts and feelings. They were no longer just hotel employees who would normally remain anonymous. It was more as if I was a welcome guest in their home rather than a mere lodger in their place of business.

Our animated conversation brought to mind Dr. King's wise counsel. I was privileged to witness "the bursting hearts" of people who were themselves hungry to fill a vacuum and willing to come forward to bond with others like them. Gill Clark's honest and thoughtful conversation illustrated why it was important that I not fight simply for a single voice. It was more crucial to fight so that she and others like her could be heard. When they got to speak, they gave crucial feedback on exactly what is and is not controversial. Their eagerness to engage inspired me. But even more, I found that Gill Clark and her co-workers said what needs to be said better than the lawyers or the politicians because they spoke from the heart and from their own experience.

IT TOOK FORTY-THREE YEARS, but finally I understood what my father had always known and what my mother was still teaching me. My father told me bedtime and dinner table stories that taught me the importance of my voice; my mother nurtured the skills of listening. It took forty-three years, but by 1993, I had become a Virago.

I claimed my role as my father's Virago, the young girl who would ask, "Why?" and be told in a nonsense rhyme that "Y is a crooked letter, cut off the tail, leaves V. V stands for Virago, just like you!" My father's bedtime stories had never been more clear: I had to become who I am. I now understood what I was raised to be. As a little girl, I was the troublemaker when I asked so many questions; as a woman, I put forward troubling ideas. My ideas meant trouble because they too involved asking questions, questions that were unfamiliar, provocative, and designed to get people to challenge deeply held assumptions.

I not only asked the "Why?" that prompted my father's West

Indian rhyme, I now asked, "Why not?" I tried not only to speak but to hear. I always included a question and answer session whenever I gave a lecture or a talk. I appreciated the opportunity that listening to questions gave me to learn. The audience's personal stories and reactions to my ideas continued to enrich my thinking for days and months thereafter. I made sure to write down the nuggets of wisdom generously provided by the people in the audience. My notes from one audience would help me provoke my next audience into thinking of new ways of looking at the same ideas. My notes were also a way of respecting the genuine curiosity and often intriguing perspective of people who had come not only to listen but to speak. My notes were a tool for enlisting the audience's knowledge and inviting them to discover the power of their own voice.

It was my note taking that LDF cooperating attorney Bill Quigley said he had first noticed about me. When Bill and I met with our clients, with witnesses, or with other lawyers involved in major voting rights cases in Louisiana in the 1980s, he enjoyed watching me "process and provoke, all the while taking the most copious notes of anyone" he had ever seen. "I was struck by you and your note taking and your ability to process and provoke back in our earlier days," Bill said later, when he saw me in 1997. Despite the danger that lawyers taking notes then take charge, I added "quite a lot of levitas and gravitas," he concluded jocularly.

That was my job—to pry open a conversation and provoke the participants into moving forward, based on what they and others were saying. That was also what I had told Roger Wilkins when he first interviewed me in 1984: I saw myself as an "energizer of movement." My goal was to synthesize what others were saying and then feed it back to them in ways that would mobilize much-needed social action. That was my way of finding the voice of resistance and more inclusive transformation.

It was a voice I had heard expressed in the vigorous advocacy of many cooperating lawyers throughout the South, people with whom I had worked and from whom I had learned so much. G. K. Butterfield in Wilson, North Carolina; James Ferguson in Charlotte, North Carolina; and J. L. Chestnut in Selma, Alabama, are black lawyers whose independence of thought and dynamic oratory inspired and enlightened me. Yet I also knew that well-spoken orators like Fergie or Ches do not "move the people" if they take all the notes and then do all the talking. Director of the Chicago Lawyers Committee for Civil Rights, Clyde Murphy often tells his lawyers that "sometimes the most important thing you can bring to a meeting is your silence." Like G. K. Butterfield, civil rights lawyers on occasion need to "have a little prayer meeting" with themselves, to avoid the pitfalls of dependency that their status can engender. Even outspoken lawyers like J. L. Chestnut have been forced to come to terms with the way establishment conventions disable them from seeing what was so clear to Dr. King in Selma, Alabama, in 1965 —the importance of direct action and public education to supplement test-case litigation.

Like Chestnut in Selma in 1965 and Murphy in Chicago in 1997, I began to see how I and other civil rights lawyers, thinkers, and activists could benefit if we attended community meetings and simply listened. Murphy's advice also resonated with the wisdom of Martin Luther King, Jr., who said, "[W]e've got to understand people, first, and then analyze their problems. If we really pay attention to those we want to help; if we listen to them; if we let them tell us about themselves—how they live, what they want out of life—we'll be on much more solid ground when we start 'planning' our 'action,' our 'programs,' than if we march ahead, to our own music, and treat 'them' as if they're only meant to pay attention to us, anyway."

Dr. King was not urging us to poll people to fit their views into a preformulated set of arbitrary questions and answers. Nor was he suggesting that it was too much talk that was the problem. He was reminding us that the wrong people are too often doing all the talking. Mark Schmitt, former policy director for Senator Bill Bradley, had it exactly right when he recently wrote in an informal memorandum: "It's as if we have three-fifths of a broad, lively public debate in this country, ranging from the far-right to just about the Al Gore position on an over-simplified political spectrum. The remainder of the debate exists, but it is academic, or theoretical, or stale, or narrow, or obscure, or not inclusive." It was Schmitt's last point that captured my experience.

We have, as Schmitt described, only a small, stunted debate, from the far right to President Clinton and the New Democrats. An entire spectrum of progressive opinion is missing. Moreover, even within the debate as it is narrowly constructed, most of what we hear are vacuous pronouncements from politicians and pundits. Little public air time is available to grass-roots organizers, community activists, or the real stakeholders in the conversation—the people whose daily lives might be directly affected by public decisions and public talk.

I began to see my job as opening up that conversation both to new ideas and to different people. By listening and then responding to the muted voices of Gill Clark or former clients Maggie Bozeman and Spencer Hogue, I try to stimulate what engineers call a positive feedback process. In collaboration with others, I seek to disseminate their stories to a wider audience and reframe their insights in light of a new social justice vision. The elderly black woman in the bookstore was right: A window had closed but a door is open.

From a momentary crisis, I retrieved the opportunity to become who I am. I am neither the anointed leader nor the appointed spokesperson. If anything, I heed South African president Nelson Mandela's model of pushing forward from behind. Mandela tells the story of the shepherd who identifies two or three young energetic sheep that are headed in the right direction. The shepherd allows these active sheep to forge a path. The shepherd's role is to coax the rest of the flock to follow together as a herd and to make sure the young sheep do not lead the flock into danger. Like the shepherd, I identify ideas that seem to lead us in the right direction, but I also am careful to position myself at the back of the flock. It is important to find others who will confirm the path and ensure that none are left behind.

My father had long ago planted the idea that I am a Virago. My mother suggested that I not waste energy being angry, but rather spend time learning how to listen better to what others had to say. My sister Marie told me that the philosophy of this century would eventually become the common sense of the next.

Roger Wilkins put it all together. I had to become a woman with an issue, not a grievance. The issue is racial justice. The idea is that we need a new kind of conversation to talk about it.

I began to call more persistently for a national conversation on race. I had expressed the germ of this idea when I wrote to the president proposing a White House Racial Justice Summit.

Over the next two years, "Why We Need a National Conversation on Race" became a call to action. The idea had germinated in several speeches in the fall of 1993 and 1994, including one at the National Press Club in November 1994. It was an idea that I developed further, working on a seminar with my colleague Professor Susan Sturm, engaging with Susan in experimental conversations funded by the Ford and Mott foundations, and gaining insights from audience responses to lectures and op-eds over the next several years.

I started by talking about racial attitudes. Some of the discomfort that ordinarily accompanies talk about race simply masks *racial bias* across the political spectrum, I said. I quoted a 1994 National Science Foundation–funded study, which found that liberal and conservative whites were almost equally willing to express negative characterizations of blacks. Forty-five percent of white liberals and 51 percent of white conservatives agreed that blacks are aggressive or violent; 44 percent of the conservatives and 41 percent of the liberals said blacks are "boastful." Much of this bias, I concluded, reflects the absence of an honest dialogue about race across racial and ethnic groups, which, despite background equivalencies, live fundamentally different and separate lives.

Whereas thirty years ago, about one-quarter of blacks saw no immediate resolution to the problem of race, now over 50 percent of blacks think things are getting worse. Only 8 percent of college-educated blacks feel things got better in the last ten years; 70 percent think things got worse. (These statistics were from a May 1991 Gallup poll.) Middle-class, college-educated blacks, I noted, report continuing encounters with racial prejudice and discrimination, which for the most part remain invisible to their white counterparts. Yet many blacks do not talk about their own experience with discrimination. They fear, as the journalist Ellis Cose discovered in *The Rage of a Privileged Class*, being punished twice: first for being black; second for being angry. I relayed the story of one of my students at Penn Law School, who, in the 1980s in a public middle school in New Jersey, was treated to a Halloween party in which a fellow student dressed up as a member of the KKK, complete with hood and cross. The Klan costume received first prize! But my student, who is black, was tentative about even telling this story to her classmates. She assumed everyone had such a story to tell. So the experiences of many black people remain invisible, although they seethe quietly inside.

If we could find a public space within which to communicate, blacks, whites, Asians, and Latinos might find common ground. Common ground means a common place but not necessarily one in which we are exactly the same. Indeed, it is awareness of our very differences that allows us to begin to solve problems together. We need, for example, to hear more from Asians and Latinos, who are often invisible in the discussion of race. Race, for many Latinos, is a hybrid experience: neither white nor black, they still identify as a racial minority. Their experience "living on the hyphen," as one of my Cuban-American students describes it, might suggest new ways of thinking about racial categories. On the other hand, we also desperately need to understand the living legacy of slavery and Jim Crow, which specifically targeted blacks and nurtured myths of racial inferiority that still dominate so many of our subconscious racial attitudes.

But over time I realized that this cannot be a "Why can't we all get along?" invitation to dialogue. Nor can it be a plea for individuals to overcome personal bigotry through social color blindness. Though racial bias is still a major problem, the great challenges of race cannot, in my mind, be addressed simply by focusing on "race relations" between individuals or groups. Certainly, improved race relations is important, but race-based inequities cannot be addressed simply by opting not to "see" race or to become individually color-blind. Color blindness is a vision defect; it is not a solution to centuries of discrimination based on race.

In an October 21, 1997, *New York Times* column, Jane Brody describes color blindness as an abnormal medical condition. In extreme cases, the person with this disability sees only "what a normal-sighted person would see in the dark." Unlike shape, size, and texture, the "color of an object exists only in the eyes of the beholder." What this "least recognized and most ignored of all vision defects" reveals is that color is as much the subject of community agreement as it is individual interpretation of measurable wavelengths of light.

Social color blindness can track the medical condition in positive ways. For example, those people who profess themselves to be racially color-blind disassociate their feelings about individuals from racial stereotypes or prejudices. They don't permit themselves to interpret or judge people based solely on visual color cues whose significance "exists only in the eyes of the beholder." For all people that is a good thing. But that is not our only goal. The issue of race is bigger and more complex than any one individual's prejudice, guilt, entitlement, or reaction to perceptual cues.

Indeed, when color blindness becomes the driving force for *all* social policy, it generalizes inappropriately from the vision defect for which it is named. It freezes the current social costs of historic race consciousness into a permanent condition. Color blindness becomes an ideological position that ignores the real effects color has had and limits its proponents to seeing only "what a normal-sighted person would see in the dark." It is like saying to someone in a wheelchair that you don't see them as any different from you, but feel driven on principle to oppose curb cuts that would enable their mobility because it would offend the equality norm.

Troy Duster, a sociologist at the University of California, Berkeley, helped me understand the limitations of color blindness as a single or universal public policy solution when he started me thinking how much race, for people of color, is like water. It exists in different states, depending upon external conditions. Below 32 degrees Fahrenheit, it is frozen; above 212 degrees Fahrenheit, it is a vapor. Between those extremes it is more or less fluid, tending to crystallize at one end and evaporate at the other. When we talk about race, we may be talking about one thing in the way that when we talk about water we are talking about one thing, but race affects poor people and rich people differently. Poor people are like ice, frozen and often immobilized by the conjunction of race and class. Rich blacks are more like steam; they can move almost autonomously. But they are not completely invisible and do suffer when racial stereotypes interrupt their otherwise privileged status. Even when professionally attired and minding their own business, many blacks cannot hail a cab, shop in a store, or drive their own vehicles without being treated as criminals by the taxi driver, the store clerk, or local police. Yet, there are social conditions that ameliorate the impact of race on those who historically have been disadvantaged by it. At one end, those with a college education and good jobs can still enjoy a better life. By turning up the heat, bringing in educational and economic resources, we may be able to evaporate some of the most offensive and disadvantaging effects of race. It doesn't disappear, but it is certainly a less prominent factor.

In other words, race matters even for many middle-class blacks. Melvin Oliver and Thomas Shapiro, in their book *Black Wealth, White Wealth,* identify a wealth disadvantage not just an income disadvantage that affects all blacks, even those who are high achievers. They find a huge net worth gap between blacks and whites that reflects intergenerational wealth transfers and not just different income levels. Whites with professional credentials have a "$105,010 edge over blacks with the same mobility credentials." Because "the ability to accumulate wealth" was denied African Americans by law and social custom during two hundred fifty years of slavery, even relatively well-off blacks do not have the same access as their white counterparts to resources enjoyed by many whites, such as parental assistance that "comes in the form of gifts, interest-free loans, or loans that are never paid back." Oliver and Shapiro call for monetary reparations to address the "historic structuring of racial inequality and, in particular, wealth" that "has been aggravated during each new generation."

Along the dynamic continuum that the race-as-water metaphor evokes, both the working poor and middle-class blacks experience race very differently from their white friends or colleagues. Neither race as a sign of inclusion nor race as a sign of exclusion disappears for them simply because we decide not to talk about it. Even for relatively conservative blacks living in the largest black working-class enclave in New York City, racism is "a powerful force in the larger world," as James Traub writes in the October 19, 1997, *New York Times Magazine.* Similarly, despite their apparent material success, those black lawyers, academics, and corporate executives whom Ellis Cose interviewed for *The Rage of a Privileged Class* suffer a tangible net worth differential and, in addition, continue to feel they are trespassing in a world dominated by race, bristling with heavily coded signals and informal networks of exclusion. To refuse to see race is to refuse to acknowledge their everyday lives.

This is not to say that race and racism are the defining features of the lives of all people of color. Nor does it mean that all difference is racially assigned or that individuals acting in good faith make no difference at all. Whether they are Ellis Cose's embittered though privileged blacks or James Traub's working-class strivers, many see individual autonomy and choice as valuable assets.

Yet some also see how easy it is for individuals, acting alone, to misperceive structural problems as their own fault or completely responsive to their own will. While individuals can make a difference, it is important to recognize that when they don't, they need not internalize systemic failure as rage, anger, or guilt. Especially those in a "frozen state" may become easily frustrated if they insist on navigating life's challenges solely as autonomous, free-floating individuals. To their own detriment, they forget the mutual support that comes when connected to a larger cause or a loving community.

Race is a multifaceted construction that both affirms and degrades simultaneously. It interacts with other forces, including class, status, and gender. Like water, race exhibits different properties depending upon internal and external context. Like medical color blindness, the significance of race is often in the eyes of the beholder. For many white people, race has been used to exclude "nonwhites" and to affirm those who are included. Those whites, whether liberal or neoconservative, who want to get beyond race justifiably want to get beyond the sense of excluding people unfairly. For them, to say race matters is to say prejudice and bias are tolerable. The only way in which they "know" race is as a means of exclusion and discrimination against nonwhites.

But for many people of color, while race is used to exclude them from majority status, it also at the same time affirms in them a sense of belonging to a community. Like water in its frozen state, they may have little choice about being connected. Yet that absence of choice, or what University of Chicago professor Michael Dawson calls "linked fate," can become a source of psychic comfort. The sense of common oppression offers protection and solace; it helps channel anger into collective action rather than internalized rage or depression. It can create a community of inclusion, not exclusion.

This was certainly my experience growing up. I belonged when I went to visit my father's family. I was not only kin but welcomed, loved, greeted with tight hugs. Similarly, I enjoyed a natural affinity with the black kids in junior high school who reached out to me, included me in their parties, made me feel at home. When I went south as an LDF lawyer, once again I felt energized and empowered by my connections to black clients and cooperating attorneys. We partnered together in a collective struggle for racial justice.

Though segregation diminished both blacks and whites in its wrenching rules, limited opportunities, and distorted values, the black witnesses in the Marion Three case in Selma, Alabama, for example, created a sense of community in the midst of great despair. Because they are both outnumbered and even more vulnerable as isolated individuals, many people of color realize the value, indeed, the necessity, of collective struggle. None of these witnesses romanticized the cosseted community in which they lived. Yet they felt that the only freedom and power they had came from being connected to a community that would protect them. That, in effect, was what inspired my law review articles, in which I sought power sharing or taking-turns arrangements that would build and renew local community organizations and grass-roots mobilization.

Race, in this sense, is a reminder that we need to affirm the power of community in reinforcing individual freedom and capacity. One of the lessons I had learned as a child of an interracial marriage, as a junior high school student riding the school bus in Queens, and as a civil rights lawyer in Selma is the wondrous feeling of belonging that comes when a community takes you in. Many of those for whom race has been salient are not only victims of segregation or oppression. They have also managed to create "something out of nothing," something joyous and affirming.

To say that race matters because on the positive side it can mobilize or affirm, that it is important to overcome a sense of being marginalized or degraded, does not mean that race simply creates a biological wall around an illusion or "social construction." My mother was also em- braced and welcomed by my father's family. So were lawyers like Penda Hair and Pam Karlan. All were white women who sensed a shared obligation to stand shoulder to shoulder with black clients, friends, and colleagues, earning the trust of a community to which they would ordinarily be outsiders. Their actions and commitments confirmed their membership in this community even if their race did not. While they may have been white to everyone else, their membership in this mostly black community was signaled by their willingness to engage with a community in struggle.

I had also experienced a joyful sense of community in a multiracial setting in high school, when the whole school competed by class in a chorus format called "Sing." Each class picked a theme and rewrote the lyrics to popular songs around that theme. Every class member was automatically in the chorus, without regard to one's ability to carry a tune. What was important was a willingness to come to rehearsals, learn the new words, and practice the accompanying hand motions until we could do them in a synchronized fashion. As we each lifted our voice, we felt a power surging forth that not only filled the auditorium but created a special bond none of us would easily forget.

Thus, the issue of race is not only about individual attitudes or stereotyped thinking. It is multifaceted. It has positive, affirming as- pects. Race is about many things. It is about building community and mobilizing people around a perceived sense of injustice or a set of shared goals. It is also an issue of institutionalized power and dysfunctional social policymaking. Race matters because it signals visible problems with the way the majority configured and distributed power. But it also matters because it allowed me to see the blessings of community, of feeling connected to other people. We need to talk about race both to remind ourselves of the potential power of community and because we need to discuss the major public policy crises confronting our society.

ONE DAY not too long after the president withdrew my nomination, a dark-skinned black man in his early thirties, an attendant in a West Philadelphia parking lot, shouted to me from a distance of two hundred feet, "Are you the one that was supposed to be appointed to Clinton's cabinet?" Although my interlocutor had not gotten the title exactly right, I nodded. He then got very excited and continued the exchange, pumping both his arms in the air for emphasis. "I know why you didn't get that job," he announced proudly. "You were too black. You were just too black." He smiled broadly at me, pleased with his analysis. Then he repeated the phrase, emphasizing the first word: "*Too* black." Without hesitation or ambiguity, this brown-skinned working-class man told me, a very light-skinned African-American woman law professor, that he intuitively understood my transgression.

Questions about the future of American democracy can't ignore race and be true to the challenges we face. But by choosing to discuss democracy and race at the same time, I immediately became a racial partisan. That made me "too black" for those in the political mainstream, including the press. My ideas challenged the image of a country that has already achieved color blindness. They suggest there is more work to be done.

Though my experience as a "Quota Queen" was brief, it showed how large our fear of race really is. If those of us "with a race" speak, we will surely use the opportunity to whip up hidden resentments and fears. Thus, I was "too black" to be allowed to be heard. Being seen was enough. Moreover, once I became the Quota Queen, the message was clear: I should not even be seen for long.

Because so many people conceive of power as fundamentally oppositional and hierarchical, they understood me as a threat, as someone who was simply trying to give blacks a chance to rule over whites. Because power can only be seen in our culture as divided between winners and losers, someone had to lose. The Mexican-American journalist Raoul Lowery Contreras wrote a telling opinion piece for the *Eastside Sun* in Los Angeles while the nomination was pending in 1993. After twisting my words into an unrecognizable verbal pretzel, Contreras accused me of promoting fascism. In his view, I

> would put the Black community above all others in its desire for a political Grail. . . . In this process, Mexican Americans would lose what is rightfully ours. . . . But C. Lani Guinier would not allow us to do what so many groups have done before in the U.S. She would give the shrinking percentage of Blacks (in the general population) political

votes and influence far beyond their statistical place in the U.S. That power would have to come from somewhere and I doubt if white America would let go of such power . . . the Lani Guiniers of the world . . . would simply steal this power from the fastest growing and more prosperous groups (Hispanics and Asian Americans) and hand it to less prosperous, yet numerous and geographically well-placed Blacks.

In Contreras's zero-sum world, one group could only gain power by "stealing" it from another.

Because more of us had not spoken aloud with an inclusive explanation of the problem, we had inadvertently cooperated with the right-wing version that suggested that in a winner-take-all society, when people of color win, white people lose. Or as Raoul Lowery Contreras concluded, when a black person speaks out for more democracy, that must mean she wants other minority groups to lose.

Those of us advocating racial justice were hamstrung because we were heard as advocating a strategy of "us" versus "them." In the words of the parking attendant, I was "too black." For many in the "political mainstream," that meant my thumb was on the scale to fix the results, not to improve the processes of democracy. They allowed the right wing to define me as a racial separatist, and then, consistent with a win/lose scorecard, seemed unable to see the story as anything other than one of "whites lose if blacks win, and Guinier favors blacks."

In that kind of fight, people of color are both poor and outnumbered. Recognizing this inescapable fact meant that we have to try a new kind of conversation. This conversation would not be reduced to racial victims or entitlements; it would not see race as only one thing. Instead, it has to acknowledge the dynamics of race as frozen, fluid, or vapor depending upon other forces like class and gender. It also has to recognize the backdrop of fear that frames our racial discourse—the fear that people of color will do to whites what has been done to them. Or, conversely, the skepticism that conversations on race are just for people of color, since whites don't have a race or can't see others' race.

For the Philadelphia parking attendant, that I was "too black" was a source of pride. I was for black people. I was for him and people like him. But if I wanted to be understood more generally, I had to figure out a way to take my ideas about positive-sum solutions to invite others into the discussion, too.

I HAD FOUGHT FOR racial justice as part of the community formed by southern civil rights clients and cooperating attorneys with whom I worked as a lawyer for the Legal Defense Fund. Most of the people in that community, people like Julius Chambers, James Ferguson, Rose Sanders, J. L. Chestnut, Maggie Bozeman, and Albert Turner, were black, or at least people of color. But not all. Many of those community members were white civil rights lawyers like Penda Hair, Pam Karlan, Leslie Winner, Armand Derfner, Jim Blacksher, and Bill Quigley. I then discovered other allies outside the civil rights community after I became a law professor, and even more so after I left Washington in 1993.

One such important ally was my faculty colleague and collaborator, Professor Susan Sturm. Susan spent numerous hours with me upon my return in June 1993 to the University of Pennsylvania Law School, helping me to record my experiences with the nomination while still vivid; but even more, talking with me about those experiences.

Susan is a brilliant, methodical thinker. Susan helped me see that, while my primary community, even my audience, may be people of color, I had to worry about how I was being heard by others who are also listening. It is absolutely crucial, Susan agreed, to talk about race. But, she cautioned, it is equally important to remember that an audience in a segregated society will hear things differently and probably not as you intended. Those of us who think it is important to discuss race need to show why. We need to explain how race can become a window on fundamental problems that those of all colors may also experience. Talk of race cannot be pigeonholed as just a plea for the inclusion of a disadvantaged few into a static, rigid, and limited hierarchy. Instead, talk of race must be the beginning of serious conversation about how and for whom our society and polity is structured.

Susan's advice brought to mind something Leon Wieseltier, the literary editor of *The New Republic,* said about Justice Ginsberg's approach to women's rights: "it's the classical Jewish way of arguing against intolerance—that you argue against exceptions from fairness not in the name of the particular exception but in the name of the general principle." It also reminded me that Roger Wilkins's wise counsel applied not just to me personally but to a vision of justice more broadly. I should use the insights gained from my own experience as a window on a larger set of issues that affect many Americans.

Susan was not urging me to remove race from the picture. Nor was she suggesting that we should stop talking about it. She was in fact pushing me to take on those critics of race talk who claim that all talk of race is toxic and polarizing. For them, race talk leads to name-calling, which invariably makes white people feel guilty or alienated. Susan was saying that if race is real in the way it affects some people, then we had to worry about *how* we talk about race, not *whether* to talk about it. She was challenging me to speak in a language and with a vision that showed how problems long identified with people of color actually affect Americans of all races. She was encouraging me to extend Professor Gerald Torres's miner's canary metaphor beyond gerrymandered election districts. Many other problems that converge around people of color are also a visible signal of the dangerous atmosphere in the mines, not just a sign of the canary's vulnerability.

Race is the sentinel subject. Their very vulnerability enables many people of color, especially those who are less privileged, to function as a sponge soaking up the toxins in our political and social culture. We can blame individuals and communities of color for absorbing and reflecting back to us the full sweep of devastating social problems. Or, we can engage in collective brainstorming to identify and attempt to seek real solutions, so many of which are hidden in the racial subtext of fear of crime, welfare, drugs, and preferences or quotas—the code for "unqualified" beneficiaries of affirmative action.

If we think about affirmative action in higher education, for example, as the miner's canary, we can use the experience of people of color to open up more opportunities for everyone. I began to include in my speeches a thought experiment: Imagine white, working-class Americans as our allies. They too have often been unfairly excluded from a chance to make a contribution or to fulfill their dreams. Unfortunately, they have been conditioned to think that it is the canary who is taking their place in colleges and universities or holding them back from professional advancement. Yet the real problem confronting working-class whites is similar to the problem facing students of color: many public and private colleges employ selection criteria that favor applicants from upper-income families, whether children of alumni or simply children of privilege. This is a protocol of preferences that disadvantages both people of color *and* working-class whites.

Factors that correlate with parental income figure prominently in the current selection system. For example, Cheryl Hopwood, the white woman who successfully challenged the University of Texas Law School's affirmative action plan in 1996 in federal court, challenged only the admission of sixty-two out of the ninety-three black and Latino students accepted into the Texas Law School in 1992. But that year, when the law school rejected Ms. Hopwood, more than 130 white students were admitted who had lower test scores and grade-point averages than she did. Her grades and scores were discounted because she went to a community college and a state university. The University of Texas took points away from Ms. Hopwood, who grew up under difficult circumstances and worked her way through school, because she graduated from a less competitive but more affordable public college.

That Cheryl Hopwood's complaint challenged only the admission of blacks and Latinos ignored two significant aspects of the real problem. First, we are basing admission for all students on criteria that correspond with family income and past opportunity. Second, these same criteria may be efficient (in that they give admissions officers and faculty a quantitative measure by which to rank students), but they do not necessarily predict actual capacity to perform.

What many in the academy call "merit" really reflects an overemphasis on quantitative measures, driven by the college or university's fear of losing points in the *U.S. News & World Report*'s annual rankings of the nation's schools, 12 percent of which is based on slight differences among admittees' test scores. But the aptitude tests involved (the SAT and LSAT, for example) are only slightly better than random selection at predicting school achievement for all students. A representative of the company that makes up the LSAT admitted that it is about 9 percent better than random in predicting first-year law school performance nationwide. Research that Professors Jane Balin and Michelle Fine and I did at the University of Pennsylvania also found that LSAT scores are weak predictors of *all* students' first-year grades.

Our overreliance on timed paper-and-pencil tests favors students who do well on such tests—and those tend to be the students (disproportionately men and boys) who are good at quick, strategic guessing with less than perfect information and those from well-off families. Girls routinely score 30 to 50 points lower on the math SAT, for example, in part because many try to reason through a problem rather than simply guess the right answer. Yet their college math grades are the same as those of the higher-scoring boys. Upper-income applicants, most of whom are white, tend to score highest on the SAT and LSAT. But within every racial and ethnic group, test scores go up with family income. Those who go to better schools and enjoy greater exposure to books and travel do better on these tests. Their higher test scores often reflect the opportunities they have had (such as coaching or practice taking the test), and not necessarily how well they are likely to do in their next school or on the job.

Grades, work portfolios, evidence of motivation, teamwork skills, and perseverance are actually better predictors of college and law school achievement and, even more, of likely success after graduation. This is because a student's drive to succeed—along with an opportunity to do so—is often a better indicator of future success than test scores. Indeed, a recent Harvard study of graduates over three decades found that students with low SAT scores and blue-collar backgrounds tended to be more successful, with "success" defined by income, community involvement, and professional satisfaction. Similarly, a group of 300,000 military recruits in 1976 failed the battery of tests administered by the armed services but were admitted because of a calibration error. These "potentially ineligibles" completed training and were promoted at rates only slightly lower than those who passed the test.

What the experience of people of color and women who have been admitted pursuant to affirmative action programs demonstrates is that those who are motivated to succeed, and who are given the opportunity to do so, can catch up despite a late start or weaker test scores. A study of doctors trained at the medical school of the University of California, Davis, published in October 1997 in the *Journal of the American Medical Association*, found that students admitted to Davis between 1968 and 1987 with race, ethnicity, or unusual experience as a consideration went on to careers that were indistinguishable from those admitted on academic grades or test scores alone. The group performed less well as medical students but equally well as hospital residents and physicians. Similarly, researchers looking at a twenty-five-year policy of open admissions enrollment at the City University of New York found that the school was one of the largest sources in the United States of undergraduate students going on to earn doctorates, even though many of its undergraduates come from relatively poor backgrounds and take twice as long to complete their bachelor's degree.

Affirmative action in this sense is neither the real problem nor the whole solution. We talk about admissions' criteria only in the context of race or ethnicity because the test scores of students of color are often lower than those of whites as a group. That should not come as a surprise, given that many blacks and Latinos come from economically deprived backgrounds and have been educated in school districts that are still largely segregated. But the fact is that these admissions scores do not work to demonstrate functional merit for anyone, meaning the capacity to excel in the workplace or as a citizen in a democracy.

The experience of students of color—those who overcome weaker academic records and lower test scores to perform just as well on the job and in their professions—suggests that we should upsize the pool by substituting for test scores criteria often used to admit affirmative action applicants. Rather than admitting everyone using a single paper-and-pencil test that correlates with wealth and fails to predict success, all students could, in fact, be admitted by applying the kinds of individualized evaluations too often employed *only* for affirmative action admittees. Faculty and admissions officers could actually read each applicant's files and apply the same three-dimensional criteria to *all applicants* that affirmative action programs routinely use to discover diamonds in the rough—evidence of individual motivation, initiative in overcoming disadvantage, or teamwork and leadership skills. Or, if efficiency does not permit individualized assessments for the entire class, then schools might admit a small first-year class with an expanded program for upper class students applying to transfer from community colleges or less-prestigious institutions who have demonstrated ability to excel when given the opportunity. Or large universities could consider a cutoff to admit those with basic qualifications and an excellent work ethic. For example, Texas recently passed a law admitting all students in the top 10 percent of their high school classes to any of the state institutions of higher learning. Other schools have contemplated using a lottery to choose among qualified candidates who meet a bare threshold for admission. While random selection is clearly arbitrary, at least it is an honest way of making arbitrary decisions about how to distribute a scarce resource.

That was the second virtue in seeing race as the miner's canary. If the first lesson is that current selection conventions arbitrarily prefer those from privileged backgrounds and fail to include all people who can succeed, the second lesson is that the debate about affirmative action was in large measure a debate about allocating resources. By starting to talk about race, as Ted Koppel has been doing with his *Nightline* series "America in Black and White," Americans could, for example, begin to see the connections between higher education and the allocation of resources more generally. Koppel was prompted to do a show in response to two frightening statistics in Washington, D.C. First, he announced a study by the National Center on Institutions and Alternatives finding that one out of every two black men in D.C. is now under the supervision of the criminal justice system. Second, the study found that while 13 percent of drug users are black, 74 percent of those arrested as drug offenders are black. The *Nightline* staff highlighted these racially charged statistics in the setup piece to a show in August 1997, as the camera showcased the faces of two kindergarten children, one white and one black—one with a bright future, the other with a strong chance of dying young, especially by a handgun, before he is thirty.

But while the *Nightline* program may have started with race, listeners soon learned that race masks class and the distribution of social privilege. The truly alarming statistics about black men and the criminal justice system, I suggested on the show, actually contain lessons for all of us. They show how race allows us to ignore the total cost to all taxpayers of current social policy, both in monetary expenditures for damage control and the huge social cost of living in fear. I referred to Reverend Jesse Jackson's revealing discovery (reprinted in a William Raspberry column) that money that could be used to fund education is now being used instead to fund prisons.

Reverend Jackson visited Glennbrook South High School in suburban Chicago, I said. He witnessed a gorgeous campus with well-paid teachers, a sparkling clean physical plant, and a field house "that houses community activities as well as school athletics." Most important, the school—a public school—had an educational ethos that everyone can learn. For those slow learners, Jackson's Glennbrook guide explained, we "match them with the latest computers and let them borrow the computers' brains for a while." Glennbrook spent $11,000 per pupil annually and boasted a mere 2 percent dropout rate.

Those engaged in a conversation on race might follow Reverend Jackson (literally or figuratively) from Glennbrook South to Chicago to visit the new Cook County Jail, built at a cost of $67,000 per cell, and maintained at an annual cost of $22,000 for each of its fifteen hundred inmates. Unlike Glennbrook South's 98 percent graduation rate, 90 percent of the inmates at the Cook County Jail are high school dropouts, and at least that many are functionally illiterate.

Our racial fear and loathing, in other words, camouflage a disruptive social policy in which we track some kids from kindergarten to college and others from kindergarten to prison. Not only does such a policy have unfair social costs; it is also one fraught with significant, though hidden, financial costs. Americans pay more at the back end to warehouse an increasingly large population of adult prisoners (most of whom have not committed violent crimes) than they might at the front end to educate all American youngsters to make a contribution to our society.

Crime consistently rates as one of the primary issues of concern to voters, yet people's views on public safety appear to be shaped much more by local television news and politicians than by actual changes in the crime rates. Elected officials at all levels of government are increasingly using the issue of crime to coerce consensus, pretending to address many social problems through longer sentences and harsher treatment of offenders. As a consequence, the United States has the highest incarceration rate of any country in the world with the exception of Russia. Yet 60 percent of our prison population is serving time for nonviolent offenses. The prevailing view of drug addiction as a criminal rather than a public health issue has been a principal cause of high incarceration rates in the United States.

As Milton Friedman, the Nobelist in economics, writes, quoting a 1995 speech by Sher Hosonko, then Connecticut director of addiction services: "Today in this country we incarcerate 3,109 black men for every 100,000 of them in the population [whereas] pre–Nelson Mandela South Africa—under an overt public policy of apartheid—incarcerated 729 black men for every 100,000." Friedman concludes that the "horrendous growth" in our prison population stems primarily from the use of long criminal sentences to punish nonviolent drug use, a policy which "has generated specific evils during the past quarter century." He cites as one of these the corruption of relatively low paid police and other government officials who "succumb to the temptation to pick up easy money" just as their predecessors did during "our earlier attempt at alcohol prohibition."

Yet some of us speak about the problem as if it only involves sentencing disparities, when we need to discuss the larger implications of using the criminal justice system as our primary instrument of social policy in urban areas. We need to talk about the cost to all taxpayers of our excessive drive toward incarceration, both as a matter of an unfair and inhumane criminal justice policy, and even more as a dysfunctional social policy, which is straining state and city budgets, and not surprisingly, reinforcing massive disparities in our educational system. As Victor Hugo predicted more than 140 years ago: Every time you build a prison, you close a school. In California, the number of prisoners has grown from 19,000 two decades ago to 150,000 today. Already, California and Florida spend more to incarcerate people than to educate their college-age populations. We dismiss the cost as a necessary response to black social pathologies. We don't focus on how our social policies create and reinforce those pathologies. Our fear of race—whether of being called racist or being associated with racial dysfunction—becomes just another excuse.

It was apparently no accident, therefore, that Proposition 209 to ban "preferences" was successful in California, following the "three-strikes" law and other initiatives to shift resources to subsidize lengthy prison terms. In 1995, for the very first time, California, which used to boast a premier higher educational system, began spending more money to build prisons than to build colleges. California's entire budget for community colleges is now the same as the state budget for prisons, according to California Community College chancellor Thomas Nussbaum. These figures do not count additional money spent by either the federal government or local counties on prisons and jails. With fewer resources and more applicants, it was no wonder that admissions to college became a fierce fight. But because we are so afraid of race, many of us lost sight of these linkages.

We need a much bigger conversation about the role of higher education in a democracy, a need that is obscured by our failure to talk directly about race. The issue of race enables opponents of affirmative action to camouflage the true nature of what is really at stake: whether we can afford to track one group of kids to college and another to prison; whether we are extending opportunity to all who can take advantage of it; whether institutions of higher learning—or public elementary and secondary schools—are oriented toward training all of our citizens for the challenges of the twenty-first century. We engage in a narrow debate about "unqualified" applicants or "preferences" when we need a broader conversation to rethink the role of a public educational policy that assumes a single kind of testable intelligence is more important than effort, values efficiency over relevant information, and therefore admits and trains only a fraction of our citizens who can do the work and succeed.

If we were willing to talk about race as the beginning of a much larger conversation, we might also learn from Edward Luttwak, an American foreign policy analyst who recently visited Japan. He went to a Japanese gas station, where four young men rushed over to service his car, check the tires, wash the windows, pump the gas. Luttwak realized he was paying for this service through the inflated price of gas, a price kept high by the Japanese government to subsidize temporary employment for those who need help with the transition from high school to work. When Luttwak returned to the United States, he found the price of gas much cheaper but the same four young men were, if not literally, implicitly hanging out at the gas station. They offered him no service, but, as Luttwak recounted in a 1994 *Washington Post* essay, he was paying them anyway through his tax dollars, which went to pay for courts and judges in the criminal justice system or for the administration of a welfare system; through the high rates of his car insurance; and if he were really unlucky, through his own blood. One society sees those men as part of its community; the other sees them as outsiders.

A conversation that starts with race can then move on to reframe the issue of the disproportionate and alarming number of black men in prison in a way that appeals to the broad American sense of fairness. The issue of fairness in the criminal justice system directly connects up to all people. If we open up a bigger public conversation that begins with race, more people could begin to understand the linkages between our educational policies and the tremendous costs borne by taxpayers, as well as those young men who are being tracked from kindergarten to jail.

The formal equality that had animated so much of the civil rights movement of the 1960s and 1970s is not entirely responsive to 1990s problems. We need to start with race and use the visibility of racial unfairness as an infrared light that allows us to see in the dark. Race illuminates the problems of unequal distribution of resources, but it masks those problems as well. For example, by making the problem of social inequality primarily a problem of race, affirmative action or the high rates of incarceration of black men allows some to pretend that just the color coding is wrong, rather than the substantive decisions that are affecting everyone.

In speaking out I began to see that race should permeate our conversation; but not race in the traditional biological sense of how you look determines what you think. Race does not simply mean that white people are always treated better than black people or that people of color are never treated fairly in this society. We need to talk about the way in which our construction of race both positively and negatively affects our gender relationships, our economic relationships, our political relationships. We have to grapple with race as a window on much more systematic unfairness, to show what *all* people could learn from the indignities inflicted on people of color. These aren't mere social indignities but systemic and deeply ingrained patterns of privilege that in fact disadvantage many poor and working-class whites as well. A conversation about race could be a political moment to open up a bigger conversation about justice, power, and community.

There is a value to speaking out, but it is important to reconsider the way we are stating our views. Susan's advice and Gerald's metaphors resonate with those of Peter Cicchino. We need to find ways to frame the issues of civil rights once again as a moral crusade. We need a faith story and a church.

The challenge is to expand and explain our notion of community, to include more of those who are willing to struggle together for racial justice. If we can find or create an electronic town square in which to hold a new kind of public conversation, we might begin to understand race by linking that understanding to issues of class, gender, and power. We could then offer people their own chance to confront racially charged issues together and consider solutions through community action.

I BELIEVE THAT people gain incentives to solve the real problems in their communities when guided by an inclusive vision of social justice. A deeper understanding of the meaning of justice illuminates the connections between crime and education, between challenges to affirmative action and prison construction, between full employment and fair employment. But what might such a conversation look like? What would a good conversation need? The short answer is: A collaborative environment. To have a different kind of conversation, trust and a willingness to take risks must both be possible. Most important is a different kind of public space that would create sufficient and sustained access so people could feel safe to be honest and to be able to change their minds. We needed a safe space—what the psychologist Lila Coleburn terms "a cold shower and warm bath."

That people were both hungry for a safe yet public space and could use it to brainstorm effectively about local problems reminded me of the research I had seen on jury deliberations. Those juries that didn't vote first, but discussed the different perspectives that each participant put on the table, were more likely to come to agreement faster and with a greater sense of personal fulfillment than those who immediately took a straw poll before they began deliberations. As each member of the jury said what he or she remembered about the case they'd just heard, people recalled certain aspects but missed others, selectively remembering information that tended to corroborate their own limited frames of reference or preconceived ideas. People had different questions, some of which were answered by others as the discussion progressed. But because they started first by talking, and then only later voted, jurors were able to learn from each other and to communicate across their differences.

Septima Clark's citizenship schools are helpful reminders of the democratic capacity of lay people who interact in a "safe" space. Clark organized schools where community members taught their neighbors how to read and write in order to pass literacy tests in the South in the 1950s and 1960s. To reach people who were uneducated but willing to learn, she turned to beauticians in particular. In the segregated South, beauticians had a measure of economic independence and their place of business was a community center. Not surprisingly, the first teacher she hired to run a citizenship school was a beautician, Bernice Robinson.

Clark and Robinson held schools "in people's kitchens, in beauty parlors, and under trees in the summertime." Those citizenship schools, however, were not just about the mechanics of literacy. By using examples from local newspapers or their own household correspondence, participants could see themselves as members of the public, just as important as the white people who always ran things. These schools were laboratories, where local black people could experiment with collaborative and critical thinking. They shifted roles, from passive observer to active problem solver. They were empowered. What they had to say or do could make a difference.

The citizenship schools were also places to discover local leaders like Spencer Hogue in Marion, Alabama. He and his wife Jane opened up their living room and taught many people, including her own father, how to read. "They loved us for that," Spencer remembered.

Septima Clark's citizenship schools prepared blacks to take literacy tests. But that was not their major accomplishment. As one local sharecropper told SNCC organizer Bob Moses, the most important accomplishment of the civil rights movement, as far as blacks in Mississippi were concerned, was not the vote. It was the opportunity to meet. Coming together in small groups at citizenship schools or attending large mass meetings in black churches gave people a way to speak their stories and amplify their voices. Voting, which was a means of expressing that voice, could never substitute for the process of formulating, articulating, or pursuing a citizen-oriented, community-based agenda. The vote was crucial, but it wasn't all. In retrospect, maybe not even most.

That Clark's learning communities are—just like trial juries—instruments of democracy was demonstrated more recently through what Professor James Fishkin of the University of Texas calls a "deliberative poll." Instead of merely polling a random sample of respondents over the telephone or one-on-one in a formal interview, Fishkin invited a group to travel to the university to deliberate face-to-face with each other. Fishkin convened people in a common place around policy issues in much the same way we convene a jury of our peers to decide court cases. He provided an opportunity for a representative cross section of people to come into a public space and do something important, without politicians pontificating or the media telling people what to think. Fishkin's experiment in public dialogue is outcome-oriented in that people are encouraged to come to considered judgments, but, unlike legislative debate or television-style forums, it is more synthetic and respectful of different ways of moving forward.

One of the deliberative, face-to-face polls he did prior to the 1996 election included a very conservative white farmer from the Southwest and a black woman from New York who was on welfare. The first thing the farmer did when he walked in the room was to point his finger and say to the black woman from New York: "You are the source of all of our problems." At the end of three days of deliberation, the farmer turned to the same woman and said: "What are the three most important words in the English language? 'I was wrong.'"

A seminar on race and gender that Susan Sturm and I co-teach also showed the value of sustained communication and opportunities for brainstorming in a safe space. We found that students became much more honest and engaged when they deliberated about racially charged issues over time. Midway through the semester, the students were invited to describe a personal story about injustice. A white student described being mugged by a group of African Americans and Latinos outside his high school. The student and some of his buddies were attacked on their way to get lunch, after they had crossed the street in front of the magnet public school, Bronx High School of Science, they attended.

Initially self-conscious about retelling his story aloud to his classmates, the white student interpreted the attack as racially motivated. His voice became more self-possessed, however, when no one in the class responded in a predictable or contemptuous manner. Instead, a black student answered his story with a story of her own. She and a group of her high school classmates were routinely teased and harassed by other blacks on the subway in Brooklyn, en route to another magnet public high school, Brooklyn Tech. The "Techies"—noticeable because of the slide rules extending from their book bags—were also black. Her interpretation was different. While she agreed that the assailants' race was common to both stories, it was not the whole story. The conflict for her was about class as much as race. Her point was that both stories illustrated the class dimension of race. Yet, too often, as in her white law school classmate's mind, race had masked class.

I soon discovered people already engaged in local and regional initiatives, experiments in collaborative problem solving and community conversation. Modeling itself after discussion groups in Sweden, an organization called the Study Circles Resource Center in Pomfret, Connecticut, is encouraging local communities to become laboratories for deliberation and problem solving. Small groups of people convene once a week for at least six weeks in libraries, union halls, and other "public" spaces to reinforce the notion that even though these sessions are off the record, they are about public issues. They may invite a government official in to provide information. They may consult with other experts. But in the end, these citizens find that it is their own voice and their own understanding that is most valuable.

In Oklahoma, the League of Women Voters and several other organizations initiated a statewide study circle program on criminal justice and corrections. Over one thousand citizens joined judges, sheriffs, and legislators to discuss the twin challenges of skyrocketing corrections costs and failing public confidence in the justice system. The study circles occurred in thirteen communities, and over fifty state and local civic organizations and churches cosponsored the "Balancing Justice" project. According to *Focus on Study Circles,* the Fall 1997 newsletter:

> A month after the study circles were completed, House Bill 1213, one of the most radical revisions of the criminal justice system in the history of the state, was enacted into law. The bill upheld the two major policy themes identified by the study circle participants, authorized $5 million to be spent on community corrections programs, and mandated a much greater degree of citizen involvement in setting local corrections policy.

"The Balancing Justice study circle program made a huge difference because it helped to create an atmosphere where we could try new things in the state of Oklahoma," said Senator Cal Hobson, who sponsored the legislation.

In Sweden, at least a quarter of the country's population is usually involved in a study circle. Through study circles, citizens in the United States are inventing methods for resolving difficult community conflicts, providing important input to legislators, and identifying new and innovative ways of thinking about community issues. Even when formed in a sense of crisis, groups quickly move on from airing grievances to probing causes like perceived institutional racism. Religious organizations rank first and national media last in order of importance in helping these groups foster serious dialogue.

To me, the jury research, the citizenship schools, Fishkin's "deliberative polls," the unusual law school classroom Susan and I created each year, and the study circles' problem-solving efforts all suggest that busy people with no particular expertise can rise to the task of engaged deliberation when given the opportunity to meet and play a role in public life. Indeed, when people meet together to solve problems, even those without special knowledge can often come to an informed, creative, and workable solution. This is why brainstorming can be so empowering not only to the group's ability to make innovative decisions but to the individual's sense of her enriched role in public life. In other words, serious talk has value if it connects up to a vision of racial justice and an interactive, problem-oriented process for discussing local challenges in concrete terms.

This is about giving people a safe space where they feel empowered to resolve issues, not just to win arguments. After all, a genuine democracy must encourage *all* its citizens to participate in a process of formulating, discussing, and deciding public issues that are important to them and directly affect their lives. Such continuous participation is necessary to bring decent, poor, working-class, and middle-income citizens into the political process. Opportunities to participate, not just to vote, provide individuals the essential means to discover their real needs as social human beings. In other words, as the political theorist Peter Bachrach concludes, "political participation plays a dual role: it not only catalyzes opinion but also creates it." We know, for example, Bachrach says,

> that as persons from lower classes become active within organizations, they become more active in politics. . . . Persons who in their everyday life—in their clubs, professional organizations, and social activity—have the opportunity of formulating and honing their opinions are in a position to determine where their interests lie. . . . It is not until socially disadvantaged groups become involved in structuring their own channels of communication and their own decision-making forums that they will begin to gain self-awareness.

"It's a trip, Lani. It's a trip," my friend Charisse had said when Representatives Cynthia McKinney and Chaka Fattah had left my house in July 1995. "They are finally beginning to hear what you are saying."

Maybe Charisse was right.

If she is, we will begin to have many conversations the success of which will be measured by the willingness of people across the nation to join. Whether a series of mini-conversations or ongoing, regional convocations, the focus will be on people grappling together with issues that have a racial text or subtext in their own neighborhoods and communities. From these many conversations and many small initiatives, national issues may evolve—especially if those of us with a public voice successfully convert local stories of struggle into sustaining metaphors for justice.

These conversations and collaborations might take place in living rooms or around kitchen tables. Or they might, like Septima Clark's citizenship schools, follow Dr. King's admonition to make "every barbershop a school." They could occur simultaneously on college campuses, in union halls, church basements, and library multipurpose rooms, each focused on issues of concern to the respective participants. They could be statewide conversations, like those in Oklahoma, to think about specific criminal justice reforms with the option of returning if necessary to fine-tune or reconsider. They could solicit the perspectives of progressives like Reverend Jesse Jackson or moderates such as foreign policy analyst Edward Luttwak. Or they could focus on the experiences of local activists, neighborhood organizations, or community leaders. In content and forum they can be as varied as the people who engage in them.

Conversations on race, in other words, can vindicate democracy in the way that juries vindicate the law. Of course, citizen juries convened to discuss racially charged issues need access to expert opinion. They need reading material and background information. They need guidance to discuss the way race camouflages the devastating costs of current social and economic policies. With the benefit of a facilitator—someone like Septima Clark's local citizenship schoolteacher—participants could learn new information as well as become familiar with the power of their own voice and own experience.

Ideally, these conversations would share a number of features in common: One, they would involve ordinary people expressing their own experiences. Two, they would be serious conversations that continued until trust develops; they would occur among people with a commitment to express themselves over time. Three, participants would be encouraged to talk about and through race, to treat race as a lens on broader social issues. These are conversations that are aimed at solving public problems, not just at establishing interracial rapport. People would come together to make change, not merely to make friends. Four, these conversations would take place with the understanding that no single group can presume to have all the answers. Five, they would be a process, not a quick fix. Six, they would energize both the so-called victims and the presumed beneficiaries of racism, as long as each believed in fair play and was willing to be part of a multiracial collaboration. And seven, they would require a continued commitment to work together at the local, regional, and national level until solutions are created that can be tested over time.

But not all conversations would share all seven features. They might occur on multiple levels simultaneously. Some of the conversations would be small, anonymous, and ongoing. Others would engage the media, challenging television, radio, and print organizations to experiment with a more public-spirited style of journalism. Not to do so would betray them as obstacles rather than facilitators of democracy. Journalists could join with community organizations, business leaders, and local officials to give visibility to a brainstorming process in which citizens assumed leadership. This could only occur with media cooperation to assure the presence of all relevant stakeholders and to open up the debate to new ideas and new people. Like a jazz composition, dissonances as much as harmonies are to the point. As journalist Steve Montiel of the Maynard Institute in Oakland observes, the notes that are not played are as important as those that are.

I now know something that I did not realize in 1993 when I first urged President Clinton to convene a Racial Justice Summit. I learned since then that we did not need more top-down policy discussions about racial justice in America. Conversations on race could not succeed as a single, "scripted" performance or high-profile event aimed at teaching tolerance or accommodation with an unjust status quo. Nor do I now think the answer lies in inviting the regular cast of characters to engage in serious talk in a public setting. Without further introspection about the role of journalists in a democracy, the conventional talking-heads format is more likely to paralyze than to promote a conversation. Too often, reporters write their story and only then interview "sources" to plug holes in what they have already written. They are not listening in order to hear a genuinely different or refreshing perspective. They are waiting to get a sound bite, a pithy statement that fits a preexisting frame. As a result, they train us to speak aloud not to be understood, but to be judged.

The demands of high-visibility public performance stifle rather than engage genuine debate. As Steven Holmes recently wrote for *The New York Times* in describing one of President Clinton's racial advisory board meetings, the public format was less than conducive to freewheeling discussions. The participants were intimidated by the presence of reporters who were "ready to pounce at any sign of disagreement or provocative comment."

If we want to escape the sound-bite culture, it is critical to think hard about a "safe" space for interactive, multidimensional, and problem-oriented conversations. We need to imagine an intermediate space that is not about winning formal policy votes or showcasing controversy. We need a public space that is neither government nor the marketplace and a public conversation that is a prologue to action and not mere spectacle or distraction. Otherwise, journalists would likely revert to a headline, gotcha style of reporting, regurgitating conventional wisdom without recognizing that America needs more than the conventional wisdom.

After all, the only people Americans now trust are people like themselves, other "ordinary" people. Unlike politicians, journalists, and lawyers, ordinary citizens who speak out invite trust when, like Gill Clark and her co-workers, they speak from the heart and from their own experiences. But to get people to join with others like themselves and to stick with something even when it is hard, they need something to do, not just to listen to. They need information that invites a thoughtful response and that helps them understand that they too have a role to play in shaping and making decisions that affect all of our lives. They need, in other words, opportunities to participate in intermediate public spaces—churches, civic associations, neighborhood groups—and incentives to work together to bridge the social, political, and racial distance they presently experience. We are not a public, the historian Thomas Bender reminds us, unless we have work to do together.

Yet conversations on race cannot be limited to study circles or a special atmosphere in an unusual law school classroom. They are an important part of an ongoing national experiment in that the problem of race touches every nook and cranny of our great country. This process will almost certainly not resemble the mass movements of Selma, Alabama, in 1965. Those movements were right for their time, but their time is not now. For now, the objectives are more modest, but the long-range goals are just as ambitious.

The goals of the conversations, wherever they take place, would be to rebuild communities, to reconnect concerned citizens, and ultimately to provide laboratories for social justice. They would seek to rekindle the sense of struggle and the concept of participatory democracy that was at the heart of the early civil rights mass movement. In this instance, the burgeoning idea that animates these conversations is that democracy—like learning—is often social, interactive, cooperative, and ongoing, as opposed to individualistic, isolated, competitive, and static.

A conversation on race, therefore, has multiple objectives: to raise people's awareness of how race masks issues of resource distribution, to give potential allies a stake in our struggle, and, most important, to encourage those with a fighting spirit to remain hopeful. While the process and concept are still evolving, the idea of a conversation linking issues of race, class, fairness, and power builds on several enduring lessons from the past.

First, local conversations have an instrumental value. Organizing around local initiatives gets people involved and keeps them involved. Second, local organizing helps develop and empower individuals as full-fledged citizens in a democracy. Engaging the issues of race, class, fairness, and power with others, can, as King wished, enable "every houseworker and every laborer [to become] a demonstrator, a voter, a canvasser and a student" and find "the dignity in political and social action" that is missing from others parts of their lives.

Finally, we need allies. Once again Dr. King had it just right: by freeing ourselves, black people would be freeing white people too. These conversations will help us all see that.

Whatever their format, serious and committed conversations, just like serious and committed local activism, would not all look alike. Ideally they would track the seven conditions I listed earlier. At minimum, however, they should each involve three factors: (1) a willingness to include a range of people (as individuals and as members of organized, interested groups such as neighborhood associations and the NAACP) in efforts to solve problems over time; (2) continued interaction around concrete local challenges, informed by an understanding of the way race links issues of gender, power, and class; and (3) the capacity to deliberate and collaborate again and again. Wherever and however it occurs, this process of public education and brainstorming, sharing solutions, and then experimenting in the field is never totally finished. You have to keep coming back as new problems emerge.

As Professor Jim Carey of the Columbia School of Journalism once told me, a successful conversation is one that we want to continue. It is one that will continue even after we leave.

IT WAS THE EXPERIENCE of not being able to speak for myself while others attacked me, my ideas, and ultimately my community that reminded me of the value of community and the role of many people in building that community. I had always drawn strength from the Albert Turners, the Spencer Hogues, the Maggie Bozemans, the J. L. Chestnuts, and the Septima Clarks who have struggled to change America and in important ways have succeeded so admirably. To retrieve my voice, I needed to go back to where I had found theirs.

By returning to the lessons I learned from the real civil rights clients I had represented, I ultimately survived my own personal tutorial in the politics of racial justice. I was forced back in time. I tried to reimagine the civil rights activism that began in the black Baptist churches of the South in the 1950s. That was an activism that led to a national movement of civic protest and personal renewal. I had been a lawyer for that movement, for people who believed in democracy and wanted to bring it home. I had mostly represented black people who had been intimidated into silent suffering, and who were released from silence by the legal process and by their own actions. I had watched them fight the system, trying to coax it into allowing them to participate, not just by voting but by having a say in the decisions that affected their lives.

In that movement, I had found community. In my effort to understand better the movement's successes and failures, I was reminded that the capacity to struggle and to fight back occurs when people feel connected to a community. Community makes you whole. Real life takes place in a community. Yet it is not a homogeneous community that I found. It is a community committed to people of color, but not by virtue of the color of our skin. It is a community held together by a passion for justice that connects us to the energy, insight, and faith of people of color—all colors.

From Septima Clark's citizenship schools, to the mass meetings that helped J. L. Chestnut retain "the edge," to the spirited audience at the NAACP Convention in 1993 that chanted as an organist played "The Battle Hymn of the Republic," to Professor James Fishkin's experiment in citizen deliberation, ordinary people take their task quite seriously when they lift their voices in unison. Even if no one else is listening, their voices somehow still matter. I began to understand the imperative of making space for the many still silent voices.

The challenge ahead is to lift more voices. Whether it is the mass meetings in the segregated South or the "Sing" competition in a public high school in Queens, each of us becomes more powerful when we work together. In 1982, I had seen a ragtag group of lobbyists and litigators practice exactly what we tried to get Congress to enact in the Voting Rights Act amendments. Where others saw chaos, we saw democracy.

Similarly, I witnessed the amazing power of collective voice in the shadow of the Edmund Pettus Bridge, as we emerged from the courthouse in Selma, singing spirituals to celebrate the jury verdict of acquittal in the Marion Three case. There too I realized that when we struggle with others, we gain a sense of our own power to resist injustice and to make things better for more than ourselves. I knew even from my recent lecture experiences that sustained face-to-face interaction was key. When I spoke, I was neither preaching nor singing. That fact didn't matter; the audience and I often felt we were making music together.

I began to see how the civil rights movement itself has been silenced, and how we need to reconnect to the true source of our voices in order to be heard once again. If we succeed, it will be because Americans from all walks of life join together, moved by a new vision of social justice that they themselves have made. I believe that can happen: especially if we lift every voice.

SOURCES

THE LION'S SHARE of information came from five sources: (1) contemporaneous notes and tapes that I made of events; (2) contemporaneous newspaper clippings, magazine articles, e-mail messages, and memoranda (including those made available to me by Alvin Benn of *The Montgomery Advertiser* office in Selma, Alabama; those collected and collated by Gwen McKinney of McKinney and McDowell, Washington, D.C.; those subsequently passed on to me from their own files by Dayna Cunningham, Carolyn Osolinik, and Penda Hair, as well as those documents I compiled during the pendency of the nomination from informal memoranda, faxes or notes given me during courtesy calls); (3) trial transcripts and public records regarding civil rights cases in Alabama, North Carolina, and Arkansas made available to me by the NAACP Legal Defense Fund, Inc., from its public records in New York and by the Federal Records Center in Atlanta, Georgia; (4) the congressional hearing records from the 1981–82 extension of the Voting Rights Act; and (5) interviews that I personally conducted with the following individuals.

Former NAACP LDF staff lawyers:

Dayna Cunningham (New York, N.Y.)
Penda Hair (Washington, D.C.)
Pamela Karlan (Boston, Mass., and Charlottesville, Va.)
Deval Patrick (Washington, D.C.)

NAACP LDF cooperating attorneys, local civil rights lawyers and judges, and LDF clients and local activists:

Frank Ballance (Wilson, N.C.)
Acie Byrd (Washington, D.C.)
G. K. Butterfield (Wilson, N.C.)
Julius Chambers (Durham, N.C.)
J. L. Chestnut (Selma, Ala.)
James Ferguson (Charlotte, N.C.)
Spencer Hogue (Marion, Ala.)
Olly Neal (Marianna, Ark.)
Hank Sanders (Selma, Ala.)
Rose Sanders (Selma, Ala.)
Albert Turner (Marion, Ala.)
Evelyn Turner (Marion, Ala.)
Robert Turner (Marion, Ala.)
Leslie Winner (Charlotte, N.C.)

I also interviewed and/or collected information from Professor Susan P. Sturm (University of Pennsylvania Law School), Professor Roger Wilkins (George Mason University), Professor Eddie Correia (Northeastern University Law School), Iwalani Smith Mottl (Maui, Hawaii), Eugenia Guinier (Cambridge, Massachusetts), and Reverend Nelson Johnson (All Faith Church, Greensboro, North Carolina).

I received and relied on e-mail messages, interview notes, articles, and informal memoranda from former LDF cooperating attorney Bill Quigley (New Orleans, Louisiana); Rob Richie, Executive Director, Center for Voting and Democracy, who e-mailed me notes of interviews that Dan Johnson conducted wtih Emil Jones and Arthur Berman, and who provided a virtual encyclopedia of information on election systems; Carolyn Osolinik, who shipped me her files from the nomination; and Mark Schmitt, formerly on the staff of Senator Bill Bradley and now a fellow with the Open Society Institute.

Stephanie Camp, a Ph.D. student in history at the University of Pennsylvania, conducted telephone interviews with most of the people I later interviewed in person. She also conducted and took notes on her own conversations with the following people: Attorney Howard Moore, Oakland, California; Attorney Dennis Balske, formerly Legal Director, Southern Poverty Law Center, Montgomery, Alabama, now Assistant Federal Public Defender, Portland, Oregon; Attorney Margaret Carey, formerly with the Center for Constitutional Rights and now practicing in Mississippi; Judge John England, Tuscaloosa, Alabama; Professor Harry Watson, Raleigh, North Carolina; and Alice Ballance, Warrington, North Carolina.

No effort has been made to make this bibliography exhaustive. Section I includes books whose general ideas, organizing concepts, or supplementary details were of real significance in shaping the account. Section II lists articles, speeches, and studies that were especially useful. I cite in section III those legal cases that are mentioned or alluded to in the text. The works and organizations in section IV are listed to assist readers seeking additional information from those working in the field.

I. Books

Amy, Douglas. *Real Choices/New Voices: The Case for Proportional Representation Elections in the United States.* New York: Columbia University Press, 1993.

Applebome, Peter. *Dixie Rising: How the South Is Shaping American Values, Politics and Culture.* New York: Times Books, 1996.

Branch, Taylor. *Parting the Waters: America in the King Years 1954–63.* New York: Simon and Schuster, 1988.

Brown, Cynthia Stokes. *Ready from Within: A First-Person Narrative: Septima Clark and The Civil Rights Movement.* Trenton, N.J.: Africa World Press, Inc., 1996.

Carson, Clayborne. *In Struggle: SNCC and the Black Awakening of the 1960s.* Cambridge: Harvard University Press, 1981.

Chafe, William. *Civilities and Civil Rights: Greensboro, North Carolina, and the Black Struggle for Freedom.* New York: Oxford University Press, 1980.

Chestnut, J. L., Jr., and Julia Cass. *Black in Selma: The Uncommon Life of J. L. Chestnut, Jr.* New York: Farrar, Straus & Giroux, 1990.

Cose, Ellis. *The Rage of a Privileged Class.* New York: HarperCollins, 1993.

Dalton, Harlon. *Racial Healing.* New York: Doubleday, 1995.

Davidson, Chandler, ed. *Minority Vote Dilution.* Washington, D.C.: Howard University Press, 1984.

Dawson, Michael C. *Behind the Mule: Race and Class in African-American Politics.* Princeton, N.J.: Princeton University Press, 1994.

Frank, Robert H., and Philip J. Cook. *The Winner-Take-All Society.* New York: The Free Press, 1995.

Gardener, Howard. *Leading Minds: An Anatomy of Leadership.* New York: Basic Books, 1995.

Garrow, David J. *Protest at Selma: Martin Luther King, Jr., and the Voting Rights Act of 1965.* New Haven: Yale University Press, 1978.

————. *Bearing the Cross: Martin Luther King, Jr., and the Southern Christian Leadership Conference.* New York: Vintage Books, 1988.

Greenberg, Jack. *Crusaders in the Courts: How a Dedicated Band of Lawyers Fought for the Civil Rights Revolution.* New York: Basic Books, 1994.

Greene, Melissa Fay. *Praying for Sheetrock.* New York: Ballantine Books, 1991.

Grofman, Bernard, and Chandler Davidson, eds. *Controversies in Minority Voting: A 25-Year Perspective on the Voting Rights Act of 1965.* Washington, D.C.: Brookings Institution, 1992.

Guinier, Lani, *Tyranny of the Majority.* New York: The Free Press, 1994.

Guinier, Lani, Michelle Fine, and Jane Balin. *Becoming Gentlemen: Women, Law School and Institutional Change.* Boston: Beacon Press, 1997.

Hamilton, Richard F. *Who Voted for Hitler?* Princeton, N.J.: Princeton University Press, 1982.

Hampton, Henry, and Steve Fayer. *Voices of Freedom: An Oral History of the Civil Rights Movement from the 1950s Through the 1980s.* New York: Bantam Books, 1990.

Jamieson, Kathleen Hall. *Beyond the Double Bind: Women and Leadership.* New York: Oxford University Press, 1995.

Jaynes, Gerald David, and Robin M. Williams, Jr. *A Common Destiny: Blacks and American Society.* Washington, D.C.: National Academy Press, 1989.

King, Martin Luther, Jr. *Why We Can't Wait.* New York: New American Library, 1964.

————. *Where Do We Go From Here: Chaos or Community?* New York: Harper & Row, 1967.

Kluger, Richard. *Simple Justice: The History of Brown v. Board of Education and Black America's Struggle for Equality.* New York: Random House, 1975.

Kousser, J. Morgan. *The Shaping of Southern Politics.* New Haven: Yale University Press, 1974.

Lasch, Christopher. *The Revolt of the Elites and the Betrayal of Democracy.* New York: W. W. Norton, 1995.

Lawson, Steven R. *Black Ballots: Voting Rights in the South, 1944–1969.* New York: Columbia University Press, 1976.

Lijphart, Arend. *Democracy in Plural Societies.* New Haven: Yale University Press, 1977.

Lipsitz, George. *A Life in the Struggle: Ivory Perry and the Culture of Opposition.* Philadelphia: Temple University Press, 1988.

Mandela, Nelson. *Long Walk to Freedom.* Boston: Little, Brown, 1994.

McCarthy, Sheryl. *Why Are the Heroes Always White?: Columns.* Kansas City: Andrews and McMeel, 1995.

McGerr, Michael. *The Decline of Popular Politics: The American North, 1865–1928.* New York: Oxford University Press, 1986.

Mommsen, Hans. *The Rise and Fall of Weimar Democracy.* Translated by Elborg Forster and Larry Eugene Jones. Chapel Hill: University of North Carolina Press, 1996.

Norrell, Robert J. *Reaping the Whirlwind: The Civil Rights Movement in Tuskegee.* New York: Vintage Books, 1985.

Oliver, Melvin L., and Thomas M. Shapiro. *Black Wealth/White Wealth: A New Perspective on Racial Inequality.* New York: Routledge, 1995.

O'Reilly, Kenneth. *Nixon's Piano: Presidents and Racial Politics from Washington to Clinton.* New York: The Free Press, 1995.

Pateman, Carol. *Participation and Democratic Theory.* London: Cambridge University Press, 1970.

Pertschuk, Michael. *The Giant Killers.* New York: W. W. Norton, 1986.

Piven, Frances Fox, and Richard Cloward. *Poor People's Movements: Why They Succeed, How They Fail.* New York: Pantheon Books, 1977.

———. *Why Americans Don't Vote.* New York: Pantheon Books, 1988.

Powell, G. Bingham. *Contemporary Democracies: Participation, Stability, and Violence.* Cambridge: Harvard University Press, 1982.

Raines, Howell. *My Soul Is Rested.* New York: Bantam, 1978.

Reynolds, Andrew, and Ben Reilly. *The International Handbook of Electoral System Design.* Stockholm: IDEA, 1997.

Rosenberg, Gerald N. *The Hollow Hope: Can Courts Bring About Social Change?* Chicago: The University of Chicago Press, 1991.

Rule, Wilma, and Joseph F. Zimmerman, eds. *United States Electoral Systems: Their Impact on Women and Minorities.* New York: Greenwood Press, 1992.

Salzman, Jack, with Adina Back and Gretchen Sullivan Sorin, eds. *Bridges and Boundaries: African Americans and American Jews.* New York: George Braziller and The Jewish Museum, 1992.

Taagepera, Rein, and Matthew Soberg Shugart. *Seats and Votes: The Effects and Determinants of Electoral Systems.* New Haven: Yale University Press, 1989.

Texeira, Ruy A. *The Disappearing American Voter.* Washington: Brookings Institution, 1992.

Tingsten, Herbert. *Political Behavior: Studies in Election Statistics.* London: P. S. King & Son, 1937.

Verba, Sidney, Norman Nie, and Jae-On Kim. *Participation and Political Equality: A Seven Nation Comparison.* Cambridge: Cambridge University Press, 1978.

Walzer, Michael. *On Toleration.* New Haven: Yale University Press, 1997.

Watters, Pat, and Reese Cleghorn. *Climbing Jacob's Ladder: The Arrival of Negroes in Southern Politics.* New York: Harcourt, Brace & World, 1967.

Weisbrot, Robert. *Freedom Bound: A History of America's Civil Rights Movement.* New York: W. W. Norton, 1990.

Wilkins, Roger. *A Man's Life: An Autobiography.* New York: Simon & Schuster, 1982.

Williams, Juan. *Eyes on the Prize: America's Civil Rights Years, 1954–1965.* New York: Penguin Books, 1987.

Wofford, Harris. *Of Kennedys and Kings.* New York: Farrar, Straus & Giroux, 1980.

Wolfinger, Raymond, and Steven Rosenstone. *Who Votes?* New Haven: Yale University Press, 1980.

Young, Andrew. *An Easy Burden: The Civil Rights Movement and the Transformation of America.* New York: HarperCollins, 1996.

II. Articles, Essays, Newsletters, Op-eds, Speeches, and Studies

"ADL Seeks Clarification of Guinier's Position on Voting Rights," U.S. Newswire, 7 May 1993.

Aleinikoff, T. Alexander, and Richard H. Pildes, "In Defense of Lani Guinier," *The Wall Street Journal*, 13 May 1993.

Anderson, Christopher J., and Christine A. Guillory. "Political Institutions and Satisfaction with Democracy: A Cross-National Analysis of Consensus and Majoritarian Systems." *American Political Science Review* 91 (March 1997): 66–81.

"Anti-Defamation League Statement on Nomination of Lani Guinier to Be Assistant Attorney General for Civil Rights," U.S. Newswire, 26 May 1993.

Appiah, K. Anthony, "The Multiculturalist Misunderstanding," *New York Review*, 9 October 1997.

Apple, R. W., Jr., "President Blames Himself for Furor Over Nominee: Says He Was Wrong to Let Pressure Mount Before He Acted," *The New York Times*, 5 June 1993.

Applebome, Peter, "Where Ideas That Hurt Nominee Thrive," *The New York Times*, 5 June 1993.

Bachrach, Peter. "Interest, Participation and Democratic Theory." In *Participation in Politics*, edited by J. Roland Pennock and John W. Chapman. New York: Lieber-Atherton, 1975.

Baker, Ella. "Developing Community Leadership." In *Black Women in White America: A Documentary History*, edited by Gerda Lerner. New York: Pantheon Books, 1972.

Balz, Dan, "Decision Played Out as a Painful Rerun: For the President, Latest Embarrassment Is Both Personal and Political," *The Washington Post*, 4 June 1993.

Birnbaum, Jeffrey H., and Joe Davidson, "Clinton Pulls Plug on Choice for Rights Post," *The Wall Street Journal*, 4 June 1993.

Bobo, Lawrence, and Ryan A. Smith, "From Jim Crow Racism to Laissez-Faire Racism: An Essay on the Transformation of Racial Attitudes in America," 3 May 1994.

Boldt, David R., "Guinier's Writings Would Have Hurt Her," *Philadelphia Inquirer*, 6 June 1993.

Bolick, Clint, "Clinton's Quota Queens," *The Wall Street Journal*, 30 April 1993.

Bone, Hugh, and Belle Zeller. "The Repeal of P.R. in New York City." *American Political Science Review* (December 1948): 1127–48.

Brischetto, Robert, "Cumulative Voting at Work in Texas," Voting and Democracy Report: 1995.

———, "The Rise of Cumulative Voting," *The Texas Observer*, 28 July 1995.

Broder, John M., "White House Launches Effort to Save Justice Dept. Nominee,"*Los Angeles Times*, 27 May 1993.

Brody, Jane E., "When Eyes Betray Color Vision," *The New York Times*, 21 October 1997.

Bronner, Ethan, "Study of Doctors Sees Little Effect of Affirmative Action on Careers," *The New York Times*, 8 October 1997.

Brownstein, Ronald, "Nomination May Add Race Issue to Democrats' Schism," *Los Angeles Times*, 26 May 1993.

Butterfield, Fox, "Study Links Violence Rate to Cohesion in Community," *The New York Times*, 17 August 1997.

———, "Crime Keeps on Falling, but Prisons Keep on Filling," *The New York Times*, 28 September 1997.

Carlson, Margaret, "Where is 'My Center'?" *Time*, 14 June 1993.

The Center on Crime, Communities & Culture. "Education as Prevention," Research Brief, Occasional Paper Series, no. 2, September 1997.

Center for Voting and Democracy. "Monopoly Politics," July 1997.

"A Civil Rights Struggle Ahead," *The New York Times*, 23 May 1993.

Clift, Eleanor, "A Hard Right Turn," *Newsweek*, 14 June 1993.

Cohn, Bob, "Crowning a 'Quota Queen'?" *Newsweek*, 24 May 1993.

Colburn, David R., and George E. Pozzetta. "Race, Ethnicity and the Evolution of Political Legitimacy." In *The 1960's: From Memory to History*, edited by David Farber. Chapel Hill: University of North Carolina Press, 1994.

Coleman, William T., Jr., "Three's Company: Guinier, Reagan, Bush," *The New York Times*, 4 June 1993.

Contreras, Raoul Lowery, "The Stench of Fascism," *Eastside Sun* (Los Angeles), 27 May 1993.

Dionne, E. J., Jr., "Guinier: She Came, She Saw, He Dumped Her," *The Washington Post*, 8 June 1993.

Dowd, Maureen, "Clinton's Reversals: As President Drops Justice Nominee, Many Wonder What He Stands For," *The New York Times*, 4 June 1993.

Dryzek, John S. "Political Inclusion and the Dynamics of Democratization," *American Political Science Review* (September 1996): 475.

Du Bois, Paul Martin, and Jonathan J. Hutson, "Bridging the Racial Divide: A Report on Interracial Dialogue in America," for the Interracial Democracy Program of the Center for Living Democracy, September 1997.

Duster, Troy. "The New Crisis of Legitimacy in Controls, Prisons, and Legal Structures." *The American Sociologist* (Spring 1995): 20–29.

Dyzenhaus, David. "Legal Theory in the Collapse of Weimar: Contemporary Lessons?" *American Political Science Review* 91 (March 1997): 121–34.

Editorial, "The Lani Guinier Affair," *The Washington Post*, 6 June 1993.

Engstrom, Richard L. "Modified Multi-Seat Election Systems as Remedies for Minority Vote Dilution." *Stetson Law Review* 21:3 (Summer 1992): 743–70.

Engstrom, Richard L., Delbert A. Taebel, and Richard L. Cole. "Cumulative Voting as a Remedy for Minority Vote Dilution: The Case of Alamogordo, New Mexico." *Journal of Law and Politics* 5:3 (Spring 1989): 469–97.

Everson, David. "The Effects of the 'Cutback' on the Representation of Women and Minorities in the Illinois General Assembly." In *United States Electoral Systems: Their Impact on Women and Minorities*, edited by Wilma Rule and Joseph F. Zimmerman. New York: Greenwood Press, 1992.

"Excerpts from Lani Guinier's News Conference," *The Washington Post*, 5 June 1993.

Focus on Study Circles, "Laboratories for Democracy," The Newsletter of the Study Circles Resource Center, vol. 8, no. 4, Fall 1997.

Fredrickson, George M., "America's Caste System: Will It Change?" *New York Review*, 23 October 1997.

Friedman, Milton, "There's No Justice in the War on Drugs," *The New York Times*, 11 January 1998.

Gigot, Paul, "Hillary's Choice on Civil Rights: Back to the Future," *The Wall Street Journal*, 7 May 1993.

———, "Guinier Is Going, No, She's Staying, No, Going . . ." *The Wall Street Journal*, 4 June 1993.

Goldberg, Laura, "A Nomination 'Nibbled to Death,' " *USA Today*, 4 June 1993.

Goldstein, Steve, "Penn's Guinier: Clinton's Controversial Choice," *Philadelphia Inquirer*, 23 May 1993.

———, "Clinton's Friend from Yale Law School Days Asked for a Hearing, but She Was Denied One," *Philadelphia Inquirer*, 5 June 1993.

Goodman, Howard, "For Lani Guinier, a Forum to Finally Make Her Case," *Philadelphia Inquirer*, 13 June 1993.

Gottlieb, Martin, "The 'Golden Age' of the City Council," *The New York Times*, 11 August 1991.

————, "Guinier's 'Low-Tech' Lynching." *Political Woman*, 1, no. 9 (July 1993).

Guinier, Lani, "Who's Afraid of Lani Guinier?" *The New York Times Magazine*, 27 February 1994.

————, "What Color Is Your Gerrymander?" *The Washington Post*, 27 March 1994.

————,"Don't Blame the Gerrymander," *The New York Times Magazine*, 8 January 1995.

————, "Can't We Talk? Beyond Winner Take All in Democracy's Conversation," *The Nation*, 23 January 1995.

————. "The Miner's Canary: Race and the Democratic Process." *Dissent* 521 (Fall 1995).

————. "More Democracy." *University of Chicago Legal Forum* (1995).

Hagerty, James A., "Supporters of PR to Keep Up Battle," *The New York Times*, 3 November 1947.

Heintz, Jim, "Voter Turnout Study Yields Surprises," *Honolulu Advertiser*, 3 July 1997.

Hester, Jere, "Pres' Civil Rights Furor," *Daily News*, 31 May 1993.

"High Registration Cheers PR Friends; Total is 2,356,248," *The New York Times*, 13 October 1947.

"Idea Woman," *The New Yorker*, 14 June 1993.

Ifill, Gwen, "Anatomy of the Failure to Confirm a Nominee," *The New York Times*, 5 June 1993.

Isikoff, Michael, "Clinton Nominates 7 to Justice; Housekeeper Issue Raised," *The Washington Post*, 30 April 1993.

————, "Confirmation Battle Looms Over Guinier," *The Washington Post*, 21 May 1993.

————, "White House Affirms Support of Guinier," *The Washington Post*, 28 May 1993.

Jarrett, Vernon, "Black Professionals Should Be Defending Lani Guinier," *Chicago Sun-Times*, 3 June 1993.

"Judiciary Committee Confirmation Hearings This Week," *Morning Edition*, National Public Radio, Washington, D.C., 17 May 1993.

Karlan, Pamela S., and Peyton McCrary. "Without Fear and Without Research: Abigail Thernstrom on the Voting Rights Act." *Journal of Law and Politics* 4 (1988): 751–77.

Kelly, Michael, "The Guinier Affair Aggravates Clinton Credibility Problem," *The New York Times*, 6 June 1993.

Kelly, Robin. "The Black Poor and the Politics of Opposition in a New South City, 1929–1970." In *The "Underclass" Debate: Views from History*, edited by Michael Katz. Princeton: Princeton University Press, 1993.

King, Colbert, "Bill Clinton's Treatment of Lani Guinier," *The Washington Post*, 6 June 1993.

Klaidman, Daniel, "Guinier's Backers Play Defense as Confirmation Battle Looms," *Legal Times*, 24 May 1993.

Kramer, Michael, "Another Blown Opportunity," *Time*, 14 June 1993.

Kristof, Nicholas D., "Where Children Rule: Why are Japan's primary schools better than ours? Students lead classes. They even clean the bathrooms. Everything they learn they teach themselves," *The New York Times Magazine*, 17 August 1997.

Kurtz, Howard, "First Lady's Press Picks," *The Washington Post*, 8 May 1993.

Labaton, Stephen, "N.A.A.C.P. Embraces a Nominee Abandoned," *The New York Times*, 14 July 1997.

Leo, John, "A Controversial Choice at Justice," *U.S. News & World Report*, 17 May 1993.

Lewis, Anthony, "Anatomy of a Smear: The Lynching of Lani Guinier," *The New York Times*, 4 June 1993.

———, "Depriving the Nation," *The New York Times*, 27 September 1993.

Lewis, Neil, "Guerrilla Fighter for Civil Rights," *The New York Times*, 5 May 1993.

———, "Lani Guinier's Agenda Provokes Old Enemies," *The New York Times*, 9 May 1993.

———, "Civil Rights Nominee's Words Make Her a Target," *The New York Times*, 14 May 1993.

———, "Clinton Faces a Battle Over Civil Rights Nominee," *The New York Times*, 21 May 1993.

———, "Aides Say Clinton Will Drop Nominee for Post on Rights," *The New York Times*, 3 June 1993.

———, "Facing Opposition, Clinton Abandons Rights Nomination," *The New York Times*, 4 June 1993.

———, "Clinton Acts to Cut Losses Over Abandoning Nominee," *The New York Times*, 5 June 1993.

Lijphart, Arend. "Unequal Participation: Democracy's Unresolved Dilemma." *American Political Science Review* (March 1997): 1–14.

Lotke, Eric, *National Center on Institutions and Alternatives Study on Blacks and Criminal Justice*, Washington, D.C., 26 August 1997.

Luttwak, Edward N., "Will Success Spoil America?: Why the Pols Don't Get Our Real Crisis of Values," *The Washington Post*, 27 November 1994.

Mansbridge, Jane. "The Limits of Friendship." In *Participation and Politics*, edited by J. Roland Pennock and John W. Chapman. New York: Lieber-Atherton, 1975.

Mansnerus, Laura, "At the Bar: After her 'public torture,' Lani Guinier finds acclaim and 'solidarity' in many places," *The New York Times*, 3 September 1993.

Marcus, Ruth, "Clinton Withdraws Nomination of Guinier: Legal Writings Controversy Dooms Choice," *The Washington Post*, 4 June 1993.

Marcus, Ruth, and Michael Isikoff, "Administration Leaves Guinier in Limbo: Clinton May Withdraw Name; Nominee Presses for Senate Hearing," *The Washington Post*, 3 June 1993.

Margolick, David, "Musty Academic Speculation or Blueprint for Political Action," *The New York Times*, 4 June 1993.

Mauro, Tony, "Ideas on the Edge Topple Guinier from Nomination," *USA Today*, 4 June 1993.

Mezzacappa, Dale, "How Tests Fail Our Children," *Philadelphia Inquirer Magazine*, 30 November 1997.

Moore, Acel, "Let's Look at Guinier's Record, Not Just Law Review Misquotes," *Philadelphia Inquirer*, 27 May 1993.

Moore, Linda Wright, "The Chance She Never Got," *Philadelphia Daily News*, 10 June 1993.

Moscow, Warren, "Election Will Decide Pro's and Con's of PR," *The New York Times*, 19 October 1947.

"The Nomination of Lani Guinier." Statement by Senator Dole. Congressional Record S6171. (20 May 1993).

Nussbaum, Chancellor Thomas J., "The State of the California Community Colleges." Address delivered at Sacramento, California, 19 September 1997.

Ost, David, "Solidarity and Public Space in Poland: From Civil Society to Bourgeois Society." Paper prepared for Annenberg School for Communication Scholars Conference on Public Space, March 1–4, 1995.

Page, Clarence, "The Smearing of Lani Guinier," *Chicago Tribune*, 30 May 1993.

Payne, Charles. "Ella Baker and Models of Social Change." *Signs: Journal of Women in Culture and Society*, 14, no. 4 (1989).

Pildes, Richard, and Kristen Donoghue. "Cumulative Voting in the United States." *University of Chicago Legal Forum* (November 1995).

Polak, Maralyn Lois, "An American's Dilemma," *Philadelphia Inquirer Magazine*, 8 January 1995.

Quigley, William P. "Reflections of Community Organizers: Lawyering for Empowerment of Community Organizations." *Ohio North University Law Review*, 21 (1995): 454.

Quindlen, Anna, "Political Illiteracy," *The New York Times*, 6 June 1993.

Raspberry, William, "Clinton's Cold Feet," *The Washington Post*, 4 June 1993.

———, "Sermon on a Bus," *The Washington Post*, 7 March 1997.

"Republican Heads Set to Join War on PR," *The New York Times*, 4 October 1947.

"Republican Leaders Join in Fight for Repeal of PR System in City," *The New York Times*, 17 October 1947.

"Rights Nominee Gains Support," *Philadelphia Daily News*, 27 May 1993.

Rosenthal, A. M., "Clinton Voter Stays Glad!" *The New York Times*, 28 May 1993.

Rule, Wilma. "Parliaments of, by and for the People: Except for Women?" In *Electoral Systems in Comparative Perspective: Their Impact on Women and Minorities*, edited by Wilma Rule and Joseph F. Zimmerman. Westport, Conn.: Greenwood Press, 1994.

Russakoff, Dale. "Lani Guinier's Second Act," *The Washington Post Magazine*, 12 December 1993.

"Sampson Likens PR to Hitler Law," *The New York Times*, 1 November 1947.

Savage, David, "Paper Trail Could Block Nominee for Justice Post," *Los Angeles Times*, 22 May 1993.

Seelye, Katharine Q., "Group Seeks to Alter S.A.T.'s to Raise Girls' Scores," *The New York Times*, 14 March 1997.

Seper, Jerry, "Justice Nominee Once Defeated Clinton in Suit," *The Washington Times*, 1 May 1993.

———, "Guinier Backers, Foes Speak Out," *The Washington Times*, 27 May 1993.

———, "White House Lobbies as Barbs Fly at Guinier," *The Washington Times*, 28 May 1993.

Shapiro, Bruce, "Getting Guinier," *The Nation*, 31 May 1995.

Sherman, Mark, "Proportional Voting Called Redistricting Solution," *The Atlanta Journal/The Atlanta Constitution*, 6 August 1995.

Stanley, Harold W. "Runoff Primaries and Black Political Influence." In *Blacks in Southern Politics*, edited by Lawrence W. Moreland, Robert P. Steed, and Tod A. Baker. New York: Praeger, 1987.

"Statement of the American Jewish Congress on Nomination of Lani Guinier to Be Assistant Attorney General for Civil Rights," U.S. Newswire, 26 May 1993.

Still, Edward. "Alternatives to Single-Member Districts." In *Minority Vote Dilution*, edited by Chandler Davidson. Washington, D.C.: Howard University Press, 1984.

Sturm, Susan, and Lani Guinier. "The Future of Affirmative Action: Reclaiming the Innovative Ideal." *California Law Review* 84 (July 1996): 953.

Taylor, Stuart, Jr., "DOJ Nominee's 'Authentic' Black Views," *Legal Times*, 17 May 1993.

"Text of President Clinton's Comments on Withdrawal of Guinier Nomination," *The Washington Post*, 4 June 1993.

Thompson, Phil, "Universalism & Deconcentration: Why Race Still Matters in Poverty and Economic Development," 10 September 1995.

Torry, Jack, "Writings Damaged Guinier," *Toledo Blade*, 6 June 1993.

Twersky, David, "Jews Collide With Clinton Over Guinier," *Forward*, 21 May 1993.

United States Commission on Civil Rights. "The Voting Rights Act: Ten Years After." Washington, D.C.: U.S. Government Printing Office, 1975.

———. "The Voting Rights Act: Unfulfilled Promises." Washington, D.C.: U.S. Government Printing Office, 1981.

U.S. House of Representatives, Committee on the Judiciary. "Extension of the Voting Rights Act," hearings before the Subcommittee on Civil and Constitutional Rights, 6, 7, 13, 20, 27, 28 May; 3, 5, 10, 12, 16, 17, 18, 23, 24, 25 June; and 13 July 1981. Parts 1 and 2.

Von Drehle, David, "Lani, We Hardly Knew Ye: The Lawyer Who Burned Briefly —But Too Bright for Her Own Good," *The Washington Post*, 4 June 1993.

———. "The Undoing of Lani Guinier: Academic Life and Political Death: A Paper Trail Cast in Two Lights," *Philadelphia Inquirer*, 6 June 1993.

Walzer, Michael. "Multiculturalism and Individualism." *Dissent* (Spring 1994).

Wattenberg, Ben, "To Survive, Clinton Must Be Reborn as a Moderate," *Sacramento Bee*, 21 May 1993.

Weymouth, Lally, "Lani Guinier: Radical Justice," *The Washington Post*, 25 May 1993.

Wilkins, Roger, "Lani Guinier Is a New Kind of Civil Rights Lawyer with an Old-fashioned Goal: . . . And Justice for All," *Esquire*, December 1984.

Williams, Patricia, "Lani, We Hardly Knew Ye: How the Right Wing Created a Monster Out of a Civil Rights Advocate and Bill Clinton Ran in Terror," *Village Voice*, 15 June 1993.

Willing, Richard. "Choice for Rights Post Is Sparking D.C. Brawl," *Detroit News and Free Press*, 16 May 1993.

Woodhouse, Barbara Bennett, "The Right-wing Smear Attacks on Lani Guinier," *Philadelphia Inquirer*, 26 May 1993.

III. Cases

Thornburg v. *Gingles*, 590 F. Supp. 334 (ED N.C. 1984)(three-judge court), aff'd, 478 U.S. 30 (1986).

Whitfield v. Democratic Party, 686 F. Supp. 1365 (ED Ark. 1988), aff'd on reh'g by an equally divided court, 902 F2d 15 (8th Cir 1990) (enbanc).

United States v. Spiver Gordon, 817 F2d 1538 (11th Cir 1987).

United States v. Turner, Hogue, & Turner, Cr. No. 85-00014 (SD Ala. 5 July 1985) (jury trial).

Bozeman v. Lambert, Civ. A. 83-H-579-N (MD Ala. 13 April 1984), aff'd, (No. 84-7286)(11th Cir 6 May 1985) (unpub.).

Haskins v. Wilson County, N. 82-19-Civ-8 (ED N.C. 16 August 1985).

Johnson v. Halifax County, 594 F. Supp. 161 (ED N.C. 1984).

Major v. Treen, 574 F. Supp. 345 (ED La. 1983) (three-judge court).

Booker v. United States, 655 F2d 562 (4th Cir 1981).

IV. Other Sources

For more information about Local Conversations on Race, contact:
Center for Living Democracy, RR#1 Black Fox Road, Brattleboro, VT 05301. Phone (802) 254-1234; fax (802) 254-1227; e-mail cld@sover.net (Published "Bridging the Racial Divide: A Report on Interracial Dialogue in America," 30 September 1997.)

Study Circles Resource Center, Pomfret, Conn. Phone (860) 928-2616; fax (860) 928-3713; e-mail scrc@neca.com (Sarah Campbell, deputy director). Excellent model for citizen brainstorming, often leading to collaborative action and influential town hall discussion.

Other possible sources of information include:

Common Ground, Rocky Mount, N.C. Phone (919) 442-5111; fax (919) 442-5068 (Steve Evans, executive director). Affiliated with chamber of commerce, examines the impact of race on community and public issues.

Three Valleys Project, Portland, Oregon. Phone (503) 281-1667; fax (503) 249-1969 (Sharif Abdullah, director). Facilitates Latino-Anglo dialogues on issues of race, ethnicity, and class; a project of the Rockefeller Foundation, it publishes a bilingual newsletter.

Center for Healing of Racism, Houston, Texas. Phone (713) 520-8226; fax (713) 526-3037 (Cherry Steinwinder, executive director). Produces newsletter, hosts a video film festival, presents school programs, and creates safe environment to talk about racism.

Project Change, San Francisco, Calif. Phone (415) 501-7725; fax (415) 501-6575. Originally launched in 1991 by the Levi Strauss Foundation, aimed at eliminating prejudice and racism in Levi Strauss plant communities; has worked with multiracial coalitions in Albuquerque, N.M.; El Paso, Texas; Valdosta, Ga.; and Knoxville, Tenn.

The National Conference, New York, N.Y. Phone (212) 206-0006; fax (212) 255-6177 (Wayne Winborn, director of program & policy research). Has 61 regional offices nationwide that regularly sponsor informal conversations among diverse community groups.

Hope in the Cities, Richmond, Va. Phone (804) 358-1764; fax (804) 358-1769, e-mail 102732.1363@compuserve.com. Issued "A Call to Community" in 1996, stating that America needs and deserves honest conversations about race; is working with groups in Los Angeles, Philadelphia, Pittsburgh, Cincinnati, and Chicago.

For more information about alternative election systems and proportional representation initiatives in the United States, contact:

Center for Voting and Democracy, P.O. Box 60037, Washington, D.C. 20039. Phone (301) 270-4616; fax (301) 270-4133; e-mail FairVote@compuserve.com; web site: http://www.igc.org/cvd/ (Rob Richie, executive director). This is a nonpartisan educational institution that provides information about proportional representation, other election systems, and is a good source of information about current activity and local organizations working for this reform.

For international comparisons, write:

Institute for Democracy and Electoral Assistance, Stromsborg, S-103 34 Stockholm, Sweden. Phone +46 8 698 3700; fax +46 8 20 24 22; e-mail info@int-idea.se; web site: http://www.int-idea.se

For additional, basic reading material:

Douglas Amy. *Proportional Representation: The Case for a Better Election System.* Northampton, Mass.: Crescent Street Press, 1997. This is an excellent pamphlet on proportional representation.

Proportional Representation Library. Web site: http://www.mtholyoke.edu/acad/polit/damy/prlib.htm (Includes extensive bibliography from beginning readings to more sophisticated articles.)

INDEX

Journal of the American Medical Association, 297
Justice Department, U.S., 26, 32, 33, 40, 43, 44, 50, 53, 76, 79, 92, 133, 134, 163, 174, 177, 184, 186–87, 189, 196, 221, 256
Civil Rights Division of, 27, 30, 34, 70, 74, 86, 141, 143, 156, 179
Public Affairs Department of, 190

Kamen, Al, 49
Karlan, Pamela, 228–32, 233, 235, 236, 291, 294
Katzenbach, Nicholas, 174, 178, 179
Keith, Damon J., 70, 71
Kennedy, Bill, 26
Kennedy, Edward M., 96, 120
Kennedy, John F., 137, 152, 174
Kennedy, Robert F., 30, 126, 163
Kennedy administration, 173–74
Kerner Commission, 157
Kerrison, Ray, 54, 55
King, Colby, 99
King, Coretta Scott, 215
King, Martin Luther, Jr., 53, 71, 85, 90, 160, 166, 169, 172, 173, 181, 182, 184, 222, 223, 228, 232, 239, 247, 276, 280–81, 283, 285, 307, 309
Chestnut's meeting with, 170–71
"I Have a Dream" speech of, 137
Johnson's meetings with, 174–75, 177
New York Times letter of, 175
Voting Rights Act and, 174–75
King, Pat, 143
Klimesz, Marie, 34
Kluger, Richard, 232
Kmart, 240–44, 245
Knesset, Israeli, 268–69
Knights of the White Camellia, 171
Knopf, Siegfried, 89
Kohl, Herbert H., 99, 118
Koppel, Ted, 98, 107–11, 111, 298
Ku Klux Klan, 171, 190, 191, 287

Lafayette, Bernard, 175, 181
Lasch, Christopher, 278
Leadership Conference on Civil Rights, 73, 78–79, 82–83, 122, 143, 150
League of Women Voters, 73, 84, 265
Leahy, Patrick, 96

Lee, Willie, 189, 192–93
Legal Services Corporation, 78
Legal Times, 38
Leo, John, 38
Lesbian and Gay Youth Project, 245
Lewis, John, 175, 177, 178
Liebman, James, 194, 209
Lijphart, Arend, 269
Lillie, Charisse, 142, 281, 306
Lincoln, Abraham, 155
"linked fate," 290
Lipsky, Seth, 31
Los Angeles Times, 48
Lowell, Abbe, 92, 130
Lowell, A. Lawrence, 59–60
Lowery, Joseph, 137–38, 186
Luttwak, Edward, 301, 307
Lynde and Harry Bradley Foundation, 38

McCarthy, Sheryl, 269–70
McCarthyism, 69
McFadden, Nancy, 101, 104, 106–7, 124
McKinney, Cynthia, 261, 279–81, 306
McLarty, Thomas F. "Mack," 115, 124
Madison, James, 37
Magruder, Julious, 229
Major, Barbara, 221
Major v. Treen, 36
Mandela, Nelson, 258, 286
March on Washington (1963), 152
March on Washington (1993), 137
Marcus, Ruth, 99
Marion Three case, 186–218, 220, 221, 227, 246–47, 256
absentee ballot process and, 186–188, 189, 190, 192, 193, 195, 196
Bozeman case and, 204, 206
character witnesses in, 214–15
Chestnut-Meese meeting and, 191–92
Chestnut's closing argument in, 216, 218
civil rights leadership and, 203
community support and, 203–4, 212–13
defendants' voluntary testimony in, 199–202
defense lawyers in, 194–95